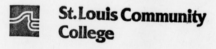

The Victims of Democracy

The Victims of Democracy

Malcolm X and the Black Revolution

by Eugene Victor Wolfenstein

University of California Press

Berkeley Los Angeles London

University of California Press
Berkeley and Los Angeles, California

University of California Press, Ltd.
London, England
© 1981 The Regents of the University of California

Library of Congress Cataloging in Publication Data

Wolfenstein, Eugene Victor.
    The victims of democracy: Malcolm X and the black revolution.
    Bibliography: p.
    Includes index.
    1. Little, Malcolm, 1925–1965. 2. Black Muslims—Biography. 3. Afro-
Americans—Biography. 4. Afro-Americans—Race identity. I. Title.
BP223.Z8L579   361.2'092'4 [B]   79-63551
ISBN 0-520-03903-3

Contents

Preface

WHEN MALCOLM X was in prison and after he had been converted to Islam through Elijah Muhammad's ministry, he dedicated himself to documenting Muhammad's teachings in books. The present inquiry is an attempt to document in books the truths contained in *The Autobiography of Malcolm X* and in Malcolm's collected speeches. It is, however, an interpretive and critical documentary.

There are various ways in which this book falls short of the mark I set for it. Its most important limit, however, was given in advance of the inquiry itself for, at least in a racist society, no white person can claim an existential appreciation of the black experience. But I am quite convinced that all of us have vital lessons to learn from Malcolm X and the black revolutionary movement. This book is a public record of my attempt to learn these lessons. It is not a substitute for *The Autobiography of Malcolm X*, his speeches, and the other primary materials upon which it relies.

I should add a few words about the origins of the inquiry. In the early 1960s I began to use psychoanalytic theory as a way of understanding the relationship between personality and politics. In so doing I adopted a version of Max Weber's methodology and borrowed certain theoretical notions from Erik H. Erikson and Harold D. Lasswell. Erikson had extended the psychogenetic dimension of Freud's theory into a conception of the human life-cycle. In particular, he developed the idea of an adolescent identity crisis, perhaps accompanied by a moratorium (a temporary cessation of socially expected activities) from which the individual emerges with a culturally significant vocation and self-definition. Lasswell's formula of "private motives displaced on public objects and rationalized in terms of

the public interest" provided an appropriate psychodynamic and political complement to the idea of identity-formation. When these
psychogenetic and psychodynamic notions were utilized within an
ideal-type method, which legitimated bracketing research with an
"everything else being equal" clause, it became possible to derive
propositions about various types of political participants: leaders,
followers, theorists, revolutionaries.

The Black Revolution and the war in Vietnam broke in upon and
in time undermined this approach to political life. These events
were clearly interconnected and multi-determined. Viewing my
own work in their light, it appeared that bracketing a field of psycho-
political inquiry created an artificial subject-matter which substituted for and precluded the understanding of the real one. Marx's
dialectical method, which aims at the comprehension of an historically developing totality of social relationships, seemed to be more
adequately determinative of this reality. Moreover, when examined
from a Marxist perspective, it became evident that Erikson had no
theory of the historical process, but only a psychoanalytic theory on
the one hand and an interest in historical events on the other. It also
could be argued that Lasswell's formula reversed the real relationship between personality and politics: perhaps political interests are
first reflected into the private sphere, then internalized as character
structure, and only subsequently displaced again into the public
realm.

With these issues in mind, I took up the works of Wilhelm Reich,
Erich Fromm, Herbert Marcuse, Jean-Paul Sartre, and Frantz Fanon,
but I soon concluded that the critical appropriation of their ideas
was less vital than a thorough re-immersion in the theories of Marx
and Freud. Correspondingly, when I decided to investigate the relationship between Malcolm X and the Black Revolution, I also decided to lay aside any Freudian-Marxist conceptions which were not
absolutely necessary for purposes of interpretation. Thus the present inquiry is primarily a confrontation between Marx and Freud
and Malcolm X. It contains few references to the other writers I have
mentioned (except for Fanon, whose special bearing on the subject is
evident). The reader who is familiar with their work will, however,
recognize their ideas playing their part behind the scenes.

I am grateful to Richard Ashcraft, Clyde Daniels Halisi, Norman
Jacobson, Barry Silver, and Jon Tierce for their insightful and sympa-
thetic criticism. I am also grateful to Alain Hénon and Jane-Ellen
Long for their editorial judgment and skill. I have a special debt to

my wife, Judith Wolfenstein, who from first to last has been my best and most understanding critic.

Financial support for this project was provided by the John Simon Guggenheim Foundation.

This book is dedicated to my aunt, the late Martha Wolfenstein, who will always represent to me the highest ideals of the psychoanalytic vocation.

CHAPTER I

The Problem

IN 1944 MALCOLM X was a small-time Harlem hustler known as Detroit Red. Two years later he was a prisoner in Massachusetts' Charlestown State Prison, miserably cursing God, the Bible, and his imprisonment. In 1962 he was a Muslim minister, a follower of Elijah Muhammad, preaching hellfire and damnation to white America, redemption and salvation to the Nation of Islam. And in 1964 he formed the OAAU, the Organization of Afro-American Unity. At the organization's founding rally in Harlem on June 28 of that year, Malcolm proclaimed that the OAAU's purpose was to unite African-heritage peoples

> to fight a common enemy . . . to fight whoever gets in our way, to bring about the complete independence of people of African descent in the Western Hemisphere, and first here in the United States, and bring about the freedom of these people by any means necessary.[1]

This action, an important moment of Malcolm's individual experience, was also a significant moment in the history of the Black Revolution. Our purpose is to grasp it as the unity of both these aspects and as a product of its own process of development.

We will find that realizing this purpose requires the mediation of a simultaneously Marxist and psychoanalytic theory of race, racism, and racial liberation.

The problem of the inquiry, as jointly determined by its subject matter and its theoretical orientation, may then be formulated: *how does racism falsify the consciousness of the racially oppressed; and* *how do racially oppressed individuals free themselves from both the falsification of their consciousness and the racist domination of their practical activity?* *

The inquiry may be approached from another direction. Speaking at Harvard in 1964, Malcolm X argued that the black victims of American democracy do not have the "same form or system of logic or reason" as their oppressors. "What is logical to the oppressor isn't logical to the oppressed. And what is reason to the oppressor isn't reason to the oppressed."² Karl Marx put forward a similar position in the postface to the second edition of *Capital*, Volume I. A rational form of dialectical method, he said, "is a scandal and an abomination to the bourgeoisie and its doctrinaire spokesmen, because it includes in its positive understanding of what exists a simultaneous recognition of its negation, its inevitable destruction; because it regards every historically developed form as being in a fluid state, in motion, and therefore grasps its transient aspect as well; and because it does not let itself be impressed by anything, being in its essence critical and revolutionary."³ Our investigation is intended to be "critical and revolutionary" in this sense. It is an attempt to analyze American democracy from the perspective of its victims and with the logic of the oppressed.

This introduction is meant to be a propaedeutic for the inquiry as a whole. We will begin by representing Malcolm's consciousness of his historical situation. Next, as a response to the representation of Malcolm's consciousness, we will dissolve our general formulation of the problem into a more workable set of investigative concerns. This process of problem-formation will also permit us to justify a Marxist and psychoanalytic approach to our subject matter. To anticipate its results:

1. Given that Malcolm contributed significantly to the black revolutionary movement, what is the precise nature of that contribution? Stated another way, how are his characteristic individual and racial pride; the racially militant and politically radical tendencies in his theory and practice; and the charismatic quality of his leadership related to each other?

2. The black revolutionary movement, taken together with the

* As a first approximation, the *Black Revolution* may be broadly defined as the struggle of black people for liberation from racist oppression. More narrowly, it is the self-consciously militant and/or radical movement toward black liberation of the 1960s and early 1970s. *False consciousness* may be defined as a systematically distorted understanding of and resistance to corrective learning from experience, i.e., from everyday activity.

vicious circle of racist domination, may be designated *the problematic of racist oppression*. Here we will ask: what is the relationship between class and race in constituting the vicious circle; and what is the relationship between reformist and revolutionary tendencies in the struggle for racial liberation?

3. When placed in historical perspective, the problematic of racist oppression becomes the problem of false consciousness, i.e., the problem of establishing principles of historical development and human nature sufficient to determine judgments concerning the reality, rationality, and responsibility of choices of political action.

We will conclude the introduction with some comments on the method, limits, and organization of the inquiry.

Malcolm X and the Black Revolution: A Preliminary Representation

Malcolm X was born Malcolm Little in Omaha, Nebraska, on May 25, 1925. He fell to assassins' bullets in a Harlem auditorium on February 21, 1965. He spent his youth hustling the streets of Boston and New York, but he "rose from hoodlum, thief, dope peddlar, and pimp to become the most dynamic leader of the Black Revolution."[4] His autobiography, detailing this rise, became after his death in 1965 a kind of black synoptic gospel, the words and deeds of a man who symbolizes the terrible racial division of our society. It also vividly describes Malcolm in his role as the leading organizer and spokesman for Elijah Muhammad's Lost/Found Nation of Islam in the West. In this role, he brought into the Nation large numbers of people from the black ghettoes, people who had been left virtually untouched by the organizing activity of the civil rights movement. In addition, he carried to members of the black intelligentsia Muhammad's message of a revitalized black nationalism. With this base of support among the oppressed urban masses and with at least the tacit support of many of the more militant black artists, intellectuals, and leaders, he mounted a powerful polemical attack against both "white world supremacy" and the integrationist aspirations and nonviolent tactics of the civil rights movement. From the pulpits of the Nation of Islam, in its official newspaper (which he himself had founded), on radio and television programs, and at public forums across the land, Malcolm reached black, white, and interracial audiences with his angry and skillful articulation of Muhammad's message. Finally, during the year of life remaining to him after he left the Nation in 1964, Malcolm wove together most of the theoretical and practical strands that would form the matrix of the black revolutionary movement in the coming years: Afro-American unity (political and cultural), Black Power, Black Pride, and Malcolm's orientation toward political action—"freedom by any means necessary."

If *The Autobiography of Malcolm X* is the synoptic gospel of the Black Revolution, the preserved speeches of his last year are its Pauline epistles. The former inspires by personal example; the latter lead on to collective action. The *Autobiography* draws the reader into a personal world reconstructed by memory and self-reflection; the speeches bring one into the forum of public debate, polemical encounter and proselytizing activity. Together, the autobiography and the speeches provide us with a conscious experience that is simultaneously deep and broad, reflective and active, personal and political.

Where, then, do we begin our representation of Malcolm's consciousness, and how are we to proceed once the beginning has been established? If we were to honor biographical convention, we would begin with the earliest memories reported in Malcolm's autobiography. Any interest we might have in these memories is, however, dependent upon our prior interest in Malcolm's contribution to the black revolutionary movement. Our political interest determines that we begin with Afro-American consciousness and its organizational embodiment, the OAAU. But the OAAU cannot be adequately represented without considering the forms of consciousness preceding it. As Hegel observed, "The mere result attained [is not] the concrete whole, but the result along with the process of arriving at it."[5] And as Malcolm argued, to understand why anyone is what he is, "his whole life, from birth, must be reviewed. All of our experiences fuse into our personality. Everything that has ever happened is an ingredient."[6] Accordingly, we will begin with the OAAU and regress through the forms of Malcolm's consciousness until we arrive at his earliest memories. In this way—i.e., through a technique of regressive representation—our political interest will determine our biographical starting point.

The content of this regressive representation of Malcolm's consciousness may be briefly noted. After we have outlined the theory and intended practice of the OAAU, we will describe Malcolm's polemical attack upon the middle-class leadership and integrationist aspirations of the civil rights movement. Historically, this attack connects his last years in the Nation of Islam to his period of independent political leadership. Next we will turn to Elijah Muhammad's version of the Islamic world view, hence to the foundation of Malcolm's consciousness during his years of membership in the Nation. Finally we will specify certain linkages between these adult forms of Malcolm's consciousness and his earliest childhood memory.

In December, 1964, Malcolm remarked that the assassination of President Kennedy was a case of "chickens coming home to roost." Such comments were not unusual at the time. Sorrowful reflections on the violence of American life were a common part of the national mood of mourning. But Malcolm's mood was not mournful. He believed that the death of the president was a just, if only partial, retribution for the sufferings the "white devil" had inflicted upon black people, a view his leader, Elijah Muhammad, presumably shared. After all, Muhammad taught that the white man was a devil and that Allah would destroy him. But the Prophet, not wishing to bring the wrath of the white world down upon his Nation of Islam, disassociated himself from this comment by suspending Malcolm from the Nation for ninety days. As the three months passed, it became evident that Malcolm would not be reinstated.

Later, we shall investigate why Muhammad and his leading disciple came to a parting of the ways. In any case, Malcolm now had to formulate an independent course of action, one that would take into account not only the various forms of white racist power, but also the demonstrated strengths and weaknesses of the civil rights movement and the Nation of Islam. The members of the "Movement" had confronted Southern racists, bravely absorbing physical abuse in an attempted nonviolent revolution. Their goal was the desegregation of American society. The Muslims had meanwhile been building a nation within the nation's ghettoes. Their stated goals were to defend themselves against racist attack and exploitation, and to separate black from white America. As this period drew to a close, it was becoming clear both that the nonviolent revolution had failed and that the Nation was no nation. Since the Movement, despite its activism, had won only token victories, questions were being raised about the validity of both its nonviolent means and its integrationist ends. The Muslims, despite their militant posture, were politically disengaged and therefore vulnerable to the charge of talking tough while doing nothing. Not only Malcolm but black people in general needed a new plan of attack.

Malcolm's first response to the situation was to form Muslim Mosque, Inc. (MMI). MMI was to be a direct alternative to the Nation of Islam, but its political orientation was to be black nationalist rather than black separatist. A couple of months later, Malcolm traveled to the Middle East and to sub-Saharan Africa. There he was much impressed by the revolutionary fervor and pride of the Africans he met, and by the apparent ability of governments ranging from radical to conservative to work together for common goals in the Organization of African Unity. He also picked up intimations of a more extensive solidarity: one African leader remarked to him that "the world's course will change the day African-heritage peoples come together as brothers."[7] When he returned from Africa he brought with him this idea of a revolutionary unity of all African-heritage peoples.

The premise of Malcolm's radically pan-Africanist conception was that "This is not an era where one who is oppressed is looking toward the oppressor to give him some system or form of logic or reason. What is logical to the oppressor isn't logical to the oppressed. And what is reason to the oppressor isn't reason to the oppressed." It follows that "there just has to be a new system of reason and logic devised by us who are at the bottom if we want to get some results in this struggle that is called 'the Negro revolution.'"[8] This position contains both a critique and a construction—an attack upon the oppressor's logic that should result in revolutionary action.

The white man's logic, Malcolm argued, is based on one fundamental supposition, namely, white over black. Whatever else may be variable in human experience, the one constant is white superiority. The history of civilization is white history, the only genuine morality derives from white Christianity and the only legitimate sovereignty is that of white ruling powers. Humanity and whiteness are coextensive. Consequently the height of black ambition is to become white, to integrate. Physically, the black man hopes for light skin, straight hair, an aquiline nose; spiritually, he accepts white history, values, and dominion, looking only for the opportunity to say "our" past, "our" religion, "our" government. Like the slave who said "we" "whenever the master said we," the modern Uncle Tom echoes the white man's words.[9] Just as the slave exists *for* his master, the contemporary Negro exists *for* the white man, and hence is responsible only to him. More: his very existence is *from* the white man. The Negro is an artifact, a creation of the white man for his own purposes: "Whenever you see somebody who calls himself a

Negro, he's a product of Western civilization."[10] He therefore cannot reject his dependency without severing his tenuous connection with humanity. Better to be subhuman than inhuman, a slave than a jungle beast, a second-class citizen than a ghetto criminal. Concretely, this means that the Negro acts according to the ostensible rules of society while the white man acts according to the real ones. The Negro speaks the language of morality, the white man the language of power. The Negro has the responsibilities of a man and the rights of a beast; the white man has the responsibilities of a beast and the rights of a man. Thus the existing logic entails total negation of black humanity: "As long as you call yourself a Negro, nothing is yours."[11] This negation must itself be negated if black self-affirmative action is to be possible.

Malcolm's attack upon the white man's logic began with the empirical claim that white has not always dominated black: at an earlier period "on the African continent . . . there was always a higher level of culture and civilization than that which existed in Europe at the same time."[12] This being so, it cannot be claimed that white over black is an eternal law of nature. It is instead, an historical variable. Moreover, if one examines the historical process through which white dominion was established, one discovers that the high moral claims of the white man were inversely reflected in the criminal character of his actions. The "founding fathers from England came from the prisons of England; they were prostitutes, they were murderers and thieves and liars."[13] From such people nothing could be expected other than what in fact they did: "As soon as they got over here . . . they created one of the most criminal societies that has ever existed on earth since time began."[14] And the proof of this proposition was close at hand: "If you doubt it, when you go home at night, look in the mirror at yourself, and you'll see the victim of that criminal system that was created by them."[15] In short, the collective experience of black people in America was sufficient evidence of white criminality. They therefore owed the Man neither love nor respect. They were free to reject the hypocritically held values of white society, and to reject the white man's demand that they be "respectable and responsible when they holler against what white men are doing to them."[16]

Malcolm's Afro-American perspective thus enabled him to reject the moral claims of white America. Because, unlike Elijah Muhammad, he was not willing to wait for Allah to destroy the white world, he also had to demonstrate that black people had the power to overthrow their oppressors. The terms of such a demonstration were set by those civil rights leaders who had consistently argued that Malcolm was an irresponsible demagogue, who failed to recognize the realities of the American situation. Because black people were in the minority, a black revolution could not succeed: the only hope was to work for liberal reform in a cooperative, nonviolent effort with white allies. But, Malcolm rejoined, moderation would be necessary only if black people were a minority, while in fact they are the great majority of the world's population:

> As long as the black man in America thinks of himself as a minority, as an underdog, he can't shout but so loud. . . . He never gets irresponsible. He never goes beyond what the power structure thinks is the right voice to shout in. But when you begin to connect yourself on the world stage with the whole of dark mankind, you see that you're the majority and this majority is waking up and rising up and becoming strong, then when you deal with this man, you won't deal with him like he's your boss or he's better than you or stronger than you. You put him right where he belongs.[17]

After centuries of white rule, "the dark world is rising." This in turn means that the white world is declining:

> It's impossible for the dark world to increase in its power and strength without the power and strength of the white world decreasing. This is just the way it is, it's almost mathematics. If there is only so much power, and all of it has been over there, well, the only way this man's going to get some over here is to take it away from those over there.[18]

Furthermore, the white man "knows that he didn't do right when he had all the power, and if the base of power changes, those into whose hands it falls may know how to really do right."[19] Because there is a finite amount of power in the world, and because the white man has used his power immorally, it follows that he can only escape retribution by trying desperately to preserve what power he still has. This in turn implies the major operative rule of politial struggle, the rule obscured by the ideological veil of responsible and nonviolent protest: "It's not the nature of power to back up in the face of anything but some more power."[20]

When this has been understood, a "new game" begins, in which the first rule is that *anything goes*. Black people, recognizing that they are the majority and that time is on their side, will be willing to pay the necessary price for freedom—the price of death:

> The price to make others respect your human rights is death. You have to be ready to die or you have to be ready to take the lives of others. This is what old Patrick Henry meant when he said liberty or death. . . . If you're not for that you're not for freedom. It means you don't even want to be a human being. You don't want to pay the price that is necessary.[21]

Malcolm's reasoning tends toward the conclusion that the oppressor must expect violent resistance to oppressive actions and that the oppressed must be willing to kill or die for freedom. It does not necessarily follow that the revolutionary process will be violent: if the black man demonstrates his willingness to use any means necessary to win his freedom, the white man may back down. One has to reckon, however, with the more likely alternative.

In sum, if the historical premise is bondage and the conclusion is to be freedom, the mediating activity or middle term must be revolutionary action. This in turn entails organization. Malcolm's organization, the OAAU, was to have had a double nature: it was to be an alliance of all the forces working for black liberation in America, and was to coordinate its actions with those of the Organization of African Unity; and it was to be a cohesive political organization, under Malcolm's leadership and oriented toward black community renewal and self-defense. Especially in this latter form, it was similar to the Black Power concept that developed after Malcolm's death. As indicated above, its guiding principle was to be "freedom by any means necessary," by "the ballot or the bullet."[22]

An assassin's bullets took Malcolm's life before he was able to advance the OAAU much beyond the planning stage. Moreover, by the end of his life his conception of the revolutionary situation was changing somewhat. At the beginning of his last year, he had believed that political struggles were essentially racial. For example, when asked his opinion of the Marxist conception of imperialism, he responded:

> It is true that when a nation loses its markets . . . it's in trouble. And this is one of the basic factors behind America's problem. . . . [Still], I don't know too much about Karl Marx, but . . . in Spengler's *Hour of Decision*, it's about revolution, and his thesis is that the initial stages of the

world revolution would make people be forced to line up along class lines. But then after a while the class lines would run out and it would be a lineup based upon race. Well, I think he wrote this in the early thirties. And it has actually taken place.[23]

But when Malcolm was in Ghana in May, the Algerian ambassador asked him to describe his philosophy. He replied, "Black nationalism." According to Malcolm, the Algerian then asked, "Where did that leave him? Because he was white. . . . Where does that leave revolutionaries in Morocco, Egypt, Iraq, Mauritania? So he showed me where I was alienating people who were true revolutionaries."[24] Thus when Malcolm founded the OAAU it was pan-Africanist rather than black nationalist, and in his speeches he began to emphasize the parallels between European/American exploitation of Africa and the exploitation of Afro-Americans. He no longer argued that it was "the American white *man* who is a racist" but, rather, that "it's the American political, economic and social *atmosphere* that automatically nourishes a racist psychology in the white man."[25] To eliminate racism the whole system must be transformed:

A chicken just doesn't have it within its system to produce a duck egg. It can't do it. It can only produce according to what that particular system was constructed to produce. The system in this country cannot produce freedom for an Afro-American. It is impossible for this system, this economic system, this political system, this social system, as it stands, to produce freedom right now for the black man in this country. And if a chicken did produce a duck egg, I'm quite sure you would say it was certainly a revolutionary chicken![26]

If not black nationalism, what, then, was the alternative to the American system? During his travels Malcolm had been struck by the fact that "all of the countries that are emerging today from under the shackles of colonialism are turning toward socialism."[27] This, he believed, was no accident: "Most of the countries that were colonial powers were capitalist countries, and the last bulwark of capitalism today is America. . . [And] you can't have capitalism without racism."[28] This did not mean Malcolm was turning toward an orthodox Marxist view of impending class-based revolution; instead, he foresaw a "showdown between the economic systems that exist on this earth which almost boil down along racial lines."[29] But while there would be a strong racial bias along the line of conflict, the conflict itself would not be racial:

> I believe that there will ultimately be a clash between the oppressed and those that do the oppressing. I believe there will be a clash between those who want freedom, justice and equality for everyone, and those who want to continue the systems of exploitation. I believe there will be that kind of clash, but I don't think that it will be based upon the color of the skin.[30]

Not race, but common suffering, was the basis for unity. Like the successful Algerian rebels, other oppressed peoples were coming to realize that "oppression made them brothers; exploitation made them brothers; degradation made them brothers; . . . humiliation made them brothers."[31] They were also coming to understand the need to "fight a common enemy." And among them, Afro-Americans were learning that they did not have "anything to lose but discrimination and segregation."[32]

The leaders of the civil rights movement did not think black people had nothing to lose. They believed that there was a world to be won within the American system, that the Negro revolution was the realization of the American Revolution. Malcolm was severely critical of this view, both before and after he left the Nation of Islam. He argued that the Negro revolution was in fact counter-revolutionary, that "Negro" meant "nonviolent," and that a nonviolent revolution is a contradiction in terms:

> The only revolution in which the goal is loving your enemy is the Negro revolution. It's the only revolution in which the goal is a desegregated lunch counter, a desegregated theater, a desegregated park, and a desegregated public toilet; you can sit down next to white folks—on the toilet. That's no revolution.[33]

The harsh realities of black life are not changed by demonstrations, or even by the passage of minimally enforced civil rights legislation: "The masses of our people still have bad housing, bad schooling, and inferior jobs, jobs that don't compensate with sufficient salaries for them to carry on their life in this world. So the problem for the masses has gone absolutely unsolved."[34] Even worse, insofar as it was successful the nonviolent revolution was perpetuating these conditions. Its token victories were only "devices to lessen the danger of an explosion, but not designed to remove the material that's going to explode."[35] As in the case of the March on Washington, the government uses the civil rights movement to control the black community:

> The white liberals control the Negro and the Negro vote by controlling the Negro civil rights leaders. As long as they control the Negro civil rights leaders, they can also control and contain the Negro's struggle, and they can control the Negro's so-called revolt.[36]

Civil rights leaders, along with the press and the media, were conduits for spreading the reality-distorting and politically debilitating liberal ideology. The liberal carrot is that progress is being made, the stick that "we're the underdog, and that we don't have a chance, and that we should do it nonviolently and carefully; otherwise, we'll get hurt or we'll get wasted."[37] Thus admonished, the black masses are supposed to fall in line behind their responsible leaders and cling fiercely to their white allies.

The Negro revolution, moreover, accentuates class divisions within the black community. It helps to create a "so-called upper class Negro" whose interests appear to be at odds with those of the masses.[38] In fact, Malcolm contended, upper-class Negroes are merely "the modern counterpart of that slavery-time Uncle Tom"; they are "twentieth century house Negro[es]."[39] Unlike the field Negro, who knew from the welts on his back that the white man was his enemy, the house Negro was totally identified with his master: "Whenever the master said 'we,' he said 'we.' That's how you can tell a house Negro."[40] In exchange for better food, cast-off clothing, and the privilege of living in his master's attic or cellar, this Uncle Tom gave up any idea of becoming a free man. He sold the slave's birthright—the right to escape or rebel—for a mess of pottage:

> If someone came to that house Negro and said, "Let's separate, let's run," the house Negro would look at that person like he was crazy and tell him, "Run where? How would I live, how would I eat if my master didn't feed me? How would I clothe myself if my master wasn't here to give me some clothes?[41]

In the same way, the modern Uncle Tom is identified with and dependent upon his white master. He, too, values proximity to the white man—that is, integration—above all. He, too, rejects and ridicules those who, like Elijah Muhammad, call upon the black man to separate himself from the declining white world.

As in the days of slavery, however, this class of Negroes is in the minority. The majority is the mass "of black people . . . who are the offshoot of the field Negro, . . . who benefit in no way, shape, or form whatsoever from this thing that is called democracy."[42] Like the field Negro who jumped at any chance to escape, the modern "mass level type" Negro is similarly responsive to the call for separation: he says, "Let's separate. We are catching hell in this system we are now in. Let's separate."[43] He is not willing to wait for the realization of the American dream, for the realization of Martin Luther King's dream. To a Harvard audience Malcolm said:

> What is a dream to you is a nightmare to us. What is hope
> to you has long since become hopeless to our people. And as
> this attitude develops, not so much on Sugar Hill [in
> Harlem]—although it's there too—but in the ghetto, in the
> alley where the masses of our people live . . . you have a new
> situation on your hands.[44]

American values, in other words, were more and more openly revealing their double meaning . . . one white and one black, one positive and one negative. Prosperity for the white man was poverty for the black; democracy for the one was a police state for the other; freedom for one was bondage for the other. Understanding this, the masses were becoming progressively angrier and more impatient, tired of hoping for what had been promised to them a hundred years ago, in no mood to stay under the control of their responsible leaders or listen to the smooth talk of liberal politicians. They were ready to join the Nation of Islam; or, in Malcolm's words, they were saying, "We'll blow the world skyhigh if we're not respected and recognized and treated the same as other human beings."[45]

Unlike the integrationist, this "new Negro," the impatient black man, did not distinguish between liberals and conservatives. Northern liberals and their Negro adherents were as bad if not worse than the Southern racists:

> The white conservatives aren't friends of the Negro . . . but
> they at least don't try to hide it. They are like wolves; they
> show their teeth in a snarl that keeps the Negro always
> aware of where he stands with them. But the white liberals

are foxes, who also show their teeth to the Negro but pretend that they are smiling. . . . [And] the job of the Negro
civil rights leader is to make the Negro forget that the wolf
and the fox both belong to the same family.[46]

The sheep's clothing was no longer sufficient to hide the rapacity of
the wild dog. Through the long history of broken promises linking
the Emancipation Proclamation to the March on Washington, black
people had been learning to penetrate the white man's ideological
disguises. They were aided in this effort by the teachings of Elijah
Muhammad. As Malcolm put it, the Prophet's "greatest greatness"
was that "he is the *first*, the *only* black leader to identify . . . *who* is
our enemy. . . . Our *enemy* is the *white man*."[47] And not only were
all white men the enemy, but they were also enemies of *all* black
people. Just as the distinction between liberal and conservative was
beginning to collapse, so too the divisions within the black community were being overcome. Even black people on Sugar Hill were beginning to realize that

any Negro in the community can be stopped in the street.
"Put your hands up," and they pat you down. Might be a
doctor, a lawyer, a preacher or some other kind of Uncle
Tom, but despite your professional standing, you'll find that
you're the same victim as the man who's in the alley.[48]

It made sense for black people to "unite—on the basis of what we
have in common. And what we have foremost in common is that
enemy—the white man."[49]

Here we have reached the vital center of Malcolm's conception of
Muhammad's doctrine: the facts of the American experience are
comprehensible only from the initial premise that the white man is
the black man's enemy. Given this premise, black people can develop a common logic of action, can unite against their enemy.[*]
Moreover, the implications of this clarified understanding were vital
for white people as well. They had to learn, and were in bitter fact
learning, that the black man considered them to be the enemy. The
ghetto disturbances of 1963 and 1964 brought about a painful awak-

---

[*] As we have seen and shall see further, the unity thus derived does not entail a program any more specific than the abstract unity itself, the shared perception of the
enemy. No particular plan of action follows from it; consequently, Malcolm and
Muhammad could arrive at very different conclusions from at least apparently identical starting points.

ening for many white Americans. This fact in itself supported the position, which Malcolm had long maintained, that there "never was any *communication*" between the races:

> You need some proof? Well, then, why was it that when Negroes did start revolting across America, virtually all of America was caught up in surprise or even shock? I would hate to be general of an army as badly informed as the American white man has been about the Negro in this country.[50]

For several years Malcolm had been arguing that the white man was blinding himself to the realities of the racial situation. The veil of lies in which he shrouded the black masses also prevented *him* from understanding their condition: "In many communities, especially small communities, white people have created a benevolent image of themselves as having had so much 'good will toward our Negroes.'"[51] In the larger cities, they had kept black people "sealed up" in the ghettoes, "out of sight somewhere, around the corner."[52] The mediating factor common to both cases was that "the local Negro 'leader,' in order to survive as a 'leader,' kept reassuring the local white man, in effect, 'Everything's all right, everything's right in hand, boss.'"[53] If, however, he was having trouble keeping things quiet, or needed some form of bounty to distribute to his followers, he asked, "'Er, boss, some of the people talking about we sure need a better school, boss.' And if the local Negroes haven't been causing any 'trouble,' the 'benevolent' white man might nod and give them a school or some jobs."[54] This permitted "the white man to feel 'noble' about throwing a few crumbs to the black man, instead of feeling guilty about the local community's system of cruelly exploiting Negroes."[55]

The determining principle in this design was, of course, white power. The white man controls the Negro leader, through whom in turn he controls the black masses. He tells the leader what to tell the people, thereby hoping to maintain domestic tranquility. The leader follows orders because his power is dependent upon the white man's support. Then, because the white man wants both to exploit the masses *and* to feel noble while so doing, the Negro leader must lie not only to his people but also to his boss. He becomes the classic "yes-man," and the country's "very atmosphere" is filled with "racial mirages, clichés and lies."[56]

Malcolm's task in this situation, first as Elijah Muhammad's spokesman and then as chairman of the OAAU, was to replace the mediation of the Negro leader with his own. He sought to form himself into a two-way medium for honest communication between black and white. The oppressed masses would thereby learn the true nature of their condition and the true character of the white oppressor. In consequence, their rejection of the existing system, now spontaneous and sporadic, would become increasingly organized and self-conscious. The oppressor would learn that his house was aflame and only emergency measures would put out the fire: "I'm only warning you of a powder-keg situation. You can take it or leave it. If you take the warning, perhaps you can still save yourself."[57] When he was a follower of Muhammad, Malcolm's message was that the white man could save himself by granting the Nation a land of its own, thus making partial reparation for the long years of exploitation. When he was on his own, his message was that the white man had to meet the black people's demands for a genuine transformation of American society. But in neither instance was Malcolm optimistic about the white man taking the warning:

> Yet instead of the white man blaming himself for the anger
> of the Negro, he . . . has the audacity to blame us. When we
> warn you how angry the Negro is becoming, you, instead
> of thanking us for giving you a little warning, try to accuse
> us of stirring up the Negro. Don't you know that if your
> house is burning, you shouldn't accuse me of setting the
> fire! Thank me rather for letting you know what's happen-
> ing, or what's going to happen, before it's too late.[58]

In truth, no one man or small group of men could start the fire. There are, after all, no ghetto rebellions without ghettoes.

The great sin of the white liberals and Negro leaders was their attempt to ignore the ghettoes, to perpetuate the myth that freedom could be found north of the Mason-Dixon line. For Malcolm, "America is Mississippi. There's no such thing as the South—it's America."[59] Both as a Black Muslim and afterward, Malcolm hammered home this point: the continued existence of the ghettoes demonstrated that the North was not the promised land, that there was a *national* condition virtually as oppressive as slavery itself. Consequently, there could be no hope for black people within the existing American system. Either they would have to follow Elijah Muhammad out of white America, like the Israelite children following Moses out of Egypt (as Malcolm put it, "Moses never taught integration, Moses taught separation");[60] or they would have to rebel against their masters. There was no basis for compromise.

Malcolm's attacks upon white racism, his critique of the Negro revolution, and his conception of Afro-American history were all developed from the perspective of the black masses. They were also derived from the doctrines of Elijah Muhammad. Muhammad was a chiliastic prophet who preached that the collective black man was god, the white man was the devil, and history was the story of the black man's life in paradise, his subsequent sufferings at the hands of the white devil, and his impending salvation. Although ultimately Malcolm abandoned Muhammad's racial theodicy in favor of Islamic orthodoxy and a secular vision of black liberation, for many years it constituted the foundation of his consciousness. Indeed, it provided a framework within which he was able to develop a coherent conception of black history. This conception stressed the existence of highly developed African and Asian civilizations while Europe was still neolithic; the gradual growth and expansion of white power through trickery and brutality; the use of guns and the policy of "divide and rule" to conquer Africa; the bestiality of the slave trade and of slavery itself; the white man's murder, rape, physical brutalization, and exploitation of black people both during and after slavery; the corrupting and demoralizing influence of Christianity on blacks; the need, therefore, to reject white values, to restore a black identity, and to become independent of the existing society; and, finally, the belief that the age of white world supremacy was coming to an end.

Muhammad's theology and the black man's history were well designed to appeal to the suffering black masses, many of whom had been raised as Christians, had need of religious consolation, and had good reason to believe that the white man was the power of evil. But neither the theology nor the history would have had so much appeal for ghetto blacks without the practical program through which Muhammad taught his followers to "wake up, clean up, and stand up."[61] The conversion experience of Benjamin Goodman, who found his way into the Nation through Malcolm and who later followed Malcolm into the OAAU, provides us with an example of how these practical aspects of the doctrine met the needs of the black masses.

In 1958 Goodman was working in downtown Manhattan, with hair conked (straightened and greased), "trying very hard to be hip."[62] He had heard of Malcolm, but his "idea of him was confused and, undoubtedly, erroneous."[63] Then, in the spring of that year, a Muslim named Hinton Johnson was beaten by police and arrested while witnessing an altercation between an officer and another black man. When he learned of the incident, Malcolm led a group of Muslims down to the local precinct station. As they stood outside, surrounding the building, Malcolm entered and demanded the ministerial right to visit the arrested man. Having gained this end and seen that Johnson was badly injured, Malcolm prevailed upon the police to transfer Johnson to a hospital for treatment. After he received medical attention, Johnson was returned to his cell. At this point, as one report stated, "Mr. X left the station house, gave one brief command to his followers, and they disappeared as if in thin air."[64] The next day Malcolm reappeared for the arraignment with his followers, a lawyer, and the necessary bail bond. Johnson was released.

Goodman states: "It was this incident that really brought Malcolm X and the Muslims to my attention."[65] Impressed by both the strength and the discipline of the Muslim action, he went one Sunday to Temple Number Seven in Harlem, where Malcolm was minister. Upon entering, he was searched for concealed weapons and his breath was checked for the smell of alcohol. This, he learned, was standard practice. Having passed the tests, he was permitted to proceed to the meeting room, where he was overwhelmed by a succession of impressions: "the 'uprightness,' the sobriety of the brothers walking around"; the Arabic greeting "As-Salaam-Alaikum," which struck him as "strange"; and, most of all, Malcolm's teachings about slavery. "I was spellbound. . . . I had never in my life heard a man speak like that, and I knew then that something in my life had changed, or was about to change. I had been like a boat adrift, and I had found my course."[66] Goodman had been *awakened*; he accepted the message and applied for membership. This involved, first, copying a form letter to Muhammad, in which he affirmed that he had attended meetings and "believed in the truths" he had heard. The letter had to be copied perfectly. Then he had to abandon his conk; reform his style of dress from hip to sober and simple; give up cigarettes, alcohol, and all other "drugs"; stop using profanity or speaking disrespectfully to women; and abjure "poisonous" foods, such as pork or cornbread. He learned to pray, facing Mecca, five times daily; to perform daily rituals of personal cleanliness; to attend meetings at least twice weekly; and to work for the Temple whenever possible. Thus his waking up was followed by *cleaning up*. Finally, after six months of probation, he was admitted to full membership as Benjamin 2X.[67]

The "X" is undoubtedly the most potent symbol of the Muslim life. As Goodman observes of his own first reaction to it: "That 'X' really struck me, and I kept repeating it to myself, as though there were something magic about it."[68] It immediately conveyed the idea that its bearer was somehow different, and superior, to people with conventional last names. To ascertain its true meaning entailed learning Muhammad's version of Islamic doctrine, in particular, the "Black Man's History": the "X" is "substituted for the slave name given to our forebears by the plantation owners, 'X' being the unknown factor, since we did not know what our rightful names were."[69] As slaves, black people had been stripped of their names and their tribal identities. Although the name of a believer's original tribe was sometimes revealed to Muhammad (thus Malcolm was Malik el-Shabazz), usually this knowledge was out of reach. In this sense the "X" symbolizes paradise lost, with the reminder that the devil is responsible for the loss. It also embodies the idea that its bearer is an ex-slave, an ex-Negro; that is, he acknowledges his past slavery, and thereby entitles himself to a justified hatred of the slavemaster. At the same time, he rejects the mental slavery of the present—the collective identity of Negro and the individual one signified by his "Christian," or "slave" last name. On this level the "X" testifies to its bearer's strength, to his ability to transcend the limits imposed upon him by his enemy. Further, the "X" indicates his adoption into the Muslim family: all Muslims are brothers and sisters, the children of Elijah Muhammad who, as one minister put it, is their "mother and father."[70] Finally, it identifies him as a citizen of the Nation of Islam and a believer in the divinity of Allah. Goodman says that by the time he received his "X" he "was a changed person, inside and out."[71] He was someone who, through Malcolm and Elijah Muhammad, had re-created himself. Where before he had been the passive object of another's interest, he was now the subject, the active force, in his own life. By negating the weak, individual self-image that negated him, he had affirmed a powerful, collective self-conception.

The most intense experience of this collective self, the moment when Muslim believers could feel fully united through their mutual participation in Allah's love and power, was the weekly or twice-weekly meeting. Especially when the word was being given by Muhammad or Malcolm, the listeners would be fused into a transpersonal unity. At a less emotional level, even everyday life was infused with collective meaning. Through the five daily prayers, believers would "join the world's 725 million Muslims in communicating with God." [72] The routines of home life, from the order in which family members used the bathroom in the morning to what food was placed on the table at night, were ritualized. As we saw in Goodman's process of initiation, most aspects of personal behavior were doctrinally regulated. Moreover, the Nation provided its members with a genuine community. In Detroit and Chicago, for example, children could attend the University of Islam, a Muslim parochial school, instead of public school. Most temples offered a variety of adult education courses, ranging from the black man's history to the "domestic sciences" taught in the Muslim Girls Training and General Civilization Class (M.G.T.-G.C.C.). For men there was in addition the opportunity, if they qualified, to be trained as members of the Fruit of Islam, the elite guard of the Nation. And the major centers of the Nation had Muslim restaurants, grocery stores, and certain other retail outlets, providing both employment and the chance to keep the money earned by Muslims circulating within the Nation.

The paramilitary Fruit of Islam and the Muslim economic institutions embodied the third of Muhammad's promises to his followers. After waking up and cleaning up, they would be able to stand up; that is, they would be economically secure and able to defend themselves from attack. Muhammad argued that a major part of the Negro's "sickness" was that he was a beggar rather than a producer, dependent rather than self-sufficient; hence he forbade his followers to buy on credit—a road back into virtual slavery to the white man —and he encouraged them to build business enterprises, either under the aegis of the Nation or independently. To aid them in such endeavors he gave them an "Economic Blueprint," consisting of five basic principles. First, "know thyself . . . recognize that you are a member of the Creator's Nation . . . recognize the necessity for unity." This implies, second, the importance of pooling "your resources, physically as well as financially." Next, one must not criticize anything that is black-owned or black-operated. Rather, one should spend one's money "with one's own kind," to enrich the black man, not the white man. Fourth, because "jealousy destroys from within," no black man should be envious of another's success. Finally, "observe the operations of the white man. He is successful. He makes no excuses for his failures. He works hard—in a collective manner. You do the same." [73]

The "blueprint" makes clear that Muhammad's program consisted in part of stealing the white man's thunder. Just as black people would be in fact what the white man was only in theory with respect to morality, so they would emulate and then surpass him in economic rationality. Similarly, as the white man never hesitated to defend himself when attacked, neither would the members of the Nation. According to Malcolm:

> We are never aggressors. . . . We strive for peaceful relations with everyone. BUT—[we teach our people] if anyone attacks you, *lay down your life!* . . . Never be the aggressor, never look for trouble. But if any man molests you, may Allah bless you! [74]

As the last phrase indicates, self-defense was sanctioned by religion. Every Muslim had the right, and the obligation, to do unto others as they did unto him. In practice, this right was vested in the Fruit of Islam; the response to any attack was to be collective rather than individual, as it was, for example, in the Hinton Johnson incident. Through their united effort black people would be freed from the clutches of the white devil.

By combining these economic and defensive principles with his program of self-purification and revitalization, the Prophet sought to build a strengthened and independent black community, united nationwide under his leadership. Although there were obvious limits to what could be achieved—limits reflected in Muhammad's instructions to his followers to be conscientious employees no matter who was their boss, and to obey the law—his plan yielded substantial results. As Malcolm put it, for ghetto blacks whose minds had been "whitened out" and whose bodies had been thoroughly corrupted by drugs and alcohol, Muhammad's "truth" was "a two-edged sword. It cuts into you. It causes you great pain, but if you can take the truth, it will cure you and save you from what otherwise would be certain death." [75]

Malcolm had personal reasons for believing in Muhammad's two-edged sword. He had been a convicted criminal when he encountered the Prophet's truth. Through his conversion he had been able to transform himself from a nihilistic street hustler into a disciplined, hard-working, and morally impeccable Muslim minister. Concerning his own conversion he argued that "'the white man is the devil' is a perfect echo of [the] black convict's lifelong experience." [76] He also observed that "only guilt admitted accepts truth," and that "the very enormity of my previous life's guilt" created the necessary precondition for enlightenment. By his "guilt" Malcolm meant his years of living by the hustling code on the streets of Roxbury and Harlem.* In saying that his "lifelong experience" prepared him to believe the white man is a devil, he was looking back past his hustling years to his childhood: to the eighth-grade English teacher who told him that, despite his evident intelligence, "a lawyer— that's no realistic goal for a nigger";[77] before that, to the state welfare authorities whom he blamed for driving his mother insane and breaking up his family after his father's death; to the white racists who killed his father, and who had previously burned down the family home. This latter event, "the nightmare night in 1929," was Malcolm's "earliest vivid memory":

> I remember being suddenly snatched awake into a frightening confusion of pistol shots and shouting and smoke and flames. My father had shouted and shot at the white men who had set the fire and were running away. Our home was burning down around us. We were lunging and bumping and tumbling all over each other trying to escape. My mother, with the baby in her arms, just made it into the yard before the house crashed in, showering sparks. I remember we were outside in the night in our underwear, crying and yelling our heads off. The white police and firemen came and stood around watching as the house burned down to the ground.[78]

In sum: when we begin with the OAAU, we end with Malcolm's earliest experience of racist oppression, and see the roots of his commitment to racial liberation in his childhood.

Militancy vs. Radicalism:
The Question of Malcolm's Historical
Significance

The OAAU thus signifies the whole of Malcolm's life-history, and, more generally, it points us toward the Black Revolution, especially those moments in its history which followed Mal-

---

* The hustling code was Malcolm's first self-chosen form of consciousness. Its basic postulates are that everything is a hustle, i.e., a self-interested deception by one person of another; that, therefore, no one can trust anyone else; that it is a disgrace for

colm's death. Afro-American consciousness was fundamental to the black revolutionaries, as was Malcolm's secularized version of black community renewal and self-defense. Moreover, Malcolm himself came to symbolize the angry pride so characteristic of the revolutionary leaders. This is not to say that these elements were exclusively Malcolm's contribution to the revolutionary cause. His Afro-American consciousness, for example, has a long prior history: from Martin R. Delany to W. E. B. DuBois, there extends a direct line of concern with the question of African origin and possible destiny. The rapid process of decolonization in the postwar period gave this tradition new life. Many black Americans were inspired by and interested in finding ways of relating to the emerging African nations. Several black leaders besides Malcolm sought support for the American struggle from these countries. Malcolm, however, was the most persistent and most successful in heightening black American consciousness of the African cultural heritage, and in linking the national struggle to the international one. He is therefore most closely identified with the contemporary development of Afro-Americanism.

The second major theme in Malcolm's work—what came to be called Black Power—has also been part of the tradition of American black nationalism.[79] The particular form it has taken, however, is clearly Malcolmite. James Farmer, for example, admitted shortly before leaving CORE that "figures like the late Malcolm X have influenced us perceptibly."[80] With the younger members of the Movement, Malcolm's call for black community self-determination and self-defense, coupled with an uncompromising challenge to racism in the society at large, reached a most receptive audience. It is Malcolm's language that echoes in the final warning of Stokely Carmichael and Charles Hamilton's Black Power:

> Whatever the consequences, there is a growing—a rapidly growing—body of black people determined to "T.C.B."—

---

one hustler to be duped by another; and that eventually one must expect to kill or be killed, indeed, to kill and be killed.

The hustling code thus differs markedly from either Muhammad's theodicy or Malcolm's conception of Afro-American unity. It is grounded in self-interest rather than racial interest; it is nihilistic rather than religious or revolutionary. Moreover, unlike Malcolm's later world views, it is not a systematic theoretical mediation of actual or intended practice, but, instead, a more or less direct reflection into consciousness of hustling as a way of life. Accordingly we will forego representing it in more detail until our interpretive work brings us to Malcolm's life in the hustling society.

take care of business. They will not be stopped in their drive to achieve dignity, to achieve their share of power, indeed, to become their own men and women—in this time and in this land—by whatever means necessary.[81]

The Afro-American and Black Power themes provide us with a general way of describing the ideological content of Malcolm's work, but do not express its full significance. Malcolm also had a personal impact on people that went beyond the program he was articulating. Ossie Davis reports, for example, that after he eulogized Malcolm at his funeral, numerous black people wrote to him, commending him for the action:

> Most all of them took special pains to disagree with much or all of what Malcolm said and what he stood for. . . . [But] with one singing exception, they all, every last, black, glory-hugging one of them knew that Malcolm—whatever else he was or was not—Malcolm was a man.[82]

In believing they disagreed with what Malcolm said, many people were probably fusing and confusing his Black Muslim pronouncements with his subsequent position. At least, the relative popularity of Afro-American and Black Power concepts during the late 1960s indicates that more people would agree with the latter than with the former. Yet, despite the differences (which we will be at pains to specify later on) there is an underlying unity between these two phases and, indeed, between them and the younger, pre-Muslim Malcolm portrayed in the *Autobiography of Malcolm X*. Malcolm was a proud and angry man, who over time turned his anger into a slashing critique of American racist practices and of any Negro justification for tolerating them. In paraphrase: Be proud you are black, don't apologize for it; make the white man apologize, in fact, make him compensate you for the oppression to which you have been subjected. More—fight to end that oppression, make yourselves into a free people by any means necessary.

We now have some sense of Malcolm's significance: an individual/collective history—his life and work as such, along with its immediate consequences for the consciousness and conscious activity of his contemporaries; and a legacy—those aspects of his activity which have been carried beyond the limits of his lifetime. This significance can be summarized as Afro-American Unity, Black Power, and Black Pride. The theoretical framework of Black Power is

Afro-American Unity; one form of the actualization of Afro-American Unity is Black Power. Together they help to generate Black Pride, upon which they are themselves predicated. These three concepts are, in other words, interpenetrating aspects of Malcolm's racial consciousness. But if they suffice to establish that Malcolm's life-work was historically significant, they do not provide standards for judging the relative significance or the theoretical meaning of Malcolm's various activities. For example, some would say that pride was Malcolm's most significant contribution to the revolt; in fact, that his historical meaning resides in that contribution:

> Malcolm helped to alter the style and thought of the black revolt of the 1960's, even when . . . [its leaders during his lifetime] denied him a place in its certified leadership. He left another, more lasting bequest as well—the example of that unchained, unbowed black manhood. "Like somebody said," one of Malcolm's movement friends told me, "I never heard nobody call Malcolm X 'nigger.'"[83]

Without a reasoned position and the relevant evidential material (which Peter Goldman, the writer of this passage, fails to provide), such a judgment is in fact a mere assertion. We can only observe that, in a still undetermined manner, Black Pride and Afro-American consciousness were interrelated. Which is to say, we may take Goldman's position not as a conclusive judgment but, rather, as a question: what was the relationship between pride and principle in Malcolm's practical activity, and in the practice of the Black Revolution? To give the question a more general form, what was the relationship between character and consciousness in these practices?

A second question grows directly out of the first: given that Malcolm did contribute valuable elements to the "style and thought of the black revolt," what was the relative value of these elements? In this regard we are confronted with precisely contradictory judgments. On one side there is the Reverend Albert Cleage, who argues that Malcolm's signal contribution was to teach black people the "first basic principle" that "the white man is your enemy." On that principle, Cleage contends, black people can "build a total philosophy, a total course of action for struggle"[84]—a community-based, black nationalist or separatist struggle for power. As for Malcolm's Afro-Americanism, Cleage acknowledges that Malcolm wanted to "relate the struggle of black people in America to black people everywhere." But he does not believe that Malcolm was seriously interested in relating it to "the struggles of oppressed people everywhere."[85] Malcolm's importance is misinterpreted if one focuses on "the last moments of confusion, when he was getting ready to be assassinated," and says that "the confused little statements he made in those last moments were his life."[86]

On the other side from Cleage are people like George Breitman, who argues that "Malcolm was a radical both before and after leaving the Black Muslims. After, he was a revolutionary—increasingly anti-capitalist and pro-socialist as well as anti-imperialist."[87] The Essien-Udoms share this position. They argue that "by the time of his untimely death Malcolm X had moved from black nationalism to internationalism, and had completely identified himself as well as the Afro-American struggle with the revolution of the 'wretched of the earth'—the exploited people of the Third World. He had become a foe of the international capitalism system and a staunch Pan-Africanist."[88] Moreover, "Malcolm was not thinking solely in racial terms toward the end of his life. He very clearly indicated that the oppressed might find allies both in America and in Europe that were opposed to the capitalist system."[89]

One may readily surmise from the tone of Breitman's and the Essien-Udoms' remarks that they consider Malcolm's movement from black nationalism and racial militancy to international socialism and political radicalism to have been a progressive development. Cleage views that shift, insofar as he acknowledges its existence, as a regression caused by the pressure of the threat of imminent death. The universal agreement that Malcolm infused a previously lacking racial pride into the freedom movement breaks down into opposing evaluations of the principles through which that spiritual force was expressed. We are, accordingly, given the problem of determining the relationship between these two forms of consciousness.

A third question now arises from the conjunction of the first two. Malcolm's characteristic pride, expressed in the form of militant and/or radical conscious activity, gave him an almost magnetic quality of personal power and prestige. This quality is reflected in John Henrik Clarke's judgment that "Malcolm X . . . was a remarkably gifted and charismatic leader whose hostility and resentment symbolized the dreadful stamp of the black ghetto, but a man whose philosophies of racial determination and whose pragmatic comments made him unacceptable as a participant in peaceful social change."[90] He had, in other words, "the authority of the extraordinary and personal *gift of grace* (charisma), the absolutely personal devotion and personal confidence in revelation, heroism, or other qualities of individual leadership."[91] His followers were bound to him by their recognition of that gift. But charisma and the charismatic relationship, as Max Weber here defines them, are not determinative concepts: they identify a certain quality, but they do not explain it. Consequently, our question becomes: what is the relationship among Malcolm's characteristic pride, his militant and radical forms of conscious activity, and his charismatic power and authority?

The Problematic of Racist Oppression

The terms in which we have now formulated our problem force us to consider the relationship between political consciousness and social context. As Karl Mannheim reasons: "What is new in the achievement of the personally unique 'charismatic' individual can only be utilized for the collective life when, from the very beginning, it is in contact with some important current problem, and when from the start its meanings are rooted genetically in collective purposes."[92] Hence we must now consider Malcolm's leadership within the context of his particular social and political situation, within the problematic of racist oppression.

The problematic of racist oppression has two aspects. First, if we view race from an abstract, anthropological perspective, we recognize that a race is a natural or biological category which, as such, is devoid of political meaning. But racism is a relationship of domination and subordination based upon skin color. Consequently, we are interested in explaining this transformation of a natural category into a criterion of social valuation and devaluation. Second, the illusion of a naturally determined social differentiation between racial collectivities manifestly deprives the subordinated group of its human value. Thus from the perspectives both of racially oppressed people and of any consistent conception of human value, racism must be eradicated.

Such a definition of racism would not seem to be significantly controversial. When we attempt to give some theoretical content to the definitional form, however, we are once again confronted by opposing views. On the one hand, there is a liberal, reform-oriented conception of race relations; on the other, a revolutionary conception. The former position has been most notably articulated by Gunnar Myrdal and his associates in *An American Dilemma*. Myrdal's premise is that:

The American Negro problem is a problem in the heart of
the American. It is there that the interracial tension has its
focus. It is there that the decisive struggle goes on. . . . The
"American Dilemma," referred to in the title of this book, is
[this] ever-raging conflict between, on the one hand, the
values preserved on the general plane which we shall call
the "American Creed," where the American thinks, talks
and acts under the influence of high national and Christian
precepts, and, on the other hand, the valuations on specific
planes of individual and group living, where personal and
local interests; economic, social, and sexual jealousies; considerations of community prestige and conformity; group
prejudice against particular persons or types of people; and
all sorts of miscellaneous wants, impulses and habits dominate his outlook.[93]

American racism is a moral contradiction, an unresolved tension between the universal rights of man and the manifold particularities of
everyday experience. In Myrdal's view, it is the product of a vicious
circle of cumulative causation which preserves the Negro people as
an inferior caste within what is otherwise a relatively open if still
class-structured society. Cumulative causation exists when, in a relationship between any two factors, a change in one of them "will
cause a change in the other factor, too, and start a process of interaction where the change in one factor will continuously be supported
by the reaction of the other factor. . . . The whole system will be
moving in the direction of the primary change, but much further."[94]
In the instance of American racism, "white prejudice and discrimination keep the Negro low in standards of living, health, education,
manners and morals. This, in turn, gives support to white prejudice."[95]*

This dynamic relationship both presupposes and reinforces the
caste position of Negroes, meaning by the term *caste* a social status
consisting of "such drastic restrictions of free competition in the
various spheres of life that the individual in the lower caste cannot,
by any means, change his status, except by a secret and illegitimate
'passing,' which is only possible to the few who have the physical
appearance of members of the upper caste."[96] We therefore have a
self-perpetuating system of social injustice. But "such a harsh devia-

---

* Later we will adapt the concept of the vicious circle to our own ends, but in the
process its meaning will be significantly altered.

tion from the ordinary American social structure and the American Creed could not occur without a certain internal conflict and without a system of false beliefs and blindnesses aided by certain mechanical controls in law and social structure."[97] The "false beliefs" or "popular theories" of race, "because of the rationalizing function they serve, are heavily loaded with emotions," especially sexual fears and phantasies; but "people also want to be rational" and can be expected to respond favorably to educational efforts.[98] Similarly, the mechanical deficiencies in the system may be remedied by intelligent social engineering oriented toward cumulative causation in a liberal direction. In other words, Myrdal is looking toward a genuine "New Deal" for the Negro people, and therefore ends on this optimistic, if hypothetical, note:

> If America in actual practice could show the world a progressive trend by which the Negro became finally integrated into modern democracy, all mankind would be given faith again—it would have reason to believe that peace, progress and order are feasible. And America would have a spiritual power many times stronger than all her financial and military resources—the power of the trust and support of all good people on earth.[99]

One might say that the civil rights movement during its phase of nonviolent direct action was an attempt to realize Myrdal's vision. Although it had roots in the black American experience and drew its inspiration from Gandhi's *Satyagraha* campaigns, its leaders viewed its purpose as the realization of the American dream.

The opposing position is argued most forcefully by Oliver C. Cox in *Caste, Class, and Race*. Cox begins by observing that Myrdal's belief in the universal acceptance and potency of the "American Creed" was not shared by James Madison, who was one of its originators. Madison began instead from the presupposition that "those who have and those who are without property have ever formed distinct interests in society."[100] Hence "Myrdal is abstract and unreal because he implicitly homogeneates the material interests of the American people and then declares animistically, 'America is continually struggling for its soul.'"[101] But in fact the struggle is between the American ruling class and the working masses, a struggle for political power. It follows that there is no "dilemma" in Myrdal's sense, "for it seems quite obvious that none of the great imperialist democracies either can or intends to practice its democratic ideals among its subject peoples."[102] As for the vicious circle: to be sure, race prejudice and Negro standards are interrelated; but both of them "are consistently dependent variables. They are both produced by the calculated economic interests of the Southern oligarchy."[103] Indeed, "the poor whites themselves may be thought of as the primary instrument of the ruling class in subjugating the Negroes."[104] The use of the term *caste* is obscurantist:

> Our primary objection to the use of the caste belief in the study of race relations rests not so much upon its scientific untenability as upon its insidious potentialities. It lumps all white people and all Negroes into two antagonistic groups struggling in the interest of a mysterious god called caste. This is very much to the liking of the exploiters of labor, since it tends to confuse them in an emotional matrix with all the people.[105]

The term caste is thus akin to the idea that sexual fears and obsessions are basic determinants of racism, when in fact "sex is not 'basic' in race relations, but it is basic in the system of rationalization which supports racial antagonism."[106] In this way "sexual obsession functions in the fundamental interest of economic exploitation."[107] Finally, not education and reform but aggressive propaganda and class struggle must be used to eradicate racism: "The problem of racial exploitation, then, will most probably be settled as part of the world proletarian struggle for democracy; every advance of the masses will be an actual potential advance for the colored people."[108] The vicious circle will be broken by proletarian revolution.

Myrdal and Cox clearly have opposing views of the problem. Indeed, the difference between them is even greater than we have indicated, for *An American Dilemma* is explicitly an argument against the kind of class-analytical position Cox develops. "The Marxian solidarity between the toilers of the earth will," Myrdal contends, "have a long way to go as far as the solidarity of the poor white Americans with the toiling Negroes." Especially in the South, "these two groups, . . . placed in an intensified competition with each other, lacking every trace of primary solidarity, and marked off from each other by color and tradition, could not possibly clasp hands. There is a Swedish proverb: when the feed-box is empty, the horses will bite each other."[109] Intra-class competition precludes inter-class conflict; Myrdal's and Cox's arguments are mutually exclusive.

Earlier we found that radicalism and militancy seemed to exclude each other; now we find ourselves confronting opposed reformist and revolutionary interpretations of racism and racial liberation. For purposes of investigation, however, we may dissolve the polemical opposition into a question: what is the relationship between reformist and revolutionary tendencies in the struggle for racial liberation? We may note that Myrdal's own analysis of the lack of working-class consciousness is not incompatible with Cox's conception of the determining force of ruling-class interest in American life, while Myrdal's concept of caste is at best another name for the phenomenon it is intended to explain. But neither we nor Cox can deny Myrdal's observation that black and white have yet to unite in proletarian class struggle. We must admit that the working class is so divided along racial lines that actual working-class consciousness reflects this division more clearly than it does its economic foundation. Hence a second question can be added to the first: what is the relationship between class and race in the vicious circle of racist oppression?

The Problem of False Consciousness

We saw earlier that Malcolm, especially during his last year, seemed to be evolving toward an anti-capitalist, African socialist position. He was also sensitive to and recognized the importance of class (or classlike) divisions within the black community. However, his astute psychological analysis of the "Negro" identity prevents us from taking a purely political-economic approach to his philosophy. In parallel fashion, Cox's critique of Myrdal strengthens our interest in a Marxist analysis of class conflict. But clearly, the subjective factors in the vicious circle cannot simply be identified with or reduced to class determinations. If such a reduction were possible, the theoretical and practical problem of racism would not arise. The actual consciousness of the working class would be class consciousness in the Marxist sense, and there would be an end to the matter. The racist system of "false beliefs" and "popular theories" is not class consciousness, however, but the *falsification* of class relationships in consciousness. Indeed, racism signifies the more general problem of false consciousness—of the active resistance by members of the working class to the recognition of their objective class-interests. We therefore require a theoretical understanding of this resistance to learning the lessons of everyday life. Psychoanalysis is one such theory.

The relevance of psychoanalysis to our inquiry may be suggested in another way. It follows from the idea of false consciousness as defined above that we are seeking to uncover the distortive mediation joining the extremes of class structure and conscious belief. This middle term must satisfy two conditions. First, it must preclude the identification of class structure with consciousness while simultaneously determining the interpenetration of these polarities; that is, it cannot be either class or consciousness, but must instead be a function of the former and a tendency toward the latter. We therefore need a conception of class-structured unconscious mental functioning. Second, this middle term must deal with the sexual obsession which Cox admits plays its disruptive role in the class struggle, and with the emotion with which Myrdal claims racist beliefs are "heavily laden." Psychoanalysis, because it provides an understanding of sexual and other obsessions in terms of unconscious mental functioning, has the potential of meeting both conditions.

In other words, psychoanalysis provides a possible solution to the problem of how class relationships are falsified in consciousness. We are also interested in how false consciousness is overcome, and this interest raises the problem of determining the relationship between racial consciousness and class consciousness. Racial consciousness of the type embodied in the OAAU or the Nation of Islam arises in opposition to racism and is therefore differentiated from the latter *eo ipso*. But it is not, at least manifestly, class consciousness. If, for example, we view Malcolm's political radicalism as tending toward class consciousness and his earlier militancy as the limiting form of racial consciousness, we have a new form of the debate between these two positions. In such a renewed debate, the militant would argue that radicalism leads to interracial alliances which invariably disadvantage black people, while the radical would argue that militancy isolates black people in their blackness, deprives them of all possible allies, and likewise is to their disadvantage. Each would appear to the other to be blind to the realities of the existing situation, hence to be irrational and irresponsible with respect to the interests of black people.

At this juncture the debate ends inconclusively: because the relationship between racial and class consciousness has not been determined, we cannot decide if radicalism and militancy really exclude each other, much less if they are engaged in a life-and-death struggle. But insofar as the terms of the debate reveal the problematical nature of acting rationally in a given situation, they suggest a particular line of inquiry. Each party is accusing the other of false consciousness while simultaneously ascribing truth to its own position. Both sides would agree, however, that a form of consciousness can be judged "true" only if it yields a realistic picture of an existing situation and thereby creates the possibility of rational and responsible political action. But just as any existing situation is a moment of the historical process, so any judgment concerning the rationality of political action must be derived from the laws or principles of historical development. Consequently, the formulation and/or explication of such laws is the theoretical precondition for solving the problem of false consciousness.

The elements of Marxist and psychoanalytic theory we need for our work will emerge in due course. A critical exposition of certain concepts developed by Wilhelm Reich and Frantz Fanon will, however, help us to define more precisely our investigative aims.

In "Dialectical Materialism and Psychoanalysis," Reich argues that "the economic structure of society—through many intermediary links such as the class association of the parents, the economic conditions of the family, its ideology, the parents' relationship to one another, etc.—enters into a reciprocal relation with the instincts, or ego, of the newborn." [110] Class structure determines character structure; character structure reinforces class structure. The Marxist conception of society is here brought into contact with the Freudian conception of the individual. Reich goes on to argue that the bourgeois ruling class "has a reality principle which serves the perpetuation of its power," so that "if the proletariat is brought up to accept this reality principle . . . this means an affirmation of the proletariat's exploitation and of capitalist society as a whole." [111] Insofar as a member of the proletariat has internalized the bourgeois reality principle, his own character structure prevents him from achieving class consciousness; that is, under these conditions the proletarian loses or is alienated from his potential for class-conscious activity—his conscious activity is falsified. As Fanon says concerning racist oppression, the black man wears a white mask. [112] He has been taught that to be white is to be human, and he wishes to be human. The consequence is self-hatred: shame that he is black, guilt if he attempts to pass for white. It follows that liberation from false consciousness necessitates overthrowing the reality principle of the oppressing class or throwing off the mask of the white racist oppressor. In the limiting instance this means that the objective violence of class or racist oppression, which has been reflected into the character structure of the oppressed individual, must be turned back against its perpetrator. Fanon argues that in a colonial world created by violence and maintained through the internalization of violence by the colonized population, "decolonisation is always a violent phenomenon." [113]

In a sense, our inquiry will be an elaboration of these propositions. It will not be an empirical testing of their validity, for two reasons. First, as a point of method, we do not wish to impose these postulated relationships upon Malcolm's life experience in advance, but will, rather, be concerned to see how they emerge through the analysis of that experience.* Second, we can ascertain through a critical reflection of these propositions that they state problems as well as solutions. Most importantly, Reich's basic position is a confounding of two problems and hence a solution to neither. On the one hand, he is interested in how the individual is theoretically and empirically connected to society. On the other, he is interested in how objective or economic forces are connected to subjective or emotional ones. He thinks, however, that the problem is to connect a *subjective individual* with an *objective society*, with the consequence that he cannot even raise the question of the *objectivity of the individual* and the *subjectivity of society*. Unless this question has been raised and adequately answered, a subjective individual and an objective society must continue to exclude each other. It follows that psychoanalysis is taken to be an individual psychology, which can at best be juxtaposed against a Marxist political economy. Such an outcome has the advantage of precluding either a psychoanalytic or a political economic reductionism, but it also precludes the possibility of comprehending how the individual is linked to society and how subjectivity is related to objectivity. Thus Reich's formulation has a theoretically determined society at one pole, a theoretically determined individual at the other, but only pre-theoretical, empirical linkages in between. The most important of these linkages for Reich, namely, the family, is seen from both perspectives but comprehended by neither; but we must comprehend the family

---

* We will take up this methodological issue in the next section of this chapter.

and other middle terms if we are to have a coherent Marxist psycho-analytic theory and practice. Accordingly, we must try to develop a set of concepts through which we can comprehend the objectivity as well as the subjectivity of the individual, the subjectivity as well as the objectivity of society, and the simultaneously objective-subjective mediations of these polarities.

Fanon formulated the problem in terms similar to our own. He believed that "only a psychoanalytical interpretation of the black problem can lay bare the anomalies of affect that are responsible for the structure of the complex."[114] But if "the black man wants to be white," if there is an "inferiority complex," then "it is the outcome of a double process: —primarily, economic; —subsequently, the internalization—or better, the epidermalization—of this inferiority."[115] Therefore if the black man's alienation is to be ended, there must be a "total understanding" of the problem: "On the objective level as on the subjective level, a solution has to be supplied."[116]

Initially, Fanon believed that the "massive psychoexistential complex" created by the "juxtaposition of the white and black races" could be destroyed by analysis.[117] Later, he concluded that the solution involved the spontaneous, violent rebellion of the wretched of the earth and the subsequent transformation of this unself-conscious impulse toward national liberation into a genuinely national culture through the mediation of organized political activity. From beginning to end, his theorizing was firmly grounded in practice, yet the energy and unifying tendency of that practice was not ultimately reflected in theory. Although he recognized that the falsification of black consciousness and the shattering of false consciousness were objectively and subjectively determined, he did not attempt to establish theoretical principles which would determine the conscious unity of these tendencies as a life-process, as dialectically structured activity. Consequently, his brilliant analysis of the complex, highly problematical de-colonization process is readily misinterpreted as a disconnected series of assertions and impressions, or even as a panegyric to violence. In our own analysis of the construction and destruction of the vicious circle of racist oppression, we will orient ourselves toward the development of the requisite theoretical principles and, in so doing, we will also be searching for the unifying premises for a Marxist psychoanalysis. That is, we will attempt to establish principles of historical development and human nature sufficient to determine the relationship between objective and subjective forces at the individual, socially universal, and intermediate levels of analysis; to determine this relationship as a dialectical process, as conscious life-activity; and, by so doing, to determine our judgment of the reality, rationality, and responsibility of Malcolm's theory and practice.

Comments on the Method, Limits, and Organization of the Inquiry

A method is a way of working. If theorizing is what we are doing, then our method is how we are doing it. A method is dialectical if, as Marx states, "it includes in its positive understanding of what exists a simultaneous recognition of its negation, its inevitable destruction." In other words, a dialectical method grasps its object as becoming, as coming-to-be and ceasing-to-be: as coming-to-be through ceasing-to-be, and ceasing-to-be through coming-to-be. It takes things as process, as internally contradictory or self-oppositional activity through which a potential is actualized. When an object under investigation does not appear to be dialectical in this sense, or when the laws of its self-transformation are unknown, then the method must also be phenomenological. It must be a critical analysis of appearances, i.e., a breaking-down of the object as given in experience and a reduction of the resulting elements or determinations to their most abstract, general form. Once such a critical analysis has been completed, a synthetical reconstruction of the object—including its appearances—becomes possible. To cite Marx once more: "Along the first path the full conception . . . [is] evaporated to yield an abstract determination; along the second, the abstract determination leads to a reproduction of the concrete by way of thought." [118]

Dialectical method thus consists of two phases or modes: an analytical, regressive, or phenomenological mode; and a synthetical, progressive, or logical mode.* In actuality, it is impossible to utilize one without also using the other, but we may differentiate them on the basis of their starting points. Phenomenology begins with the object as given in experience, with what Marx terms a "chaotic conception of the whole." [119] Logical exposition begins with the general principles, laws, or abstractions uncovered in the course of phe-

---

* This distinction between phenomenology and logic originated in the relationship between Hegel's *The Phenomenology of Mind* and his *A Science of Logic*, and was developed further by Marx in the text cited above.

nomenological investigation. Together they constitute a circle, in which the beginning is the apparent or "imagined concrete" and the ending is the concrete as a "rich totality of many determinations and relations."[120]

Defined in these terms, the present investigation is phenomenological. We begin with Malcolm's consciousness and conscious activity as a record of his experience. We will attempt to analyze this manifold of activity with the aim of laying bare its underlying meaning and determinants. But within the process of dissolving "the chaotic conception of the whole" into its abstracted form we will periodically return to the concrete. It is our hope that in the course of this return Malcolm's conscious activity will emerge as a "totality of many determinations and relations."

Having said something about what our inquiry is (or at least is intended) to be, we should add a few words about what it is not. It is not an empirical testing of propositions. From an empiricist's perspective it is more nearly an exercise in hypothesis-formation than in hypothesis-confirmation. Moreover, the empirical representations evolved in the course of the investigation are of varying solidity. It has often been necessary to sacrifice depth for breadth. Such a sacrifice is justified, at least in my opinion, if it permits us to construct a unifying conception of an actual historical situation.

With respect to empirical reliability, the most important questions concern *The Autobiography of Malcolm X*. Was Malcolm representing himself accurately? Was Alex Haley, his biographical amanuensis, representing him accurately? From a purely empirical standpoint, I believe the answer to both questions is generally affirmative. Throughout the *Autobiography* . . . there is a clear and self-consciously drawn distinction between fact and opinion. Furthermore, both men had a passion for accuracy and order, as is evident in Haley's epilogue as well as in the body of the text. Finally, and I think most convincingly, the relationship with Haley and the process of self-reflection this involved were integral parts of Malcolm's personal evolution. By permitting him to develop a knowledge of himself as a distinct individual, they were instrumental in helping to free him from his unquestioning devotion to Elijah Muhammad. It is extremely unlikely that such a process of individuation could have been premised upon major falsification of the life-historical record.

This last point raises another issue. We will see later on that Malcolm's relationship with Haley had something of a psychoanalytic quality. The *Autobiography* . . . is a record of the more or less psychoanalytic interaction of the two men. It is Malcolm's reconstruction and interpretation of his world from a particular point of view and at a particular time. It does not exhaust the possible meanings of the recorded events. We must therefore consider in what ways his interpretations conceal as well as reveal meaning, or provide us with one meaning instead of another. We must also recognize that the interpretations he constructed have their own validity quite apart from any judgment we may make of them. As in a psychoanalytic interaction, they are moments in a process of self-transformation. This confers a truth-value upon them that goes beyond anything to be found within the mode of theoretical reflection. Indeed, our own psychoanalytic interpretations of Malcolm's activity, just because they are formed outside the context of therapeutic interaction, cannot be considered true, but only more or less plausible. At best, we may hope to provide a coherent, internally consistent, and empirically inclusive view of his character and emotional development.

The preceding statement of the relationship between interpretive meanings and practical truth is derived from Marx's conception of *praxis*: "The question whether objective truth can be attributed to human thinking is not a question of theory but is a practical question."[121] Or again: "Social life is essentially practical. All mysteries which mislead theory into mysticism find their rational solution in human practice and in the comprehension of this practice."[122] It follows that our prior statements concerning psychoanalytic interpretations apply equally to historical ones. This does not mean there are no intratheoretical criteria for distinguishing good interpretations from bad, or more powerful theories from less powerful ones: one can, for example, evaluate the claims of rival theories through mutual critique and the comparative testing of their empirical propositions. But in the present instance and for reasons of economy, a number of Marxist and psychoanalytic concepts are taken as given. They are developed within the investigative process as interpretive responses to represented subject matter, but they are not themselves subjected to a critical analysis. Similarly, certain complicated issues that arise within these theories—e.g., the relationship of the state to the capitalist class, or of the labor-value of commodities to their market prices—will not be addressed. And at times, in order to provide an adequate interpretive structure without unduly expanding the scope of our work, we will have recourse to schematic presentations instead of more fully elaborated empirical-conceptual formulations.

The final limit of the inquiry is its most important limitation, i.e., the problems and contradictions involved when a white writer (or a white reader) attempts to understand the experience of black people. But, as I noted in the preface, I believe we all, black and white alike, have lessons to learn from Malcolm X and the black revolutionary movement.

Having defined our method of working and the limits of our work, how are we to structure the work itself? From our brief, regressive representation of Malcolm's consciousness we determined that our starting point must be his first remembered experience, namely, the "nightmare night" of the Black Legion attack. It is also evident that in the course of our work we must return to Malcolm's founding of the OAAU, and to the Black Revolution of the 1960s. Moreover, our subject matter requires that we will consistently be advancing from individual experience or specific events through the particular meanings of these experiences and events to their more general determinations, and back again. In like fashion, our theoretical orientation requires that at each step along the way we attempt to establish the objective and subjective meanings of these various forms of conscious activity. Finally, when viewed from the perspective of the problematic of racist oppression and the related problem of false consciousness, Malcolm's life history falls into two distinct phases: The first, extending from his birth to his imprisonment in Charlestown Prison, was a period of intensifying alienation and falsification of consciousness, of regression or descent into the depths of a racially oppressive society. As such it constitutes a negation of Malcolm's potential for racially self-conscious activity. The second phase, the negation of this negation, is the period during which Malcolm progressively overcame the alienation and falsification of his self-conscious activity, beginning with his conversion to Islam while he was still in prison. Our inquiry as a whole is designed to reveal the unity of or relationship between these two phases of development.

More specifically, in Chapter II ("The Nightmare Night") we will be analyzing Malcolm's first memory as an event in American racial history, a confrontation between the Ku Klux Klan (and its derivatives) and the United Negro Improvement Association (the Garvey Movement). This will involve developing a conceptual relationship between alienated labor and class interests; alienated emotional forces and mass motives; and the above-mentioned opposing forms of collective racial activity. Then in Chapter III ("The Seventh Son") we will analyze the same event as a moment in Little family history and as a determinant of Malcolm's character, conscience, and consciousness. We will find that the more general conditions of social alienation analyzed in Chapter II were reflected into the life of the family and into Malcolm's individual identity. In this chapter we will also advance in time to the death of Malcolm's father, when Malcolm was six years old. Taken in combination, Chapters II and III will form an interpretation of Malcolm's early childhood, of the initial development of his potential for self-conscious activity within a social and familial situation of falsified conscious activity.

In Chapters IV ("The Vicious Circle") and V ("Never Trust Anybody") we will analyze the further falsification or regressive development of that potential. Chapter IV will be concerned with the disintegration of Malcolm's natal family, his juvenile delinquency, his attempted reform while living with a white family, and the fateful confrontation with the respected teacher that proved to Malcolm that his reform had been to no avail. We will see that these events were conditioned by the impact upon black people of the American welfare state, as it was developing during the Depression; that this impact was subjectively expressed in the form of a constellation of racial stereotypes; and that Malcolm ultimately rejected the role that had been assigned to him in this stereotypical drama. In Chapter V we will interpret Malcolm's further regression, from hipster to hustler to criminal nihilist. Here the broader framework will be the ghettoized situation of black people, especially as it was influenced by the transformation of the welfare state into a warfare state during World War II.

Chapter VI ("Only Guilt Admitted") will constitute the turning point in our inquiry. Our subject matter will be Malcolm's conversion to Islam, i.e., the racial-religious negation of his self-negating criminal-nihilist identity. In Chapter VII ("We Have a Common Enemy") we will analyze Malcolm's developing racial self-consciousness as it proceeded from the ground of racial-religious self-identification and as it was conditioned by the integrationist and separatist tendencies in the movement toward racial liberation. In Chapter VIII ("Think for Yourself") we will come to the painful process of reflective or self-conscious activity through which Malcolm came to recognize the necessity of leaving the Nation of Islam. This will bring us in Chapter IX ("Freedom By Any Means Necessary") to Malcolm's founding of the OAAU; to our direct appraisal of the reality, rationality, and responsibility of his chosen mode of political activity; and (very briefly) to the struggle for racial liberation as it developed after Malcolm's death. Finally, in Chapter X ("The Logic of

Democracy") we will summarize the various propositions which constitute our contribution to a theory of racial and human liberation.

A few last words before we proceed: we are going to be representing and interpreting Malcolm's individual-collective experience in terms of consciousness and conscious activity. It may therefore be useful to provide a preliminary definition of these terms. Webster defines *activity* as "any process which an organism carries on or participates in by virtue of being alive." *Activity* is the life-process itself; consequently, it is inherently dialectical. *Consciousness* is activity characterized by a self's being (as the dictionary has it) "aware of that of which another is aware," in a state of mental wakefulness. Somewhat more restrictively, any particular form of consciousness is a way of looking at things; ultimately, such forms become theoretical structures or even world views. Such highly articulated or crystallized structures of consciousness, however, presuppose the more fluid process of *conscious activity*, that is, sensuous interaction characterized by the attention of a self to its object or by the mutual recognition of two or more selves. Conscious activity mediated by consciousness of itself is *self-conscious activity*. Finally, we can speak of consciousness in the special sense of the thought-form which remains to us after a conscious subject has ceased being active, either in a particular way (when the person's activity has taken on a new form) or altogether (when the person has died). In this case consciousness is an activity which continues to live in memory only.

CHAPTER II

The Nightmare Night

MALCOLM'S FATHER, EARL LITTLE, was "a big, six-foot four, very black man. He had only one eye."[1] He was from Reynolds, Georgia, had a third- or fourth-grade education, and "he had seen four of his six brothers die by violence, three of them killed by white men, including one by lynching."[2] His intense exposure to racist violence was "among the reasons [why he] had decided to risk and dedicate his life to help disseminate [the Garveyite] philosophy...." He believed, "as did Marcus Garvey, that freedom, independence and self-respect could never be achieved by the Negro in North America, and that therefore the Negro should leave America to the white man and return to his African land of origin."[3] Until that day of homecoming, black people should strive to be independent of the white man, to be economically self-sustaining. In accordance with this latter principle, Little had moved to Lansing, Michigan, in the late 1920s, looking for a place where his family could own their own home, raise their own food, and maybe build a small business of some kind.

Little's basic source of income was his Baptist preaching. He was a "jackleg preacher," not an ordained minister, and he "never pastored in any regular church of his own."[4] But he had sufficient inspiration, or at least was sufficiently inspiring, to make a tolerably good living from church collections (and occasional odd jobs). He was able to buy the family a home outside of the Lansing Negro district, and to start accumulating a small amount of capital for his projected business. In fact, the combination of his militancy and relative prosperity led "some stupid local Uncle Tom Negroes ... to funnel stories about his revolutionary beliefs to the local white people...."

Soon, everywhere [he] went, Black Legionnaires were reviling him as an 'uppity nigger' for wanting to own a store, for living outside the Lansing Negro district, for spreading unrest and dissension among 'the good niggers.'"[5] Shortly thereafter came the "nightmare night" in 1929 which was Malcolm's "earliest vivid memory":

> I remember being suddenly snatched awake into a frighten-
> ing confusion of pistol shots and shouting and smoke and
> flames. My father had shouted and shot at the two white
> men who had set the fire and were running away. Our home
> was burning down around us. We were lunging and bumping
> and tumbling all over each other trying to escape. My
> mother, with the baby in her arms, just made it into the
> yard before the house crashed in, showering sparks. I re-
> member we were outside in the night in our underwear, cry-
> ing and yelling our heads off. The white police and firemen
> came and stood around watching as the house burned down
> to the ground.[6]

The attacking Black Legion was a local variant of the Ku Klux Klan: "Formed ostensibly to seek jobs for Southern whites, the Legion was anti-Negro, anti-Semitic and anti-union."[7] In its heyday it had "several thousand" members and a reputation for being even more "sinister and violent" than the Klan itself. It operated freely in Southern Michigan and Ohio until 1936, when seven of its members were convicted of murdering a young WPA worker. That Earl Little should have been anathema to members of such an organization is hardly surprising; and, considering the violent character of the Legion, the nature of the attack is equally comprehensible. Instead of burning a cross in front of the house, they burned the house itself, thereby delivering a warning to Little and to the "good niggers" of the area to abjure any kind of uppity behavior. And if by chance the Little family had perished in the flames, that would have been all to the good.

Thus Malcolm's consciousness began in a moment of racist violence. Even earlier, in fact, his father's Garveyism, which here provoked the Legion to violence, had resulted in a confrontation with the KKK itself. As Malcolm tells the story:

> When my mother was pregnant with me, she told me later,
> a party of hooded Ku Klux Klan riders galloped up to our
> home in Omaha, Nebraska, one night. Surrounding the
> house, brandishing their shotguns and rifles, they shouted

for my father to come out. My mother went to the front
door and opened it. Standing where they could see her preg-
nant condition, she told them that she was alone with her
three small children, and that my father was away, preaching, in Milwaukee. The Klansmen shouted threats and
warnings at her that we had better get out of town because
"the good Christian white people" were not going to stand
for my father's "spreading trouble" among the "good"
Negroes of Omaha with the "back to Africa" preachings of
Marcus Garvey.[8]

The riders then "galloped around the house, shattering every win-
dowpane with their gun butts [and] finally rode off into the night,
their torches flaring."* The attack in Lansing was not an isolated
incident. Indeed, from our representation of these two events it is
evident that they must be understood as skirmishes in an ongoing
war between Garveyites and members of the Klan.

At this juncture two paths are open to us: either to explore what
the "nightmare night" meant to Malcolm, i.e., approach it as a moment of life history, or to seek to establish its social historical meaning. Since our interest in Malcolm ultimately depends upon his relationship to the Black Revolution, the meaning of his life history is
likewise dependent upon its social determination. We will therefore
work our way out from the event to its general historical determinants, beginning with a representation of the KKK and the Garvey
Movement. Within the historical context thus established, we will
explore its meaning as a moment in the life of Malcolm's family and
with respect to his own developing consciousness.

"Up, You Mighty Race!"

In 1914 the Klan was only a memory, an historical but
not a living presence. Its rebirth was occasioned by the heroic depiction of the Klan in D. W. Griffith's *The Birth of a Nation*. Released

---

* When he returned from his journey, Malcolm's father decided to wait until his wife
had given birth, and then to move. After Malcolm was born "on May 19, 1925, in an
Omaha hospital," the family moved, first to Milwaukee and then to Lansing. Malcolm states that he is not sure why his father decided to leave Omaha, for "he was not
a frightened Negro." One might surmise, however, that this push from the Klan was
complemented by the pull of greener financial pastures to the north.

on March 3, 1915, the first full-length American motion picture was in part the story of "a vanquished South, rescued at the last moment from the tentacles of scalawags, carpetbaggers, drunken Union soldiers and unprincipled freedmen by the hard-riding horsemen of the Ku Klux Klan."[9] Toward the end of the year, as word of the epic drama preceded the film into the modern South, William J. ("Colonel") Simmons, an Atlanta fraternal organizer, received a charter from the state of Georgia for the "Invisible Empire, the Knights of the Ku Klux Klan."

Despite the advance publicity provided by Griffith's film, the Klan did not do well during its first four years of renewed existence. As late as the spring of 1920, it had fewer than two thousand members. At that point it was joined by two imaginative and avaricious promoters, Edward Young Clarke and Elizabeth Tyler, who "reasoned correctly that it could greatly broaden its appeal by exploiting the fears and prejudices of uncritical minds against the Catholic, the Jew, the Negro, the Oriental, and the recent immigrant."[10] Simmons was quickly won over to this more aggressive program; he agreed to pay Clarke $2.50 for each new recruit brought into the organization.

Using the booster techniques of the modern salesman and the administrative procedures of a large corporation, in eighteen months Clarke increased the Klan's membership to over one hundred thousand. He also won for the organization the not-always-kindly attention of the big city newspapers. In the fall of 1921 the New York *World* published an exposé of the Invisible Empire, accusing it of major financial irregularities and of "152 separate outrages, . . . including four murders, forty-one floggings, and twenty-seven tar and feather parties."[11] This story led to a Congressional investigation, but the proceedings were terminated abruptly when Simmons denied all the charges—and when "Atlanta Representative W. D. Upshaw introduced a bill calling for a similar investigation of the Knights of Columbus and other 'secret' societies."[12] The investigation had failed, and more than failed: "The publicity was a boon to recruiting. Many persons outside the East were inclined to look with favor upon the secret order merely because a great New York daily had seen fit to condemn it. . . . Within four months [of the hearings] more than two hundred local chapters were chartered, and within one year membership burgeoned from one hundred thousand to almost one million."[13] By the end of 1924 there were probably one and a half million Klansmen; one contemporary observer estimated that there were close to four million.[14] The Invisible Empire had become a powerful national organization, as strong in the lower-middle-class and working-class neighborhoods of many major cities as it was in the small towns of the South and Midwest, where it had originally found its greatest support. It controlled and/or exerted major influence upon many local and even several state governments. It was, in fact, strong enough to prevent passage of a motion condemning it at the National Convention of the Democratic Party in 1924.

According to its second Imperial Wizard, Hiram Wesley Evans, the Klan's strength derived from the fact that it spoke for "the great mass of Americans of the old pioneer stock," for "Nordic Americans."[15] He stated the same principle doctrinally: "The Klan goes back to the American racial instincts, and to the common sense which is their first product, as the basis for its beliefs and methods."[16] There were three of these "great racial instincts": "loyalty to the white race, to the traditions of America, and to the spirit of Protestantism."[17] The most important was native Americanism, "patriotism." Patriotism entailed not only that political power must be wielded by Nordic Americans and that the contaminating effects of foreign or alien culture and belief must be avoided, but also that the "pioneer stock" had to be maintained in all its purity, for "mongrelization" weakens and corrupts the race. Second, "the world has been so made that each race must fight for its life, must conquer, accept slavery or die."[18] Hence the "white race must be supreme, not only in America but in the world." From the combination of these "instincts" followed the Klan's "common sense" attitude toward Negroes:

> The Negro, the Klan considers a special duty and problem of the white American. Unlike Eastern European immigrants, he is among us through no wish of his; we owe it to him and to ourselves to give him full protection and opportunity. But his limitations are evident; we will not permit him to gain sufficient power to control our civilization. Neither will we delude him with promises of social equality which we know can never be realized. The Klan looks forward to the day when the Negro problem will have been solved on some much saner basis than miscegenation, and when every State will enforce laws making any sex relations between a white and a colored person a crime.[19]

Finally, the Klan was determined that "Rome shall not rule America."

The KKK did not always articulate its principles in such a tolerant manner. A popular Klan broadside stated them this way:

Every criminal, every gambler, every thug, every libertine, every girl ruiner, every home wrecker, every wife beater, every dope peddler, every moonshiner, every crooked politician, every pagan Papist priest, every shyster lawyer, every K. of C., every white slaver, every brothel madam, every Roman controlled newspaper, every black spider—is fighting the Klan. Think it over. Which side are you on? [20]

With respect to black people, Klan lecturer R. H. Sawyer spoke even more violently: "The Negro, in whose blood flows the mad desire for race amalgamation, is more dangerous than a wild beast and he must and will be controlled." [21] And the first Imperial Wizard drew the obvious practical conclusion from this position. At meetings of Atlanta's Nathan Redford Forest Klan No. 1, "it was Simmons' custom to draw two revolvers, place them on the table before him, and shout to his subjects, 'Bring on your niggers!'" [22]

In most respects, the Klan's activities resembled those of many other fraternal orders, civic organizations, and political pressure groups. It developed a wholesome feeling of Klannishness among its members at its Karnivals, Klanvokations, initiations, and other ceremonial occasions. It gave flags and financial contributions to churches; supported one-hundred-percent-American candidates for political office; and, in accordance with its representation of the American common man, advocated an extension of the public school system and the exclusion of foreign immigrants. It was for temperance, moral purity, motherhood, and the "old-time religion"; it was against Darwinism, liberalism, or any other form of corrupt big-city modernism. It demonstrated its support for these positions in open meetings and parades, as well as by direct political campaigning and lobbying. But the Klan's willingness to use coercive means to gain its ends was its distinguishing characteristic. The intimidating presence and violent actions of hooded Knights bearing weapons and/or flaming crosses were the organization's most complete expression. Yet even these practices do not divorce it fully from a broader segment of the American population. As John Hope Franklin observes:

> White citizens, in and out of the Klan, poured out a wrath
> upon the Negro population shortly after [the World War]
> that could hardly be viewed as fit punishment even for a
> treasonable group of persons. More than 70 Negroes were
> lynched during the first year of the post-war period. . . .

Fourteen Negroes were burned publicly, eleven of whom were burned alive. In utter despair a Negro editor of Charlestown, South Carolina, cried out, "There is scarcely a day that passes that newspapers don't tell about a Negro soldier lynched in his uniform. Why do they lynch Negroes anyhow? With a white judge, a white jury, white public sentiment, white officers of the law, it is just as impossible for a Negro accused of a crime, or even suspected of a crime, to escape the white man's vengeance or his justice as it would be for a fawn to escape that wanders into a den of hungry lions." [23]

In other words, there was no clear, categorical distinction between the Klan and white America in general, or between Klan power and legal authority: "The Klan was typically American. It prospered and grew to power by capitalizing on forces already existent in American society: our readiness to ascribe all good or all evil to those religions, races and economic philosophies with which we agree or disagree, and our tendency to profess the highest ideals while actually exhibiting the basest of prejudices." [24]

Viewed from the position we have now defined, the nightmare night appears as a product of American white racism mediated through the actions of a Klan-like organization. It was a typical actualization of the Klan mentality, a mentality not limited to those who were members of the KKK: after the Black Legion attack Earl Little "was called in and questioned about a permit for the pistol with which he had shot at the white men who set the fire." [25] The police evidently hoped to disarm the defender and thereby to defend his attackers.

Our examination of the KKK has led us back to Earl Little, both as an individual and as a member of the UNIA (Garvey's Universal Negro Improvement Association). Now, if we accept Malcolm's inference, one of the critical forces creating this individual-collective identity was racist violence: in Earl Little's case, the deaths of his brothers, one by lynching, were "among the reasons [why he] had decided to dedicate and risk his life" to spreading the Garveyite message. His experience in this regard was not unique, although it may have been unusually intense. The wave of Klan and Klan-like violence noted above provided a major impetus toward the development of the organization: "Membership in the Garvey movement soared into the hundreds of thousands [by the early 1920s], with much of this growth a consequence of the race wars of 1919."[26] Thus for Little and many others, joining the UNIA was an act of self-definition against white American racism, a declaration of the intention not to be anonymous, passive, and defenseless victims of Klan-like violence.

Garvey founded the UNIA in his native Jamaica in 1914. Through an earlier association with African nationalists, and after reading Booker T. Washington's *Up from Slavery*, he conceived the project of "uniting all the Negro peoples of the world into one great body to establish a country and Government absolutely their own." The UNIA was to be that body.

For three years the organization attracted relatively little attention, but in 1917, with headquarters now located in Harlem and with a core membership of West Indian immigrants, it began a period of rapid growth. By his own estimate, Garvey had gained six million adherents by 1922, and even his enemies conceded him one million. In any case, he had the support of a very large percentage of the country's 10.5 million black people; indeed, other Negro leaders were worried by his success. He was able to reach, as they were not, the newly emerging urban masses, "the children of the soil—the descendants of plantation hands, without voice, without leadership, and with little basis for self-pride."[27] And he reached them with a formulation of and solution to the racial problem that was antithetical to the integrationist position being argued by such groups as the NAACP.

In Garvey's view, as in Colonel Simmons's, the black and white races were fundamentally incompatible; but it was the black race that was superior, and that was corrupted and weakened by "race amalgamation." Garvey in fact distrusted Negroes of mixed blood. Writing about the UNIA in 1923, C. S. Johnson commented:

> Essentially this is a movement of pure blood Negroes. It is their revanche. Mixed bloods—mulattoes—have received a shade more consideration at the hands of white America. This is partly a question of kinship, partly the caprice of scientific theory, partly physical similarity, partly traditional advantage in wage opportunities.[28]

This tendency toward caste distinction was even more pronounced in Jamaica, with "the whites superior to the mulattoes, but in association with them; the mulattoes superior to the blacks and aggressively so; the blacks at the bottom,—smoldering, resentful."[29] Coming from that situation, feeling that resentment, and viewing

the United States as similarly structured, Garvey argued that Negro
leaders, W. E. B. DuBois's Talented Tenth, were at best naive and at
worst the white man's accomplices. The white man would never
grant equality to the black man. That being the case,

> if you cannot live alongside the white man in peace, if you
> cannot get the same chance and opportunity alongside the
> white man, even tho you are his fellow citizen; if he claims
> that you are not entitled to this chance and opportunity be-
> cause the country is his by force of numbers, then find a
> country of your own and rise to the highest position within
> that country.[30]

To Garvey, this seemed the necessary conclusion, given the existing
historical premises. His challenge to the Negro leadership was, in
essence, "Which side are you on?"

As the passage just cited indicates, Garvey was not urging a violent confrontation with the white American majority, nor even a
major political one. Basing his position upon the fact of black minority status, he argued that black people could not expect to have a
dominant voice in political affairs or to win in an armed struggle.
Therefore, the prudent course was to avoid trouble when possible
and defend themselves when necessary. This attitude determined
the Garveyite policy vis-à-vis the Klan, as formulated at the 1924
UNIA Convention:

> I. Resolved, that the Fourth International convention of
> the Negro peoples of the world regards the alleged attitude
> of the Ku Klux Klan to the Negro as fairly representative of
> the feelings of the majority of the white race toward us, and
> places on record its conviction that the only solution to this
> critical situation is that of the UNIA, namely, the securing
> for ourselves as speedily as possible a government of our
> own on African soil.
> II. Moved, that it shall be the policy of the UNIA to pro-
> tect against the brutalities and atrocities alleged to be per-
> petrated upon the members of the Negro race by the Ku
> Klux Klan or any other organization.[31]

Garvey viewed the Klan as we have viewed it: as typically American. Black people could no more challenge it than they could challenge the United States government itself—at least, not from within the United States. An international struggle was required, one

which would ultimately culminate in the liberation of Africa and the creation of a pan-Negro nation.

This Africanist orientation did not mean that all American and West Indian Negroes should immediately leave for Africa:

> We are not preaching any doctrines to ask all Negroes of Harlem and of the United States to leave for Africa. The majority of us may remain here, but we must send our scientists, our mechanics, and our artisans, and let them build railroads, let them build the great educational and other institutions necessary, and, when they are constructed, the time will come for the command to be given, 'Come Home!'[32]

The UNIA's purpose was

> to establish a universal confraternity among the race; to promote the spirit of pride and love; to reclaim the fallen; to administer to and assist the needy; to assist in civilizing the backward tribes of Africa; to assist in the development of independent Negro nations and communities; to establish a central nation for the race; to establish commissaries or agencies in the principal countries and cities of the world for the representation of all Negroes; to promote a conscientious spirit of worship among the native tribes of Africa; to establish universities, colleges, academies and schools for racial education and culture of the people; to work for better conditions among Negroes everywhere.[33]

In the words of the UNIA motto, "One God! One Aim! One Destiny!" Garvey and his top aides took extensive speaking tours to spread this message, and they reached an even larger audience through the UNIA's weekly newspaper, *The Negro World*, which "became the world's most widely read black weekly in the early 1920's, with a circulation reaching nearly two hundred thousand."[34] Moreover, Garvey's orientation was practical as well as polemical. He was vitally concerned to transform his vision into reality, actually to construct a self-determining black nation. Accordingly, he attempted to establish economic, social, religious, and political institutions that would serve both as defensive bulwarks against attack within the existing historical situation and as tools for changing that situation.

The UNIA's economic activities were coordinated by the Negro Factories Corporation, formed in 1919 and funded by the sale of

shares, at five dollars each, to UNIA members. The capital thus accumulated was sufficient to permit the ownership and operation of a
number of cooperative enterprises, including "grocery stores, restaurants, laundries, garment factories, dress shops, a greeting card company, a millinery, a phonograph record company and a publishing
house"[35]—and, most spectacularly as well as least successfully, the
Black Star Steamship Company, designed to link in trade and transportation "the ebony-hued sons of Ethiopia in the Western Hemi-
sphere with their brothers across the sea."[36]

Some of these enterprises were administered directly by the national offices of the organization and others were managed locally;
all were integral parts of the collective life of UNIA communities.
The center of activity in these communities, at least the major
ones—New York, Philadelphia, Pittsburgh, Cleveland, Cincinnati,
Detroit, and Chicago—was the UNIA Liberty Hall. These halls,

> wherever located, served the needs of the people: Sunday
> morning worship, afternoon Sunday Schools, Public Meet-
> ings at nights, and concerts and dances were held, especially
> on holidays and Saturday nights. Notice boards were put up
> where one could look for a room, a job or a lost article. In
> localities where there were many members out of work
> there were 'Soup Kitchens' to give them a warm meal daily.
> Often there were portable screens for a corner of the Hall
> where men who could not be temporarily housed with fel-
> low members could sleep on benches at nights. In the freez-
> ing winter days stoves had to be kept going to accommodate
> the cold and homeless, until they 'got on their feet' again.[37]

Like the Nation of Islam, the UNIA was thus virtually a polity; unlike the Nation, it was not a theocracy. After 1921 there was the op-
tion of joining the African Orthodox Church and worshipping a
black God the Father, a black Virgin Mary, and a black Christ; but
men like Earl Little, who found their religious calling in the Baptist or the Methodist church, were not required to surrender their
faith.[38]

As the term "polity" suggests, the UNIA was conceived as a pro-
totypical black nation. The basis for practical activity was established in 1920 at the First International Convention of the Negro
Peoples of the World, which was in essence a constitutional convention for a pan-Negro nation. Attended by over two thousand delegates representing twenty-five countries on four continents, in a
month of intensive work it produced a Declaration of Rights for the

Negro People of the World that was both a bill of grievances and a framework for self-government.

The Declaration's empirical premise was that "nowhere in the world, with few exceptions, are black men accorded equal treatment with white men," that, for example, in the United States "our race is denied the right of public trial accorded to other races when accused of a crime, but are lynched and burned by mobs." Consequently— and also inherently—there must be an independent Negro nation:

> Be it known to all men that whereas, all men are created equal and entitled to the rights of life, liberty and the pursuit of happiness, and because of this we, the duly elected representatives of the Negro peoples of the world, invoking the aid of the just and mighty God do declare all men, women and children of our blood throughout the world free citizens, and do claim them as free citizens of Africa, the Motherland of all Negroes.[39]

From this constitutional premise were developed both principles of interracial conduct deemed binding upon existing nations, and the project of national self-determination. Other countries were called upon to "accept and acknowledge Negro representatives who shall be sent to the said governments to represent the general welfare of the Negro peoples," and to grant Negroes all the rights accruing to members of other races. As for national self-determination, the central goals were defined as follows:

> 13. We believe in the freedom of Africa for the Negro people of the world, and by the principle of Europe for the Europeans and Asia for the Asiatics, we also demand Africa for the Africans at home and abroad.
>
> 14. We believe in the inherent right of the Negro to possess himself of Africa, and that his possession of same shall not be regarded as an infringement on any claim by any race or nation.
>
> 15. We strongly condemn the cupidity of those nations of the world who, by open aggression or secret schemes, have seized the territories and inexhaustible natural wealth of Africa, and we place on record our most solemn determination to reclaim the treasures and possessions of the vast continent of our forefathers.[40]

In sum, through the Declaration the UNIA was defined as a nation in the process of becoming itself. Claiming from the outset the prerogatives of sovereignty, it declared its intention of putting these principles into practice.*

Viewed from within this organizational conception, the more festive or ritualized moments of the Convention, as well as Garvey's more general polemical efforts, become intelligible as means to the end of nationhood—just as the KKK rituals were means to the end of maintaining white Anglo-Saxon Protestant supremacy. The most significant events of the UNIA Convention were a massive rally at Madison Square Garden and a full-dress parade of UNIA legions that brought Harlem to a standstill. As described by one participant:

> Hundreds of thousands of people took part . . . and watched the parade from windows (for which many had to pay) and sidewalks. The onlookers could not help but catch the spirit of the occasion; they clapped, waved flags and cheered themselves hoarse. . . . Here indeed were New Negroes on the march, with a goal to be reached, and a determined look in their eyes to achieve it.[41]†

On such an occasion, one might well feel the imminent, indeed the immanent, truth of Garvey's powerful exhortation, "Up, you mighty race, you can accomplish what you will!"

If one were not present at the Convention, something of its mood and meaning could be experienced indirectly through the proselytizing of UNIA activists. Malcolm reports that at his father's Garvey meetings,

> big, shiny photographs of Marcus Garvey . . . were passed from hand to hand. . . . The pictures showed what seemed to me millions of Negroes thronged in parade behind Garvey riding in a fine car, a big black man dressed in a dazzling

---

* This political program was taken both seriously and literally. Executive officers for the new nation were elected, with Garvey as provisional president, and members henceforth tried to think and act as citizens of Africa: "All [UNIA] employees belonged to the UNIA civil service; divisions even had civil service commissions to examine job applicants. Some positions carried monetary rewards; others entailed service in the branch police force, as youth group leaders, or in some other service function. . . . There was also an Association court system. Members with a poor work record, or given to wife-beating, alcoholism or similar offenses, appeared before an Association judge, were provided with a defense lawyer, and were tried before a jury of the division members. . . . [And] if a follower in a small town [decided] to move to the big city, he would probably write the secretary general's bureau of passports to obtain a UNIA passport" (Vincent, Black Power, p. 167).

† The term "New Negro" is discussed below, pp. 61 ff.

uniform with gold braid on it, and he was wearing a thrilling hat with tall plumes. I remember hearing that he had black followers not only in the United States but all around the world, and I remember how the meetings always closed with my father saying, several times, and the people chanting after him, "Up, you mighty race!"[42]

But by the time of the meetings Malcolm remembered, the UNIA was already far past its prime. Like the Klan, it was plagued by internal dissension, lack of managerial talent, and outright corruption. The finances of the Black Star line were so tangled that federal authorities were able to prosecute Garvey on charges of fraudulent solicitation of funds through the United States mails. Although the case against Garvey himself was less than substantial, he was convicted and imprisoned (in 1925). His sentence was commuted in 1927, but he was deported as an undesirable alien immediately thereafter. Without his active leadership, the UNIA's decline was accelerated; it soon ceased to be a major force in American life.

By the late 1920s the Klan was also in decline. Governmental action against it was never as forceful as that against the UNIA, but the behavior of its leaders—who embezzled funds, abused the powers of their offices, and violated with great regularity the Invisible Empire's proclaimed principles of moral decency—brought the organization into general disrepute. The nightmare night was accordingly a confrontation between two dying racial movements, one embodied in the stubborn pride and anger of Earl Little, and the other in the increasingly bitter white supremacism of the Black Legion. The protagonists were like two soldiers fighting for their countries on a lonely and distant battlefield, not knowing that both nations had already been defeated by a third.

Class, Race, and the Great Migration

We began this phase of our work by forming an image of an event involving certain individuals. We now recognize it as resulting from the conflicting interests of two national racial movements, organizationally embodied in the UNIA and the KKK and mediated through the activity of Earl Little and the Black Legionnaires. But this interpretation through contextualization is not yet complete. We have seen that the nightmare night occurred late in the history of the two organizations, and that these organizations were parallel (and in the event we are considering, convergent) movements within the same historical period: the UNIA and the KKK both rose to power in the immediate aftermath of the World War, and both fell from national prominence as the postwar era advanced. It has also been shown that the two groups were manifestations of widespread tendencies in American life—that the KKK was a form of a pervasive white racism, and that the UNIA crystallized the yearnings of millions of black people for racial self-determination. We thus see that we cannot confine our inquiry to the organizations themselves, but must extend it to a more general consideration of the character of the American people during this historical era.

The UNIA, we may recall, was a movement of "the children of the soil, the descendants of plantation hands," of "the blacks at the bottom." But its greatest strength was in urban areas, especially Northern urban areas. This juxtaposition signifies the "great migration" northward which began between 1910 and 1920 and which was in time to transform the racial demography of America. (Even during this ten-year period there was a net gain of 330,000 in the Negro population of the North.)[43] Moreover, the great migration was part of a larger demographic movement. During that decade the percentage of the national population living in urban areas increased from 45.7 to 51.2 percent—a change reflected in and reflective of changes in the composition of the labor force. In 1910 32.4 percent of American workers were farmers or farm laborers; in 1920 these occupations accounted for only 25.5 percent of the labor force. At the same time the number of lower-salaried and industrial workers in the labor force rose from 44.5 to 51.2 percent;[44] the number of wage laborers in general went from 71.9 to 73.9 percent; and the number of self-employed entrepreneurs declined from 26.3 to 23.5 percent of the working population.[45]

This pattern of increasing urbanization and proletarianization was certainly not confined to the second decade of the twentieth century; it is a long-term and fundamental trend in American history. But viewed from a black perspective, these years were a critical moment in the transition from rural peasant to urban proletarian life. And while a variety of general historical forces and particular events combined in determining this movement, two are of basic importance: the World War and the depressed condition of the Southern cotton economy.

In the period prior to the outbreak of hostilities in Europe, the United States had been facing severe economic difficulties. Then

came the war and, with it, a great wave of prosperity. From a combination of money borrowed and securities sold by the Allied
powers, over five billion dollars entered the economy between 1915
and 1917. The major part of this added purchasing power was of
course used for guns and munitions, but the Allies also bought
much more wheat flour, meat, and sugar than they had during the
preceding period.[46] There was, however, no war boom in the cotton
market. Before the war, the United States exported three-fifths of its
cotton—mostly to England, France, Belgium, Russia, and Germany;
during the war, the German market was lost, the other markets con-
tracted, and foreign competition for the remaining outlets increased.
Consequently the price of American cotton fell, production fell off,
and the demand for agricultural labor in cotton declined. Because
there had long been a population surplus in the rural South, and
hence an abundant supply of labor (especially black labor) relative to
demand, wages had always approached the minimum amount necessary to keep a worker alive and functioning. Now the surplus of
labor supply over labor demand increased even more, and wages
reached a low of seventy-five cents a day.[47] Moreover, the reduced demand for cotton was sharply felt by the black "peasant" class—those
tenant farmers and sharecroppers who worked the least fertile lands,
the farms having the highest costs of production and yielding the
lowest margins of profit.* Thus the war weakened the already tenuous hold on survival of the black peasant and agricultural worker.

There was an additional reason for the unprofitable nature of cotton production during these years. The disasters of war were compounded by natural disaster: a massive boll weevil invasion. Huddie
Ledbetter (Leadbelly) told the story simply and graphically:

> Talk about de lates',
> De lates' of this song,
> Dese devilish boll weevils,
> Dey gonna rob you of a home,
> Dey lookin' for a home,
> Dey lookin' for a home.
>
> The first time I seed de boll weevil,
> He was sittin' on de square.

* That is, those who worked small, relatively independent farms. But black tenants
and sharecroppers frequently worked on the large plantations in exchange for pay-
ment in kind or for the minimal amounts of food and shelter needed for survival during their period of employment. These workers were really in a state of peonage,
caught midway between slavery and wage labor.

The nex' time I seed him,
He was spreadin' ev'ywhere—
He was lookin' for a home,
He was lookin' for a home.

After several verses in which the infestation of a family's farm is described, "De Ballit of de Boll Weevil" concludes:

Farmer tol' de merchant,
"I didn't make but one bale.
Before I let you have that one,
I'll suffer an' die in jail—
I'll have a home,
I'll have a home."[48]

When the boll weevil found a home in the cotton fields, the tenant farmer often lost his. Then, too, there were floods in the summer of 1915 and drought in 1916 and 1917. In sum, during the early war years an impetus for emigration from the South came into existence. Like the boll weevil that symbolized their troubles, many black people were "lookin' for a home."

At the same time that there was a push away from the land in the South, there was a pull toward the cities of the North. The war generated an enormous demand for manufactured goods, especially military supplies; it drew men out of the labor market and into the armed services; and it brought foreign immigration to a virtual standstill. In combination these factors produced a labor shortage in the North coincident with the surplus in the South: while wages were falling, unemployment was increasing, and farms were being lost in the South, wages were climbing and unemployment was disappearing in the North. As Myrdal observes, the war "widen[ed] tremendously the already existing differences in opportunity for a Negro in the two regions."[49] Southerners in general and black people in particular were quick to perceive the growing disparity. By the summer of 1916, emigration from the South had become a black exodus, as the "children of the soil"[50] laid aside their hoes and cotton sacks, scraped together the money for train fare, and set out hopefully for the promised land.*

This economic push-pull of Southern agricultural poverty and

* The figure of 330,000 for the growth of the Negro population of the North and West during the decade does not take into account those who moved back and forth during the period: the actual number of people involved in the migration must have been considerably greater.

Northern industrial prosperity was not the only determinant of the migration. A contemporary investigator reported: "Better wages . . . has without doubt been the immediately impelling influence that has taken the Negro into the North in such large numbers." But "the treatment accorded the Negro always stood second, when not first, among the reasons given by Negroes for leaving the South."[51] The term "treatment" refers, of course, to the full range of oppressive social and political practices that accompanied the economic exploitation of black people in the South, to the "injustice in the Southern courts, the lack of privileges, disenfranchisement, segregation and lynching."[52] Perhaps most of all it refers to the degrading, emasculating, and infantilizing practice of treating all black people as children. The weight of these oppressive practices had never been borne gladly; but it was all the more unbearable when black men were being drafted into the armed services, when they were expected to fight like men in order to preserve a system that treated them like boys.

At first, the North was seen as the antithesis of the Southern system of victimization, as a land of democratic opportunity, freedom, justice, and equality. Northern city life was in fact a marked improvement over rural existence in the South. As one migrant who had found a home in Philadelphia wrote back to a friend:

> I am making very good I make $75 per month . . . [and] I
> dont have to mister every little white boy comes along I
> havent heard a white man call a colored nigger you no
> now—since I been in the state of Pa. I can ride in the
> electric street and steam cars any where I get a seat. I dont
> care to mix with white what I mean I am not crazy about
> being with white folks, but if I have to pay the same fare I
> have learn to want the same acomidation.[53]

Such letters, as well as word-of-mouth communication, induced others to follow where one had led. Further, labor recruiters from Northern industries and the Negro press played a critical role in bringing the possibilities of self-improvement to the conscious attention of Southern Negroes; the "outside agitators" of their day, they helped to transform individual migration into a social movement.

Thus the "great migration" of the black peasantry into the Northern cities comes to be understood as a resolution of the contradiction between the existing Southern system of victimization (economic exploitation, social segregation, legal discrimination, po-

litical disenfranchisement, personal degradation, and physical violation) and a vision of democratic liberation (opportunity, equality,
justice, citizenship, manhood, and safety) in the North. We have also
gained some understanding of why Earl Little left the South, thereby
becoming a potential member of the UNIA and an object of Black
Legion animosity: it is a good guess that he was part of the wartime
migration. His character and background were typical of those who
left the South during the war: he was the kind of proud and ambitious man who would find Southern life especially limiting and
degrading; he was from a rural area, and had undoubtedly worked in
and around agriculture; and he had little formal education, but a
wealth of practical knowledge, including an intimate knowledge of
Southern treatment. Moreover, Malcolm's narrative, while it does
not preclude the possibility of a somewhat earlier regional shift,
does place Little in the North by the time the conflict ended. The
indeterminacy of the precise time of Little's emigration only forces
us to recognize that the migration was not simply a wartime experience. There was substantial interregional movement before the war,
and intensified movement thereafter. The war period constituted a
turning point in the migratory process, but it did not cause the migration, any more than it caused the basic social conditions that un-
derlay it.

It seems likely, indeed, that Little's antagonists in the confrontation were, in the more extended sense, also a part of the migration.
The treatment of poor whites in the South was little better than that
accorded to blacks. Of course, they had one advantage:

> A South politician preaches to the poor, white man,
> "You got more than the blacks, don't complain,
> You're better than him,
>   you been born with white skin," they explain.[54]

But during the war years that explanation did not adequately compensate the poor white man for his reduced economic opportunities.
So when the labor recruiters called—and it was mainly to white
workers and tenant farmers that they directed their appeals—many
white people answered, carrying North not only their aspirations
but also their carefully inculcated prejudices. This population, we
may suppose, was particularly vulnerable to the influence of the
KKK. More specifically, we remember that the Legion was "formed
ostensibly to seek jobs for Southern workers." Leaving aside for the
moment other implications of this statement, we may infer from it
that the Legion's membership was drawn largely from this migra-

tory population of white Southerners who came North looking for work in the burgeoning automotive industry.

The next question is: what happened to these migrants once they reached the North that made membership in organizations like the UNIA and the Klan desirable and even necessary? Most obviously, for black people it was the experience of violent racist attacks. Even during the war, when black men were fighting and dying for democracy in Europe, their brothers and sisters were dying *from* democracy at home. As Southern blacks, and black people in general, began to work at what had formerly been white jobs and to seek homes in what had formerly been white residential areas, they met with intense resistance:

> At least 38 Negroes lost their lives at the hands of lynching parties in 1917, while in the following year the number had risen to 58. . . . In Tennessee more than 3,000 spectators responded to the invitation of a newspaper to come out and witness the burning of a "live Negro." In East Saint Louis, Illinois, at least 40 Negroes lost their lives in a riot that grew out of the employment of Negroes in a factory holding government contracts. Negroes were stabbed, clubbed, and hanged; and one two-year-old Negro child was shot and thrown in the doorway of a burning building.[55]

These racist attacks did not diminish when the war ended; but by 1919, Negro servicemen were returning, armed with a new militancy and confidence, to the country they had defended. W. E. B. DuBois, then editor of the NAACP journal *The Crisis*, articulated their mood when he wrote in the spring of that year:

> This country of ours, despite all its better souls have done and dreamed, is yet a shameful land.
> It *lynches*. . . . It *disfranchises* its own citizens. . . . It encourages *ignorance*. . . . It steals from us. . . . It insults us. . . .
> We *return*. We *return from the fighting*. We *return fighting*.
> Make way for Democracy! We saved it in France, and by the Great Jehovah, we will save it in the U.S.A., or know the reason why.[56]

A "New Negro" had been born, on the battlefields of France and in the factories of Chicago, Detroit, New York, Saint Louis. When the wave of racist terror rose to floodtide heights during the "Red Summer" of 1919, black people fought back. By the end of the year, there had been approximately twenty-five race riots in the urban areas; and while black deaths greatly outnumbered white, both sides were thoroughly bloodied.

We now understand what that contemporary observer meant when he spoke of the Garvey legions as "New Negroes on the march." It was Garvey who most effectively organized those members of the emergent black urban population who were no longer willing to be the passive victims of democracy. On the other side, it was the Klan that played most effectively upon the emotions of those white people who felt threatened by the New Negro.

There was, of course, no real threat to white people from black people. But as noted above, in the Northern cities there was interracial competition for both jobs and housing. Drake and Cayton comment that in Chicago during World War I:

> The sudden influx of Negroes . . . immediately resolved itself into a struggle for living space. Between 1900 and 1914, the Black Belt and its satellite areas had absorbed over ten thousand Negroes without serious difficulty. Now the saturation point was reached, and although the migrants had jobs, there were literally no houses to accommodate them. . . . The Black Belt had to expand, and this situation aroused exaggerated fears throughout the city.[57]

In the "invaded areas," bombs were sometimes thrown at Negro homes, and the "conflict over space often came to a head where Negroes and whites met in public places."[58] The Chicago riot of 1919, in which thirty-eight lives were lost and over five hundred people were injured, grew out of one such public confrontation. Similarly, Jackson argues that racial conflict was most intense in the residential "zones of emergence"; and that consequently the Invisible Empire thrived in such areas:

> Unable to afford a fine home far removed from minority problems, the potential Klansman . . . was forced by economic necessity to live in older transitional areas close to his place of employment. He was bewildered by the rapid pace of life and frustrated by his inability to slow the changes which seemed so constant and oppressive. He perhaps remembered an earlier neighborhood transition and was frightened at the prospect of a Negro or a Pole coming

into his block and causing him to sell his house at a low price. Unable to escape and hesitant to act alone, the threatened citizen welcomed the security and respectability of a large group.[59]

Thus the Klan grew in reaction to black residential expansion.

Bringing this general point down to cases, the black population of Detroit (the stronghold of the Black Legion) went from 5,741 in 1910 to 40,000 in 1920 and 125,000 in 1930. Not surprisingly, the major racial confrontation during this period occurred when a black doctor moved into a white neighborhood. The Legion's hatred for Earl Little is illuminated by this event, for one of Little's major sins was that he built his home outside the Lansing Negro district. From the Legion's perspective, he was violating a fundamental territorial imperative.

The antagonism between the UNIA and the KKK or the Black Legion is thus partially explicable as a struggle for urban living space. That struggle in turn reflects the entry of the black "peasantry" into the urban job-market, a market which had previously been monopolized by white workers (although not solely by "native Americans"). Especially during the war years, when labor shortages resulted in racially fluid job definitions, blacks became eligible for work in the same industries as whites. Of course, members of the two races occupied different positions within such industries and within the common labor-market. Jobs were usually hierarchically structured by race; the wage rate, even for comparable jobs, was racially differentiated in most places; and blacks were typically the last hired and first fired. Despite this racial differential, however, a common working-class identity was developing, with the logical consequence that a tendency toward territorial identity developed as well. Most white workers fought vigorously or even violently against being thus identified with black people, while black workers sought to solidify their precarious position in the formerly all-white world. Hence the interracial conflict we have been describing was an intra-class antagonism, a competitive struggle between racially differentiated segments of the urban proletariat. The UNIA and the KKK were organizational expressions of this antithetical relationship, and the confrontation between Little and the Legionnaires was an actualization of that organizational antithesis.

By this interpretation, economic competition is seen as a determinant of the event through the twofold mediation of residential and organizational rivalry. Presently we shall see that inter-class movement as well as intra-class competition was an important determinant of the destruction of the Little home. At this juncture, however, another issue commands our attention: given that the UNIA and the KKK reflected their members' dependence upon the urban labor market, one might expect the internal movement of the market, the ebbs and flows in the demand for labor, to have had an impact upon the variable fortunes of the two organizations. Such a relationship does indeed exist. Because the need for an organizational identity is strongest when a situation is both variable and difficult, the UNIA and the KKK grew most rapidly between late 1920 and 1922, during a time when an insufficient demand for commodities was accompanied by a correspondingly low demand for labor. The competition for the few available jobs was intense; and because black people were often willing to work for lower wages than white people (that is, because they usually were given work only if they accepted lower pay), the native American fear of and hostility toward blacks, as well as toward immigrant members of the work force, was heightened. The KKK was responsive to these anxieties, and in fact served as a terroristic agency for the suppression of aspiring non-native or non-white workers. On the other side, the UNIA responded to the fears and hopes of the black worker, whose confidence in progress within the existing system was severely undermined by the harsh facts of economic life during this period and by the ferocity of the reaction to his presence in formerly all-white neighborhoods and places of employment. After 1923, when the demand for labor stabilized on a middle ground between the wartime high and the postwar low and when members of both races had made a preliminary adjustment to the new conditions of urban working-class life, the organizations faded in importance.* Consequently, the confrontation between Malcolm's father and the

---

* The estimated unemployment figures for the period provide a kind of statistical image of this historical pattern:

1915:	9.7%	1919:	2.3%	1923:	3.2%	1927:	4.1%
1916:	4.8	1920:	4.0	1924:	5.5	1928:	4.4
1917:	4.8	1921:	11.9	1925:	4.0	1929:	3.2
1918:	1.4	1922:	7.6	1926:	1.9		

[From Historical Statistics of the United States, p. 73; cited in Baran and Sweezy, Monopoly Capital (New York: Monthly Review Press, 1966), p. 232.] It may be noted that while these figures accurately depict the relative demand for labor over time, they probably understate the absolute levels of unemployment existing during the period. One economist calculates that: "The jobless constituted 13% of the labor

Black Legion was of strictly individual or local significance. At that time there could no longer be national reverberations from such a clash.

We have seen that the parallel rise and fall of the UNIA and the KKK is explicable in terms of the supply of and demand for labor in the nation during the 1920s: variations in the labor market produced changes in the way of life of both black and white workers, which in turn generated a particular substantive and temporal configuration of interracial hostility and organizational activity. Stated somewhat more generally, the market situation during the war and the years following set the limits within which the other situational determinants of KKK and UNIA activity could exert their particular influences. But, further, both organizations were oriented toward the transcendence or transformation of the existing situation. From this it follows that the members of the two movements must have been or have appeared to have been relatively disadvantaged in the exchange of market values; otherwise they would have had no *interest* in transformative activity.

In this way we come to the question of who gained and lost in the exchange between the buyers and sellers of labor-power during the 1920s. Simply stated: "While the poor did not grow poorer, the rich grew richer more rapidly than the poor did."[60] Between 1923 and 1929, for example, the top 5 percent of income recipients increased their share of income payments from 22.9 to 26.1 percent, a gain of 14 percent. The basis for this increase was, of course, ownership of the means of production: the relatively larger income of the rich was primarily a reflection of a 27 percent expansion of dividends, interest, and rent during these years, compared to a 21 percent expansion of wages. Thus while the 1920s were years of growing national prosperity, "property income was . . . the leading beneficiary of the advance. In 1929 it constituted about one fifth of the total sums distributed."[61]

Capital's gain was labor's relative loss. At no time during the decade did a majority of workers earn enough to live at the so-called "American standard."[62] And at certain times—most notably during the postwar depression, when the UNIA and the KKK experienced their membership booms—the position of the wage-laborer declined

force in 1924 and 1925, 11% in 1926, 12% in 1927, 13% in 1928 and 10% in 1929" [cited in Irving Bernstein, *The Lean Years* (Baltimore: Penguin, 1970), p. 59].

in relation to both that of the owner of productive property and his own prior level of well-being (i.e., the standard of 1917–1920).* In Marx's words: "We see, therefore, that even if we remain *within the relation of capital and wage labor, the interests of capital and the interests of labor are diametrically opposed.*"[63]

The opposing interests of wage-labor and capital, although evident in the process of exchange, originate in the process of production. The capitalist extracts, or attempts to extract, a surplus value from the worker's productive activity.[64] Because the amount of that surplus equals the difference between the total new value the worker produces through the expenditure of his labor-power and the value-equivalent of his wages, the capitalist has every interest in depressing wages to the lowest possible level.† Conversely, the worker has a short-term interest in raising the wage rate and a long-term interest in abolishing the capitalist system.

There is, of course, another and even more general way of expressing both the relationship between the market (exchange) and the work-place (production), and the relationship between capital and wage-labor. Capitalism is a social system based upon alienated labor. When the worker sells his labor-power, he is alienating his potential for humanly productive activity, and consequently he is alienated in the productive process as well as from the product of his productive activity. Surplus value measures his alienation from his product, and the extent (and productivity) of his time spent in laboring measures his alienation in the productive process. The concept of alienation thus expresses in a general way what Marx more specifically formulated as the "buying and selling of labor-power." And because what is alienated from the worker is appropriated by the capitalist, alienation also expresses the antagonistic class relationship of bourgeoisie and proletariat. Hence from a Marxist stand-

---

* The pattern of economic advance followed by economic retreat—or, more abstractly, of a rising level of satisfaction followed by a sharp decline—has long been recognized as a major determinant of revolutionary upheaval. We shall consider this phenomenon more closely in connection with the civil rights movement and the Black Revolution.

† The exchange value of a commodity may be divided into three parts: constant capital (raw material, machinery, and other forces of production), that is, previously crystallized labor-power, the value of which is preserved through being transferred to the commodity; variable capital (wages), that is, living labor-power, the value of which is reproduced in the commodity; and surplus value (potential profit), that is, the new value created by the worker for which he is not compensated. It is evident that if the total value of the commodity and the value of constant capital are given, then variable capital and surplus value must be inversely proportional.

point, the abolition of private property and the end of alienation mutually entail each other.

Viewed in this manner, it becomes clear that the determining force in the historical situation of the UNIA and the KKK was the interest of the American bourgeoisie, the property-owning and politically ruling class.[65] The realization of this class interest was at the same time the negation of the interest of the proletariat, the emergent urban working class. The two organizations expressed the suppressed longings of this oppressed class, its antipathy for the common enemy, and its interest in situational transformation. The KKK saw the enemy as modernism, while the UNIA saw it as white America; but hidden beneath these divergent images was the ruling elite of the capitalist system. Thus from the standpoint of class interests it would seem that the UNIA and the KKK "should" have been allies. Instead, they were antagonists, fighting each other instead of the common enemy. The question is, therefore, why did such an internal division of the working class occur?

The answer can be partially derived from our prior analysis. The greater the supply of labor relative to demand, the more will the sellers of labor power compete among themselves by accepting a lower price for their work; the capitalist's interest is well served if he either finds in existence or can create such a labor-market situation. As we saw earlier, during the First World War, when labor was in critically short supply and wages were correspondingly high, agents were sent South to recruit new workers. The immediate purpose of these efforts was to keep the war machine turning; the long-run consequence was to accelerate the liberation of the black peasant and sharecropper from his condition of semi-feudal bondage and thereby to increase permanently the size of the urban work-force. Further, both during the war and afterward, other methods were used to increase or maintain the supply of labor. Because labor unions, by transforming competitive workers into a cooperative work-force, regulate and restrict the supply of exploitable labor, they were fiercely opposed by American industrialists, who used the workers themselves as instruments of class warfare: strikes were broken with scab labor; the hungry worker of the present was used to insure that workers would remain hungry in the future. And along the picket lines a penumbra of color developed. In the explosive 1919 strike against the steel industry, for example, "between 30,000 and 40,000 black workers were brought into the steel districts as strikebreakers."[66] Before the war, blacks had been excluded from the unions as firmly as they had been from most industrial firms; it is therefore not surprising that they seized the opportunity to preserve and if possible accentuate the wartime employment situation. However, the immediate result of scabbing (both black and white) was to break the strikes and weaken the unions, which in turn helped to preserve the existing system of intra-class competition and tended to deepen the white worker's hostility toward his black rival. Thus in one sense the interracial hostility and violence of 1919 is explicable as a deflection from or a by-product of the inter-class conflict of the same year.

In addition to increasing or at least preserving the supply of labor through judicious use of monetary incentives and suppressive force, the owner of the means of production may attempt to decrease his demand for labor by raising his level of productivity. If he can produce more product with fewer workers (i.e., reduce the number of man-hours of labor-power materialized in his commodity), he can reduce the wage component of his costs of production, and indeed the cost of production overall. Further, if the reduction is sufficiently great, he can afford to pay the workers a higher wage than he did formerly while still maintaining or increasing his margin of profit. At the same time, given a stable or growing labor force, he is increasing the number of workers who are competing for employment.

The stimulus for increased productivity is obviously greatest when labor is in short supply. Thus, in response to the market situation during and after the war there developed a marked tendency toward the augmented use of inanimate sources of power, new and better kinds of machinery, and new ways of organizing production.* As one contemporary businessman remarked, "High wages, thrust upon us by the war, and always opposed by those in charge of our business, have lowered our manufacturing costs, by making us apply machinery and power to tasks formerly done by hand."[67] This gratifying result for the industrialist was also of benefit to his workers, whose real wages rose during the decade—albeit not as fast as the industrialist's profits. But these great advances in the division or specialization of labor also accentuated the internal division of the laboring class. The gap between the employed and the unemployed

---

* The impact of electricity and the internal combustion engine, the moving assembly line, and so-called "scientific management" of the industrial process in general and automobile manufacture in particular amounted to something of a technological revolution. It may be added that the Model T, i.e., the inexpensive automobile, had a transforming effect on the American way of life and a sustaining impact upon the U.S. economy throughout most of the decade.

widened; and already during this period, black workers were beginning to be disproportionately represented among those without employment.

In sum, efforts to realize the interests of the bourgeoisie through increasing labor supply while decreasing labor demand tended to enlarge both the American proletariat in general and the industrial reserve army (the army of the unemployed) in particular, although the latter tendency was partially offset by the expansion of the economy. Intra-class and interracial antagonism was one consequence of the bourgeois advantage in inter-class competition. At the same time and more specifically, the mutual opposition of the UNIA and the KKK resulted from a process of inter-class movement. The black peasantry was advancing into the urban proletariat. The UNIA crystallized the aspirations and organized the energies generated by that advance: its program reflected the New Negro's social progress. The KKK, on the other hand, was the vehicle of a declining class. The increasing efficiency and concentration of industrial capital was undermining the one-man firm as surely as mechanized agriculture was destroying the one-family farm. "Americans of the old pioneer stock" were becoming déclassé, losing their petit-bourgeois status and sinking into the proletariat.[68] The KKK embodied their fears and regrets: its program was a reflection of the present in the image of a past time when Everyman, every white, Protestant man, was economically self-made and self-sufficient. Although this past was partially mythic and in any case distant, although many if not most Klansmen had never been independent entrepreneurs, the typical White Knight or Black Legionnaire identified himself with the descending petite bourgeoisie and blamed the ascending black man (and the foreign-born worker) for his loss of status. The Garveyite, and black people in general, returned that hostility in kind. Moreover, the UNIA doctrine of economic self-determination contributed to this hostility by encouraging the petit-bourgeois ambitions of many of its members. Earl Little's dream of owning a small farm and retail business, for example, reflected Garvey's teaching that black people should become "independent of the white man." To be sure, this doctrine could not be collectively realized: the same forces that were destroying the white petite bourgeoisie precluded the development of a genuine black equivalent.* But it may readily be sur-

* Two points may be added. First, such projects as the Negro Factories Corporation and the Black Star Line do not come under consideration here. They expressed some combination of bourgeois and socialist aspirations, but they were not petit-bourgeois. Second, given that the term "petit-bourgeois" defines a relationship of independent,

mised that the embattled native American would have especially resented any attempt on the part of a black man to enter his own lost
estate: having been recently expelled from the garden of productive
private property, he now guarded its gates with a flaming cross. Thus
armed, he was ready, willing, and sometimes able to turn the dreams
of men like Earl Little into nightmares.

White Racism and Charismatic Group-Emotion

The mutual animosity of the UNIA and the KKK,
which at one historical moment was materialized in the attack upon
and unsuccessful defense of the Little home, can now be seen as resulting ultimately from the conflict of class interests in American
society. Yet despite its relatively comprehensive and extensive
quality, this explanation is not entirely adequate. We can explain in
strictly objective (political-economic) terms the opposition of one
class to another, based upon differential relationships to social productive forces; structural oppositions within the working class, as,
for example, between the employed and/or unionized workers and
members of the industrial reserve army, or between skilled and unskilled workers; and the opposition of every individual to every
other individual in the general competition for either work or profit.
But the lines of racial division in American society are not congruent with any of these objective divisions; racial antagonisms are
not, in fact, comprehensible in purely objective terms. Of course,
bourgeois interests were served by exploiting the existing racial division of the working class. White racism, as an instrument of divide-
and-rule, was and is a rational means to bourgeois ends. And given
this division or, more precisely, white racist domination, there is
nothing objectively problematical in the fact that black people organized in their own interest and for their own defense. But white racism is not rational from the standpoint of the white proletariat,
whose objective enemy is not the black worker but the bourgeoisie.

---

individual ownership to forces of production, the decline of the traditional petite
bourgeoisie in no way precludes the rise of a new middle class—when this latter term
is used to define a pattern of consumption or way of life, not a direct relationship to
productive forces. Thus the black middle class, which played a vital role in the Black
Revolution, was largely proletarian. Its aspirations, however, had certain petit-bourgeois characteristics.

This is not to deny that white racism, by the post-World-War-I period, had a long prior history: one might want to say that white workers inherited, rather than formed, such beliefs. But when one attempts to derive white racism from prior historical circumstances, one must still be able to explain the efficacy of the ideology which justified, e.g., slavery and the slave trade in the first instance. One cannot be content with a regression from theoretical explanation to empirical correlation. Finally, and most obviously, there is no basis in perception or experience for white people's phantasies concerning black people—for believing, e.g., that the "Negro, in whose blood flows the mad desire for race amalgamation, is more dangerous than a wild beast." Thus from several perspectives, white racism is an irrational belief system and, in organizations like the KKK, an irrational form of collective activity. We therefore require an explanation of objectively irrational conscious activity.

This requirement can also be stated in other terms. Class interests have here emerged as the objective ground of conscious activity. But the relationship between this ground and its actualization would be unproblematical only if the latter could be directly inferred or deduced from the former—if, so to speak, the language of conscious activity could be univocally derived from a grammar of interest. For in that case any subjective or motivational mediation of the extremes could be safely ignored. Motives would appear to constitute a purely passive or neutral medium through which the determinative value of an interest would be transferred without loss to practice. Conversely, when the form and content of conscious activity cannot be directly derived from the objective ground, then the process of motivational mediation not only transfers but also transforms the initial value. Our problem therefore becomes to explicate the psychological process through which working-class interests were transformed into white racist consciousness.*

* Two points may be added: (1) Our purpose is not to write a psycho-history of white racism, but to assess how racism, as it is objectively and subjectively determined, determines in turn the situation of black people. (2) It might be argued that there is a prior issue. We have observed that more than one class interest can be embodied in a single social movement. Doesn't this incongruence of class and organizational lines suggest the subjective mediation of an objective ground? The answer is: not in the sense that presently concerns us. Inter-class organizations are adequately comprehensible in terms of interests so long as they embody the time-honored principle, "The enemy of my enemy is my friend." In the case of the UNIA, peasant, proletarian, and even the black petite bourgeoisie had a common interest in opposing the big bourgeoisie. In the case of the Klan, although there was an historical antagonism between small-scale proprietors and wage-laborers, in the contemporary context that conflict

Given that our approach to this matter is to be psychoanalytic and that, at least initially, we are concerned with forms of collective activity like the KKK, we may begin this phase of the inquiry with Freud's "two theses" that in groups like churches and armies there is an "intensification of the affects" and an "inhibition of the intellect."[69] An individual becoming a member of such a group ceases to think or to judge independently, but instead comes to accept, unquestioningly, totally, and passionately, its laws and commandments. Now this is manifestly the phenomenon with which we are concerned, ascribed to organizations like the KKK, which might be described as a kind of church militant. How, then, does Freud explain this conjuncture?*

The basic hypothesis is that "love relationships . . . constitute the essence of the group mind": members of a group are sexually bound to each other and to their leader or leading idea.[70] Under certain conditions—most importantly, under the influence of a powerful leader—this emotional connection usurps all other relational possibilities.

Freud, following Gustav LeBon, observes that in the limiting case of leadership based upon "personal prestige," the leader exerts a "mysterious and irresistible power" over the members of the group. He produces "a feeling like that of 'fascination' in hypnosis" that "paralyzes our critical faculty." This "magnetic magic" is, however, "dependent upon [the leader's] success, and is lost in the event of failure."[71] Or, to interpose what may be a more familiar representation of the phenomenon, we have before us a depiction of Max Weber's charismatic leader, an individual whose legitimate authority rests upon a personal quality "by virtue of which he is set apart from ordinary men and treated as endowed with supernatural, superhuman, or at least specifically exceptional powers or qualities."[72] The potential adherent recognizes this quality through divine reve-

---

of interest was more than offset by the need to oppose the common enemy. Moreover, the petite bourgeoisie was becoming proletarian, and consequently the residual divergence of interest was rapidly disappearing. The problem is not, therefore, that the two movements crossed class lines; it is that they crossed them separately and perceived them only dimly—i.e., that both the petit-bourgeois and proletarian Klansmen saw themselves in the light of the "pioneer" past instead of the working-class present, that in this distorting light friends and enemies seemed distinguishable only by skin color; and that black people were forced to work from within and against these same regressive categories.

* What follows is a much compressed and, in some respects, an interpreted version of Freud's argument.

lation or some kind of miraculous proof, and henceforth is *obliged* to actualize his adherency. But the relationship, which is emotional in character, lasts only so long as the leader continues to be blessed by success.

Naming, of course, is not explaining; and, in fact, neither LeBon nor Weber understood the phenomenon they depicted. Freud helps us to understand it through a three-step analysis. First, he notes that in extreme cases of "being in love" there is "the phenomenon of sexual overvaluation—the fact that the loved object enjoys a certain amount of freedom from criticism, and that all its characteristics are valued more highly than those of people who are not loved." [73] This falsification of judgment results from a tendency toward idealization in love relations, a tendency to "substitute [the beloved] for some unattained ego ideal of our own. We love it on account of the perfections which we have striven to reach for our own ego, and which we should now like to procure in this roundabout way as a means of satisfying our narcissism." [74] Further, under the influence of what we now see as an externally mediated form of self-love, "the ego becomes more and more unassuming and modest, and the object more and more sublime and precious, until at last it gets possession of the entire self-love of the ego, whose self-sacrifice thus follows as a natural consequence. The object has, so to speak, consumed the ego." Or, rather, "the object has been put in the place of the ego ideal." [75] Consequently, "the functions allotted to the ego ideal entirely cease to operate. The criticism exercised by that agency is silent; everything that the object does and asks for is right and blameless." [76]

Here it must be noted that there is a conceptual uncertainty beclouding Freud's generally lucid analysis: the functions of the ego and the ego ideal, their boundaries as it were, are ill-defined. Much would be revealed through a critical investigation of this definitional difficulty; but for our present purposes it is sufficient to observe that being in love can involve the projection onto another of just the idealized, morally reasoning self, or of the reasoning self altogether.* Only in the latter case does the basis exist for Freud's sec-

---

* For clarity's sake, let me indicate how I use the basic psychoanalytic vocabulary. The concepts which state the qualitative and quantitative aspects of emotional energies (the so-called "economic" concepts) I view as the ground of analytic theory. The dynamic and genetic concepts, which are bound together as tightly as time and space, mediate this ground. Structural concepts are, then, the realization of the theoretical process. To perform this function, however, the latter must constitute a dialectical unity. This is possible if the *ego* is seen as a manifold of activity extending from un-

ond analytical step, the movement from "being in love" to hypnosis, to the introjection of the other, now enriched with its projectively acquired powers.[77] The hypnotic penetration of the self by the other is complete only when the other takes full possession of the conscious self, when it becomes the self's consciousness: when this happens, the self as such is reduced to unconsciousness; it simply responds emotionally to the introjected other. Indeed, at the limit the distinction between self and other, between object-love and identification, is annihilated. A sensation of oneness is all that remains.

The third step—from an analysis of the individual to that of the group—is easily taken. As Freud observes: "The hypnotic relation is . . . a group formation with two members."[78] Hence it may be posited that the group mentality is premised upon an idealizing love for the leader and is consummated in an hypnotic union with him. Further, the situational requisites of this consummation are readily specified: the hypnotic attraction is most powerful at moments of collective triumph or ritual exultation. Conversely, it is weakest when the group member is involved in mundane activities or when the leader fails to gain an announced end, thereby damaging the illusion of his omnipotence. Finally, the nature of the attachment of group members to each other can be inferred from this conception: they are bound to each other through their mutual love for and identification with the same object; they love and identify with each other "for His Name's sake."

Thus we arrive at an understanding of the enhanced emotionality/reduced intellectuality characteristic of groups like the KKK; and in the process, of the feeling of solidarity (or collective identity) which membership in such organizations produces. The tendency of group members to accept illusions as realities is also understandable: because the leader of the group is its consciousness, he has the power to define reality.

Our analysis is still incomplete, however. We have described the hypnotic effect of charismatic leadership, and to some extent its dynamics; we have yet to uncover its genetic basis. Here, again, Freud

---

conscious fusion with the physical self through pre-conscious processes (which are to be understood primarily in dynamic-genetic terms) to the complexities of consciousness and conscious activity. The term *id* is then reserved for the alienated or unconscious-repressed self, while the term *super-ego* designates the self-judgmental aspect of the ego. Id and super-ego are thus opposing forces, which develop concomitantly and which, through the contradictions their development entails, internally differentiate or structure the ego.

provides us with the necessary starting point: "Hypnosis," he observes, "has something positively *uncanny* about it."[79] It is this quality that distinguishes it from even the more extreme forms of identification and being in love. The question therefore becomes: from what source does the impression of uncanniness derive?

Freud's answer is that the sensation of uncanniness comes from the return of "something old and familiar that has undergone repression."[80] Forces from the past, although not announcing themselves as such, suffuse and take possession of the present, transforming it into an intense and timeless escape from the mundane world. Not the past recaptured, but the past recapturing, is the essence of the uncanny.

But what is it that has been repressed in the past, and that has now returned? What forces are at work here? Clearly, they are not conscious thoughts and desires, either current or recalled; for there is no mystery in the manifest. Nor can they be the innocent designs of this time or another, for in that case there would be no need for either the original repression or the later disguise. Hence, they must be morally or rationally unacceptable desires. Viewing the matter both psychoanalytically and psychogenetically, these must be the sexual and aggressive impulses of earliest childhood, the powerful and ambivalent emotions that bind children to their parents. These are the forces that are driven from the realms of consciousness to imprisonment in the unconscious by the judgments of conscience, by the internalized (and also unconsciously functioning) agent of parental authority. These are the forces that, as the uncanny, reappear in forms borrowed from the present moment.*

What, then, makes possible this return of the repressed? In the case of hypnosis, it is evidently the hypnotist himself who liberates these forces from their subterranean internment and provides them with a legitimate identity. He performs this magical feat by "putting himself in the place of the subject's parents"; that is to say, by laying claim to the moral authority of conscience and the reality-defining power of consciousness.[81] The phenomenon described above, the process of projection-introjection in hypnosis, is seen to have a basis in the introjection of parental authority during early childhood and the consequent repression of primitive sexual and aggressive desires. The overall psychodynamic structure of hypnosis may thus be formulated as *repression-projection-introjection*. More concretely:

---

* In the next chapter, when we have an adequate empirical basis for so doing, we will examine more closely the phenomenon of repression.

when the hypnotist becomes the subject's consciousness, he acts as a mirror that reflects repressed impulses back into the self in the form of rational-moral imperatives.

We now have a better understanding of the love that binds the subject to the hypnotist, the follower to the charismatic leader. But at this point two new problems arise. First, if both sexual and aggressive impulses are called forth by the charismatic leader, what becomes of the aggression? The sexual impulses are sufficiently well accounted for, but the object of aggression has yet to be defined. Second, the leader's authority must have a cognitive as well as an emotional content. His followers believe not only in him but also in the idea he embodies. Moreover, it is exactly this idea or set of ideas that provide the cloak of rationality in which the repressed impulses are concealed. We must, therefore, specify the relationship between the manifest or conscious content of collective dreams and the repressed desires we have found lying beneath them.

Actually, the solutions to these problems lie close at hand. First, with respect to aggression, we observed earlier that the KKK had a double nature: one existence in itself, and one directed against others. We were able to describe both the organization's internal life and its relations with its enemies. We then uncovered a latent group-structure beneath the manifest organizational one, an internal structure defined or determined by the pressure of repressed sexual impulses; but the external relationship has only been represented at the manifest, organizational level. Thus we are presented with latent aggression lacking a manifest content, on the one hand, and manifest hostility lacking an unconscious basis, on the other.

Stated this way, it is evident that we have before us two sides of the same phenomenon, that the relationship of such organizations to outsiders has a basis in repressed aggression. The group member first projects the unconscious hostility which was originally aimed at his or her parents onto the hypnotic leader, then the leader authorizes the displacement of that hostility away from both the group member and himself, toward a designated enemy. Thus the outsider, like the hypnotic leader, becomes a mirror of the self; but in this instance the reflected image does not return into the self, but remains external, an alien and threatening presence. Thus, the overall psychodynamic process of the group's foreign relations is *repression-projection-displacement*.

It now appears that the activities of the KKK were determined by the force of repressed emotional energies through the mediation of the projection and re-introjection of sexual tendencies and the projection and displacement of aggressive ones. But such a formulation is too simple, for as Myrdal stressed and Cox acknowledged, the alien group (the object of racist belief) is perceived as a sexual as well as an aggressive threat. The alien male is a rapacious devil; the female is a seductive witch—which is to say, the image of the racial enemy is a crystallization of aggressively dominated or limited sexual tendencies. It is formed through the projection and displacement of the group member's infantile self, of the sadistic child who survives within even the most compassionate adult.* For just this reason intra-group life is freed from the pressure of unwelcome infantile sexuality, so that it takes on the character of a relatively aim-inhibited relationship. If we translate this conception into structural terms, we may state that the group is to its enemy as a combined ego/super-ego is to the id, while the group itself is "a number of individuals who have put one and the same object in the place of their ego ideal [or super-ego] and have consequently identified themselves with one another in their ego." [82]

What, then, can we say about the relationship of consciousness to this process? From the perspective we have been developing, consciousness can only be viewed as the surface of the unconscious, as a manifestation of unconscious forces. This follows directly from the notion of a group, for the determinative movement of that notion is exclusively from the unconscious to consciousness. Thus, group ideation is to be understood as rationalization, not reason; in the language of dream interpretation, as secondary elaboration, not explanation. Finally, as implied above, the leader's function is to provide a system of such rationalizations, to give a semblance of reasonableness and justification to the release of repressed desires.

Freud once noted that neurotic symptoms give "the impression of being all-powerful guests from an alien world, immortal beings intruding into the turmoil of mortal life." [83] The emotional group—or, to state the concept in dynamic rather than structural terms, group-emotion—is a kind of social neurosis. It is also the psychological content of the sociological form which Weber designated as charisma; hence we may term any collectivity of this type a *charismatic group*. A charismatic group, then, is an alienated or falsified form of

---

* Even this depiction is too simple. Because the infantile self is formed through introjective and projective interaction with the parents, when the bad infantile self is displaced outside the group the wish to rid oneself of the archaic parental image is being expressed as well. At the most primitive emotional level, the group attempts to keep everything "good" inside itself and everything "bad" outside itself. (This aspect of group relations will receive more of our attention in later chapters.)

conscious activity, i.e., the rationalized product of repressed sexual-aggressive forces mediated through an externally directed (hypnotically induced) and double-valenced emotional process—the intra-group dynamic of projection and introjection, which constitutes a super-ego/ego structure, and the inter-group dynamic of projection and displacement, which constitutes an ego/id structure. The Klan's white racism may thus be understood as an instance of charismatic group-emotion. And, keeping in mind that the Klan was only an extreme form of a more general phenomenon, we may hypothesize that institutional racism is routinized charismatic group-emotion, and that the diffuse but pervasive racist atmosphere of American life reflects the widespread individual internalization of these same emotional tendencies.

Class Interests, Group Motives, and Conscious Activity

We began our descent into the unconscious because our objective analysis did not permit us to comprehend the white-racist falsification of working-class consciousness. Conversely, our subjective analysis does not permit us to understand conscious activity except as the product of unconscious emotional forces. But when we combine these two sides of the analysis, the phenomenon of working-class white racism becomes comprehensible. The Klan's white racism is seen as *a falsification of proletarian class-consciousness developed through the mediation of charismatic group-emotion.* In this way *working-class or group motives come to serve ruling-class interests.*

White racism in general and the activity of the KKK in particular were falsifications of working-class interests. By contrast, the UNIA expressed the class-racial interest of the emerging black proletariat. It can be argued, however, that it did not express this interest in a rational form. C. S. Johnson's contention was that the UNIA was avoiding the realities of American life by escaping into the dream of a return to Africa:

> For the "Back to Africa Movement," tho visionary and
> perhaps utterly impossible of accomplishment, afforded a
> mental relaxation for the long submerged Negro peasantry.
> It was a dream—but the new psychology has taught us the

utility, the compensatory value, of dreams. These might be expected to increase in intensity in direct proportion to the impossibility of conscious realization. Assuming, as we now must, the increased desires and aspirations of Negroes and the correspondingly increased racial consciousness among white groups, what other mode of escape is possible? Balked desires, repressed longings, must have an outlet. This was an outlet.[84] *

In other words, Johnson argues that the UNIA's guiding principles were irrational, given the realities of the American situation; and he offers an explanation of such irrationality in more or less psychoanalytic terms. We are under no obligation to accept this argument, but we cannot adequately evaluate it unless we have some standard by which to judge the situational rationality of conscious activity.

What, then, is the basis for the judgment of situationally rational action? At first sight it might appear that we would judge as rational any intended action or project that is realizable within a situation, and as irrational or non-rational one that is not: that which is not realizable, which cannot come into existence, is a situational nullity, exactly an abstraction and *ipso facto* not rational. Such a formulation is consonant with conventional psychoanalytic usage: an unrealizable project is a phantasy, a daydream; if it is mistakenly thought to be realizable or confused with reality, then reality-testing has failed, conscious reasoning has been subordinated to uncon-

---

* C. S. Johnson was a leading Negro scholar of the period. His judgment of Garvey reflects the general position of the Negro middle class. [See, for example, sections 85 and 86 of Herbert Aptheker's *A Documentary History of the Negro People in the United States*, Volume 2, 1910–1932 (Secaucus, N.J.: Citadel, 1973).] It therefore implies the conflict between Garvey and those Negro leaders who desired participation in, rather than separation from, American life, hence also the conflict between such organizations as the NAACP and institutionalized white-racism. Later on such intra-racial and inter-racial conflicts will become a part of our story, but for now, our interest is in the relationship of the Garvey movement and the Klan.

It should be mentioned that Johnson also argued that Garveyism was "a black version of that same 100 percent mania that now afflicts white America, that emboldens the prophets of a 'Nordic blood renaissance.'" In part this judgment reflects the intra-racial conflict mentioned above; in part it reflects the fact that the UNIA, like the KKK, did accept pseudo-biological explanations of historically and culturally determined racial differences. But such an equation ignores the *interaction* between black and white which gives these myths their historical meaning. It is one thing to propagate such myths in the service of racist oppression; it is quite another to turn them back upon the oppressor in the service of racial liberation (see in this regard Chapters VI and VII).

scious impulse—as in the instance of the charismatic group. This is clearly what C. S. Johnson had in mind when he called our attention to the "impossibility of realization" of the UNIA and KKK dreams.

As formulated, however, this definition begs the question of whether a project of situational transformation can be judged rational, for the only project realizable and therefore rational *within* a situation is one that accepts the situation as a given, as a fixed ontological limit. The existing situation here occupies the position of a first term in a formal syllogism, which must of necessity reappear in the conclusion. In other words, the definition implies a logic that reifies the present, that establishes it as identical to a universal and timeless essence and therefore as the sole criterion of rational action. Any attempt to go beyond or outside the existing situation, as did both the UNIA and the KKK, is irrational *a priori*.

Yet the idea that a project must be realizable to be rational has a certain persuasiveness; therefore let us accept it, at least for the moment. It then becomes evident that we must reformulate the idea so that it is *related* but not *limited to* an existing situation—which is to say, we must formulate it historically. In this regard, Karl Mannheim provides us with the useful concept of a "situationally transcendent" interest or idea. As opposed to ideas that "correspond to the concretely existing and *de facto* order," a situationally transcendent idea "is incongruous with and transcends the immediate situation (and in this sense, 'departs from reality')."[85] Hence initially we are thrown back into the irrationality of any idea that goes beyond what already exists; but insofar as such an idea can be realized, can become situationally congruent through the transformation of the existing situation, then (in our terms) it is rational or (in Mannheim's terms) "utopian": "Only those orientations transcending reality will be referred to . . . as utopian which, when they pass over into conduct, tend to shatter, either partially or wholly, the order of things prevailing at the time."[86] By contrast, a situationally transcendent idea is irrational or "ideological" when in practice it remains within the existing order despite the manifest intention to go beyond it. In sum, a utopian idea is situationally transcendent and rational, in the sense of being at least contingently realizable. Historically or temporally speaking, it is *progressive*: it draws its energy from the future. An ideological idea, on the other hand, is irrational, in the sense of being absolutely unrealizable. Historically speaking, it is static or *regressive*: it draws its energy from the present, or from the past incarnate in the present, despite the conscious belief that its vision descends from heaven, is in the nature of things, or is an imminent reality.

How are class interests and group emotions related to historically progressive (situationally rational) and regressive (situationally irrational) "ideas" or forms of collective, conscious activity? First, it is evident that a class or class-racial interest which cannot be realized in or through the transformation of the existing situation must necessarily result in situationally irrational activity. And because political action based upon such interests quite literally makes no sense, these movements must rely upon charismatic group-emotion to obscure their relationship to objective reality. We can say of the members of such movements what Freud said of certain patients, that they give us an "impression of having been 'fixated' to a particular portion of their past, as though they could not manage to free themselves from it and were for that reason alienated from the present and the future."[87] By contrast, action based upon a realizable collective interest does not presuppose distorted perceptions and understandings of the existing situation. In movements based upon realizable interests, the emotional tendencies of the members may simply give subjective force to the collective project. Charismatic group-emotion may here be replaced by what might be termed organizationally or instrumentally rational motive-forces. But as we have seen, a realizable class or class-racial interest does not necessarily result in situationally rational forms of conscious activity. If a collective interest is sufficiently falsified by charismatic group-emotion, then situationally irrational activity will be the consequence. The class or racial interest is in this case rendered unrealizable through the agency of its subjective mediation rather than as a result of its objective presuppositions.*

We thus emerge with two pure "types" of collective, conscious activity: progressive movements, in which realizable interests are me-

---

* In discussions concerning the nature of class consciousness and false consciousness it is sometimes argued that workers are simply uninformed of their real interests. Leaving aside the fact that workers are often *resistant* to learning where their interests lie, my view is that class consciousness is the most general articulation of what makes sense, even common sense, out of everyday working-class experience. Hence a variety of ordinary judgments are compatible with it, are in fact its mediations. But if a worker, recognizing that he is disadvantaged, accepts regressive leadership, he will increasingly come to misperceive and misunderstand his situation, so that eventually his capacities even for ordinary action will be impaired. Conversely, if he finds progressive leadership, his rational and critical capacities will be enlarged. (Later we

diated by organizationally rational motive-forces; and regressive movements, in which either a realizable or an unrealizable interest is mediated by charismatic group-emotion. But when we come to the analysis of actual political movements like the UNIA and the KKK, we find that matters are not so simple.

Let us first consider how the Klan's unrealizable petit-bourgeois interest was converted into charismatic group-emotion. This involves looking a bit more closely at the idea of an unrealizable class interest. A moment's thought tells us that such an objective ground has contradictory implications for conscious activity. On the one hand, if a class has lost and cannot regain control over a society's forces of production, it no longer has a basis for organizing itself as a political class. On the other, if some members of that class continue to occupy their traditional positions despite their relative loss of status, then an objective basis for class action has not entirely disappeared. Consequently, no unambiguous course of action is open to members of a dying class, of a class that is no longer a class. In the current instance, if a member of the petite bourgeoisie acknowledged his proletarian future, he was denying the validity of his present position; if he affirmed his present position, he was condemning himself to political impotence. He was painfully suspended between past and future: having no ground for rational action, he fell victim to the irrationality of group emotion.

An unrealizable interest, one might therefore conclude, *is* essentially group-emotion; but in fact the notion expresses only the immanent *possibility* of subjective irrationality. It does not specify, for example, why the petit-bourgeois individual falls backward in this way instead of making a leap forward; it does not differentiate between those members of a dying class who are buried with it and those who are reborn from its demise.

Our work thus far has not provided an adequate empirical foundation for comprehending this differential response; but with respect to the regressive reaction a somewhat speculative line of argument does suggest itself.[88] We remember Jackson's observation that the potential Klansman was "bewildered by the rapid pace of life and frustrated by his inability to slow the changes which seemed so constant and oppressive. . . . Unable to escape [from his transitional neighborhood] and hesitant to act alone, the threatened citizen welcomed the security and respectability of a large group." In other

---

shall see how both tendencies were played out in Malcolm's relationship to Elijah Muhammad.)

words, we might surmise that the petit-bourgeois Klansman was traumatized by urban proletarian life. He was a man formed in the image of his class, an embodiment of its moral and rational standards. These standards, the traditional virtues of the small-town businessman and the independent yeoman farmer, were no longer relevant to his new social circumstances; but initially their irrelevancy was experienced as personal failure, as a lacerating contradiction between his sense of what he ought to be and his recognition of what he actually was. Because it was only exceptionally possible to overcome this internal contradiction by transforming his external condition, he was predisposed toward irrational alteration of his location in both space and time; that is, he was predisposed toward ego-defense through both denial and regression. He was eager to deny the existence of or blind himself to the realities of his situation; and he was inclined to regress into the comfortably uncritical and passive condition of early childhood. These two defenses were, moreover, mutually reinforcing. Working together, they established the potential for slipping into a dream world structured and determined by repressed sexual and aggressive wishes.

When such a traumatized individual came into contact with the Klan, he was ready to accept an ideological vision which legitimized his repressed wishes by articulating them in the language of his currently suppressed but traditionally respectable petit-bourgeois interest; and he was glad to lose himself in the warm anonymity of charismatic-group emotion. His unrealizable class interest, experienced as personal trauma, was thereby resocialized in the form of collective irrationality—which is also to say, his emotional denial of and regression from the present moment became the means for preserving as a living social force the objectively out-lived interests and standards of an earlier time.

Among these standards was, of course, a racist criterion of human value, transferred more or less intact from its historical home in the rural South to a new home in the urban North. As we have seen, this standard made no *immediate* sense in class-analytic terms; but it loses its problematical character if we view it as a passageway into the realm of conscious action for group-emotion. The Klan's racist ideology was, in other words, a vehicle for the expression of unconscious motives: it attached the traumatized member of the petite bourgeoisie to his lost cause by serving his unconscious emotional needs. Operating charismatically upon the minds of such individuals, it gave them a renewed collective identity and a clearly defined, and presumably inferior, enemy. The white race was formed into a group through the hypnotic introjection of sexual energy; the black race was transformed into a hostile power through the hypnotic projection of aggressive energy; and the flaming cross presided with equally charismatic, equally orgasmic intensity over both the resurrection of the former and the destruction of the latter. . . . *In hoc signo vinces!*

Charismatic group-emotion was, then, the immanent subjective potential of the unrealizable class-interest of the white American petite bourgeoisie. But this formulation does not exhaust the implications of the group mediation: through his absorption into a group-emotional world, the Klansman became racially identified with his objective enemy, the big bourgeoisie, while at the same time his aggressive tendencies were displaced, deflected, away from his oppressor onto his fellow victims of oppression. In short, Klan racism, an historically conditioned form of charismatic group-emotion, served the interests of the American ruling class, served to facilitate the extraction and realization of surplus value from wage-labor.

We have now examined the Klan in terms of its predominant class aspect; before turning to its other side, let us analyze the UNIA in a parallel manner.

How is a realizable interest converted into rationally organized activity? We may posit that members of a rising class or race experience their situation as a field of enlarged possibilities, as challenging rather than as traumatizing. Their experience engenders reality-testing rather than emotional denial, progression or growth rather than regression. As we have seen, a typical black worker moving North wrote to friends at home: "I am making very good I make $75 per month . . . [and] I dont have to mister every little white boy comes along . . . I am not crazy about being with white folks, but if I have to pay the same fare I have learn to want the same acomidation." Unlike the Klansman who found it necessary to retreat into a phantasy world constructed from the fragmentary remains of his individual-collective past, the "Negro" was learning from and growing emotionally stronger in response to his greater opportunities. But in the Red Summer of 1919 and during the economic crisis of the early 1920s, he came up hard against white racism in general and Klan racism in particular. Further individual progress within the existing situation was precluded. He was therefore forced to organize for self-defense, and for the transcendence of the situation itself. A number of organizations came into being or grew in strength at this time, of which the UNIA, far and away the largest, was the only organization that developed workable programs for the black masses, the "descendants of plantation hands." Garvey's emphasis on a return to Africa and its petit-bourgeois aspects notwithstanding, it therefore constituted a largely rational, programmatic response to the conditions of urban proletarian life.

Yet we cannot ignore the "back to Africa" or the petit-bourgeois attributes of the UNIA any more than we can disregard the proletarian side of the KKK. In the latter regard, two issues arise. First, there are those aspects of the Klan's program that were progressive, reflecting without distortion the interests of its working-class members—most notably, its emphasis on free public education. But given our analysis of the UNIA, this rational proletarian side of the KKK is no longer problematical. It is the proletarian irrationality in both movements that still requires explanation—the petit-bourgeois and racist consciousness of the proletarian Klansman and the petit-bourgeois and African Zionist consciousness of the Garveyite.*

Once again, a tentative and partial solution to the problem is suggested by our previous analysis. A proletarian interest in a capitalist society is *ipso facto* negated. The worker's situation is inherently suppressive: he is recurrently left with ambitions he cannot realize and emotions he cannot release into action. Hence an unrealized but realizable interest has a double valence. As realizable, it implies a condition of challenge, reality-testing, and progression; as unrealized, it implies frustration, avoidance, and fixation. The former tendencies outweigh the latter in the long run; but at any given time the latter may predominate or even be negatively magnified into trauma, denial, and regression. Thus in the immediate postwar period, many workers must have found their always alienating situation even more difficult, unpredictable, and anxiety-producing than usual. Although better adapted to these conditions than a failing petit-bourgeois businessman, they would have been vulnerable to the Klan's hypnotic power. Moreover, workers as well as independent entrepreneurs are nurtured on the American dream; they grow up believing that with luck and pluck they will be able to escape from the drudgery of farm or factory labor. Although we have not

---

* Two points should be noted. First, an individual could rationally aspire to petit-bourgeois status, but a racial collectivity could not. Second, Garvey's idea of a return to Africa is not irrational in the same sense as the Klan's white racism and anti-modernism. There is nothing inherently or *a priori* unrealizable about a spiritual return to Africa or an international movement toward de-colonization. Keeping in mind the experience of the Jewish people, one could even argue that the historical jury is still out on the question of a more literal black Zionism.

developed an adequate empirical basis for explaining why this phantasy prevails in the face of the overwhelming evidence that it is a phantasy, our theoretical work suggests the hypothesis that a national group-identity, a routinized charismatic mentality having a well-defined petit-bourgeois and racist content, is an important general motivational mediation of American ruling-class interests.

Thus the proletarian membership in the Klan can be comprehended as an attempt by white workers to escape from an extremely frustrating labor-market situation. Moreover, the irrational side of the UNIA is similarly explicable. Even in the best of times the urban labor-market was difficult for the black worker. It presented far greater opportunities for advancement and emotional growth than sharecropping or plantation work; but the frustration resulting from being both black and a wage-laborer constituted an ever-present pressure toward situational transcendence by any apparently possible means. The predominant consequence of this pressure was the progressive core of the UNIA program; but an outer shell of escapism somewhat obscured the inner rationality of the movement. The dream of returning to Africa was one manifestation of this tendency; the vision of petit-bourgeois respectability and self-determination was the other. Both forms of escapism were outgrowths of the economic and demographic movements of the times. The exodus from the South to the North was extended to Africa; and the movement up from peonage was extended beyond proletarian status to the petit-bourgeois estate.

The desire to escape from bourgeois oppression, with all the determinations this formulation now contains, thus emerges as our final explanation of the two racial movements and, through their mediation, of the "nightmare night." Simply stated: Earl Little wandered through much of this country, "lookin' for a home" for himself and his family—only to have that home, once found, destroyed by white men who were themselves homeless in America.

CHAPTER III

The Seventh Son

IN CHARACTERIZING the Black Legion's opposition to Earl Little's activities, Malcolm concluded that his father was first reviled and then attacked as "an 'uppity nigger' for wanting to own a store, for living outside the Lansing Negro district, for spreading unrest and dissension among the 'good niggers.'" We have taken Malcolm's interpretation seriously, and have therefore analyzed the concatenation of economic, social, and political forces signified by the nightmare night. Nonetheless, our explanation of the nightmare night is neither all-inclusive nor conclusive. First, we have investigated the event from the outside in but not from the inside out. Until we determine what it meant to Malcolm at that time, the chain of interpretation from universal social forces through particular racial movements to individual activity will be incomplete. Our interest in the relationship between the individual and society, as well as our inherent interest in Malcolm, entails that we analyze the nightmare night explicitly as a moment of his experience.

Second, particular interpretations can be no stronger than the empirical grounds from which they are derived. Where the ground has been weak, speculative connections as well as real lacunae have appeared in our theoretical reconstruction of that night. Most importantly, because we have no clear account of how Earl Little and his enemies became racially self-defined individuals and, later, members of racial movements, the possibility of working up a theoretical reflection of this process has been extremely limited. This limitation cannot be overcome with respect to the nightmare night itself; but Malcolm's autobiography does provide the empirical basis for analyzing the genesis of racial activity. It will permit us to investigate how his character-structure developed, how he became an individual with a national-racial identity, and how he became a member of a charismatically led movement. In addition, since he achieved a position of racial leadership, in the end it will permit us to analyze political movement from the perspective of the leader as well as the follower.

How, then, did Malcolm experience the nightmare night? In the first place, he did not experience it as we have hitherto reconstructed it, or as he himself later understood it: a four-year-old boy does not live his life as a self-conscious participant in and observer of a complex sociohistorical process. He lives, less self-consciously, within the microcosm of the family.

The Family

Let us begin by recalling how Malcolm described the attack. He remembered "being suddenly snatched awake into a frightening confusion of pistol shots and shouting and smoke and flames." His father was shooting at "the two white men who had set the fire and were running away." The children, Malcolm included, were "lunging and bumping and tumbling all over each other trying to escape" from the burning building; and his mother, babe in arms, barely got out of the house before it collapsed. Then "we were outside in the night in our underwear, crying and yelling our heads off." Thus Malcolm's "earliest vivid memory," a terrifying and confusing nightmare of noise, flames, and frantic activity. The experience was so intense that it brought to an end the undifferentiated succession of days that had preceded it. Measurable time, the chronological record of Malcolm's consciousness, began that night—which is also to say, Malcolm knows himself, can remember and reflect upon himself, only as the child of this moment of terror. From his own perspective, earlier events in his life are prehistoric, while all later ones will be seen in the light of this primal experience. A Manichean groundwork had been established in his character, a potential for seeing the white man as a powerful and evil force that black people had every reason to fear and hate. Although subsequent experience would lead Malcolm to realize this potential in varying ways— sometimes even by inversion—the Legion attack firmly impressed the dualism of American racial life upon his soul.

Thus the Legionnaires were the first "white devils" of Malcolm's conscious life, and the nightmare night was his first submersion in the latent content of the American dream. This much is evident in Malcolm's memory of the experience. But the meaning of the event is not exhausted by such a phenomenological representation, for two reasons. First, on formal grounds every event must be perceived as a moment in a temporal manifold, i.e., as the manifestation of past and future in the form of the present, or as the simultaneous transformation of the past into the future and the future into the past through the mediation of present activity. Second, the emotional content of this transformational process is the continuing pressure of ungratified desires and unavoidable fears, be they conscious or unconscious. The unity of content and form is theoretically determined by finding those analogic relations between successive events that are indicative of motivational continuity. Thus ideally we would have to find in the nightmare night the child Malcolm had previously been and the youth he was about to become; and we would constitute the unity of this process by first explicating the unconscious determinants of his conscious actions and then transforming the resultant relationship between conscious and unconscious forces into a conception of his character. Precisely because the Legion attack *is* a beginning, however, only certain general connections can be established between it and Malcolm as a preexisting subject.

In *The German Ideology* Marx observes that "the first premise of all human history is . . . the existence of living human individuals."[1] Elsewhere he notes: "There are characteristics which all stages of production have in common."[2] The same is true in the history of the individual: the first premise is a living human being who, as such, has certain characteristics in common with every other living human being. For present purposes, the most important such characteristic is that the earliest mother-child interaction establishes an anaclitic relationship between emotional drives and objective needs. Freud argues that when a child is nursing at its mother's breast, its "lips . . . behave like an erotogenic zone, and no doubt stimulation by the warm flow of milk is the cause of pleasurable sensation."[3] Hence "to begin with, sexual activity attaches itself to functions serving the purpose of self-preservation and does not become independent until later."[4] Leaving aside the question of whether sexual activity, or sexual-aggressive activity, is ever "independent" of self-preservative functions, it seems better to say that "at the very beginning of life . . . instinctual energy is still in an undifferentiated state."[5] Such an undifferentiated instinctual state may be described as merely *sensuous*. We may then posit that the infant has sensuous needs which must be satisfied if it is to survive. It also has the power to gain satisfaction: it cries to attract its mother's attention, sucks to take in nourishment and to quiet primitive anxieties resulting from somatic tensions, and generally encourages maternal solicitude by responding with signs of contentment to the experience of being nurtured. But as the nurturing experience indicates, sensuous needs constitute a pressure as well as a power: the very existence of a need entails the experience of frustration, hence a pressure toward activity which will end the unsatisfactory condition. For this reason Freud believed that pressure, the "amount of force or the measure of the demand for work" which an instinct represents, is any instinct's "very essence."[6]

If we now use the term *energy* to denote a need in the double sense of power and pressure, or as a potential for activity; and if we use the term *sensuous* as above, i.e., to denote the earliest form of human activity, then we may say that human individuals are sensuously energetic. And given that human activity is distinctively self-conscious (verbally structured and self-reflective), we may say that sensuous energy is a potential for self-conscious activity. By so doing, we avoid defining character in a one-sided, emotionally oriented manner. Instead, we see character as originating in the sensuous interactions of energetic human individuals, not in sexual and aggressive drives per se. The latter continue to play a basic role in our theorizing, as they must if theory is to reflect human practice, but they are viewed as arising through differentiation from sensuous energy. This process of development can then be termed *anaclitic*: the particular form taken by sexual and aggressive drives is conditioned by the infant's objective needs and by the way these needs are met. Furthermore, a moment's reflection tells us that self-preservative needs are not met simply from the outside, or at the mother's discretion. Rather, the infant *works* to satisfy its needs: crying, sucking, touching, attending to sights and sounds, manipulating objects, and learning to creep, crawl, stand, and walk are the forerunners of the work-process. In the life history of the individual, as in the history of the species, human organs are the first tools, environmentally predetermined materials are the first objects of work, and work consists in constructive and destructive activity through which the one is united with the other.[7] Sensuous energy is developed through the work-process just as much as through the development of sexual-aggressive drives (which we may term the emotional-process). In other words, we may say that sensuous energies are developed as much through objectification (the creation of inter- and intra-objective relations) as through subjectification (the creation of inter- and intra-subjective relations). Conscious and self-conscious activity can then be understood as the product of sensuously energetic human interactions mediated through mutually determining subjectification and objectification processes.

It might seem that in formulating these abstract conceptions of human species life we have left our interest in Malcolm behind. In one sense, we have. As Marx observes concerning objectification: "The so-called general preconditions of all production are nothing more than . . . abstract moments with which no real historical stage of production can be grasped."[8] Any such generalities must be worked up from and back down to historically particularized materials. Since we lack detailed information about Malcolm's first few years, we cannot adequately ground our general conceptions of that period. But by establishing Malcolm's human individuality in this fashion, we will be able to describe his activity as sensuously energetic, hence as a life-process; his work-activity in particular as integral to his character; and his conscious activity as recognizably human. This is also to say that we will be working with an idea of human nature appropriate to Marx's historical conceptions, and that we have rendered potentially comprehensible the interests and motives of individuals who participate in progressive and regressive racial movements. Thus the presentation of these more or less unmediated generalities is justified by our interest in Malcolm as a human individual and as a participant in collective racial activities.

The acceptance of these generalities does not, however, give us license to speculate very far on the pre-Oedipal (oral and anal) phases of Malcolm's development. We know, of course, that he went through these phases—that he was weaned and toilet-trained, that he learned to walk and talk, etc.—but *how* he experienced this period of his life we do not know. From what he tells us about his later childhood, we can surmise that he was a very active child, and probably not a docile one. He himself says that he learned very early to "cry out and make a fuss" until he got what he wanted from his mother.[9] Although in making this comment he was not describing his earliest years literally, it seems likely that the forceful use of the spoken word was generally characteristic of him. In addition, we know from his autobiography that the Little family moved twice between the time of Malcolm's birth and the Legion attack. Malcolm was too young to have been affected consciously by the first move, which came shortly after his birth, but he may have experienced some anxiety through his mother, if the move was upsetting to her. Anxious and homeless feelings may also have accompanied the second move. More importantly, however, Malcolm became "homeless" in another sense during this period. He lost his position as the family's youngest child, first to Reginald and then to Yvonne. His penchant for being noisy in order to attract his mother's attention may have been conditioned by the appearance of these rivals. And with his loss of maternal attention in mind, we can read his description of the children confusedly tumbling over each other during the nightmare night as an indirect complaint that there were too many children, that he was not receiving sufficiently individualized attention. Thus the nightmare night might be viewed as signifying both Malcolm's intensifying experience of the homelessness of black people in white America and the emotional homelessness of a small child who has to compete with his younger siblings for his mother's love.

We are on firmer evidential ground when we attempt to establish the relationship between Malcolm's primal experience and his subsequent memories of family life. "After that [night]," he reports, "my memories are of friction between my father and mother. They seemed to be nearly always at odds. Sometimes my father would beat her."[10] Malcolm deduced that the friction was accentuated by educational disparities: "My mother had a pretty good education. . . . But an educated woman, I suppose, can't resist the temptation to correct an uneducated man. Every now and then, when she put those smooth words on him, he would grab her."[11] Moreover, his father's wrath was visited upon the children: "My father was also belligerent toward all of the children, except me. The older ones he would beat almost savagely if they broke any of his rules—and he had so many rules it was hard to know them all."[12] And while Malcolm escaped punishment at his father's hands, he received his fair share of "whipping" from his mother.

Now, if we view this description of the internal relations of the Little family against the background of Malcolm's first memory, it is hard to avoid the conclusion that the nightmare of Malcolm's childhood was not confined to one night. The violence of the Legion attack is carried over into Earl Little's attack upon the other members of the family; and we can readily surmise that a mood of terrified confusion pervaded the home whenever the parents were at war with each other or the father was being "belligerent" to one of the children. In this sense the Legion attack was only the nightmare of everyday life in an intensified form.

The determinative force in each of these experiences was aggression (or more precisely, the aggressive form of emotional energy). But their nightmarish quality, their common content, is analogical, not identical: the Black Legion of the nightmare night is to Earl Little and his family as the Earl Little of everyday life is to his wife and children. This analogy implies not only that Little as well as his enemies had an aggressive relationship to the family, but also that he was the connecting link between the Legion and the family. We are made to realize that it was Little's uppity behavior that brought the Legion's wrath down upon the family. This was, of course, the inevitable consequence of his struggle for self-determination in a racist society. Nonetheless, his choice cast him in a double role: he both exposed his family to racist assault and attempted to defend them from their assailants. In so doing, from the standpoint of his wife and children he would not only have been identified with the family against its enemies, he would also have been identified with its enemies, against the family.

This identification might have been inconsequential, might have become one of those ghostly double images that float freely in the unconscious without ever determining the character of conscious activity, were it not for Little's aggressive behavior in the home. By his brutal attacks on his wife and children Malcolm's father solidified the double image, transformed it from a circumstantial analogy into an in-dwelling reality. He made himself, by his own hand, into both the defender and destroyer of his family. There is no mystery in this double role. Little was an explosively angry man whose anger reflected the white racist hatred surrounding him. His two roles were only opposing expressions of this same energetic potential—what we may call the bivalent aggressivity in his character. But however explicable and justifiable his aggressive actions may have been, they entailed a fateful duplication for his children: at least in Malcolm's mind and memory, his father appeared simultaneously as himself and his enemies.

In this terrifying way, and in these confusing forms, the racial antinomies of American society were impressed upon Malcolm's developing character.

Leaving aside for the moment the external and racial dimensions of the event, the nightmare night is now seen as a magnified reflection both of Earl Little's bivalent personality and of the confusion and fear produced in Malcolm by his father's violence toward his mother and the older children. It thus signifies, explicitly for us and implicitly for Malcolm, the internal relations of the Little family.

The question therefore becomes: how do we comprehend this familial relationship, in itself and as it affected the formation of Malcolm's character? Given the psychological interest with which we
began this chapter, this is also to ask: how can this empirical pattern
be conceptualized so that its genetic connection to Malcolm's later
group membership becomes theoretically specifiable? Once the
question has been posed in these terms, it becomes evident that we
should begin with what Freud had to say about the genesis of group
psychology.*

In *Group Psychology and the Analysis of the Ego* Freud referred
back to the Darwinian hypothesis, previously utilized in *Totem and
Taboo*, that "the primitive form of human society was that of a
horde ruled over despotically by a powerful male."[13] The latter, he
now went on to argue, was the first true individual: "He, at the very
beginning of the history of mankind, was the 'superman' Nietzsche
only expected from the future." His "intellectual acts were strong
and independent even in isolation, and his will needed no reinforcement from others." It follows that "his ego had few libidinal ties; he
loved no one but himself, or other people only insofar as they served
his needs."[14] The members of his horde, conversely, were emotionally and intellectually dependent upon him. They loved him
submissively, feared him absolutely, obeyed him unquestioningly,
and were bound to each other by their common bondage to their
leader. Thus for Freud the primal horde is the archetypal group as
well as the archaic form of the human family; and the father of the
horde is the precursor of both the patriarch and the hypnotic leader.

Needless to say, the Little family was not literally a horde, and Earl
Little was not a Nietzschean *übermensch* any more than he was a
primitive totemic deity. But our analysis of Malcolm's earliest memories did reveal that, in Malcolm's mind, his father was an awesome
force for good and evil, and that the family's internal relations were
defined by his actions. Thus if we use Freud's anthropological Just
So Story to conceptualize Malcolm's view of his father and his family, it forms a first theoretical mediation between Malcolm's childhood experiences and his adult activities: as the primal father is to
the hypnotic leader, so Earl Little is to Elijah Muhammad; and as the

---

* This choice places us momentarily in the field of anthropological speculation, for
Freud himself was concerned with the phylogeny of group psychology, not its ontog-
eny. But in psychoanalytic theorization it is permissible to work analogically either
from the individual to the species or the species to the individual. In the present instance we must briefly consider the hypothesized archaic heritage of the group, and
then reformulate the notion ontogenetically.

horde is to the group, so the Little family is to the Nation of Islam. The prophet was heir to the father's awesome power; the Nation re-embodied the collective identity generated by that power. Malcolm's membership in the Nation was, therefore, a return at a higher level of individual development to the family of his childhood. *

Thus far we have only described the authority structure of the horde, the form of its internal relations; we have yet to consider its content, i.e., the advantage the father gains through the exercise of his power, and the son's reaction to that advantage. According to Freud, the primal father was a violent and jealous male who kept all the females of the horde to himself. He used his brute strength and the hypnotic power of his total self-confidence to maintain a sexual monopoly, thereby forcing his sons "into abstinence and consequently into the emotional ties with him and with one another that could arise out of those of their impulsions that were inhibited in their sexual aim. He forced them, so to speak, into group psychology."15 The aim-inhibited sexual bondings we discovered in the charismatic group appear here in their primitive form, as the sexual interrelationships of a patriarchal family, specifically, of Earl Little's family. To be sure, in this real-life situation there was only one adult "female" in the "horde"; but that is only to say that the modern nuclear family is *not* in fact a horde, and that it is only from a son's infantile perspective that the father's power and sexual privileges vis-à-vis the mother take on the aura of a horde relationship.

If Malcolm's family is understandable in these terms, and if we have accounted preliminarily for its sexual content, we must next search out the aggressive impulses we would expect to be present in the precursor of an adult group-formation. Here, for the first time, the analogy between the family and the hypnotic group, or between the Littles and such racial organizations as the UNIA or the Nation of Islam, breaks down. * While it is true that the Little family group was more or less united against its external enemies, it was not thereby freed from internal rivalries and hostilities. In part this was because Earl Little directly attacked his wife and children; but the idea of a horde suggests another level of emotional meaning.

The male children of the horde loved their father, or at least were

* At least so our analogy implies. We shall have to see as we proceed whether or not Malcolm's membership in the Nation is in fact comprehensible as a life-historically mediated realization of this primordial ground.
* The reader will have noticed that thus far the family lacks the distinctive moral quality of its adult analogue. We shall see presently how the father's power over his wife and children becomes a binding moral authority—how might becomes right.

fascinated by his power, but their own feelings also mirrored his violent and jealous emotions. They lived with a constant suppressed anger, envied him his sexual prerogatives, and waited for the day when they would be strong enough, or he would be weak enough, to make possible a successful patricidal rebellion. Meanwhile their passions were most inflamed when they witnessed the so-called "primal scene"—when they saw their father having sexual intercourse with one of his wives or daughters.[16] On these occasions their latent sexual urges and hatred for their father fused into a consuming, highly erotized jealous rage.

We shall see presently that the patricidal climax of this original family tragedy has relevance for Malcolm's life history. At present, however, our concern is the son's jealousy of the father's relationship to the mother. If we suppose that Malcolm envied his father that special role, and that he either witnessed or overheard his parents while they were having sexual intercourse—an assumption that seems entirely plausible, considering the tight quarters the family habitually occupied—then we can view the nightmare night as a screen memory for the primal scene, a disguised representation or image of that other terrifying, confusing, but also sexually stimulating event. Moreover, Malcolm, in witnessing or overhearing his parents' love-making, would almost certainly have misconstrued what was happening, interpreting it as his father attacking his mother. On this reading, the Black Legion represents Earl Little "grabbing" Louise sexually as well as aggressively. Finally, we can suppose that Malcolm's jealous anger was inflamed on such occasions, so that the flames of the nightmare night symbolize his jealousy as well as white racist and paternal violence.

Malcolm

At this juncture we have represented Malcolm as a member of his family and as a child who was jealous of his father's power and sexual prerogatives. His character has been seen as little more than a sensuously mediated unity of himself and his situation. Only the newborn child, however, really exists in such a state of immediate unity with its environment. Even before the end of the first year of life, a process of individuation begins, and the child begins to determine his own character and the nature of his relationship to his family. Before the age of five this process has resulted in the formation of a self that is both distinct from and identified with its significant others; that is internally differentiated but constantly reunifying; and that acts, both intra-personally and inter-personally, in an emotionally, intellectually, and morally characteristic manner. Malcolm had at this time already developed a nascent character structure, which we can begin to uncover by representing more substantially his varying identifications and affective interactions with the other members of his family.

Earl Little married twice. He had three children from his first marriage, and three children with Louise (Wilfred, Hilda, and Philbert) before Malcolm was born. Malcolm in turn was followed by Reginald, Yvonne, Wesley and Robert. Hence Malcolm could state, "I was my father's seventh son."[17] To be sure, it would be more in line with conventional usage to say Malcolm was his parents' fourth child; but by placing himself in a patrilineage Malcolm was able to claim for himself a special black cultural position. The seventh son is a born hero, destined to be a man who can "heal the sick, raise the dead, and make the little girls talk out of their heads."[18] He is possessed of extraordinary sexual and mental powers and uncanny good luck. These are, of course, precisely the perceived or imagined attributes of the primal father (or the charismatic leader). In defining himself as the seventh son, Malcolm was therefore laying claim to his father's *mana*, as well as to the role of culture-hero.

To be the seventh son is not only a blessing, however, but also a curse. After noting that Earl Little was destined to "die by the white man's hands," Malcolm says: "It has always been my belief that I, too, will die by violence."[19] The son who ascends to the father's throne must die the father's death. Malcolm wrote these lines during the period of his break from Elijah Muhammad, at a time when thoughts of death and dreams of racial leadership were deeply intertwined in his mind—hence the tone of heroic *amor fati*. But beneath the obvious reference to his current situation, we can see the small boy's wish to inherit his father's position and his fear of the consequence of so wishing.

Although Malcolm was wishfully identified with his father's power and prerogatives, in appearance he was far more his mother's son:

> Louise Little, my mother, who was born in Grenada, in
> the British West Indies, looked like a white woman. Her
> father *was* white. She had straight black hair, and her accent

did not sound like a Negro's. Of this white father of hers, I
know nothing except her shame about it. I remember hearing her say she was glad that she had never seen him. It was,
of course, because of him that I got my reddish-brown
"mariny" color of skin, and my hair of the same color.[20]

Later on, Malcolm continues, he was "insane enough" to be proud of
looking white. "But, still later, I learned to hate every drop of that
white rapist's blood that is in me."[21] His maternal heritage, too, was
a blessing and a curse—first a reason for self-love, then for self-
hatred.

It was not only "later" that Malcolm's light skin-color played
an important and ambivalent role in his life. He was the lightest-
skinned of the Little children; in his retrospective judgment, this
fact helped to determine each parent's attitude toward him. We
noted earlier that Earl Little beat all of the children except Malcolm.
In Malcolm's opinion, it was his relative whiteness that exempted
him from punishment: "I actually believe that as anti-white as my
father was, he was subconsciously so afflicted with the white man's
brainwashing of Negroes that he inclined to favor the light ones, and
I was his lightest child."[22] Earl Little was a "white racist" *malgré
lui*, a victim of racial false consciousness. As we previously asserted,
he was partially identified, in fact and in his son's mind, with his
enemies. But Malcolm's accusation has an additional meaning.
While on the one hand he is claiming to be his father's favorite child,
on the other he is denying the authenticity of that status. If my father loved me, he is saying, he did so for the wrong reasons. Moreover, this skepticism concerning the genuineness of his father's love
has a mirrored implication, namely, that Malcolm doubted the sincerity of his own love for his father. On this reading, the statement
is an indirect confession of filial ambivalence.

In Malcolm's relationship with his mother we find the racial-
emotional equation precisely reversed: "Thinking about it now, I
feel definitely that just as my father favored me for being lighter
than the other children, my mother gave me more hell for the same
reason."[23] In other words, the play of racial forces within the family,
the mutual attraction of epidermal opposites, determined that Malcolm could be loved by his father only insofar as he was not loved by
his mother. Furthermore, if we were correct in inferring that Malcolm's retrospective recognition of the racial basis of paternal affection was not only empirically accurate but also a sign of his earlier
doubts concerning his father's love for him and his love for his fa-

ther, then by the same reasoning the present statement indicates that Malcolm believed (or wished to believe) that he and his mother did love each other, despite the manifest hostility of the relationship.

Thus far in this phase of the analysis we have considered Malcolm's perceptions of his parents' interactions with each other and with him, and the ambivalent relationship to each parent that resulted reflexively from this familial situation. Malcolm's developing character was obviously not just a mechanical effect of external causes, however; his objective situation provided him with the raw materials for subjective or self-formative activity. He was his father in essence, his mother in appearance, and he was becoming himself in actuality. In the previous section we found not only that Earl Little's power was impressed upon his son, producing a state of confused fear and admiration, but also that Malcolm desired to possess his father's power, that he wished to recreate it in and for himself. Our next step must be to unify these two phases of the argument, i.e., to determine more precisely the relationship between Malcolm as an objectively defined member of the Little family and Malcolm as a desiring individual.

Our current position can also be formulated with regard to Malcolm's autobiography. In his narrative Malcolm first presents himself, and we re-presented him, as a victim of the nightmare night. The objective and subjective dimensions of his experience here formed an immediate unity: Malcolm tells us what happened and how it felt to have it happen with the same words. Thereafter a split appears in the initial totality. Sometimes Malcolm presents himself as an observer of his situation, whose own feelings are either unstated or of secondary importance. At other times he stresses his own reactions to what is happening rather than the objective side of the experience. It is this more subjective dimension of Malcolm's self-presentation that we are now to consider.

Malcolm's description of his own feelings emerges initially from his "images" of his father's activities "outside the home."[24] The first image was of Earl Little in the role of "visiting preacher," a role Malcolm did not admire:

> My brother Philbert, the one just older than me, loved
> church, but it confused and amazed me. I would sit goggle-
> eyed at my father jumping and shouting as he preached,
> with the congregation jumping and shouting behind him,
> their souls and bodies devoted to singing and praying. Even

at that young age, I just couldn't believe in the Christian
concept of Jesus as someone divine. And no religious person,
until I was a man in my twenties—and then in prison—
could tell me anything. I had very little respect for most
people who represented religion.[25]

Malcolm was confused and terrified during the Black Legion attack;
he was "confused and amazed" by his father's preaching. He stum-
bled and tumbled out of the burning house; he also struggled to remain outside the religious frenzy that engulfed his father, his family,
and the congregation. The Baptist Sunday service thus takes its
place in the analogic series of the everyday life of the Little family
and the nightmare night, the horde-family and the primal scene—a
series which signifies the experiential realm immanently determined by Earl Little's sexual-aggressive power. Further, it shows us
Malcolm resisting that power, refusing to be swept into the whirl-
pool of group emotion, and it gives us some indication of how he
managed to maintain control over his own emotions: his proclaimed
lack of faith in Christ's divinity and lack of respect for religious people in general is a denial of his father's moral and ethical claims
upon his affection. As Malcolm was later to say of the white man,
Earl Little had no "moral basis" for his ministry of Christian love
and his preaching of divine retribution. He had no right to tell others
"'That little black train is a-comin' . . . an' you better get all your
business right!'"[26] when he personally was so far from being righteous. Little's actions within the family undercut his religious authority, although not his paternal power; and Malcolm was therefore
able to withstand paternal power when it was manifested in the
form of religious authority.

Philbert, on the other hand, loved church, i.e., loved his father in
his preacher's role. It follows from this fact that Little's paternal
brutality is not a sufficient explanation for Malcolm's rejection of
his authority. There must also have been a force in Malcolm's character that permitted and demanded resistance to his father's hypnotic power. Given our prior analysis, this force must have been his
jealousy of his father, the seventh son's desire to possess the father's
magical powers . . . and to possess his mother. In short, Malcolm's
infantile sexual passions entailed his hatred for the father who brutalized, and appeared to brutalize, his mother. It was therefore imperative that he not fall under his enemy's power; this imperative
necessitated rejection of his father's moral claims. Stated differently,
power is hypnotic only if it is morally binding, if it is might that has

become right. If it is not moralized, it remains an external force that can be legitimately resisted by any means necessary. Insofar as Malcolm could deny his father's Christian authority he could also contend against him for his power.

No sooner is this explanation offered, however, than a new problem arises. Oedipal jealousy is a psychological universal. How, then, can we explain the difference between Malcolm's and Philbert's behavior? Clearly there must be some particularizing mediation that we have hitherto overlooked.

Once the question has been raised in this manner, our attention is drawn to Malcolm's special position in the family. He was the seventh son, his father's favorite. It would seem to follow that their emotional relationship was singularly intense. But for Malcolm's part, the emotions involved were substantially Oedipal, i.e., ambivalent or contradictory. Hence we may surmise that church services, which were in themselves emotionally stimulating, called forth a rush of feeling Malcolm found it difficult to control. Malcolm may also have had more difficulty than the other children in keeping his emotions under control. If this surmise is correct, then church services would have been doubly threatening.

In sum, in order to maintain himself against his father, it was necessary for Malcolm to hold himself aloof from Christian worship. But to arrive at this formulation, we had to posit that Malcolm's love for his mother and hatred of his father were the principal determinants of his behavior. Earlier, however, we argued precisely the opposite position, namely, that Malcolm's own feelings predominantly mirrored his parents' feelings for him; and in the course of the present argument, we were forced to take into consideration Malcolm's special relationship to his father. It would seem, therefore, that we have fallen into contradiction; and, in a certain sense, we have. But the contradiction between these two moments in our work is only a theoretical reflection of an existential condition. More concretely, in the earlier instance we were representing Malcolm's manifest feelings, while in the present case we are focusing upon his latent motives. The appearance of logical contradiction results from the fact that the subordinate emotions at the former level are the dominant ones at the latter. Such an explanation is, however, satisfactory if and only if we can indicate how the balance of forces in Malcolm's character was developed and maintained. We must determine what made possible and necessary the repression of Malcolm's sexual attraction for his mother and his corresponding hostility toward his father.

Malcolm provides us with the needed empirical ground in his description of his father's other role outside the home:

> I knew the collections my father got for his preaching
> were mainly what fed and clothed us, and he also did other
> odd jobs, but still the image of him that made me proudest
> was his crusading and militant campaigning with the words
> of Marcus Garvey. As young as I was then, I knew from
> what I overheard that my father was saying something that
> made him a "tough" man. I remember an old lady, grinning
> and saying to my father, "You're scaring these white folks to
> death." [27]

Just as Earl Little the preacher was the Sunday incarnation of the brutalizing father, so Earl Little the UNIA campaigner was the everyday embodiment of the protective father. Understandably, then, Malcolm had no respect for the first image but took pride in the second: Garveyism permitted him to see his father in the light of other people's admiration, which when internally reflected gave him a sense of pride—made him proud of his father's toughness and proud to be his son. Moreover, unlike the church services, which alienated Malcolm from his father, UNIA meetings solidified the special relationship between them: "One of the reasons I've always felt that my father favored me was that to the best of my remembrance, it was only me that he took with him to the Garvey U.N.I.A. meetings which he held quietly in different people's homes." [28] Where in church Malcolm was just another member of the congregation, or of the family, at Garvey meetings he was clearly the beloved seventh son. Finally, where the church situation generated an almost overwhelming sensation of dangerous emotion, Garvey meetings gave Malcolm a feeling of quiet self-control:

> I noticed how differently they [the people at UNIA meet-
> ings] acted, although sometimes they were the same people
> who jumped and shouted in church. But in these meetings
> both they and my father were more intense, more intel-
> ligent and down to earth. It made me feel the same way. [29]

In sum, because Garveyism helped Earl Little to bring his anger under control and to direct it away from the family, it permitted Malcolm—and presumably only Malcolm—to experience the more gentle and rational side of his father's character. While he could not respect the preacher whose jumping and shouting frightened him, he could both identify with and love the tough man who "was scaring these white folks to death."

We now have before us the two poles, the antinomian extremes, of Malcolm's relationship to his father. The tendencies were not of equal strength: the second, which enabled Malcolm to control his own emotions, was the principal aspect of the contradiction. Because Garveyism brought out the positive side of his father's character and gave Malcolm unique access to his affection, it provided him with both a reason to control his sexual and aggressive impulses (the reward of paternal love), and an image of his father he could introject without fear. This internalized image of paternal authority then drew to itself some portion of Malcolm's emotional energy, and thus became the moral force in his character. Furthermore, once this force had been established, it could demand that all opposing emotional forces be driven from the field of conscious activity. Malcolm was morally formed in his father's image, and his now unwelcome sexual and aggressive impulses were repressed.

This process of self-formation necessarily involved certain unintended consequences. First, the introjection of the positive paternal image entailed the introjection of the negative aspect as well. Try as he would to keep the two sides separated, they were after all but opposing aspects of the same paternal power. The preacher consequently gained entrance to Malcolm's soul; and his conscience became a two-edged sword, an instrument of brutal self-hatred as well as of powerful self-love, of guilt as well as pride. And second, Malcolm's Oedipal ambitions were repressed but not destroyed. Imprisoned in the unconscious regions of his mind, they would constantly be seeking the opportunity to make good their escape. To take these two points in combination and derive from their product the salient theoretical conclusion: the unintended consequence of Malcolm's identification with his father was the formation of characterological ground for charismatic group-membership.

We now have a better picture of how the racial divisions of American society became forces in Malcolm's character, forces that would eventually be turned against that society. We must not, however, make the mistake of thinking that Malcolm was predestined to racial militancy, that the father's Garveyite crusade necessarily entailed either the son's Muslim ministry or his Afro-American activity. This could have been the case only if Malcolm understood that his father's power was a verbal expression of Garveyism (that the strength of the movement gave authority to the words of the individual), if he thought of himself as heir to that *social* power, *or* if over time and under his father's tutelage he came to understand the situation in these terms. But at that time Malcolm aspired only to his father's personal power and to his love. Garveyism was but the outward form of this emotional content. As Malcolm himself observes, he did not then connect his father's words with their political meaning: "I have never understood why, after hearing as much as I did of [Garveyism], I somehow never thought of the black people in Africa. My image of Africa, at that time, was of naked savages, cannibals, monkeys and tigers, and steaming jungles."[30] Finally, even if Earl Little was thinking of Malcolm as his political heir, there was to be no opportunity for such a direct laying on of hands. If in some sense his father's Garveyism was his rightful heritage, it was nonetheless one he would have to earn for himself. Malcolm would have to learn to control rather than be controlled by his conscience's two-edged sword.*

We must now determine the emotional content of Malcolm's relationship to his mother, which thus far has appeared before us only as the physical resemblance between Louise and her son, and as the inverted form of Malcolm's relationship to his father. The physical similarity was, of course, emotionally significant. As we have already seen, Louise was ashamed of her mixed blood, and she generalized her racial self-hatred into a negative predisposition toward her light-skinned son. She even tried to make him darker: Malcolm remembered that "she would tell me to get out of the house and 'let the sun shine on you so you can get some color.'"[31] In this way, as well as through physical punishment, the mother's shame was reflected into her son. Malcolm learned, or perhaps merely sensed, that he should have been someone or something other than who and what he was. But rather than trying to be that other person—to be, for example, like his older brother Wilfred, who was not only dark but also "nice and quiet"—Malcolm reacted to this existential injustice with childish defiance:

> I've said that my mother was the one who whipped me—
> at least she did whenever she wasn't ashamed to let the
> neighbors think she was killing me. For if she even acted as

* It should not be thought that the opposition between Garveyism and Christianity that Malcolm experienced through his relationship with his father was given in the nature of the two social practices *per cis*. They were not incompatible for Earl Little, or for many other Garveyites. The point here is simply that Malcolm's relationship with his father established a basis both for his later black nationalism and for his critical view of Christianity.

though she was about to raise her hand to me, I would open my mouth and let the world know about it. If anybody was passing by out on the road, she would either change her mind or just give me a few licks.[32]

Thus Malcolm was able to assert his autonomy, express his anger, and save himself from punishment by using his mother's fragile self-esteem against her. But by so doing, he was also confirming the alienated quality of their relationship.

Malcolm's protestations helped him to avoid punishment only to the same extent that they prevented him from earning his mother's love. They did, however, bring him a tangible substitute for her affection:

My older brothers and sisters had started to school when, sometimes, they would come in and ask for a buttered biscuit or something and my mother, impatiently, would tell them no. But I would cry out and make a fuss until I got what I wanted. I remember well how my mother asked me why I couldn't be a nice boy like Wilfred; but I would think to myself that Wilfred, for being so nice and quiet, often stayed hungry. So early in life, I had learned that if you want something, you had better make some noise.[33]

Having lost the contest for his mother's love to his brothers and sister, Malcolm fought all the harder for the original substance of that love. He tried to restore the nurturing relationship that initially unifies mother and child. But being fed is not, in itself, being loved: Malcolm may have satisfied his craving for buttered biscuits, but he remained emotionally hungry. As we have seen elsewhere, regressive solutions are in truth unsolved problems.

The almost tongue-in-cheek tone of political self-consciousness in Malcolm's descriptions of his "protest demonstrations" does not prevent us from seeing that they were spontaneous outbursts, not calculated tactical choices. Looking back upon his childhood, Malcolm derived a certain wry pleasure from uncovering the primitive forms of his later characteristic activities; but taken in themselves, these memories are the record of a vicious emotional circle, a self-fulfilling prophecy of maternal dissatisfaction, filial resentment and protest, and therefore the confirmation of the *a priori* maternal judgment—a prior judgment that had been brought forth covertly from a racially determined ground. They testify, in brief, to the mutual hostility of mother and son. At the same time, they necessarily bespeak

Malcolm's unrequited love for his mother, his half-acknowledged longing for her attention and affection.

This wishful side of Malcolm's relationship to his mother is more directly expressed in another of his early memories. The family at this time was living outside Lansing proper, and therefore had the space for an extensive garden. One day Malcolm decided he wanted a garden plot of his own:

> One thing in particular that I remember made me feel grateful toward my mother was that one day I went and asked her for my own garden, and she did let me have my own little plot. I loved it and took care of it well. I loved especially to grow peas. I was proud when we had them on our table. I would pull out the grass in my garden when the first little blades came up. I would patrol the rows on my hands and knees for any worms and bugs, and I would kill and bury them. And sometimes when I had everything straight and clean for my things to grow, I would lie down on my back between the two rows, and I would gaze up in the blue sky at the clouds moving and think all kinds of things.[34]

Viewed in one way, Malcolm's gardening was an occasion for regaining, through daydreaming and phantasy, at least the semblance of lost infantile bliss. As he lay on the ground, gazing "up in the sky at the clouds moving," he probably experienced something like the relaxed pleasure or oceanic feeling characteristic of the earliest mother-child interactions. At the same time, by working in his garden Malcolm was able to be a dutiful son, a contributing member of the family. His mother was bound to take pride in his work, to accept its fruits, and thereby to give Malcolm a feeling of pride in return. Viewing the matter from Malcolm's perspective, his gardening was a labor of love: he found his own value confirmed in the product of his activity; the work was sensuously pleasurable; and the project itself was freely chosen. While it was not in itself a solution to his problematical relationship with his mother, it was a progressive response to his situation. By providing food for his mother instead of demanding food from her Malcolm was for the first time converting his hunger for his mother's love into a motive for productive work.

Finally, against this background we gain renewed perspective on Louise Little herself: "My mother at that time seemed to be always working—cooking, washing, ironing, cleaning and fussing over us eight children. And she was usually either arguing with or not speaking to my father."[35] Earlier we might have read this description as a reproach to Louise for having so many children that she did not have enough time left for Malcolm. No doubt, it does have such an implication; but we can now find in it another and deeper meaning, for here in everyday terms is the suffering mother of the primal scene. The equivalent of the direct physical brutalization of the nightmare night is Louise's crushing burden of work, work multiplied by the number of children forced upon her and by Earl Little's devotion to a higher vocation than mere tilling of the soil or the woman's task of taking care of the home! These latter activities were obviously Louise's obligations, and Malcolm, by tending his garden, was accepting a share of that responsibility. In this sense he was internalizing a maternal image, making his own one of his mother's fundamental standards of self-judgment. Furthermore, in the nonverbal language of childish effort, Malcolm's gardening constituted a reproach against his father: "Even I," we can hear him saying, "am more helpful to my mother than you are!"

Malcolm's work at this time could not bring him in fact, however, the sensual pleasure he was able to experience in phantasy. In the contest with his father for his mother's love he was bound to lose. Moreover, his love for his mother, in its deepest and most urgent form, was precluded by his love for his father, by the bond of Garveyite pride that united them against her. And even more importantly, his jealous love for his mother brought with it the danger of terrible punishment—the torments of Christian guilt or (what is at root the same thing) the fear of castration. Consequently Malcolm repressed these dangerous impulses; but in the process the field of his conscious activity and his capacity for productive effort were markedly narrowed.

Thus Malcolm at age five, ready to follow in the footsteps of his older sister and brothers and go off to school. Because the family lived outside Lansing, it was an all-white school; but the children attended it without any problem:

> In those days white people in the North would usually "adopt" just a few Negroes; they didn't see them as any threat. The white kids didn't make any great thing about us either. They called us "nigger" and "darkie" and "Rastus" so much that we thought those were our natural names. But they didn't think of it as an insult; it was just the way they thought about us.[36]

The racial line cutting through American society was blurred in the interaction of the children. Racial slurs lost their derogatory connotations and became simply "natural names," devoid for the moment of social value. But the innocence of this nominal racism was more apparent than real. It would not take long for the children to learn, it would not be difficult for their teachers to teach them, that white skin was the outward manifestation of a noble soul, black skin the phenomenal sign of a base one. And most black children would learn the lesson just as thoroughly as their white counterparts.

Garveyism was intended to be a transvaluation of these racial values, a liberation of black souls from white moral chains. Its unintended consequence was a new form of racial-moral anxiety: sufficiently strong to destroy the logic of white supremacy, to crack the reified structure of racial valuations handed down from slavery, it was not strong enough to rebuild that structure on self-determined black grounds. Hence a Garveyite child like Malcolm might know that skin color was the *a priori* standard of moral judgment, the sole criterion of good and bad; but he or she could not know with sufficient certainty which color fell into each category. This ambiguity might seem to devalue the evaluative structure itself; one might conclude that skin color was no proper standard for the judgment of souls. But such a devaluation would presuppose the transformation of the social conditions, the class divisions, of which these racial categories are a skewed reflection. Because Garveyism could not accomplish *that*, the standard of skin color survived in a particularly confusing and anxiety-producing form.

In time, Malcolm would make a major contribution to the solution of the problem. He would master the language and logic of racial conflict, developing its double meanings and moral antinomies with charismatic power. He would make his father's and mother's Garveyite words his own, and in the process he would transform them into a vehicle of Afro-American self-consciousness. But not yet. For the present, he was trapped in a maze of racial ambiguities and contradictions that compounded the ambivalences inherent in his Oedipal situation. He was caught in a double, double bind.

The Oedipal bind had this character: insofar as Malcolm loved his mother, he could not love his father; insofar as he loved his father, he could not love his mother. This contradiction resulted in the morally mediated splitting of his psyche—its division into a sphere of conscious activity and one of covert unconscious activity, into a conscious ego and an unconscious id—literally into an "I" and an "It," the latter being the alienated-repressed side of the self. In the conscious realm, love for his father predominated over hatred, while resentment, if not hatred, of his mother predominated over love; in the kingdom of the unconscious repressed, a fully sensualized love for his mother and a jealous hatred of his father were the dominant forces. Thus he was bound by love and hate to each parent, and each of the two relationships was self-contradictory as well as in opposition to the other. In the language of conscience, the Garveyite pride he internalized from his father was negated by Christian guilt, while the standard of familial responsibility he took from his mother was negated by Garveyite shame.

Now, conscience (more technically, the super-ego) is simultaneously the principal divisive force in the psyche and the guarantor of its unity. It is inherently a two-edged sword: on the one hand it demands the repression of morally unacceptable impulses; on the other it permits their re-emergence in moralized and rationalized forms. Which of these sides will predominate is not, however, deducible from the Oedipal situation as such. We have already established, however, the particularity of Malcolm's situation: the racially mediated force of American ruling-class interests formed the Littles into a family ruled despotically by a bivalently aggressive father. Earl Little's anger, magnified in the process of being frustrated by the superior power of his enemies, was turned back upon the members of his family. The family in turn became a group in which the members were emotionally bound to each other through their bondage to him. But the group thus formed, formed on the basis of deflected aggression, reflected in itself and in the character of its individual members the racial divisions of the larger society—which is to say, skin color established the channels through which emotions could and could not flow. Hence Malcolm alone among the children was bound positively to his father and negatively to his mother, while at the same time his father's brutalization of his mother added fuel to the flames of his ambitions. Thus the doubling of his emotional bondage, the intensification of the moral contradiction in his character. And given the strength of the motive-forces which were doubly alienated from the conscious self, the necessity of repression was threatening to destroy the possibilities for free conscious activity.

Still, at this juncture the balance had not been decisively tipped. The contradictions in the Garveyism of everyday family life, although generative of intrapsychic antagonisms and hence of both confusion and anxiety, were nonetheless a progressive movement of interpenetrative forces. They were implicitly unifying: Earl and

Louise Little, for all their mutual antipathies, loved each other, were united against their white-racist enemies, and were able to articulate their passions and beliefs. The way was open for Malcolm, who had learned early to "make a noise" if he wanted something, to become a hard-working "race man," his mother's son and his father's heir. But as an immediate possibility, this future was foreclosed by Earl Little's death.

Earl Little Dies Alone

One afternoon in late September, 1931, when Malcolm and his older siblings returned from school, they found their parents engaged in one of their frequent quarrels.[37] According to Malcolm: "There had lately been a lot of tension around the house because of Black Legion threats."[38] But the specific point of contention was dietary. Earl Little was "a real Georgia Negro, and he believed in eating plenty of what we in Harlem today call 'soul food.'"[39] This included rabbit and pork, both of which, like soul food in general, were inexpensive both to buy and produce. But Louise would eat neither of these meats, which she considered unclean. On this occasion, Malcolm reports,

> my father had taken one of the rabbits which we were raising, and ordered my mother to cook it. We raised rabbits, but sold them to whites. My father had taken a rabbit from the rabbit pen. He had pulled off the rabbit's head. He was so strong, he needed no knife to behead chickens or rabbits. With one twist of his big black hands he simply twisted off the head and threw the bleeding-necked thing back at my mother's feet.[40]

Louise was crying, but she began to prepare the rabbit for cooking. But her husband "was so angry he slammed on out of the front door and started walking up the road toward town."[41]

Thus far there is nothing to distinguish this scene from numerous others of the same kind. External pressures were intensifying the normal intrafamilial contradictions. Louise was protesting against a violation of her beliefs concerning dietary purity; Earl was asserting the primacy of his desires (and way of life) over any opposing force. Might made right, power became law: the man won the contest by strength of arm and strength of character, making it plain in the pro-

cess what fate awaited anyone—especially any one of his sons—
who dared to challenge his position. Then, consumed by the fire of
his own anger, and perhaps a bit ashamed of once again having lost
his temper, he withdrew from the family battlefield, leaving behind
him his beaten wife and their frightened children. It was an archetypal moment of Little family life, a daytime version of a primal
scene.

This day was destined, however, to bring the death of the primal
father and, in turn, the eventual dissolution of his family:

> It was then that my mother had this vision. She had always
> been a strange woman in this sense, and had always had a
> strong intuition of things about to happen. And most of her
> children are the same way, I think. When something is
> about to happen, I can feel something, sense something.[42]

We shall return momentarily to Malcolm's self-identification with
his mother's prophetic powers. But manifestly (only manifestly) the
statement is a reflection upon rather than a moment of the event,
and must therefore await subsequent interpretation. What happened
next was that Louise

> ran screaming out onto the porch. *"Early! Early!"* She
> screamed his name. She clutched her apron in one hand, and
> ran down across the yard and into the road. My father
> turned around. He saw her. For some reason, considering
> how angry he had been when he left, he waved at her. But
> he kept on going.[43]

Earl Little waved good-bye, meaning, perhaps, "I'm too angry to
stick around, I've got to go off to town, I'll be back when I've calmed
down." But Louise had had a vision of her husband's doom, possibly
a genuine premonition, in any case a wish unconsciously converted
into an apprehension. "All the rest of the afternoon, she was not herself, crying and nervous and upset." When Earl Little was not home
by the children's bedtime, she "hugged and clutched" them, and the
children "felt strange, not knowing what to do, because she had
never acted like that."[44]

Then:

> I remember waking up to the sound of my mother's
> screaming again. When I scrambled out, I saw the police in
> the living room; they were trying to calm her down. She had
> snatched on her clothes to go with them. And all of us chil-

dren who were staring knew without anyone having to say
it that something terrible had happened to our father.[45]

Another awakening into a nightmare night, this one far more fateful
and fatal than the first. Earl Little was dead. He had been found on a
streetcar track, his body cut almost in two, his skull crashed in on
one side. "He lived two and a half hours in that condition. Negroes
then were stronger than they are now."[46] Even dying, Earl Little was
a "tough" man.

Officially, Little's death was an accident. But "Negroes in Lansing
have always whispered that he was attacked, and then laid across
some tracks for a streetcar to run over him, . . . that the white Black
Legion had finally gotten him."[47] Although the truth of the matter
cannot be established with certainty, the previous attacks upon Little and the strong probability that the police were tolerant of if not
complicitous with Black Legion activity suggests that community
opinion was correct. We will therefore assume that direct, murderous assault had succeeded where arson had failed.

As a public event, Little's death places no new demands upon us.
It was simply the last act of this particular racial tragedy. Likewise,
Malcolm's belief that his father had been murdered is not especially
problematical. It may be regarded as a cognitive reflection, in time a
memory, of a probable historical event. As a moment in his emotional life, however, it is not self-explanatory, in the first instance
because it is not apparent why he should have chosen this context
for identifying himself with his mother. But if we are correct in
treating prophecies as unconscious or pre-conscious wishes, as the
transformation of (in this case) half-acknowledged hostilities into
foreseen evil happenings, then we may take Malcolm's reflection as
an inadvertent admission that he wished for his father's death—in
which case it follows that Little's doom, as an event occurring in
Malcolm's unconscious, was an Oedipal patricide. As such, it returns us to Freud, and to the final moment in the mythic drama of
the primal horde.[48]

As the years go by, the father weakens with age, until at last there
comes a time when the youngest son—who has been sheltered by
his mother from the old man's rage—leads the band of brothers in
revolt. The father is slain and his genitals are eaten by his sons, who
seek thereby to incorporate and share his power. But the sons' remorse over killing the father they loved as well as hated inclines
them toward posthumous obedience. Accordingly, the act of incor-
poration re-establishes the father as a living force in the minds of his

children. The agency thus established is the conscience or super-
ego, henceforward signified by the phallus, which takes its vengeance by punishing the sons with a haunting sense of guilt. In
short, the brothers, and the young hero most of all, must carry the
weight of a bad conscience as the punishment for their crime and as
the price of their freedom. Thus Malcolm, the seventh son, not the
youngest son but the one destined to take his father's place, inherited from his mother her mysterious prophetic power, i.e., an omnipotence of thought such that even (or especially) unconscious
wishes are magically fulfilled.[49] With this power, he murdered his
father and consequently held himself responsible for the patricide.
Yet in truth his *deed* was only an unconscious *wish*, and his power
only a childish delusion. It was, in phantasy, a turning of passivity
into activity, a defense against experiencing himself as the helpless
victim of external circumstances. Thus by the perverse logic of social
injustice Malcolm unknowingly judged himself guilty of the crime
committed by the family's white racist enemies.

The quarrel, the murder, the funeral:

> I don't have a very clear memory of the funeral. . . . Oddly,
> the main thing I remember is that it wasn't in a church, and
> that surprised me, since my father was a preacher, and I had
> been where he preached people's funerals in churches. . . .
> And I remember that during the service a big black fly
> came down and landed on my father's face, and Wilfred
> sprang up from his chair and he shooed the fly away, and he
> came groping back to his chair . . . and the tears were
> streaming down his face. When we went by the casket, I
> remember that I thought that it looked as if my father's
> strong black face had been dusted with flour, and I wished
> they hadn't put on such a lot of it.[50]

The members of the family mourned their protector, who could no
longer protect himself from the incidental insult of an impious fly;
they wept for their beloved father, despite his various abuses of their
love. But Malcolm himself did not mourn, and he did not weep. At
least, he does not represent himself as being grief-stricken; and we
would infer from this fact that he did not remember openly weeping,
as Wilfred was. A two-sided question accordingly arises: Why did
Malcolm recall so vividly Wilfred's act of filial piety? Why didn't he
represent himself as similarly distraught?

Let us consider first Wilfred's part in the scene. We recall that he
was Malcolm's oldest full brother, dark-skinned, "nice and quiet,"

and for these reasons his mother's favorite. He was, that is to say, precisely what Malcolm was not. In general and in this particular instance, he was Malcolm's opposite. Thus in this memory he represents the feelings Malcolm did not have and the actions he therefore could not perform. Further, this could not be an external or mechanical opposition; for if Wilfred had been simply another member of the family at the funeral, then there would have been no specific reason for Malcolm to focus upon him. We must therefore see him as an alienated form or mirror-image of Malcolm: he represents the feelings Malcolm could not possess and, therefore, the actions that he did not take. He incarnates the good or ideal self that Malcolm, the bad son, could not be. And he came by this role honestly: not only had he always been the good boy, but he was now the oldest male in the family, its nearest approximation to paternal authority.

What, then, prevented Malcolm from being the dutiful and grieving son? At first glance it might appear that he simply had no last respects to offer, no feelings of sadness or remorse concerning his father's death. He had wished his father dead and his wish had come true; there was no reason to mourn. But if jealousy had been the sole determinant of his inaction, then he would not have reproached himself through comparison with Wilfred's pious behavior. His love for his father must also have been involved in his reaction. Recognizing this, we might then conclude that Malcolm was immobilized by his own ambivalence, that his contradictory emotions resolved themselves into a negation of feeling as such. But a closer examination of Malcolm's memory of the funeral sheds a different light upon his apparent lack of emotion. He reports that the funeral did *not* take place in church, that he did *not* openly mourn, and that Earl Little did *not* look like himself. In other words, we have before us Malcolm's *denial* of the reality of his father's death: he is saying, it was not a real funeral, it was not really my father, and therefore there was no reason to mourn. This was not of course a denial in the immediate perceptual sense: Malcolm acknowledged that his father was dead, that the body in the coffin was his father's corpse; but what he affirmed cognitively he denied emotionally. This negation was possible because from his perspective the death of his awesomely powerful father was a palpable absurdity, an event akin to the failure of a natural law or the death of God. Earl Little murdered by his enemies was, in Nietzsche's words, the "ghastly paradox of a crucified god."

We can infer the motive behind this denial. Malcolm "wished" that his father's face had not been dusted with powder—he wished that his father were still alive. For if his father had not been killed, then Malcolm could not have been responsible for his death; the burden of Oedipal guilt would be lifted from his shoulders. And if his father were still alive, Malcolm would be able to love him and be loved in return. Thus Malcolm did not mourn his father's death both because he wished to deny the reality of his emotional loss, and because he wished to escape the punishment for his Oedipal crime.*

There was another sense, of course, in which Earl Little was not dead. Insofar as Malcolm had introjected a paternal image and vivified it with his own emotional energies, his father was a living force in his own psyche. Wilfred may have been a partial replacement for this force in an external sense, a mirror in which Malcolm saw certain aspects of his ideal self reflected; but Malcolm's character was not formed in his brother's image. He was his father's (and his mother's) son. At the funeral, it was the paternal side of his character that predominated: like the Garveyite Earl Little, Malcolm was "tough," and he kept himself under control. Moreover, now that his father was lost to him physically, there was all the more reason to preserve him spiritually; the paternal force in Malcolm's character was strengthened by his father's death. But because this intensified identification took place in the context of a successful Oedipal rebellion, not the Garveyite but, rather, the punitive Christian image was primarily strengthened. The relationship that had previously existed between these two forces—a contradictory but self-unifying process in which the Garveyite tendency was predominant—was inverted. Consequently, the negative or divisive tendency of conscience became the principal moment, with the further result that Malcolm lost the power of moral self-unification. The Garveyite tendency became merely an attribute of his conscious and pre-conscious self, upon which his Christian conscience declared open war. Henceforward, at least until he found and was found by Elijah Muhammad, Malcolm was to be morally divided against himself. Thus it was that Earl Little's death entailed his son's self-alienation.

Earl Little was dead—no amount of denial or identification could alter that fact. The family, Malcolm included, had to live on without him. At first this task was eased economically by payments from

---

* Two further points should be made: that the death of a parent is terribly anxiety-producing, and that a denial of the loss helps to ward off this potentially traumatizing emotion; and that Malcolm's self-reproaches were undeserved: mourning properly so-called is not possible for a young child. On these and other points, see Martha Wolfenstein, "How Is Mourning Possible?" in *The Psychoanalytic Study of the Child* XXI (1966), pp. 93–123.

one of the two insurance policies Earl Little "had always been proud he carried." But the other one refused to pay, claiming that Little had committed suicide. So, as Malcolm says, "There we were. My mother was thirty-four years old now, with no husband, no provider or protector to take care of her eight children."[51] The Littles were fatherless and alone in the America of 1931.

CHAPTER IV

The Vicious Circle

"MAN IS CHARACTERIZED above all by his going beyond a situation, and by what he succeeds in making of what he has been made—even if he never recognizes himself in his objectification."[1] We now have a basic conception of Malcolm's situation and character. Most generally, his situation was American bourgeois society, a structure of opposing class interests grounded in the private ownership of social forces of production. These class interests were mediated by or particularized through the interaction of progressive and regressive political movements, which in turn determined his immediate or individual, i.e., familial situation. And within the family, his situation was defined by his position as the seventh son, the lightest one, the living embodiment of his father's pride and his mother's shame. For at its limit circumstance becomes character, the inward movement of the situation becomes the outward form of the self, the making of the self insofar as the self is objectively determined. Thus conceived, the situation forms a "field of possibles," narrower or wider, as the case may be. In Malcolm's case, the field was circumscribed or defined by a hostile white society, determined by direct racist attack, by arson and murder. Hence Malcolm was "defined negatively by the sum total of possibles that [were] impossible for him; that is, by a future more or less blocked off."[2]

Within and against this situation was Malcolm himself, an extremely intelligent and energetic young boy, inflamed by Oedipal ambitions but also working hard to bring his passions under control. His task was made more difficult by his father's brutality, which both angered and terrified him; it was made easier by his father's political activity, which permitted him to introject and make his own an image of tough but self-controlled activity, especially verbal activity. The task was also made difficult by his mother's inattention if not overt rejection, which had a regressive impact upon him; but progressive development was encouraged by the opportunity she provided him for productive work. Thus Malcolm was the product of conflicting determinations he reproduced in and as himself; he was learning to love and to work in a characteristic manner.

Stating the same point in structural terms, Malcolm's situation, as he reproduced it in the form of internal determinations, became the foundation of his character. The field of conscious activity was limited by the two-edged sword of conscience, which demanded repression or sublimation of unacceptable sexual and aggressive desires. Failure to comply with these demands resulted in feelings of either Garveyite shame or Christian guilt; conversely, when Malcolm lived up to these standards, he was rewarded with feelings of Garveyite pride and a sense of family responsibility.

Before Earl Little's death, the regressive tendency of Christian family life was opposed by the progressive tendency of Garveyite activity. The fluid contradictions of this situation created for Malcolm the potential for a certain form of self-conscious activity. Although his repressed emotions constituted a basis for group membership, the necessary condition for vulnerability to hypnotic authority, he was destined to exercise such authority himself. His father's heir, possessed also of his mother's sixth sense, he had only to become actually what he was potentially. But that possibility (for the *necessity* of destiny appears only in retrospect) was all but destroyed by his father's death. The blessing of being the seventh son became a curse; his hitherto unrepressed emotional energies were transformed into a crushing burden of unconscious guilt. At the same time, the family lost its tenuous connection to the moribund Garvey movement, and its equally tenuous hold on economic self-sufficiency. Thus Malcolm's destiny became "a future more or less blocked off." It became his project to go beyond this situation of self-negation.

Malcolm's situation, his character, and the project developing from these grounds were not exclusively his own. He was a black boy in a white land. His individual character was therefore simultaneously a character type: his individual problems amounted in sum to the problematic of racist oppression. Consequently, the project of his personal liberation was simultaneously the project of racial liberation, of breaking the vicious circle.[3]

Up to this point in our work, we have not had occasion to focus our attention upon the idea of a vicious circle. But if the vicious circle is in a general sense the problematic of racist oppression, in a narrower one it is racist oppression under conditions of economic regression; in fact Myrdal's *An American Dilemma*, from which we have appropriated the concept, primarily reflects the life of black people during the Depression of the 1930s. Hence this concept comes into clear focus as we come to Malcolm's experience during the Depression years.

The Depression

"And for as long as the first insurance money lasted, we did all right."[4] Wilfred, who was "a pretty stable fellow," quit school and began to work at whatever odd jobs he could find. Between what he earned and the insurance, the family had enough income to survive. When the insurance money ran out, however, it was no longer possible to maintain this precarious condition of sufficiency. Malcolm's mother first resorted to credit buying, and then left the home daily in search of work:

> My mother began to buy on credit. My father had always
> been very strongly against credit. "Credit is the first step
> into debt and back into slavery," he had always said. And
> then she went to work herself. She would go into Lansing
> and find different jobs—in housework, or sewing—for white
> people. They didn't realize, usually, that she was a Negro. A
> lot of white people around there didn't want Negroes in
> their houses.[5]

If an employer discovered that she was black, or if it were discovered "whose widow she was," she would be fired and would come home "crying, but trying to hide it." Thus in a double sense, Louise lived in the shadow of her late husband's struggle for racial self-determination. The crucial battle had been lost; Louise's own struggle was only a sad retreat to ultimate defeat. No work meant no money, more buying on credit, more unpaid bills, and in time an unwanted dependency upon the will of the state welfare department. Moreover, along the way toward this condition of modern slavery the children came to feel guilty for their mother's pain and ashamed of the color of their skin: "Once when one of us—I cannot remember which—had to go for something to where she was working, and the people saw us, and realized she was actually a Negro, she was fired on the spot, and she came home crying, this time not hiding it."[6] Obviously, the children were not to blame for their mother's lost job; but nonetheless they held themselves accountable for her tears.

In another time and place, the family's position might have been less difficult. If they had been living in a rural community within a more extended family structure, there might have been a substantial measure of communal support; or if Earl Little had been genuinely petit-bourgeois or an independent peasant proprietor, there would have been an inheritance of potentially profitable private property. But the Littles were now unquestionably members of the urban proletariat, and their economic fate was therefore dependent upon the demand for black wage-labor. At this time, the country was on the verge of total economic collapse; there was virtually no demand for black wage-labor, and precious little demand for labor of any other color. Hence even if their situation had not been complicated by Earl Little's political legacy, the family would have been in for hard times. Conversely, had it not been for the condition of the economy, the Littles would probably have found it somewhat less difficult to survive. The Depression set the narrow limits within which the family fortunes could vary.

Political rhetoric to the contrary notwithstanding, the Depression was not some vast *spiritus mundi*, an irrational fear of fear that suddenly and inexplicably descended upon the nation. Yet so it seemed to the American people, and so it might seem to us. For we have observed that during the 1920s America's material capacity for producing surplus value was remarkably augmented. The production of surplus value is not *ipso facto* its realization, however; a given capacity for supplying commodities does not entail a proportionate level of demand.[7] During World War I, for example, there was an enormous demand for American agricultural products. Prices were high and profit margins were substantial. New and often marginal lands were brought under cultivation, farm labor was intensified, and supply was pushed up to the level of demand. After the war this same volume of farm commodities was no longer in demand, and prices declined rapidly. It was now more difficult to realize the surplus value embodied in wheat, corn, and other staples.

Now, if in such circumstances supply could be brought back into line with demand at a price insuring a socially average rate of profit, and if this could be done without major economic dislocation, then sectional imbalances of this kind would constitute no real problem for either bourgeois economic practice or its corresponding theory. But in fact the restoration of market equilibrium is rarely painless. In the present case, although it would have been rational for agricultural entrepreneurs in general to reduce supply, no individual farmer could afford to curtail production. He had to *increase* production, hoping to realize thereby an acceptable amount of profit, albeit at a lower rate of return. As a result, the agricultural sector continued to produce substantially more surplus value than it could realize.

Agriculture was not the only area of the economy characterized by a persistent imbalance between supply and demand. Bituminous coal and textiles were both chronically depressed throughout the decade. Then after 1926/27, the tendency toward underconsumption spread rapidly. Residential construction, for example, "which had been increasing ever since 1921, began to decrease between 1926 and 1927, and kept falling thereafter."[8] This does not mean that the public's desire for better housing had been exhausted, but "it does mean that only a fraction of the population was able to buy or rent new houses or new apartments at the prices charged, and that the number which could do so provided an upper limit to the market."[9] That limit was being reached during the latter years of the decade. Similarly, and even more fatefully, the automobile market was also approaching its limit, a limit that could no longer be expanded even through the expansion of credit:

> During the years of prosperity the market for cars and other forms of durable consumers' goods had been considerably widened by the growth of installment credit. Many more people bought these goods than would have done so if they had had to save the total price in cash before making the purchases. Installment buying could not, however, obviate the eventual retardation of expansion. There was certain to come a time when all the families who would utilize installment loans were loaded up with all the debt they could carry.[10]

Consequently, it is not surprising that between 1927 and 1929 only about 83 percent of the nation's manufacturing capacity was actually being utilized, i.e., was needed to meet demand within the existing structure of prices and profits.[11] Despite this curtailment of the amount of commodities actually supplied (in comparison to the potential for supplying them), in 1929 "industry was caught with large supplies of goods it could not sell."[12] Thus by that year there existed a far greater capacity for producing surplus value than for realizing it, a contradiction between the material productive forces of American society and the relations of production within which they could be employed. The result of this contradiction was the economic crisis of the 1930s, an "industrial earthquake" in which the "trading world" could only "maintain itself by sacrificing a part of wealth, of products and even of productive forces to the gods of the nether world."[13]

We have already seen that workers are alienated in the process as well as from the product of capitalist production. Capital accumulation is precisely the alienation of labor. But, as Marx observes, "Capital does not only *live* on labour. A lord, at once aristocratic and barbarous, it drags with it into the grave the corpses of its slaves, whole hecatombs of workers who perish in the crises."[14] Thus we must now explore the impact of the Depression upon the American working class in general and the black proletariat in particular.

A depression is a qualitative reduction in a society's level of economic well-being. It can be measured by a variety of standards, but the fundamental criterion is the degree of nonutilization of economically productive energies. These energies exist in two forms: congealed labor-power—forces of production in the strict sense of the term—and living labor-power, the available work-energy of the proletariat. Hence capacity utilization and unemployment figures reveal most clearly the extent to which a society is incapable of realizing the surplus value it is capable of producing. During the 1930s the depression of both indices was truly staggering, especially in the critical years of 1932–1934, when about one out of every four workers was jobless and almost fifty percent of the country's industrial capacity was not being utilized.* These economic conditions in turn

* The following figures show the parallel movement of capacity utilization and unemployment during the decade:

	Capacity Utilization	Unemployment
1930	66%	8.8%
1931	53	16.1
1932	42	24.0
1933	52	25.0
1934	58	21.6
1935	68	19.9
1936	80	16.5
1937	83	13.8
1938	60	18.7
1939	72	16.5

bred a host of social ills. Family savings were quickly exhausted, credit was used up, possessions were repossessed, and mortgages were foreclosed. Children and adults alike went to bed hungry, and were deprived of proper medical care and other social services. Many were forced to beg or steal in order to survive; children were forced to leave school to look for work. Social life in all its dimensions was severely disrupted. As these conditions intensified, the mood of the people swung from anxiety and fear through anger and melancholy to either hopelessness or the will to collective political-economic action.

Economic depression thus entailed social, psychological, and, as we shall see, political disruption. This was true for American society in general, and it was doubly true for Black America. Throughout the decade the unemployment of black workers was substantially greater than that of their white counterparts. In 1935/36, for example, it is estimated that "36 percent of colored males and 28 percent of colored females were seeking work or were on emergency work, compared with 21 percent of white males and 19 percent of white females."[15] Moreover, black workers lost not only their individual jobs but also their foothold in the industrial labor market: "The number of Negroes in manufacturing, mechanical and mining occupations fell off from 1,100,000 in 1930 to 738,000 in 1940, and the number in wholesale and retail trade declined from 398,000 to 288,000."[16] In part these declines reflected the overall depression of the economy; but more significantly they resulted from the "widespread white invasion of Negro jobs by unemployed whites, often with the assistance of employers, unions and lawmakers."[17] The result was that blacks were increasingly confined to jobs as unskilled laborers or servants, i.e., to the lowest-paid, lowest-status jobs, the ones most vulnerable to elimination through technological innovation. In sum, "between 1935 and 1945, the Negro proletariat seemed doomed to become a *lumpen-proletariat*."[18]

We shall turn momentarily to another of the major forces tending toward the creation of a black lumpen-proletariat; "and in the following chapter, we shall examine *lumpen* life—the hustling society—in some detail. For the present, it is sufficient to note that the evil consequences of joblessness were magnified for the black population as compared to the white, while individuals and families suffered according to the idiosyncracies of their situations. In the

---

The first set of figures is from Baran and Sweezy, *Monopoly Capital*, p. 242. The second is from Broadus Mitchell, *Depression Decade* (New York: Harper and Row, 1947), p. 451.

case of the Littles, once their insurance money was gone and their credit depleted they increasingly went hungry:

> There were times when there wasn't even a nickel and we would be so hungry we were dizzy. My mother would boil a big pot of dandelion greens, and we would eat that. I remember that some small-minded neighbor put it out, and children would tease us, that we ate "fried grass." Sometimes, if we were lucky, we would have oatmeal or corn meal mush three times a day. Or mush in the morning and cornbread at night.[19]

Sometimes, when he got hungry enough, Malcolm would drop by another family's home at dinnertime, hoping to be invited to stay for the meal. At other times he would steal a "treat" from the food-vending bins in front of Lansing grocery stores. The family as a whole "began to go swiftly downhill"; in this way the Littles experienced as their personal misfortune the pervasive bad luck of the nation in general and Black America in particular.

At first, the masses of the people were willing to accept the idea that hard times were a matter of ill fortune and joblessness a question of personal responsibility. But as time passed and the blight spread—and when it spread unevenly, destroying the well-being of poor families but only complicating life somewhat for the rich ones—people began to seek political remedies for their ills. A number of regressive and progressive social movements developed, from Father Coughlin's fascistic National Union of Social Justice through Huey Long's populistic "Share the Wealth" organization and Upton Sinclair's utopian socialist EPIC Campaign to the Communist Party. The latter, working closely with the union movement, was a clearly proletarian, class-conscious, and historically rational response to the existing situation. Most of the other movements of the period reflected, to a greater or lesser degree, the traumatic impact of the Depression upon the petite bourgeoisie, as well as upon those with petit-bourgeois memories and aspirations. But even the most regressive of the major organizations had gone beyond the simple anti-modernism and racism of the Klan. All of them recognized that the transformation of the existing situation entailed political-economic action. At least to this extent, the Depression had made it evident that "the anatomy of . . . civil society . . . has to be sought in political economy," that "the mode of production of material life conditions the general process of social, political and intellectual life."[20]

The economic facts of life were of course as evident to black people as they were to white people. There were even moments when a unified black-and-white revolution seemed to be a possibility, when members of both races worked together to fight racism on all fronts and to overturn the capitalist system.[21] Only a small percentage of the black population were able to participate in these activities, however, with the consequence that most black people were forced into an entirely individual or at best familial struggle for survival. It is thus not surprising that some of them retreated from the frustration of fragmented proletarian existence into the comforting warmth of Father Divine's Heaven or similar religious pseudo-communities. Nor is it surprising that when Elijah Muhammad attempted to revive the defunct Moorish Temple movement in the form of a Nation of Islam, he worked hard to provide his organization with a sound economic program. He knew there could be no heaven on earth for people with empty stomachs, and that there would be hungry black people until the time when they were no longer forced to take the crumbs from the white man's table.

But dependency on the Man was the order of the day. Although the lessons of political economy were being learned, they were rarely being learned in their totality. Quite apart from the inherent complexities of the subject matter, this was because the situation of economic depression has contradictory implications for the development of class consciousness. Insofar as it is economically regressive and hence psychologically traumatizing, it creates the necessary conditions for such regressive movements as fascism; but insofar as it is radically regressive, insofar as it lays bare the root structure of capitalism, it generates the possibility of overcoming that traumatization through progressive action. Thus periods of economic crisis are also periods of political disruption and fluidity, periods defined by the play of contradictory forces.

It does not follow, however, that one or the other of these forces must necessarily triumph. At least under certain circumstances, there exists the possibility of temporarily reifying the situation. A compromise can be worked out between the radical demands of the working class and the conservative desires of the ruling class. Instead of proclaiming that social classes owe nothing to each other, that it's "root, hog, or die," and that the government therefore has no major economic responsibilities, the state announces that henceforth the losers will be permitted, even enabled, to survive, despite their manifest incapacity . . . so long as they do not challenge the bourgeois right to name the game and deal the cards. Thus in 1932, in the name of a "new deal" for the forgotten man, the American welfare state was born. The great morning, presaged a century before in Hegel's *Philosophy of Right*, developed experimentally in Bismarckian Germany, and apparently liberalized by Keynes, had finally arrived.

The welfare programs undertaken by the Roosevelt administration were quite modest, especially when measured against the size of the human and economic problems they were supposed to solve. But they were sufficient to prevent the immediate demise of American capitalism, and they had a number of important longer-run implications. From our perspective the most consequential was the destructive impact of relief programs on black people.

As we observed earlier, black workers suffered greater unemployment than their white counterparts, and consequently had a greater need for public work or welfare assistance: "In the middle of the 'thirties, roughly one-half of Negro families in the urban North were on relief. This usually was three to four times more than the corresponding proportion of whites."[22] Needless to say, many self-respecting white people gladly ignored the fact that this disproportion resulted from the racist restriction of employment opportunities and leaped to the conclusion that, as they had always said, Negroes were naturally lazy, born slaves, unwilling and unable to work unless compelled to do so by a member of the master race. In the words Hegel used to describe the impoverished sections of the European working class, they were a "rabble of paupers," lacking all "sense of right and wrong, of honesty and the self-respect which makes a man insist on maintaining himself by his own work and effort."[23] Of course, Hegel, unlike the American racist, recognized that pauperism was one pole of a social antinomy, the other being "the concentration of disproportionate wealth in the hands of a few."[24] One man's poverty and shame (or shamelessness) was another man's plenty and pride, or arrogance. Neither Hegel nor the white racist, however, differentiated between those members of the working class who were forced into pauperism and onto the relief rolls, but who fought to preserve their self-respect and who were not only willing but desperately eager to work, and that much smaller number who, having been either broken or enraged by their misery, joined the "dangerous class" of (as Marx put it) "vagabonds, discharged soldiers, discharged jailbirds, escaped galley slaves, swindlers, mountebanks, *lazzaroni*, pickpockets, tricksters, gamblers, *maquereaus* [procurers], brothel keepers, porters, *literati*, organ-grinders, rag-pickers, knife-grinders, tinkers, beggars."[25] It is certainly true that an individual can be driven from one category to the next, from the lower levels of the industrial reserve army into the *lumpen-proletariat*, and that the children of impoverished parents are all too likely to drift into the life of the streets and back alleys. This was what was to happen to Malcolm. But the stereotype of Negroes as a rabble of paupers is formed by subsuming the whole under a small part—in Malcolm's words, by looking "upon the Negro community as a community of criminals."[26]*

In sum, one consequence of the New Deal welfare programs was the reinforcement of certain white-racist stereotypes. Another was that public relief did become "one of the major Negro occupations; all through the 'thirties it was surpassed only by agriculture and possibly by domestic service."[27] Because even alienated labor was precluded by the combination of depression and discrimination, many black people were forced to become professional paupers. Relatively few people were actually criminalized by this pressure, but it had a disintegrative or regressive impact upon both family relationships and individual character. Few were able to bear the burden lightly. The experience of the Little family was fairly typical:

> Then, in about late 1934 . . . some kind of psychological deterioration hit our family circle and began to eat away our pride. Perhaps it was the constant tangible evidence that we were destitute. We had known other families who had gone on relief. We had known without anyone in our home ever expressing it that we had felt prouder not to be at the depot where the free food was passed out. And, now, we were among them. At school, the "on relief" finger suddenly pointed at us, too, and sometimes it was said aloud.[28]

Despite the hunger and humiliation, most members of the family managed to remain both mentally intact and law-abiding citizens. But Malcolm and his mother began to lose control. It "took its toll" on Louise that she was "accepting charity"; and it was at this time that Malcolm began to stay away from home. In each case, moreover, a vicious circle had been formed. Louise was on a downhill course that would end in her insanity and the fragmentation of her

* In the next chapter we will examine the impoverishment of the mass of black people in the context of ghettoization or internal colonialization.

family; and Malcolm reports that "the more I began to stay away from home and visit people and steal from stores, the more aggressive I became in my inclinations. I never wanted to wait for anything."[29] Thus the Great Depression, through the mediation of the welfare system, destroyed the Little family and further undermined Malcolm's character.

"As bad as I was . . ."

We have now developed an interpretation of the Little family's situation during the 1930s. Next we must investigate how Malcolm internalized these external determinants.

The objective ground or limit of Malcolm's experience was established by the activities of the "state Welfare people," who became after Earl Little's death the paternal force in the Little family. Little had been the principal mediator between the family and the larger society. He provided for its economic needs and, for better or worse, he kept it in contact with the currents of racial movement in American life. After his death, the family lost all contact with the racial situation outside of Lansing,* and neither Louise nor Wilfred was able to maintain the family as a viable economic unit. The welfare people became the family's major provider, and *ipso facto* its controlling power: the Littles were subjected to welfare *paternalism* in the most literal sense of the word.

Earl Little was sometimes brutal to his wife and children, subjecting them to a dehumanizing form of paternal power; but he never depersonalized them, never objectified them. The welfare people, however, seemed determined to turn persons into things, subjects into objects. They would come to the house, no doubt in accordance with standard bureaucratic procedures, and ask Louise "a thousand questions." The very fact that questions were being raised was bad enough, but the way they were being raised was worse: the investigators "acted and looked at her, and at us, and around in our house, in a way that had about it the feeling—at least for me—that we were not people. In their eyesight we were just *things*, that was all."[30] And not only things, but *their* things, commodities they purchased with the monthly welfare check: "They acted as if they owned us, as if we were their private property."[31] In other words, the Littles were

---

* For this reason the NAACP, the Nation, and other racial organizations are not directly relevant to this phase of our work.

the victims of a peculiar form of capitalist appropriation: they had become animate objects owned by the state, virtual *slaves* of the welfare system. Because they were members of the proletariat, possessing nothing of exchangeable value beyond their labor-power, and because they could no more exchange their labor-power for wages than the economic system as a whole could realize the surplus value it had been producing, they were *de facto* valueless, at least on the open market. Hence their value could be set arbitrarily by the state; so many dollars, so much food marked "Not To Be Sold"[32] per month. And having been purchased at that price, they were henceforward the property of the state.

The slavery thus objectively imposed was subjectively confirmed. Because the Littles were without value to the state but, rather, received their value from it as a gift of grace, they were forced to accept the system's judgment of their worth. Louise tried to escape the condemnations of her welfare judges: "She would talk back sharply to the state Welfare people, telling them that she was a grown woman, able to raise her children, that it wasn't necessary for them to keep coming around so much, meddling in our lives."[33] But she was poor and therefore impotent; and her impotence was irrefutable proof that the welfare people had justice on their side. Moreover, because she was a Garveyite, she had always been especially proud of her economic self-sufficiency. Now that basis of her self-respect had been destroyed. When she looked into the eyes of her state-appointed judges she saw reflected in their contempt her own feelings of shame. "And her feelings," Malcolm observed, "were communicated to us."[34]

In sum, through their mother's humiliation, the children came to be ashamed of being themselves, of being members of their own family. But even that was not the end of the matter. Like the bourgeoisie of which they were the administrative manifestation, the welfare people ruled the family by a policy of divide-and-rule. Over Louise's protestations, they "began insisting upon drawing us older children aside and asking us questions, or telling us things—against our mother and against each other," trying to "plant the seeds of division" by asking "such things as who was smarter than the other."[35] But their principal goal was to alienate Louise from her children and from herself. In this regard their technique was to play on the children's hunger: through their questioning they would encourage the children in turn to question "why, if the state was willing to give us packages of meat, sacks of potatoes and fruit, and cans of all kinds of things, our mother obviously hated to accept."[36] The children were being taught to blame their mother for their hunger and to doubt the sincerity of her love for them; and when Louise saw the attitudes of the welfare people reflected in her children's eyes, she found it that much more difficult to continue her resistance to the bureaucratic usurpation of her maternal prerogatives. Her shame over being poor became her guilt for being a bad mother, and her haunting sense of unmet responsibilities further undermined her pride. Increasingly, therefore, the welfare people were able to interpose themselves as the effective head of her household.

Unable to defeat her enemies in direct combat, Louise sought to escape from the trap of poverty, shame, and guilt by other means. For a while in 1935/36 she had a lover, a replacement for her late husband—a "large, dark man" whose affection and attention gave her spirits a lift. But after about a year, he "finally backed away from taking on the responsibility of those eight mouths to feed."[37] He jilted her, and this was a "terrible shock," the "beginning of the end of reality."[38] Somewhat earlier, she had joined the Seventh Day Adventist Church, and had gained a certain amount of strength from its chiliastic vision. But in the end her adherency contributed to her downfall. One of the things that had initially attracted her to the religion was its devotion to Mosaic dietary law, which sanctified her own conceptions. Accordingly, when a neighbor offered her a free butchered pig, she refused. This was incomprehensible to the welfare people: "They were as vicious as vultures. They had no feelings, understanding, compassion or respect for my mother. They told us, 'She's crazy for refusing food.' Right then was when our home, our unity began to disintegrate."[39] And Louise's inner unity began to disintegrate as well. She was lost in a house of mirrors, surrounded by multiple images of her own failure; she "began to sit around and walk around talking to herself—almost as though she was unaware that [her children] were there."[40] She became "less responsive" to them, "less responsible" for their well-being, and the house became "less tidy." The situation was, in Malcolm's words, "increasingly terrifying": "We children watched our anchor giving way. It was something terrible that you couldn't get your hands on, yet you couldn't get away from. It was sensing that something was going to happen."[41] Finally Louise had to be institutionalized, and the children were dispersed to various foster homes. They also became directly the property of the state:

> A Judge McClellan from Lansing had authority over me and
> all of my brothers and sisters. We were "state children,"

court wards; he had the full say-so over us. A white man in charge of a black man's children! Nothing but legal, modern slavery—however kindly intentioned.[42]

The welfare game had been played to the end.

Thus the state welfare system, in its possession of the Little family, can with justice be termed capitalist slavery, a most peculiar combination of Southern slavery and Northern capitalism. It produced neither cotton nor automobiles; by law it owned nothing and employed no one beyond its administrative staff. But it did preserve through fusion the paternalism of the one and the divide-and-rule policy of the other. To be sure, these two forms of ruling-class practice are at root the same. The slavemaster understood that an intact family was a base of resistance to his power. Accordingly, he fragmented family units and, in so doing, fragmented individual character structure. The result, when this policy was successful, was an isolated slave who was physically and emotionally dependent upon his master. In parallel fashion the capitalist, using the mechanism of the market instead of the sting of the lash, divided the working class against itself, transformed collective identities into self-negating stereotypes, broke down the unity of even the nuclear family, and alienated the individual from his own sensuous energies. As we have seen in the case of the Littles, the family was first divided by the prejudices of skin color. Then its paternal guardian was murdered by the pitiful, ragtag ghosts of Southern Reconstruction. Now the welfare people proceeded to destroy the family altogether. Because Louise had neither income nor emotional support, they were able to depersonalize her. They alienated her from her pride, then from her maternal responsibilities and her children's respect, and finally from her mental powers. And because the children lost their mother, they also lost the life of their family. Thus in the end the welfare state, through its bureaucratic and juridical intermediaries, took legal possession of both the mother and her children.*

---

* In *White Racism* (New York: Vintage, 1970), Joel Kovel develops an interesting distinction between what he terms "dominative" and "aversive" racism. The former was characteristic of the slave-owning South; the latter is characteristic of the North in particular and industrial society in general. The dominative relationship he sees as being based upon a brutal but also sensual Oedipal-level phantasy, the aversive relationship upon a moralized regression to anal phantasy. Hence the white Southerner views blacks in sexual-aggressive terms, while the Northerner objectifies them, projects his own fecal images onto them.

If we assume that the KKK and the Black Legion were "dominative" racists and the welfare people were "aversive" racists, then Kovel's distinction can be applied to our

Hitherto we have represented and interpreted the disintegration of the Little family without considering Malcolm's own role in this melancholy drama. We have therefore to tell the tale again, this time bringing into focus the part he played.

After their father's death, Wilfred and Hilda willingly took on adult responsibilities, while Malcolm and Philbert "just fought all the time"—fought each other at home, and white classmates at school. These fights were sometimes "racial in nature," the nominal racism of the preceding period having begun to develop a substantive meaning; but at this point the fights still "might be about anything."[43]

In other words, when his father died Malcolm first fell back into his characteristic patterns of activity. But as time passed and the family's economic condition worsened, Malcolm began to change. Although he made small contributions to the family's well-being by running errands and by shooting rabbits or catching frogs to sell to the neighbors, he also began to beg meals from the Gohannas (more prosperous family friends); to steal "treats" from the Lansing stores and to stay away from home; and to become more aggressive in his "inclinations." He persisted in this behavior despite the fact that the welfare people used it as proof that he wasn't being taken care of by his mother, and even threatened to place him in a foster home if he didn't settle down. His mother, whose position with the authorities was being undermined by his actions, would whip him for stealing; but Malcolm would just try to "alarm the neighborhood" with his yelling, and then resume his aggressive ways. He did not, however, attempt to ward off his mother's blows with blows of his own. Finally he was taken to live with the Gohannas; and shortly thereafter the family was conclusively fragmented.

Such are the main facts. From them it is evident that Malcolm's conscience was not yet sufficiently strong to perform its two-edged function without external reinforcement. He could be in control of himself only when his parents were in control of themselves and attentive to him. Now that Earl Little was dead, Malcolm was without his love and disciplining power; and Louise, without a husband to

---

subject matter. But it is surely better to see the dominative racist—to use what may only be a metaphor—as orally fixated, someone whose sexual-aggressive phantasies are a thin cover over a pre-anal character structure. The aversive racist is one level higher on the developmental line. The benevolent paternalists we are going to encounter in the next section of this chapter go a step beyond the aversive level: they are normal, good people whose racism exists in spite of themselves, really as a direct reflection of an objectively racist system.

provide for the family and serve as its ruling power, was forced to fill both roles, with the result that the children received less maternal attention. Racist violence had transformed Malcolm and his siblings into neglected children: Malcolm was left to his own moral resources, which were inadequate to meet the demands being placed upon them.

Yet it is not sufficient to say that Malcolm's behavior was the product of racist violence mediated by parental neglect, for it is clear from the *Autobiography* that the immediate precipitant of Malcolm's actions was hunger. The family simply did not have enough food, and so Malcolm was driven to seek sustenance elsewhere. Dizzy with hunger or finding it difficult to stomach "fried grass," Malcolm begged or stole in an attempt to satisfy his voracious appetite. And if stealing was wrong and begging undignified, then so be it. In Brecht's words, *"Erst Kommt das Fressen, dann kommt die Moral"*: First comes food, then come morals![44]

Malcolm, needing to eat, sacrificed his morals in general and his pride in particular for food; but if food comes first, morals come second. Malcolm was the proud son of proud, Garveyite parents who had cherished their economic independence as much as their racial autonomy. So he ate the dandelion greens, but he resented the comments of "small-minded" neighbors and the teasing of his schoolmates. He hungered after the welfare department's food, but he was ashamed when the "on relief" finger was pointed at him and his family. He would stop at a neighbor's house at dinnertime, hoping for a good meal; but he never asked to be fed, and he was grateful that these families (in his words) "never embarrassed me by letting on" that they knew why he was there.[45] He swallowed his pride in order to survive, but he was not shameless.

In sum, family poverty, mediated by neglect, resulted in Malcolm performing apparently shameless actions of which he was in fact ashamed. But food was emotionally as well as physically significant for Malcolm (as indeed it is for children in general, but the children of poor parents in particular). Being fed by his mother meant being loved by her, and providing food for her meant loving her in return: when his mother was unable to feed him properly Malcolm felt unloved—despite the fact that he knew why the family lacked food. Or, at least, sometimes he knew; at other times it appeared to him that his mother was refusing good food for no good reason. Malcolm really couldn't understand why Louise did not want the welfare food. He was tempted to accept the welfare people's claim that she was crazy, and their insinuation that she did not love her children.

Thus when he went begging or stealing he was trying to appease a double hunger, a hunger for food and a hunger for love. Both appetites were satisfied at the Gohannas' house: they were "nice, older people" whom Malcolm especially liked, and who liked him. In a peculiar way, both appetites were also satisfied by his stealing, which brought him his mother's attention as well as food. To be sure, that attention was in the form of whippings; but such punishments had always carried the covert connotation of mutual affection. Thus Malcolm's misdeeds brought him the reward of maternal love in the outward form of punishment. Finally, we can see in his actions an attempt to change that outward form. Both at this time and earlier, Malcolm yelled loudly whenever his mother whipped him, making it embarrassing for her to punish him. His visits to the Gohannas and his petty thievery may have been a particular instance of this general maneuver, i.e., an unconsciously motivated effort to embarrass his mother by calling attention to himself as a neglected child, with the hope that somehow this would force her to change her unloving ways. But of course, any such change was beyond her power, and Malcolm's protestations were correspondingly powerless to accomplish their proper purpose. They had, however, an unintended and fateful consequence.

Malcolm turned beggar and thief for love of his mother. That on the one hand. On the other, his love was manifestly unrequited, and therefore ambivalent. Unconsciously if not consciously, love turns to hate when it is unduly frustrated. It follows that the normal Oedipal ambivalence would have been accentuated in Malcolm's case by his mother's negative predisposition toward him, and further augmented as a result of her increasing economic and emotional incapacity. He had cause for anger, the anger that accompanies unfulfilled romantic love. Consequently it must have been a source of both pain (consciously) and pleasure (unconsciously) that his bad behavior was embarrassing to her; and there must have been a bitter satisfaction in the fact that when the welfare people "went after" his mother, he was the "first target" because his stealing implied that he "was not being taken care of properly."

Viewed from this perspective, Malcolm's actions were the expression of his ambivalent feelings for his mother. As such, they were inherently guilt-inducing. His love for his mother, in combination with his moral identification with her, entailed that these hostile actions would be repugnant to his better self, to his conscience. Hence the aggression that motivated them was turned back against the I, so that a vicious circle was set in motion. Hostile actions generated remorse and guilt, and this internal, aggressive pressure led in turn to further hostile actions. This circle might have been broken if Louise had remained healthy and the family had remained intact. Then there might have been an opportunity for the more loving side of Malcolm's character to gain control over the more hostile one.* But the larger circle of his family situation continued its downspin, and he was therefore trapped in the deepening abyss of his own shame and guilt. He wanted desperately to escape from this terrifying and traumatizing unity of self and situation. Hence as his mother declined, he increasingly stayed away from home; and when he was finally sent to live with the Gohannas, he was glad, "at least in a surface way."[46] But below the surface his guilt had been compounded: he held himself accountable for not wanting to be with his mother and the other children when they were down and out. In this way the original sins "committed" against his father became offenses against the family as a whole. Malcolm's moral alienation was nearly complete; his capacity for self-control was nearly exhausted.

Looking back on those hard times, Malcolm's conclusion was that had it not been for the vulture-like interference of the state welfare people, the family would not have disintegrated—despite his own irresponsible behavior: "We could have made it, we could have stayed together. As bad as I was, as much trouble and worry as I caused my mother, I loved her."[47] Clearly, Malcolm did love his mother and he did regret the pain he caused her. The melancholy feeling evoked in the reader by his telling of her tale is sufficient proof of that. And he is correct in placing the blame for the family's disintegration upon the shoulders of the welfare people, at least if they are seen as the mediating agents of larger political-economic forces. But it is also clear that his denial of responsibility is a nearly conscious, perhaps even fully conscious, admission of guilt: a self-condemnation for not loving his mother enough, for helping to drive her insane, and for not helping the family to stay together.

With hindsight, Malcolm was able to see himself in his situation. At the time he knew that he was being bad, but not why he was being bad. He recognized, however, that his being "bad" had a family precedent:

---

* There was one other possibility of breaking the circle: see below, pp. 137ff.

I was growing up fast, physically more so than mentally.*
As I began to be recognized more around the town, I started
to become aware of the peculiar attitude of white people toward me. I sensed that it had to do with my father. It was an
adult version of what several white children had said at
school, . . . which really expressed what their parents had
said—that the Black Legion or the Klan had killed my
father.[48]

To Malcolm, being "bad" meant being his father's son. Earl Little
had been a tough man who refused to play the game by white-racist
rules and who had been murdered for being so uppity. Malcolm was
an aggressive boy who refused to "wait for anything" and who was
already gaining a "peculiar" recognition from white people. Not
only white people "around town": we have seen that the welfare
people and, in a certain sense, his mother recognized that Malcolm
had inherited his father's tough and aggressive character. In other
words, by being bad Malcolm was confirming his identification with
his father, attempting to preserve some remnant of their shared Garveyite pride and of his own self-respect, despite the family's shameful poverty. And by so doing, he was defying those who had constituted themselves as his judges.

The seventh son has re-emerged, in the form of a young bad-man.
But we remember that Malcolm's moral patrimony was both the
unifying force of Garveyite pride and the divisive power of Christian
guilt. What had become of this latter aspect of Malcolm's conscience? The answer lies close at hand. Because the welfare people
were playing a destructive paternal role in the life of the family, they
had become the legitimate successors to the Christian Earl Little,
and to the Black Legion as well. Malcolm could project his internalized Christian paternal imago onto them, and hence displace
hostility away from himself. In short, Malcolm's defiant conduct
was grounded in a primitive form of group-emotion or, better, in a
semblance of group-emotion. It was only a semblance because the
mediating force of the Word made Flesh, of a charismatic leader or
leading idea, was missing; without that mediation, there was no
way for Malcolm to legitimate and stabilize his emotions, to bring
them under conscious control.

As we know, in the years to come Malcolm would gradually take

* It should be mentioned that at this point (1937/38, the period of transition between
his living at home and with the Gohannas), Malcolm was approaching adolescence, a
phase of life when emotional control is inherently difficult.

conscious possession of his Garveyite heritage by fighting against white Christianity; but Garveyite pride, in its unconscious form, was not a sufficient ground for overcoming Christian guilt. Indeed, when viewed from another perspective, the very activities through which Malcolm was preserving his self-respect were adding to his burden of guilt. Like his father before him, Malcolm was bringing down upon his mother the pressure of white racist harassment. Manifestly this was an unintended consequence of choices made for other reasons; but we have seen that Malcolm was bound to take a guilty pleasure in Louise's pain. Thus he was compounding his sins against his mother. He still could not be a good son to both parents.

There was, however, one narrow ground upon which Malcolm might have been able to build a less antinomian character structure. "One thing I have always been proud of," he commented, "is that I never raised my hand against my mother."[49] As "bad" as he was, as much as he was his father's son, he never attempted to brutalize his mother as his father had done. This was a basis for pride he had constructed by his own self-restraint. It was his own title to self-respect. His aggressive inclinations were still the principal driving force in his psyche, however, and they could not be totally contained. He therefore needed to find an appropriate way to utilize his aggressive energies, to convert them into a form of conscious activity of which both parents could be proud. And for a brief time in 1938, it seemed that such a way might be found.

In 1937, Joe Louis had won the heavyweight boxing title, "and all the Negroes in Lansing, like Negroes everywhere, went wildly happy with the greatest celebration of race pride our generation had ever known."[50] In Richard Wright's words:

> Four centuries of oppression, of frustrated hopes, of black bitterness, felt even in the bones of the bewildered young, were rising to the surface. Yes, unconsciously they had imputed to the brawny image of Joe Louis all the balked dreams of revenge, all the secretly visualized moments of retaliation, AND HE HAD WON![51]

The Garvey movement was dead. It could no longer express the "balked dreams" of an oppressed people. But Joe Louis was alive, and his victory connoted a new project even for, or especially for, the "bewildered young": "Every Negro boy old enough to walk wanted to be the next Brown Bomber."[52] Among them was Malcolm's brother Philbert, who practiced hard and quickly became a good amateur boxer. But this meant that Malcolm was losing his position as the "tough" member of the family. Philbert, with whom he had been fighting since babyhood, who loved church—in short, his major sibling rival—was about to become his father's successor! Moreover, his younger brother Reginald, who had always idolized him, was starting to admire Philbert instead. Malcolm therefore had everything to gain by becoming a boxer himself: an escape from poverty and anonymity, an appropriate outlet for aggression, an affirmative racial identity, an earned claim to his father's throne, a victory over one brother and the admiration of another.

He lost: to a white boy, with all of his brothers and sisters in attendance. He lost the fight, and he lost face among his peers. The white boy, he observed "did such a job on my reputation in the Negro neighborhood that I practically went into hiding . . . [and] when I did show my face again the Negroes I knew rode me so badly I knew I had to do something. But the worst of my humiliations was my younger brother Reginald's attitude: he simply never mentioned the fight. It was the way he looked at me—and avoided looking at me." [53] The only mirrors in which Malcolm could see himself heroically reflected had been broken. He tried to cement the fragments back together by taking on the white boy in a rematch; but the second was no better than the first, except that at least his family was not present to witness his downfall. His one possibility of breaking the vicious circle of self-destructive aggressive action no longer existed.

Malcolm was thus left with no choice but to continue his hopeless battle against all moral authorities:

> Not long after this, I came into a classroom with my hat on.
> I did it deliberately. The teacher, who was white, ordered me
> to keep the hat on, and walk around and around the room
> until he ordered me to stop. "That way," he said, "everyone
> can see you." [54]

The young bad-man was determined to draw all eyes to himself, to win recognition of one kind or another. He needed to see himself in the reactions of other people to him, no matter what the substance of those reactions might be. Come what may, he would not be humbled:

> I was still walking around when he got up from his desk
> and turned to the blackboard to write something on it. . . . I
> passed behind his desk, snatched up a thumbtack and deposited it on his chair. When he turned to sit back down, I was

far from the scene of the crime, circling around the rear of the room. Then he hit the tack, and I heard him holler and caught a glimpse of him spraddling up as I disappeared through the door.[55]

Unable to defeat a white boy in the ring, Malcolm attacked a white man in the classroom. Defiance, punishment, again defiance. But the white authorities were the stronger party, both morally and rationally. They not only expelled him from school, they took him to court, judged him guilty of crimes against society, and condemned him to imprisonment in a reform school. Malcolm, who had been violating their commandments solely on the basis of a blind determination not to submit, could not withstand their onslaught. He was, after all, only a thirteen-year-old boy, with an increasingly unrealizable desire to make someone proud of him, so that he could be proud of himself. When, therefore, the "white state man" who was taking him away told him that the word "reform" meant "to change and become better," and that reform schools were places where boys "could have the time to see their mistakes and start a new life and become somebody everyone could be proud of," Malcolm took him at his word.[56] In his old life—as an individual, a member of the Little family, and a Negro—he had been a failure. He had been abandoned by the gods of his childhood and, left to his own resources, he had become a hero to no one. Perhaps he would do better to serve the gods of the power which had defeated him.

Straining to Integrate

Malcolm never reached reform school. Instead, he spent a little over two years being re-formed and re-forming himself at a detention home in the nearby town of Mason. The home was run by a couple named Swerlin who, the white state man had told him, were "very good people." Malcolm agreed: "They were good people. Mrs. Swerlin was bigger than her husband, I remember, a big, buxom, laughing woman, and Mr. Swerlin was thin, with black hair, and a black mustache and a red face, quiet and polite, even to me."[57] Malcolm liked them both from the first, and they liked him, too. He also liked the fact that he had his own room in the dormitory ("the first in my life"), that all the boys and girls being detained except the most troublesome ones ate meals with the Swerlins, and that

the rest of the staff treated him well. Soon he began voluntarily to
help out around the main house, which led to more kindly attention
from the Swerlins and the privilege of being allowed to spend part of
the weekend with his brothers and sisters, away from the home.
Then in the fall of 1939, instead of being sent on to the reform
school, he was enrolled in the seventh grade of the local junior high
school, where he quickly rose to the top of his class academically.
The Swerlins also helped him find a job, so that he could earn some
regular spending money. Finally, in the second semester of the seventh grade he was elected class president, which surprised him but
which also gave him a real feeling of pride. And not only him:

> "Malcolm we're just so *proud* of you!" Mrs. Swerlin ex-
> claimed when she heard about my election. . . . Even the
> state man, Maynard Allen, who still dropped by to see me
> once in a while, had a word of praise. He said he never saw
> anybody prove better exactly what "reform" meant.[58]

The young bad-man had become a good, a very good, citizen.

Now, this rapid transition from the vicious circle of character de-
formation to the upward spiral of character reformation requires
some explanation. From our prior analysis, it would not have appeared that Malcolm had the internal basis for reformation. The
contradictions of the welfare state—the processes of decomposition
that characterized proletarian life, especially black proletarian life,
and that had taken the life of his family—had been reflected into his
psyche. He had been de-formed in the image of a disintegrating society. The Christian side of his conscience (i.e., conscience in the
narrow sense of a standard of right and wrong) had been re-projected
onto civil authorities; his self-respect had been undermined and,
along with it, his capacity for self-control; and he was consequently
under the control of his own unconscious motives—most importantly, repressed aggressive impulses that were re-emerging in a barely sublimated form. He seemed to have become a nascent *lumpen-
proletarian*. How, then, was he able to respond so positively to his
new situation?

An initial answer to this question is suggested by Malcolm's reaction to his court hearing. When he was expelled from school, he
states:

> I guess I must have had some vague idea that if I didn't have
> to go to school, I'd be allowed to stay on with the Gohannas
> and wander around town, or maybe get a job if I wanted one

for pocket money. But I got rocked on my heels when a state man whom I hadn't seen before came and got me at the Gohannas' and took me down to court.[59]

Malcolm had not expected *serious* punishment. Although he had been bad for several years, he had never gotten any punishment worse than a whipping from his mother. And in former times, he had been the only child to escape the *real* punishment that his father administered. He had been the seventh son, the lucky one. Now his luck had run out. First he lost a prizefight to a white boy, then the white authorities took him into custody. It must have seemed that his protective power, his father's *mana*, had somehow disappeared, or that his *mana* was less powerful than that of his enemies. Either way, white over black had been inductively established, established in his own experience and in every moment of his experience, as an ontological principle. Furthermore, because his very existence now was dependent upon the white man's power, his essential being increasingly became a reflection of that determining force. He was "straining to integrate," which entailed denying that he was his father's son, a member of the Little family, and a Negro. Accordingly neither he nor his siblings "talked much about" their mother and they "never mentioned" their father. Although he maintained contact with his brothers and sisters, he soon "had just about forgotten about being a Little in any family sense."[60] Most of all, he tried to forget about the color of his skin: "I didn't really have much feeling about being a Negro," he acknowledges, "because I was trying so hard, in every way I could, to be white."[61]

He would not have been able to make this effort had it not been for the Swerlins. By judicial action they had become the parental authorities in his life. The question was, what kind of "parents" would they be? If they had been punitive or rejecting parent-substitutes, they would have inherited the legacy of the Black Legion, the Christian Earl Little, Louise Little as the punishing mother, the welfare people, school authorities: the vicious circle of Malcolm's self-destructive action would have been immediately reestablished. But they were good people, and their goodness was manifested not only in the physical form of ample food and comfortable lodgings but also in the form of affectionate attention, of emotional nourishment. The standard of right and wrong which they embodied and enforced was therefore positively grounded, so that for the first time in his life Malcolm was subject to rules and regulations that were not primarily brutal power or vulture-like persecution in legal dress. The split image of Earl Little had been superseded, along with its reflection in Malcolm's proud defiance of civil authority. Moreover, in their attitude and actions the Swerlins overcame the antinomian relationship that had existed between Malcolm and each of his parents. Whereas before he had been trapped in a double, double bind—the epidermally determined bind of being able to please one parent only insofar as he displeased the other, and the bind of Oedipal ambivalence—now he received the same judgment from each parental figure for any given action, while the Oedipal tension was considerably reduced by the fact that the Swerlins were not literally his parents. Further, the Oedipal problem was attenuated (although not solved) because Mrs. Swerlin was in herself a combined version of Louise and Earl Little. She was big, strong, the dominant force in detention-home life and a "Very Important Woman about the town of Mason"; she was white (light-skinned) and a woman; and she genuinely liked Malcolm.[62] The love-starved boy who wanted to be good but needed to be proud had found someone whose affectionate praise when he was good made him feel proud. He was therefore able to displace his affections from his parents to Mrs. Swerlin in particular and the Swerlins, his school teachers, and other authorities in general; to accept their judgments as an accurate reflection of his own value; and, finally, to gain a sense of self-respect from living up to their standards of good behavior—that is, from repressing his more aggressive tendencies.

Malcolm had been reformed, had re-formed himself into "somebody everyone would be proud of." Yet there were certain strains and contradictions in his new identity. Every once in a while he would feel obliged to visit his mother in the mental hospital, which was so painful to him that he "didn't want to have to experience [it] with anyone else present," not even his brothers or sisters.[63] On the other hand, now that he was doing well, he got a "warm feeling" when he visited his siblings or the Gohannas. There were, to be sure, limits to how "well" he could do. When he went to school dances, he could "sense it almost as a physical barrier" that he "wasn't supposed to dance with any of the white girls." Conversely, he was puzzled about why some of his friends would, in his words, "get me off in a corner somewhere and push me to proposition certain white girls, sometimes their own sisters."[64] But the temptations of the flesh were not yet as powerful as they were later to become, and Malcolm had not yet learned about the role black males play in the phantasy lives of white people, both male and female. Then there were the "nigger jokes" told in class by some of his teachers, and the "cooning" from audiences when he played basketball. But these racial slurs bothered him "only vaguely." Butterfly McQueen's act in *Gone With the Wind* made him feel like "crawling under the rug"; but usually he was able to ignore the racial stereotypes, the ghosts of his individual-collective past, that were haunting his present existence. He even was able to disregard the parlor chatter about "niggers" at the Swerlins, chatter predicated upon the assumption that he was essentially deaf, dumb, and blind:

> They would talk about anything and everything with me standing right there hearing them, the same way people would talk freely in front of a pet canary. They would even talk about me, or about "niggers," as if I wouldn't understand what the word meant.[65]

Malcolm had become the Swerlins' "house nigger"—a bright nigger, but a nigger nonetheless. At that time, however, he did not understand the real nature of his position.

Years later Malcolm recognized that he had been invisible to the Swerlins:

> What I am trying to say is that it just never dawned on them that I could understand, that I wasn't a pet, but a human being. They didn't give me credit for having the same sensitivity, intellect and understanding that they would have been ready and willing to recognize in a white boy in my position. . . . Even though they appeared to have opened the door, it was still closed. Thus they never did really see *me*.[66]

They saw a composite image, part Malcolm, part "nigger" stereotype. They basically believed that "niggers" were happy living in their poverty shacks, that they preferred fancy cars to decent living quarters, that they were, in Mrs. Swerlin's words, "just that way."[67] Malcolm was visible to them only through this mystifying veil of racial misperceptions, comprehensible only through the mediating categories of falsified racial consciousness. The first principle or underlying falsification of this pseudo-logic we uncovered earlier, in Klansman Sawyer's statement that "the Negro, in whose blood flows the mad desire for race amalgamation, is more dangerous than a wild beast and he must and will be controlled." The archetypal white-racist stereotype is the Black Beast, a species linking ape to man or, better, dividing ape from man. The male of the species lusts rapaciously after virginal white women, the female is wantonly and violently sensual. In other words, the immanent force in this illusion is very primitive, predominantly aggressive but also sexual (in a word, sadistic) energy—the repressed, then projected and displaced sensual energy that determines the group's external relations.

Of course, the Swerlins and their immediate predecessors, the welfare people, did not see Malcolm and his family, or Negroes in general, as bestial savages. Rather, they fused this infantile and irrational content with more rational elements, producing compromise formations resembling dream images or neurotic symptoms. Hence the welfare people, whom we may term *malevolent paternalists*, and who will reappear in the next chapter in the form of police authorities, perceived Louise and her family as shameless, irresponsible, and irrational, as bad and/or crazy . . . children. And the Swerlins, who were *benevolent paternalists*, saw Negroes as happy and simple children, incapable of handling money wisely or power ethically, but good enough people within their natural limits. For all their good intentions, they could not help seeing Malcolm through these mediations. Or perhaps, because they liked him so much, they partially by-passed the stereotypes by thinking of him as "essentially" white, white beneath the skin. This is the process of denial that makes possible the "exception" to stereotypical categories, the exception that proves the rule. Be that as it may, the contradiction in their relationship to Malcolm was not yet explosive. He was still a boy chronologically, and benevolent paternalism was therefore hardly distinguishable—for them or for him—from genuine parental solicitude.

Yet Malcolm was not in fact deaf and blind to the racism that surrounded him. The question therefore arises: why didn't he see himself in these "nigger" images? why didn't he hear his name in the racist epithets? In the first place, these insults did not "essentially" fit. Malcolm was a smart, hardworking, and well-behaved young man, a good boy, very much in control of himself. He could think of himself as an exception. Further, his own experience inclined him to accept the double equation of White is Good and Black is Bad. This was not because the Negroes of his acquaintance were bad people; they obviously were no worse than their white equivalents. But he had been bad; and as we have seen, his bad conduct had been premised upon a familial-racial identity. In order to overcome his shame and guilt, as well as the judicial judgment which was its external confirmation, it was therefore first necessary for him to repress the aggressive impulses that were the internal source of his trouble, and then to deny his past and heritage. He had to put his former life behind him; in his situation this meant that he had to become a white boy. Because the Swerlins were good people and, more particularly, good to him, this necessity became a possibility. He was able to reintroject the parental image he had previously projected onto white authority, to re-form his conscience in (especially) Mrs. Swerlin's image. His conscience, thus reinforced, was then strong enough to demand the suppression and repression of the Bad Black Boy; and his consciousness, having been emptied of its authentic content, could at last be "whitened out." He had become, to paraphrase Fanon, a black boy wearing a white mask, a stereotypical American Negro.

In sum, the Swerlins' benevolent paternalism produced as its Other, its external reflection or negative form, Malcolm's Negro identity. Stating the point more generally, we may say that the Negro identity (like any other externally imposed and therefore stereotypically limited identity) is a character-form of group-emotion, determined through the mediation of *identification with the oppressor*.[68]* Conscience and consciousness are both whitened out, and blackness becomes firmly attached to unacceptable, predominantly aggressive, infantile emotional impulses. Black people and white people alike come to have a character-structure in which the I, including the moral I, is white, and the It is black. Within this relationship, black people can think of themselves as fully human only by denying their true racial identity, while white people secure their humanity only at the price of black dehumanization. Thus the concept of the emotional-group here emerges in the form of a *dominating-dominated intergroup relationship*. In this relationship the repressed sadistic tendencies of the dominating group become the self-hatred, the masochistic tendency, of the dominated group. Conversely, the alienated self-esteem of the dominated group becomes the narcissism of the dominating one. And through the work of secondary elaboration or rationalization, the members of both groups are held firmly in the grip of stereotypical false consciousness. This emotional process is in its totality determined by the political-economic power of the ruling class, i.e., by the American bourgeoisie's ownership of the means of production and its control of the state (including the welfare system, the courts, and the schools). Emotional alienation is determined by and is the reproductive mediation of alienated labor: the class structure of American capitalism is the

---

* The degree to which any given individual identifies with the oppressor is variable. See Chapter X, page 355.

ground from which develops a racially divided national character-structure, which in turn stereotypically falsifies working-class consciousness and thereby preserves the existing structure of bourgeois domination. Malcolm, by becoming a Negro, was learning to play his part in capitalism's dumb show of racial stereotypes, its dialectic of self-preservation.

We noted above that the contradictions in Malcolm's relationship to the Swerlins—in his Negro identity—were not initially either visible to or problematical for either party. Malcolm was able to work and love within the limits of the "good boy" stereotype, and the Swerlins were affectionately proud of the work he performed. But in the spring of 1940, the delicate structure of Malcolm's reformed character began to weaken, in the first instance because he was forcibly reminded of his familial and racial heritage. Ella, his father's "grown daughter by his first marriage," came from her home in Boston to visit her country half-brothers and sisters: "One afternoon when I got home from school . . . there she was. A commanding woman, maybe even bigger than Mrs. Swerlin, Ella wasn't just black, but like our father, she was jet black."[69] She had also inherited their father's racial pride: "She was the first really proud black woman I had ever seen in my life. She was plainly proud of her very dark skin. This was unheard of among Negroes in those days, especially in Lansing."[70] She was "commanding" in character as well as physical presence: "The way she sat, moved, talked, did everything, bespoke somebody who did and got exactly what she wanted."[71] Finally, these subjective attributes were also objectively manifested. She had come North from Georgia "with nothing, and she had worked and saved and invested in property that she built up in value."[72] Thus Malcolm's lost Garveyite soul, reincarnated in Ella, arose to challenge the presumed natural supremacy of the white race and hence the validity of his new identity. The stereotypical ground of his character began to give way beneath him.

The contradiction in Malcolm's character was further intensified by Ella's commitment to family unity. She had brought a number of the family out of Georgia to Boston, and now she was intent upon bringing the Lansing Littles back together: "'We Littles have to stick together,' Ella said. It thrilled me to hear her say that, and even more, the way she said it. I had become a mascot; our branch of the family was split to pieces."[73] Ella's words gave Malcolm a new feeling of family pride and love, they also made him ashamed of his relationship to the Swerlins, and they renewed the guilt feelings that had accompanied his original abandonment of the family. These mixed emotions were even more strongly evoked when Ella took all the children to visit their mother in the mental hospital:

> Our mother was smiling when they brought her out. She was extremely surprised when she saw Ella. They made a striking contrast, the thin near-white woman and the big black one hugging each other. I don't remember much about the rest of the visit . . . [but] we left with all of us feeling better than we ever had about the circumstances. I know that for the first time, I felt as though I had visited with someone who had some kind of physical illness that had just lingered on.[74]

Malcolm felt good to see his mother in control of herself. To some extent, the terrifying image of her disintegrated personality was robbed of its power, and he was able to love her again. He also felt a certain amount of hope that she might "get well," that she might "come back." But at the same time, this rebirth of love and hope must have reawakened feelings of guilt for his previous bad conduct. For if it is true that love for his family and guilt for his earlier actions had become inextricably intertwined in his mind, then he could not feel the one without the other. During the preceding period he had suppressed both. Now they were coming back to haunt him.

Initially, however, the positive side of Malcolm's revitalized emotions predominated, in part because Ella praised him highly for his curricular and extracurricular achievements. No doubt as a reward for his efforts, she promised him a visit to Boston that summer. So after school was over for the year, Malcolm went off to Boston—to a stunningly different world from the one with which he was familiar:

> I couldn't have feigned indifference if I tried to. . . . I didn't know the world contained as many Negroes as I saw thronging downtown Roxbury at night, especially on Saturdays. Neon lights, nightclubs, poolhalls, bars, the cars they drove! . . . I saw for the first time occasional black-white couples strolling around arm in arm. And on Sundays, . . . I saw churches for black people such as I had never seen. They were many times finer than the white church I had attended back in Mason, Michigan.[75]

The stereotype of Negro inferiority had been broken: Malcolm could no longer believe that all or almost all Negroes were inferior to all or almost all white people. Although at some level of consciousness he must have realized that white Boston overshadowed black Roxbury just as Roxbury overshadowed Lansing, his experience was sufficient to disprove the white-racist proposition that black skin and the good life were mutually exclusive. Plainly, not all Negroes were hewers of wood and drawers of water. Just as plainly, not all Negroes found it necessary to restrict their sexual choices to members of their own race. In short, there appeared to be a degree of freedom to work and to love in Roxbury that Malcolm had previously believed was precluded for black people. Moreover, this appearance of freedom was grounded in the actual existence of a black community. The Negro section of Lansing was only a neighborhood, but Roxbury was a world unto itself. Malcolm had, as he later put it, "the sense of being a real part of a mass of my own kind, for the first time." [76] He sensed himself in, saw himself reflected in, a mass of black people. The emotional energy of that mass ran through him, touched deadened racial nerves, stimulated racial reflexes that had not yet come alive. He couldn't describe this feeling at the time, either to his brothers and sisters or to himself. How could he explain that he now felt black, when he was not aware that he had been trying to feel white? He did know that something had changed: "My restlessness with Mason—and for the first time in my life a restlessness with being around white people—began as soon as I got back home and entered eighth grade." [77] Malcolm was being pulled back, and forward, into the black world.

Despite his increasing restlessness, Malcolm continued to do his school work with characteristic proficiency. Then came the fateful meeting with Mr. Ostrowski, the English teacher . . . the event Malcolm termed "the first major turning point of my life." [78]

Mr. Ostrowski was a "natural-born 'advisor' . . . about any and everything." He was especially noted for giving students advice on "how to become something in life"; and he had always been nice to Malcolm. It was therefore natural enough that he should give Malcolm some well-intentioned advice on the "something" he ought to become. One day, when they found themselves by chance alone in a classroom, Mr. Ostrowski said, "Malcolm, you ought to be thinking about a career. Have you been giving it thought?" Malcolm reports:

> The truth is, I hadn't. I never figured out why I told him, "Well, yes, sir, I've been thinking I'd like to be a lawyer." . . .
> Mr. Ostrowski looked surprised, I remember, and leaned back in his chair and clasped his hands behind his head. He kind of half-smiled and said, "Malcolm, one of life's first

needs is for us to be realistic. Don't misunderstand me, now.
We all like you here, you know that. But you've got to be
realistic about being a nigger. A lawyer—that's no realistic
goal for a nigger. You need to think about something you
can be. You're good with your hands—making things. Everybody admires your carpentry shop work. Why don't you
plan on carpentry? People like you as a person—you'd get all
kinds of work." [79]

Negroes, at least in Mason or Lansing, had to be hewers of wood,
after all! Use your hands, not your head, Malcolm—it is not realistic
for a nigger to think about a career that involves thinking.

But why not? It certainly wasn't because he lacked the mental
ability: "It was a surprising thing that I had never thought of it that
way before, but I realized that whatever I wasn't, I *was* smarter than
nearly all of those white kids." Those kids Ostrowski encouraged,
yet Malcolm he discouraged. "But apparently I was still not intelligent enough, in their eyes, to become what *I* wanted to be." Thus
the pull from the black world was complemented by a push from the
white one: "It was then that I began to change—inside." He drew
away from white people; and as he did, he began to hear the racial
slurs he had previously ignored. "Where 'nigger' slipped off my back
before, wherever I heard it now, I stopped and looked at whoever said
it." Then "I quit hearing so much 'nigger' and 'what's wrong?'—
which was the way I wanted it." [80] Finally, his emotional withdrawal
became a physical one. The Swerlins recognized that he was no
longer happy being with them, and they arranged for him to live
with a local Negro family. It was a sad departure. Mrs. Swerlin was
"wiping her eyes" as Malcolm left, and he felt "very bad." But he
left; and as soon as the school year ended, he abandoned Mason as
well. Roxbury was to be his new home.

In the following chapter we shall examine Malcolm's metamor-
phosis from aspiring lawyer to professional criminal, but first, we
should ask: why did Malcolm want to be a lawyer, and why did he
accept Ostrowski's judgment that he could not be one?

The first part is readily answered. Malcolm had been a young bad-
man. He had been caught, condemned, and confined; and he had acknowledged the validity of that legal process by re-forming his conscience in its image. It was therefore an intuitively correct choice to
want to unify himself on that moral basis—to de-energize the "bad"
side of his character and keep it under control by making the law the
substance of his conscious activity. His identification with his op-

pressor would then have been complete; his Negro identity would
have been assured. Moreover, he knew, or at least sensed, that becoming a lawyer would be an exceptional and worthy achievement.
"Lansing had no Negro lawyers . . . to hold up an image that I might
have aspired to."[81] As a lawyer, he would have been unique, the seventh son in judicial robes. Well, not entirely unique: there may have
been no Negro lawyers in Lansing, but Malcolm was under the impression that he had seen Negro men of wealth and power in Boston.
This was, however, only a general image of Negro prestige. By particularizing it to his individual situation in the form of a projected
legal career he was making it singularly and properly his own.

Now, if becoming a lawyer was the ideal choice of a career for
Malcolm, it is all the more puzzling that he was so easily discouraged. Of course, it is true that his choice was not entirely conscious.
He had not been thinking about a career: he had responded im-
pulsively to Ostrowski's question. He therefore had not gone
through the mental process of making the idea truly his own, had
not taken possession of it through self-conscious activity. If Ostrowski had encouraged him, or if Ostrowski's negative response had been
only an individual judgment, then his impulse might have matured
into a conscious motive. There were, however, no Negro lawyers in
Lansing. The law was not a Negro occupation! In fact, in 1940 there
were only 1,052 Negro lawyers in the whole country, while there
were 20,798 Negro carpenters.[82] Ostrowski was giving Malcolm
good advice. Carpentry was a realistic and, for a "nigger," a relatively
prestigious vocation. Nonetheless, this "good" advice consigned
Malcolm to a life of alienated labor. Instead of working for himself,
he was to receive work from others—he was to be dependent upon
the benevolent generosity of patronizing white people. And he was
to work with his hands instead of his head. He had demonstrated in
classroom competition his capacity for mental work; but mental
work, especially of the type he had chosen, was doubly precluded.
The law was a white, bourgeois profession, and he was a property-
less Negro. He was therefore predestined to expend his vital powers,
his work-energy, in unrewarding labor.

Malcolm's acceptance of Ostrowski's judgment was objectively
determined. However, he did choose to accept the judgment. He had
seen Boston, seen black people who were apparently lawyers, not
carpenters, and who were more impressive than Ostrowski himself.
Yet he did not directly defy his teacher's authority, persist in his ambitions, and become one of the thousand-odd Negro lawyers who

were the exception to the general rule. Hence the question still remains: why didn't Malcolm become one of this happy few?

Once again, the answer is implicit in the material we have already represented. Malcolm's experience during the preceding months had shaken the rigid foundations of his character-structure. He had been forced to remember and to feel again the painful moments of his past. The shame and guilt immanent in those moments were now rising to challenge his present sense of pride and purity; the young bad-man was re-emerging in defiance of the aspirant to a legal career. In other words, his renewed contact with the black world constituted a double ground for character development. Because it was simultaneously challenging and retraumatizing, it contained a potential both for the progressive formation of his Negro identity and for its regressive de-formation, for morally self-unifying activity and for the return of repressed sexual-aggressive impulses. These two tendencies were not, however, of equal strength. Because it had been formed from primary rather than secondary identifications and because it was reflective of more intense interpersonal relationships, the "bad" side of Malcolm's character was inherently more powerful than the "good" one. Moreover, he was now fifteen years old, physically mature for his age, and hence subject to irrational—uncontrollable and incomprehensible—ebbs and flows of sexual-aggressive feeling. The power of his repressed inclinations was thus being augmented by the untamed emotional energy of adolescent manhood, while the power of his repressive forces was being relatively diminished. He was no longer able to keep himself under control without increased external support for his Negro identity and increased possibilities for the utilization of his emotional energies. He had therefore appealed to Ostrowski, whom he liked and who encouraged young people to become a "success in life," to reaffirm the value of his reformation. But instead of the anticipated praise and encouragement, he had received only amused condescension. Instead of a renewed sense of pride, he was subjected to fresh feelings of shame and anger: success in life for a "nigger" meant being a carpenter, being a good boy until his dying day! He had been fooled, deceived, tricked. He had been led to believe that whiteness was an attribute of soul, that skin color did not matter. Now it was clear that only skin color mattered, that *therefore* his soul was irremediably black. His white mask had been stripped away. But at the same time, his teacher's appearance of paternal benevolence had disappeared.

The pantomime of Negro identity had come to an end: the contradiction between benevolent and malevolent paternalism had been one-sidedly resolved in favor of the latter. Yet for Malcolm, there had been no essential transvaluation of values. The White God had proven himself to be the White Devil after all, but He had not been dethroned. That is, Malcolm's conscience had been thoroughly whitened out. He had no racially self-determined moral ground, and hence no basis for an affirmative racial identity. Because he was still morally identified with his oppressor, he was not free either to love himself or to hate his enemy. Consequently, his anger when a white man called him "nigger" was accompanied by a familiar if indefinable sense of unconscious guilt, which in turn became a compelling need for aggressive action. The vicious circle of moralized self-hatred and subsequent self-destructive activity had been re-established. This was the truth, the ultimate meaning, of paternalist reformation.

In sum, Malcolm's Negro identity was not really a ground for the further development of his sensuous energies. It alienated him from the free use of both his emotional energy and his work-energy; hence it provided no real possibility for morally self-unifying conscious activity. Premised upon a paternalist political economy and mediated through identification with the oppressor, it entailed fixation in a posture of childlike submission to the white man's authority. It was a reified character-structure, the negation of Malcolm's potential for progressive self-determination. Since at this juncture Malcolm had no basis in conscience or consciousness for negating that negation, his character underwent a regressive development. He fell back into the vicious circle of bad conduct from which he had apparently escaped. But the young man who now was leaving Mason for Boston was not the trusting boy who had entered the town two years earlier. He had learned in the meantime that what was possible for white people was not possible for him; and he had chosen not to act as if he lacked this knowledge, not to play his assigned part in the paternalist pantomime. In this sense his decision to go to Boston was the negation of a negation: his regression into the vicious circle of uncontrolled aggressive action was simultaneously a progression beyond it. As we shall see in what follows, however, the regressive tendencies in his character were initially predominant.

CHAPTER V

Never Trust Anybody

WHEN MALCOLM DECIDED to move from Mason to Boston, he had no intention of becoming a criminal: his plan, and Ella's, was that he would get a respectable job, work hard, accumulate as much money as he could and, if possible, become a member of "so-called 'black society'."[1] He would become a "success in life" like Ella—despite Mr. Ostrowski. But despite his intentions, he was destined to become a hustler, for he had already been mesmerized by the feeling of being "a real part of a mass" of his own people. As he notes of his first days in Roxbury: "The world of grocery stores, walk-up flats, cheap restaurants, poolrooms, bars, storefront churches, and pawnshops seemed to hold a natural lure for me."[2] He was uncomfortable when he was among the more prosperous Negroes living on the "hill" that overlooked the Roxbury "town" section: "Not only was [the town] part of Roxbury much more exciting, but I felt more relaxed among Negroes who were being their natural selves and not putting on airs."[3] Malcolm only felt at home in the ghetto streets. Unless he had been content to be a "square," to find some unrewarding "slave" (job) and toil in it, he therefore had no choice but to become a member of the hustling society, i.e., of the black ghetto's *lumpen-proletariat.*

But why did Malcolm feel at home only in the "town"? Why was he uncomfortable in Ella's world? In the first place, he was a "field Negro" by heritage and life experience: the Littles had been agricultural workers in the South; and, after his father's death, his branch of the family had become part of the welfare system's "rabble of paupers." To be sure, there had been those years of Garveyite prosperity; but Earl Little's death and its consequences had almost destroyed Malcolm's Garveyite self-image—all that remained were stubborn pride, a certain toughness of character, and a burgeoning feeling of manhood. The political, economic, and racial aspects of the doctrine were no longer (if they had ever been) part of his consciousness. Moreover, Ella, like her father and like Malcolm himself, was a dominating person, "a woman whose every instinct was to run everything and everybody she had anything to do with."[4] And "everybody," Malcolm notes with wry humor, included him. It is hardly surprising that, having just escaped from one kind of paternalism, he would resist being trapped by another. Furthermore, Malcolm was not only seeking to avoid paternalism in this embodied form; he was also attempting to leave behind the whitened-out conscience that judged him to be bad on the basis of his skin color. He was looking for a place where he would not see himself reflected in the mirror of white Christian morality. Finally, he was still haunted by the guilt of his familial sins, the patricidal guilt of the seventh son, the remorse for having been his mother's bad boy. In sum, in his struggle to free himself from his moral identification with his oppressor, Malcolm became a criminal from a sense of guilt.[5]

Our task in the present chapter is to represent and interpret the period of Malcolm's alienated conscious activity—to unfold the regressive development of his character, within and as a reflection of his historical situation. First, we will consider his ascension to hip manhood, his relations with women, and his evolution from hipster to hustler. In the process we will uncover one dimension of ghetto life: its street-corner standards of masculine self-respect and recognition, its epidermal fetishism in sexual relations, and the hustling code which rationalizes and universalizes its everyday activities.[6] Next, we will examine the hustling society from the perspective of its historical situation, its internal structure, and its functional relationship to the larger society. Finally, we will come to Malcolm's life in the hustling society, his descent into criminal nihilism, and his eventual imprisonment.

The Black Man

Malcolm may have been unconsciously, even pre-consciously, inclined toward hustling as a way of life when he arrived in Boston; but he lacked the consciousness needed to realize this inclination. He needed to be "schooled," i.e., he needed someone to teach him the customs and morals of the ghetto. He soon found the necessary mentors.

While meandering through the town, Malcolm had had a brief, friendly encounter with a young man called Shorty, who racked balls in one of the local poolhalls. So one day he "slipped" into the poolroom as "inconspicuously" as he could—he was painfully aware of his "countrified" appearance and did not want to attract attention —and asked Shorty how to "go about getting a job like his." When in the ensuing conversation it turned out that both young men were from the Lansing area, that Malcolm was therefore Shorty's "homeboy," Shorty decided to take Malcolm under his wing, find him a "slave," and "school" him to the "happenings."

A job materialized almost immediately. Freddie, the shoeshine boy at the Roseland Ballroom, had "hit the big number" in the local racket and was quitting. Malcolm, Shorty's homeboy, was welcome to take over Freddie's stand. Already enamored of big-band music, Malcolm grabbed the opportunity to earn money while being involved in the nightlife of the town.

The first evening on the job, under Freddie's tutelage Malcolm received his initial lessons in hustling. He learned to "Uncle Tom" the shoeshine customers in order to get a larger tip; to make the shine rag "pop" because, although it was just a "jive noise," "cats tip better, they figure you're knocking yourself out"; to sell customers shoelaces whether they asked for them or not; and to "shame" men in the washroom into buying a towel.[7] The definition of hustling is already evident: to hustle is to make an unearned profit by giving a product or service the semblance (the outward form) of a value it does not substantively possess.* In addition, Freddie explained that income could be earned from selling prophylactics and—once he could "dig who's a cop"—liquor and reefers (marijuana) as well. Malcolm soon discovered that this additional income was the true material basis of the hustle, that "Freddie had done less shoeshining and towel-hustling than selling liquor and reefers, and putting white 'Johns' in touch with Negro whores." Thus Malcolm was schooled to the universal principle that, as Freddie formulated it at the end of the first night, "Everything in the world is a hustle."[8]

Malcolm quickly absorbed not only Freddie's teachings but also

* The connections among hustling, merchant capitalism, and monopoly marketing practices (principally advertising) are obvious: in each case, the attempt is made to sell a commodity above its exchange value, its cost of reproduction.

the general rules of town life. The "countrified" Malcolm Little transformed himself into the "hip" young cat called Red, who made all the "frantic" and "groovy" scenes around Roxbury. He learned to talk, walk, and dress hip (zoot suit, narrow belt, feathered hat, long key-chain); to drink liquor, to smoke cigarettes and marijuana; to shoot craps, play cards, bet on the numbers, and buy on credit; and to dance the lindy-hop in the approved uninhibited style. The country boy was rapidly becoming a particular type of city man.

The last vestige of Malcolm's former identity to disappear was his bushy, "hick"-style haircut. When at last his hair had grown long enough to be straightened or "conked," Shorty sent him off to buy the necessary ingredients for a do-it-yourself version. Malcolm grinned "proudly" when the local druggist asked him, "Going to lay on that first conk?" Then Shorty mixed a batch of congolene (which consists principally of lye), thoroughly vasolined Malcolm's scalp, and told Malcolm: "It's going to burn when I comb it [the congolene] in—it burns *bad*. But the longer you can stand it, the straighter the hair." Burn it did; Malcolm reports:

> The congolene just felt warm when Shorty started combing it in. But then my head caught on fire.
> I gritted my teeth and tried to pull the sides of the kitchen table together. The comb felt as if it was raking my skin off.
> My eyes watered, my nose was running. I couldn't stand it any longer; I bolted to the washbasin.[9]

Gradually the pain stopped as Shorty washed out the lye and gently combed out Malcolm's straightened hair. Then came the reward:

> My first view in the mirror blotted out the hurting. I'd seen some pretty conks, but when it's the first time, on your *own* head, the transformation, after the lifetime of kinks, is staggering.
> The mirror reflected Shorty behind me. We both were grinning and sweating. And on top of my head was this thick, smooth sheen of shining red hair—real red—as straight as any white man's.[10]

He had been fully transformed; he had become a member of the hip world, if not yet of the hustling society. It no longer mattered what was in his mind, so long as there was "whiskey aglow" in his stomach, marijuana to make his "head light," and congolene to make his hair . . . white.[11] He had learned to act his part in what he would later call the "slapstick comedy" of the Negro who "has completely lost his sense of identity, who has lost touch with himself." [12]

But wait: the boy who was ashamed to see himself mirrored in Ostrowski's half-smile is standing "lost in admiration of my hair now looking 'white,' reflected in the mirror of Shorty's room." [13] But how is this slapstick comedy different from the stereotypical dumbshow? The answer is obviously that in the one case Malcolm was losing his self-respect, in the other he was gaining it back. There was only a limited objective basis for this reevaluation. Like Sisyphus with his stone, Malcolm was expending his work-energy in alienated labor. The job at Roseland and the various jobs he held thereafter were all "slaves." But Malcolm had not accepted the particular form of slavery that Ostrowski had attempted to impose upon him; he had instead elected to slave in his own way, and in his own time and place. In this narrow sense his work was his own. Moreover, he no longer thought of his work as the active expression of his identity. Back in Mason, in his schoolboy fashion, he had lived to work; now he only worked to live. He had freed his sense of self-respect from its previous dependence upon the substance of his labor—at least for that moment.

Malcolm was doing white man's work, but he was doing it in a black man's way. Similarly, he was trying to *be* white, but in a black man's way. Although the image he saw in Shorty's mirror was only a make-believe or three-penny white man, it appeared in a mirror black men held up to themselves. He and Shorty—and hipsters in general—saw themselves reflected in and as each other, confirmed the validity of their caricature-identity through mutual recognition. To be sure, their roles were only a specification of Negro identity in general, Negro identity carried to the point where it becomes manifestly absurd; but these roles were, within certain limits, communally structured. As a result, the young men were able to educate each other, forming thereby a common consciousness. This common consciousness in turn constituted a system of conduits for emotional energy, a ground for the development of magnified narcissism through both reflected admiration and ritualized competition. Hence in the present instance Shorty could be proud of the conk he had given Malcolm and of his "homeboy's" courage, his willingness to bear the burning pain; in turn, Malcolm's pride in his own endurance and appearance was magnified by Shorty's evident approval. In this sense Malcolm's first conk was a *rite de passage*, his ceremonial initiation into the hip fraternity.

The White Woman

In most societies the passage from boyhood into manhood has two principal aspects. The first is the young man's entry into the public life of the community, a process which in many societies also determines the character of his relationships with other men. The second is his entrance into directly sexual and, ultimately, family life, into the private realm of intimate heterosexual relationships. The unity of these two sides constitutes the man's adult character.

We have considered the first aspect of this process, at least preliminarily, in the preceding paragraphs. There will be more to say on the subject later on. For the moment we need only add that Malcolm soon "outgrew" the Roseland job and took a daytime job at a drugstore on the Hill. This job was followed by work as a busboy in a downtown restaurant. Thus during the daylight hours Malcolm slaved in a typical Negro job—a low-paid, low-status service position. But after nightfall, his "real" living began and, along with it, his schooling in sexual conduct.

Malcolm is generally discreet concerning his personal sexual experience, but he is explicit about the ideal standard which determined its character: "Now at that time, in Roxbury, in any black ghetto in America, to have a white woman who wasn't a known, common whore was—for the average black man, at least—a status symbol of the first order." [14] Status or prestige rested primarily on a man's power or advantage over other men, hence on his courage, his cunning, and his "cool"; but it was based secondarily upon his sexual success, measured by three criteria: the amount of money the woman contributed to his support, the lightness of her skin, and her beauty. Beauty is of course less quantifiable than money or skin tone, more a matter of subjective preferences (or utilities, one is tempted to say); but the first two are readily measurable. They could therefore serve as a reliable rating scale of sexual achievement, the highest point on which was for a man to be fully supported by a (beautiful) white woman. This was most obviously the case in the relationships of pimps and prostitutes; but in somewhat more subtle ways all heterosexual relations were reflections of the competitive structure of male relationships. Which is to say, male-female relationships were structured as a political economy of sexual possession, in which women were used as commodities or even money, and in which a man's socio-economic status depended upon the value of his assets: two men who had women of equal value were themselves equal to each other. It follows that a black man with a white woman was the equal of a white man. His almost unavoidable inferiority in the work-economy could be overcome in the sexual one. Overcome, and more than overcome: since by white-racist law the white woman was the exclusive possession of the white man, any black man with a white woman was a successful lawbreaker, a victorious sexual rebel, and therefore more of a man than the Man he had defeated. Thus Malcolm attained not only real status among his peers but also a measure of revenge against those who had decreed that he could not be a "success in life" when he became involved with the beautiful and relatively affluent white woman he calls Sophia.

The affair began at a Roseland dance. Although Malcolm usually came to these dances unaccompanied, on this particular occasion he was escorting a decidedly "nice" girl he had met on the Hill. The two of them had just finished dancing in the "showtime" part of the evening when Malcolm found himself being "eyed" by a white woman. It was not uncommon to see white women at Negro dances, looking for "a little freelance lusting among the plentiful availability of enthusiastic Negro men"; but this woman was "almost too fine to believe."[15] She and Malcolm started dancing, and his date for the evening was "just about forgotten." He had the courtesy to take her home; but he ended the night making love to Sophia in her car.

In later years Malcolm was to be ashamed of his conduct that night. The young black woman he jilted for the older white one became a prostitute and a narcotics addict, and he blamed himself for her unhappy fate. At the time, however, he took pride in his possession of the "fine white woman" who gave him the money he spent. Yet the prestige and pride he gained from the relationship were not its essential qualities, and his choice between the two women was not in fact an act of will. Malcolm was irresistibly attracted to Sophia, that first night and for several years thereafter, and she was just as strongly drawn to him. Moreover, it is clear that the almost magnetic intensity of their mutual attraction was not idiosyncratic to them. Shorty, for example, had told Malcolm on first meeting that, in his own words, "I ain't going to lie—I dig them two-dollar white chicks."[16] And at the Roseland dances "a lot of black girls nearly got run over by some of those Negro males scrambling to get at those white women; you would have thought God had lowered some of his angels."[17] And Malcolm was later to meet a number of white women who "would get almost mesmerized by Negroes."[18]* We have therefore to determine the essential nature of his double bonding and the quality that differentiates it from other sexual interactions.

The distinguishing attribute of such relationships is plainly that skin *color* takes on sexual properties that do not naturally inhere in it. Each person is initially stimulated by the other's skin color, rather than by erotic actions or primary sexual characteristics. Thus Sophia came to Roseland looking for a Negro, and Malcolm was drawn to her despite the fact that she "didn't dance well, at least not by Negro standards."[19] To be sure, Malcolm had attracted her attention by his dancing, and she had gained his by giving him the eye. It is also true that skin color is a sensual property, and therefore a natural object for at least some sexual energy. But it would not normally constitute the ground of the relationship. There occurs, in other words, an inversion of values in which a secondary attribute becomes a primary one through the displacement onto it of emotional energy it does not inherently deserve. This we may call *epidermal fetishism*, the exaggerated love or even worship of skin color.

The next question is, why does skin color become a fetish? The answer will come easily if we ask a prior question, i.e., why is there what Marx terms a "fetishism of commodities" in which the products of human labor appear as "independent beings endowed with life, and entering into relation both with one another and the human race"?[20] According to Marx, this is because in a commodity-producing economy there really are "material relations between persons and social relations between things."[21] Human beings objectify themselves in commodities, and these objectifications then come to dominate the subjects who created them. There is, in other words, a subjectification of the object, which is reflected back into the living individual as an objectification of the subject. This inversion of subject and object is initiated in the exchange process, in the buying and selling of labor-power, which abstracts the subjectivity from the subject by transforming his work-energies into exchange values. It is consummated in the production process, which demonstrates conclusively that the worker's activity is simply another factor of pro-

---

* Malcolm makes this comment in the context of Harlem's appeal to white people of both sexes; but he was most concerned to understand the relationship between black men and white women.

duction. Thus it is that "the characters who appear on the economic stage are but personifications of the economic relations that exist between them,"[22] while economic relations take on every appearance of being a life-process.

The ghetto political economy of sexual possession and epidermal fetishism are particular instances of the commodity fetishism of bourgeois political economy. But commodity fetishism and the fetishism of skin color have intra-subjective as well as inter-subjective foundations. To make what is in fact a very long story short, we shall posit that the sensuous energies of individuals who produce and exchange commodities are reified, so that their character structures are formed in the image of the commodity.[23] They experience themselves as thing-like, and measure their own value in monetary terms. They possess, so to speak, a monetized super-ego, which commands them to repress or alienate from themselves their self-productive and self-fulfilling energies. This division of the self is then completed when they project their repressed energies onto, especially, the money-form of the commodity. Money thus becomes, as Marx remarked, both the "visible divinity" and "the common whore, the common pimp of peoples and nations."[24]

It follows from this general depiction that epidermal fetishism is a group-emotional mediation of the commodity-character of bourgeois social relations. This does not mean that it cannot occur in non-bourgeois societies; after all, both racism and fetishism antedate capitalism. But in bourgeois society, both forms of distorted consciousness are objectified and monetized. Consequently, for the type of black man with whom we are here concerned, the white woman becomes a divine prostitute; for this white woman, the black man becomes a demonic master; and both parties in the relationship accept skin color as a measure of value. Each person values the other for a quality he himself does *not* possess; each is seeking to appropriate that missing quality through sexual activity. The white woman wishes to become black, to overcome her inhibitions, to release the repressed sexual forces in her character. She is entranced by the stereotypical image of the black stud, tantalized by the fact that black men are taboo. By violating the taboo, by living out the phantasy born of the taboo itself, she turns herself into the "bad"—fallen, erotically liberated—woman she has always wanted to be. Conversely, the black man wishes to be recognized as a man instead of as a beast or a boy. He therefore wants to be white. In Fanon's words:

Out of the Blackest part of my soul, across the zebra strip-
ing of my mind, surges this desire to be suddenly *white*.
I wish to be acknowledged not as *black* but as *white*.
Now—and this is a form of recognition that Hegel had
not envisaged—who but a white woman can do this for me?
By loving me she proves that I am worthy of white love. I
am loved like a white man.
I am a white man.[25]

Thus the black man is reflected back into himself as white when he
is loved by a white woman, just as the white woman returns to herself as black through being loved by a black man. But in fact, the
double reflection is an optical illusion; the mutual recognition is a
case of mistaken identity. The black man is penetrating a woman
who is essentially black; the white woman is being penetrated by a
man who is essentially white. The would-be white man is bonded to
a would-be black woman. Each experiences in the other only the self
he or she is not but wishes to become. Their love-making is thus
a semblance, the physical interpenetration of mutually exclusive
selves, an escape from rather than a transcendence of their individual identities.

Epidermal fetishism is an alienated form of being in love and, as
such, is emotionally reifying. Skin color presides over the relationship like some archaic deity, forcing each person involved into a posture of reverence (but not of genuine respect) for the other; in other
words, skin color is idealized, withdrawn from the realm of criticism and rational evaluation and endowed with semi-magical
power, with a directly sexual prestige. Consequently, each person is
bound, quite against his or her will, to worship the other. Of course,
this is not a true relationship between two individuals, but, rather,
a doubled auto-hypnotic mirroring: each person is fascinated by his
or her own emotional energy as it is reflected back into the self
through the other *qua* epidermal fetish.*

Now if it is true that Malcolm's relationship to Sophia possessed
this hypnotic or fetishistic quality, it follows that Malcolm was
mesmerized by his repressed emotions, that he was being held captive by his infantile past. Insofar as the relationship was fetishistic,
its dynamic was a return of the repressed and its aim was possession
of his mother. Malcolm's sexual desire for the nurturing, almost-

---

* Malcolm gives us a particularly good example of this phenomenon in its pure form.
He tells of a young white woman who frequented Harlem nightclubs, and who would
go "nearly into a trance" dancing with Negroes. But she would never go beyond dancing to making love, and thus the solipsistic quality of her activity was preserved.

white woman who loved and chastised him had been repressed. In an aim-inhibited form (in the form of affection, warmth, and the desire to please) it re-emerged in his relationship to Mrs. Swerlin, who was a genuinely white and nurturing second mother to him. Now it returned to its directly sexual form in his love for Sophia, who was also white, who helped to support him, and who made him feel like a man. To a certain extent, this was a progressive emotional development, an advance from a repressed sexual attraction for his mother through an aim-inhibited love for a secondary maternal figure to a love at once sexual and aim-inhibited for Sophia. But the limiting principle in each of these relationships, and in the movement overall, was skin color; and under the aegis of this epidermal totem the movement was precisely the reverse: Malcolm's love for Sophia was reduced to his initially uncontrollable Oedipal passion.

The regressive side of the relationship has a further implication: insofar as Malcolm, in loving Sophia, was taking possession of his mother, he was exposing himself to the righteous anger of an offended paternal deity. His affair with Sophia was a guilty one, forbidden by his white Christian conscience—by the introjected primal father and all subsequent paternal authorities, internal and external. Stated another way: the epidermal fetish was to be worshipped but not possessed; God's angels were to be held inviolate. Thus his involvement with a white woman was simultaneously a violation of the incest taboo and of the superimposed sexual taboos of white racism. It follows that he could not love Sophia openly or with a clear conscience. The relationship therefore had to be hidden away in the eternal night of the hip world, in a nether region illuminated only by an amoral light.*

In sum, because Malcolm's affair with Sophia was premised upon epidermal fetishism, it was destined to intensify his moral alienation, to bind him with chains of guilt to the idols he had presumably overthrown. It was also, however, a part of his sexual education: the peculiar aspects of this relationship in particular and interracial sexual unions in general led Malcolm to work through in his own mind "the black man and white woman psychology."[26] He had a friend in New York, Sammy the Pimp, who by vocation and reputation was an expert on women. Malcolm questioned him closely on the nature of interracial sexual relations, and he also pursued the matter with several prostitutes of his acquaintance. Thus the anomalous or problematical aspect of his first love affair presented him with the occa-

---

* The moral alienation of the relationship was later to be confirmed: see below, pp. 197–198.

sion for absorbing and reformulating the sexual wisdom of the hip community.

The crucial moment in this educational process came when Sophia married another man; but thanks to Sammy, Malcolm was "entirely prepared" for the ordeal. Sammy had taught him that "white women were very practical":

> They knew that the black man had all the strikes against him, that the white man kept the black man down, under his heel, unable to get anywhere, really. The white woman wanted to be comfortable, she wanted to be looked upon with favor by her own kind, but she also wanted to have her pleasure. So some of them just married a white man for convenience and security, and kept right on going with a Negro. It wasn't that they were necessarily in love with the Negro, but they were in love with lust—particularly "taboo" lust.[27]

This proved to be the case with Sophia. She married a prosperous white man, and continued her affair with Malcolm. Thus in one sense Malcolm lost neither his love nor his sexual status; and because he kept his cool, he had in fact passed a crucial test of his hip manhood. But in another sense, he had lost, lost to the white man with whom he would now have to share her attentions. He could not fully, perhaps he did not really, possess her. The limitations on interracial sexual activity he first experienced in Lansing and Mason here re-emerged in a new and more painful form. And beneath this filtering layer of interracial images we can sense the presence of the nightmare night, feel the bitterness and anxiety of the son who is excluded by paternal right and might from his mother's marriage bed. The hip world-view helped him to deny the emotional meaning of his situation, both past and present, and in this sense it prepared him for Sophia's marriage. But more closely considered, it only helped him to understand a world he was powerless to change.

Hustling

Malcolm's education in hip living might now seem to be complete. He had learned the code of male-to-male and male-to-female conduct, and he had survived the critical practical trials of his knowledge. Yet in one important respect, his schooling was inad-

equate and his self-transformation was only half-finished: although
he had been taught that "everything in the world is a hustle," the
only hustle he actually knew, the only game he could run, was jiving
the buyers of legitimate services. The shoeshine concession had
pushed this hustle to its limit; but thereafter Malcolm had returned
to "that world of Negroes who are both servants and psychologists,
aware that white people are so obsessed with their own importance
that they will pay liberally, even dearly, for the impression of being
catered to and entertained."[28] Vocationally he was thus still a
"square," a slave to the white master. We have therefore to analyze
the process through which the hip young cat who only really lived
when he was not laboring became the hustler who lived without laboring at all. This process began with Malcolm's passage from Roxbury to Harlem.

Malcolm had wanted to visit Harlem for a long time. He remembered his father's pictures of Garvey and his legions parading through
the city; he had often seen pictures of a triumphant Joe Louis waving
to crowds from the balcony of the Theresa Hotel; and the musicians
and hustlers he admired all talked enthusiastically about the "Big
Apple." In other words, those moments in his life that were heaviest
with intimations of black manhood all gravitated around the image
of Harlem. An unexpected opportunity to see Harlem arose after the
outbreak of World War II. Like the First World War, the Second
World War strained the manpower capacities of the nation. Major industries were therefore forced to hire Negro workers; and, of course,
there were ample opportunities for young Negro men to join the
armed services—whether or not they so desired.* Consequently it
was less difficult for Negro members of the industrial reserve army
to find employment in the traditionally more stable Negro positions. Through a friend of Ella's and despite being under-age, Malcolm was able to get a job selling sandwiches on the Boston-New
York run of the New York, New Haven, and Hartford Railroad.

As he describes it, his first night in Harlem "mesmerized" him,
"narcotized" him. Most of all, he was "awed" by what he saw at the
nightspot called Small's Paradise:

> No Negro place of business had ever impressed me so
> much. Around the big, luxurious-looking circular bar were
> thirty or forty Negroes, mostly men, drinking and talking.

* Many black men did enlist in the armed forces, but the predominant attitude in the
ghetto was: "Whitey owns everything. He wants us to go and bleed for him? Let him
fight" (Malcolm X, *Autobiography*, p. 70).

> I was hit, first, by their conservative clothes and manners.
> Wherever I'd seen as many as ten Boston Negroes . . .
> drinking, there had been a big noise. But with all these
> Harlemites drinking and talking, there was just a low mur-
> mur of sound. . . . [And] every Negro I'd ever known had
> made a point of flashing whatever money he had. But these
> Harlem Negroes quietly laid a bill on the bar. . . .
> Their manners seemed natural; they were not putting on
> any airs. Within the first five minutes in Small's, I had left
> Boston and Roxbury forever.[29]

Later on, Malcolm was to discover that these were not typical Har-
lemites, that these were the "cream of the older, more mature"
numbers operators, pimps, second-story men, and the like. Be that
as it may, it is not difficult to understand why he was so impressed.
These were evidently men with real status; but unlike the members
of the Roxbury Hill community, they were not pretentious. They
were town dwellers and obviously very hip; but unlike the young
hipsters Malcolm had known, they were truly cool—mature, in control. They were, in short, a resolution of the Hill/town opposition
and, as such, living proof that a hustler could be a success in life.
Again, beneath the interpersonal structure of Malcolm's present we
can feel the force of his past: just as the Man in his various forms
was the heir to the Christian Earl Little, so these older, more mature
hustlers were the heirs-apparent to the Garveyite: they were both
themselves and the reincarnation of the self-possessed and powerful
father who loved his seventh son. Taking these two levels in their
characteristic unity, we may say that Malcolm was hypnotized by
an idealized image of his own desire to become a man of power and
prestige.

Small's Paradise was thus the high point of Malcolm's first visit to
New York, and it remained his favorite haunt for the next several
years. But during that first evening and in the days and nights to
come, he explored Harlem from top to bottom:

> I combed not only the bright-light areas, but Harlem's resi-
> dential areas from best to worst, from Sugar Hill . . . down
> to the slum blocks of old rat-trap apartment houses, just
> crawling with everything you could mention that was illegal
> and immoral.[30]

As he had initially been in Roxbury, Malcolm was fascinated by the
life of the ghetto; he was soon at home amid its daytime squalor and

its nighttime opulence, in its back alleys and on its avenues. The contradiction between these two sides of Harlem did not, however, present themselves to him as a problem. It simply seemed to be the natural order of things. Hence he paid little attention to the *Daily Worker* canvassers who tried to sell him their explanation of the situation. He was not interested in a political education, and he had no notion of trying to change the world. He was, however, very much subject to the power of black music, which by its very existence and its extraordinary beauty constitutes the aesthetic transcendence of white racist oppression. But black music, despite its sensual beauty and its in-dwelling truth—its soulful quality—provided only a temporary escape from the antinomies of Malcolm's situation. There was only one path that remained open for him: he needed truly to master the art of hustling.

Malcolm's opportunity to master hustling as a way of life arose in this manner. After a few months of selling sandwiches on the New Haven Line, he was fired for bad behavior: he had sold a lot of sandwiches, but he had also insulted a number of passengers.* He then got a job on another line, but in short order a conflict with the assistant conductor on his run ended that employment. He was about to look for another job when one of the bartenders at Small's told him there was a waiter's position open. He got the job and because he

---

* In the earlier phases of our work, we were able to follow most of the interpretive paths Malcolm's representation opened up for us. This is no longer possible. Malcolm's consciousness was developing rapidly at this time and, correspondingly, his memories of the period are rich in content: even a gloss on the text would take on encyclopaedic dimensions. Three points may, however, be briefly noted:

1. At one point when he was selling sandwiches, a white, drunken, Southern soldier tried to get him into a fight. Malcolm, smiling all the while, got him to make a fool of himself, with the result that the soldier's friends had to drag him away. Malcolm comments on the incident: "I never would forget that—that I couldn't have whipped that white man as badly with a club as I had with my mind." We would comment that the incident was also the welfare child's revenge: Malcolm was turning the tables on the Man, shaming him instead of being ashamed or beaten.

2. The above is an example of Malcolm's developing consciousness and control. On the other hand, when at some level of consciousness he wished to leave his railroad job, he allowed himself to be fired rather than deciding to quit. We have seen this unconsciously determined process of provoking authority into punitive action before—e.g., in relation to his mother and the school authorities—and we shall see it again presently.

3. Finally, we note a moment of the past revisited. Between railroad jobs Malcolm returned to Lansing to visit his family: his brothers and sisters, his mother—and Mrs. Swerlin. His siblings were impressed with their hip brother, his mother did not recognize him, and Mrs. Swerlin was as uncomfortable with Malcolm as he was with her.

was a courteous, bright, and thoroughly likable young man, soon not only the bartenders but even some of the customers began to school him. One man, a member of the Forty Thieves Gang, noticing that Malcolm dressed too flamboyantly, supplied him with a (stolen) suit cut in the more conservative manner of a real hustler; "in a paternal way," he was helping to "straighten Red out."[31] Other hustlers stressed the importance of "knowing the law people in the area" and of having the right kinds of contacts, both legal and extralegal, for various situations. Occasionally someone, "in a rare burst of confidence, or a little beyond his usual number of drinks," might describe "inside things about the particular form of hustling he pursued as a way of life."[32] Thus Malcolm "was schooled . . . by experts in such hustles as the numbers, pimping, con games of many kinds, peddling dope and thievery of all sorts, including armed robbery."[33] Most importantly, he was learning "the hustling society's first rule: that you never trusted anyone outside your own close-mouthed circle, and that you selected with time and care before you made intimates even among these."[34] Yet he was also impressed by the spontaneous generosity and understated sense of fellowship that often characterized relations in these circles; and when he came to know a number of prostitutes who lived in his apartment building, he was equally impressed by the "code of ethics and sisterliness" governing their conduct among themselves.

There is, of course, no contradiction between the "first rule" and this de facto civility—so long as the latter is strictly limited by the former, so long as (for example) an honest or generous action does not leave you dependent upon the honesty or generosity of another. But one day in early 1943 Malcolm acted from a sympathetic impulse and ignored the rule. He gave the number of one of his friends among the prostitutes to a Negro soldier sitting, in studied melancholy, at one of his tables. He "knew better," for not only was he trusting the serviceman to be in fact what he appeared to be on the surface, but he was also violating the Small's Paradise "law" prohibiting the hustling of servicemen. Moreover, something "felt wrong" in the situation itself. He was not really surprised when a short while later the police came looking for him: the "soldier" had been a "military spy." Malcolm was taken down to a local precinct station, given a warning, and released. Now, however, the police would be keeping an eye on him; and the owners of Small's, desiring no extra attention from that direction, therefore fired him.

Instead of looking for another "slave," Malcolm decided to find himself some kind of hustle. In consultation with Sammy the Pimp, he chose to sell marijuana:

> Peddling reefers . . . was the best thing. It was a relatively uninvolved lone-wolf type of operation, and one in which I could make money immediately. For anyone with even a little brains, no experience was needed, especially if one had any knack at all with people.[35]

Further, peddling required little in the way of capital; Malcolm had appropriate contacts for getting a supply of the commodity; and because he was on good terms with a large number of musicians and other hustlers, he had a good market available to him. So he borrowed some money from Sammy, bought a small amount of marijuana, and went looking for customers. By the end of the day he was able to repay the loan and "have enough profit to be in business." Then, he reports, over the next few weeks: "I kept turning over my profit, increasing my supply, and I sold reefers like a wild man. I scarcely slept. . . . A roll of money was in my pocket. . . . I felt, for the first time in my life, that great feeling of *free!*"[36] The bonds of slavery had been broken and, at the same time, his apprenticeship had come to an end: "Suddenly, now, I was the peer of the other young hustlers I had admired."[37]

Malcolm had become a hustler, become the kind of man he had been preparing himself to be. But why did his schooling end in this half-voluntary manner? Given his admiration for hustlers, his desire to be one, and the completion of his schooling, he should have *chosen* to liberate himself from servitude and thus enter the society of "free" men. This would have been the logical conclusion to a phase of progressively developing self-consciousness. Instead, he had to be expelled from Paradise.

The answer suggests itself readily enough if we remember that up to this time Malcolm had been a fairly law-abiding citizen. Moreover, although he had been attracted to hustling from the outset, he had never consciously *planned* to become a hustler. The good, white Christian voice of conscience told him to stay within the limits of the law; but as the self-formed seventh son of a tough Garveyite father, he found these limits to be limitations, and wished to go beyond them. Thus Malcolm was once again caught in the dilemma of the morally divided self, torn by antithetical compulsions to obey and disobey the heirs to parental authority—the benevolent owners of Small's and the malevolent agents of the American legal system.

And because the conflict was predominantly unconscious, an internal war between repressed sexual-aggressive forces and repressive moral counterforces, it could not be truly resolved. Instead, it dissolved into a compromise formation, an unconscious sense of guilt that manifested itself as an impulsion toward criminal activity.

As criminality from a sense of guilt, this compromise had a double object. Because Malcolm was morally identified with his oppressor, he felt guilty for the Oedipal crimes he only wished to commit and the adult crimes he had not yet committed; consequently, the actual commission of crimes confirmed his prejudgment of himself and, in the act of punishment, met the demands of his conscience, fulfilled his need for punishment. But punishment was also a reward: just as being chastised by his mother simultaneously meant being loved by her, so being expelled from Small's Paradise simultaneously meant being freed from servitude and freed for a life of crime. Again, actual criminal activity could only reconfirm the original judgment, setting the process in motion all over again.

Thus we come again upon the familiar circle of self-destructive aggressivity. However, if this regressive impulsion, which we now understand as criminality from a sense of guilt, entailed that Malcolm could not choose to leave Small's, at this juncture there was also a strong countervailing progressive tendency at work which permitted him to actualize in the conscious activity of hustling the lessons he had been learning.

What, then, was the substance of those lessons? What manner of man is a hustler? What kind of world does he inhabit? [38] The immediate unity of self and situation, the definitional limit of the hustling society, is of course that "Everything in the world is a hustle." Men exist only competitively, in a struggle for survival, and therefore every interpersonal transaction is a matter of relative advantage, of who is getting the better of whom. As Malcolm put it retrospectively in describing his own actions: "When you become an animal, a vulture, in the ghetto, as I became, you enter a world of animals and vultures. It becomes truly the survival of only the fittest." [39] Thus the ultimate edge in hustling is the willingness and ability to use violent means to gain your ends, to kill or be killed. At the periphery, the hustler becomes a warrior. Short of this extremity, advantage is secured by outwitting another person. You are always hustling, being hustled, or both—hustling but being outhustled. This implies that people and things are rarely, if ever, what they appear to be—the price of a commodity will not reflect its true value; a man's "front" will conceal his underlying character—for if there were no difference between appearance and reality, then there would be no possibility of deception. Indeed, the most successful hustler is the one who magnifies this difference to the greatest possible extent.

Hustling thus emerges as the pursuit of competitive advantage in a kill-or-be-killed world. This latter quality is accentuated by the fact that the true hustler is an outlaw, a criminal. He supplies an illegal product or service, and/or obtains his commodity illegally. He does so because "only squares [keep] on believing they can get anything by slaving."[40] That is, squares are limited to the possibilities for gain the law allows, and hence to menial jobs performed at the command of another man, usually the Man. The hustler by contrast knows that the end—freedom in the form of a big bankroll and real status—justifies any means. He therefore lives outside the law, where profit and status increase proportionately with deception and risk. By breaking the bonds of conventional moral/legal constraint, he frees himself from the slavery of ordinary ghetto life.

The hustler's freedom is purchased at a price: it follows from the premise that "Everything is a hustle" that the hustler must be constantly watchful, suspicious, and distrustful. Nothing can be taken for granted; there is no security in this world. He is in constant danger from the hustlers with whom he competes and the authorities who seek to end his illegal career. Thus the major operative principle, "hustling society's first rule," is that "You never trusted anyone outside your own close-mouthed circle," and even those within the circle could not fully be trusted. Yet because the hustler cannot live in total isolation, but is forced into contact with others simply to ply his trade, even living by this principle will not safeguard him indefinitely: "It's a law of the rackets that every criminal expects to get caught," that he only "tries to stave off the inevitable for as long as he can"; and, at least so Malcolm believed, that "After living as fully as humanly possible, one should then die violently."[41] Death can come to the individual either from the state or from other individuals:

> Full-time hustlers never can relax to appraise what they are doing or where they are bound. As in the case of any jungle, the hustler's every waking hour is lived with both the practical and subconscious knowledge that if he ever relaxes, if

he ever slows down, the other hungry, restless foxes, ferrets, wolves, and vultures out there with him won't hesitate to make him their prey.[42]

In sum, if ever there was a society approaching Hobbes's state of nature as a state of war, in which "every man is Enemy to every man," in which there is "continuall feare, and danger of violent death; And the life of man, solitary, poore, nasty, brutish, and short,"[43] the hustling society is that society.*

At this juncture we have derived from Malcolm's representation and retrospective interpretation of the hustler and his world an image of the daring criminal, a Mack-the-Knife or Stagolee, against a background of social anarchy. To take the two sides in their concrete unity, the situation reflected into the individual produces a man who is "internally restrained by nothing. He has no religion, no concept of morality, no fear—nothing. . . . [And he] is forever frustrated, restless and anxious for some 'action.' Whatever he undertakes, he commits himself to it fully, absolutely."[44] For these reasons he is "actually the most dangerous black man in America"—most dangerous to the "white power structure." He is a *lumpen-proletarian*, a bad-man who is not bound by white-bourgeois moral standards. Yet the hustler does not in fact live entirely beyond good and evil. He lives by what Malcolm himself calls the "hustling code," in which good is bad and bad is good; for to be good by official standards is to be a "square," to be subservient to the Man and thus to be less than a man. Conversely, one lexicon of Afro-American slang defines a "bad nigger" as "a black person who refuses to be meek or who rejects the social terms of poverty or oppression the culture designs for him."[45] The socially conditioned contradiction of rectitude and law vs. self-respect, which was early reflected into Malcolm's character, here re-emerges as the moral consciousness of the hustler, the hustler's conception of the world which has formed him and against which he must form himself. Thus the apparent distinction between the hustling society and society in general begins to dissolve: the moral antinomy reveals an underlying unity of class-racial opposites.

Whatever its ultimate relationship to the larger society, the hustling society is defined against the more general system. Hence its members have a common interest, reflected internally in the pre-

---

* The Hobbesian commonwealth was, of course, designed to end this anarchy. But we shall see below that the anarchy of the state of nature—the hustling society—is a reflection of the commonwealth itself.

cept that no hustler shall ever betray another hustler to any legal authority. This in turn produces the maxim that the hustler must be loyal to his few friends and, finally, that he must be loyal to himself—that, ultimately, he must guide his conduct by self-interest. But this is to say that self-interest will in the end take precedence over the interests of the group, and the interests of the group over the interests of society. Loyalty, the ethical ground of the hustling code, its affirmation of social solidarity, is a moral principle that cannot in practice be universalized, that cannot constitute an internally consistent code of ethical conduct. It follows that the operative moral-ethical principle of the hustling code, namely, honor or "face," will reflect this limiting contradiction:

> For a hustler in our sidewalk jungle world, "face" and "honor" were important. No hustler could have it known that he'd been "hyped," meaning outsmarted or made a fool of. And worse, a hustler could never afford to have it demonstrated that he could be bluffed, that he could be frightened by a threat, that he lacked nerve.[46]

Honor is the moral incarnation of prestige, and the interpersonal dimension of what is intrapersonally a feeling of pride, a sense of self-respect; hence its critical position in the code. But if on the one hand a hustler should not attempt to hype and thereby dishonor a friend —if in this sense his loyalty should be his honor—on the other he can never be absolutely sure that anyone is his friend. In fact, given the hustling society's hierarchical status-structure, any other individual must necessarily be ranked above or below him. Because true friendship can only develop from a ground of equality, it is here precluded *a priori*.

In sum, we can say that the contradiction between morality and ethics in the code reflects the antagonism between the individual and every other individual in the hustling society. Yet that society, like the code, is not without a certain internal order. First, as we have seen, there are well-understood requirements for admission and semi-regularized procedures for training new or prospective members. The membership, in turn, is organized into a kind of economy, with a functionally monopolistic sector overshadowing a more competitive one. The former is what Malcolm terms the "numbers industry," the latter the more individualistic enterprises of pimping and prostitution (the Game), banditry of various sorts, and narcotics distribution at the local level. The economy in its turn is the basis for a particular way of life, an informal but functionally efficient communications system (the "wire"), a degree of political organization, and an ideology (i.e., the hustling code).

Although the hustling society is a definite social entity, it is not an autonomous one. It is, indeed, parasitic: it absorbs surplus value produced in the capitalist economy proper rather than itself producing surplus value. In Malcolm's view, however, the parasite is welcomed by its host: "In the country's entire social, political and economic structure, the criminal, the law and the politicians [are] actually inseparable partners."[47] Thus we return to the existential premise of the hustling code and to our earlier surmise that the war of all against all is not confined to the ghetto sidewalk jungle.

State of War

Although the idea that everything is a hustle can be formulated in the abstract, one can only hustle in an actually existing historical situation. Indeed, Malcolm's schooling included lessons in the history of Harlem: "Sometimes I'd have long talks—absorbing everything—with the real old-timers, who had been around Harlem since Negroes first came there. . . . That, in fact, was one of my biggest surprises: that Harlem hadn't always been a community of Negroes."[48] He learned that successive waves of immigrants had pushed each other out of Harlem, until finally the Negroes pushed out their white predecessors; that Negroes had been ghettoed in New York in several different locations before they reached Harlem; and that the music and entertainment industry that developed in Harlem during the 1920s (during the Harlem Renaissance) had attracted "white people from all over the world," so that soon "Blacktown crawled with white people, with pimps, prostitutes, bootleggers, with hustlers of all kinds, with colorful characters, and with police and prohibition agents."[49] Then, "when it all ended with the stock market crash of 1929, Harlem had a world reputation as America's Casbah,"[50] a reputation that was still strong enough during World War II to warrant the assignment of a military morals squad to the area—i.e., "military spies" like the one Malcolm had attempted to hustle.

The history of Harlem as Malcolm learned it was the history of a ghetto in the making. As such, it exemplifies the more general phenomenon of *ghettoization*, just as Malcolm's migration from Mason to Boston and then to Harlem exemplifies the continuing migration of black people into the Northern cities.[51] The Great Migration set in motion during World War I may in fact be understood as the demographic basis of ghettoization. It had slowed somewhat during the Depression, but it had not been stopped. And as was the case during World War I, a push-pull dynamic had been involved, although of a somewhat different variety. During the war, the pull of Northern industry had been complemented by the push of Southern agricultural depression. In the 1930s, the welfare system replaced the job market as the decisive determinant of the migratory process. There was no work to be had, either South or North; but the South was harshly discriminatory in its administration of relief. Consequently many black people, deciding that welfare slavery was better than death by starvation, moved North.

After the beginning of the Second World War, the migratory flow again increased: 1.5 million black people left the South between 1940 and 1950, and the black population of Harlem grew from 458,444 to 749,680.[52] The economic stimulant was once again the greater employment possibilities in the urban North. At least, this was the case after 1943; in 1940, 13.9 percent of the labor force was still unemployed, and white workers were rehired long before black ones when industry revived in response to wartime production demand. As labor shortages began to develop, however, employment of black people increased rapidly. A substantial number of workers found skilled or semi-skilled positions, and the number of blacks employed in the public sector rose dramatically. The great majority of the black urban population, however, remained in unskilled labor, service, and domestic-service positions, and only a minute number were able to secure entry into professional, managerial, and proprietary positions.

Thus within the black work-force the lines of class division began to crystallize into a new pattern. A black middle class, consisting not only of the black bourgeoisie and petite bourgeoisie but also of the now substantial black proletariat, became clearly differentiated from the "rabble of paupers" who formed the black industrial reserve army, filled the relief rolls, or slipped into the lumpen-proletariat. The former also differentiated itself residentially from the latter (e.g., the Hill versus the town in Roxbury); and the latter was again divided between the relatively respectable areas and the back-alley homes of the most wretched of the wretched. Needless to say, the locus of political power within the community was on the Hill, but the community as a whole—be it Harlem, Roxbury, or the

South Side in Chicago—was powerless in relation to, and sharply separated from, the surrounding white domains. This condition of segregation intensified as white people fought a rearguard action against any augmentation of black political power, any expansion of black territory, and any black invasion of the white side of the urban economy.

In sum, the black population was more and more becoming a class-divided nation within a nation, a ghettoized population closely resembling the "native" populations of colonized Africa. This comparison is not incidental: it reflects the racist logic that underlies both forms of oppression. Thus the relevance of Fanon's colonial geography to the American situation:

> The colonial world is a world divided into compartments
> . . . [but] the zone where the native lives is not complementary to the zone inhabited by the settlers. The two zones are opposed, but not in the service of a higher unity. Obedient to the rules of pure Aristotelian logic, they both follow the principle of reciprocal exclusivity.[53]

For "native" read "Negro" and for "settler" read "white man," and the similarity between the two colonial relationships becomes evident. Furthermore, in each instance the two zones are simultaneously separated from and joined to each other through the instrumentalities of white bourgeois power.

In America, the welfare system and the legal system (the police, the courts, and the prisons) force the ghettoized population into a posture of resentful submission to white authority. But that resentment, the suppressed and repressed aggressive energy of the colonized man, is an explosive potential. In time it will bring crashing down the psychic structure of colonial domination, the character structure and racial identity of both lordship and bondage. At first, however, "the colonised man will . . . manifest this aggressiveness which has been deposited in his bones against his own people. This is the period when the niggers beat each other up, and the police and magistrates do not know which way to turn when faced with the astonishing waves of crime in North Africa."[54] In North America, this is the period when the individual's self-destructive aggressivity is particularized into a society of hustlers who prey parasitically upon their brothers and sisters and who view each other as actual or potential enemies. There develops a *paranoid* community: each individual sees his own aggressive intentions in his neighbor's eyes, and consequently finds it necessary to live by the hustling society's first rule. *Homo homini lupus.*

We now understand the hustling society's war of all against all as a paranoid reflection of racist domination, be it the "internal colonialism" of North America or the external colonialism of the European in North Africa.[55] But this war is also, is indeed primarily, the opposition of oppressor and oppressed. The dominating-dominated group relationship, which earlier appeared in the form of a dumb show of complementary racial stereotypes, here emerges as intergroup paranoia, a relationship of mutual suspicion magnified by the reflective movement of projected aggressive energy. In this way the toleration of Locke's civil society becomes at its limit the hostility of Hobbes's state of nature; the commodity-character of the bourgeois or proletarian individual dissolves into the paranoia of the hustler. In so saying we are not trying to collapse the relationship between these psycho-social forms into an identity. The self-interested individual in a bourgeois political economy is not necessarily paranoid: to the extent that self-interest and the interests of others are not mutually exclusive, he can cast a tolerant if invidious eye upon his neighbor. Thus Locke argues that "Every one as he is *bound to preserve himself*, and not to quit his Station wilfully; so by the like reason when his own Preservation comes not in competition, ought he, as much as he can, to preserve the rest of Mankind."[56] But this "natural" condition of mankind always has the potential of degenerating into a state of war. "And one may destroy a Man who makes War upon him, or has discovered an Enmity to his being, for the same reason, that he may kill a *Wolf* or a *Lyon;* because such Men are not under ties of the Common Law of Reason, have no other Rule, but that of Force and Violence, and so may be treated as Beasts of Prey."[57] More: once money and the accumulation of wealth are introduced into Locke's state of nature, the latter is virtually transformed into a state of war, a war between "degenerate Men" who are "no strict Observers of Equity and Justice" (who covet their neighbor's property), and those who have legitimately accumulated wealth.[58] The establishment of civil society and government is the apparent remedy for this dangerous state of affairs. But in fact, civil society legitimates and limits without eliminating the state of war. It is founded to preserve private property and accumulated wealth, which are, after all, the principal causes of war. Relapse into war is therefore as much a law of civil society as is the compact that initially creates the society itself. Hence when we come to examine the economic "anatomy of this civil society"—the objective conditions of which the "state of nature" is an ideological reflection—we discover an on-going war of all against all. The individual interests of the sellers of commodities become mutually exclusive whenever the supply of the commodity exceeds the demand for it; when there are systemic imbalances of this kind, industrial peace devolves into industrial war. In like fashion, the industrial reserve army signifies the intra-class warfare which is always latent in the proletarian condition, while the *lumpen-proletariat* makes manifest in its everyday life the mutual exclusivity of interests that underlie bourgeois civility. Thus in the hustling society the narcissistic, obsessive-compulsive, or hysterical trends which typically develop within the commodity-character structure of the bourgeois individual are replaced by paranoid suspicion and hostility. In this sense the paranoid mentality is the limiting form and recurrent potentiality of bourgeois psychology.

The paranoid mentality of the hustling society, when viewed from the perspective of the class and racial interests of black people, is clearly a regressive tendency. Yet concealed within this regressive way of life is a potential for progressive development. This is because the paranoid posture of the oppressed man is the undistorted mirroring of the paranoia of his oppressor. It may be only the immediate, unself-conscious reflection of that malign power—in which case it is subject to all the limitations of spontaneity—but it may also be the mediated reflection of the oppressor's paranoia, a position reached after the individual has played out his predetermined role in the paternalist pantomime. In this case it is already implicitly the affirmation of a new character-structure and a new collective identity; but it can become explicitly what it is implicitly only through organizational explication, i.e., through embodiment in consciously organized collective activity.

Needless to say, the hustling society is not such an organization. There was, however, a progressive racial movement organized during the war years. A. Philip Randolph's March on Washington Movement (the MOWM) was a direct response to discrimination against Negroes in the defense industries and in the armed services. Its slogan was "We loyal Negro-American citizens demand the right to work and fight for our country."[59] Beneath this surface of loyal leadership and Negro-American demands there was a new spirit stirring. Or, better, an old spirit was reviving:

Before MOWM the civil rights movement had been integrated; it was essentially an extension of the New Deal,
with no mass base among poor blacks. But Garvey had
stirred the Negro masses, they had been made militant, and
MOWM was able to build on that foundation.[60]

The memories of the last war had not died, the bitterness of the
"Red Summer" was still alive, and consequently the vision of proud
UNIA legions marching through the streets of Harlem was easily reincarnated in the prospect of a March on Washington. But the March
thus conceived was a very different affair from the one imagined by
its leaders, for its mass character was decidedly unpatriotic. "So far
as the colored peoples of the earth are concerned," commented one
black writer, "it is a toss-up between the 'democracies' and the dic-
tatorships. . . . What is there to choose between the rule of the British in India and the rule of the Germans in Austria?"[61] Or as a Negro
truckdriver in Philadelphia told a brother in uniform, "This is a
white man's government and war and it's no damned good"—for
which comment he was held on charges of treason.[62] Then there was
the man who, after Pearl Harbor, "declared that he was going to get
his eyes slanted so that the next time a white man shoved him
around he could fight back."[63] As this last comment implies, a substantial number of black people were pro-Japanese as well as anti-
American:

In 1942 and 1943 the federal government did arrest the
members of several pro-Japanese cults in Chicago, New
York, Newark, New Jersey and East St. Louis, Illinois. Although the numbers involved were small, the evidence indicated that Japanese agents had been at work among these
groups and had capitalized on Negro grievances.[64]

Among those arrested were Elijah Muhammad and over one hundred of his followers. The formal charge was draft resistance, but the
substantive one was un-Americanism.* (The members of the Nation are not allowed to bear arms except in a holy war; hence government prosecution was in truth racial and religious persecution.)
Taking this misuse of judicial power in combination with the internment of Japanese-Americans and such ugly incidents as the
"zoot-suit" riots in Los Angeles, it is hardly surprising that this
writer concluded, "Our war is not against Hitler in Europe, but
against the Hitlers in America."[65]

* An additional charge of sedition was dropped after Muhammad's arrest.

The MOWM was thus a unity of antithetical forces. To the extent that it embodied the patriotic spirit of its leaders, it was a movement within the tightening circle of the good Negro stereotype and a retreat from the more advanced position of Garveyite pan-Africanism. But its leaders recognized, as Garvey had not, that genuine progress involved confrontation with the political-economic elite of American society: in Randolph's words, "Only power can effect the enforcement and adoption of a given policy." [66] Power, he went on to note, "is the active principle of only the organized masses, the masses united for a definite purpose." [67] But the masses he was uniting did not necessarily share his purpose. Many of them were not patriots but, rather, as Malcolm commented, were more than willing to let Whitey fight his own war. Yet this progressive mass tendency, so reminiscent of Garveyism, was offset by the merely spontaneous character of the mass reaction. The consequence of this internal alienation—an alienation that could not be overcome so long as the leadership had not freed itself from loyal Negro-Americanism—was the partial cooptation of the Movement. When confronted with FDR's plea for national unity and his agreement to issue an executive order establishing a President's Committee on Fair Employment Practices, Randolph opted to compromise his own purposes and call off the March.

Although by compromising its principles and accepting a relatively token victory, the MOWM served the interests of the white ruling class, there was a double sense in which it did advance the cause of black liberation. First, as our analysis implies and as other writers have observed, the MOWM was the organizational ground from which the civil rights movement was later to develop. It established the validity of the premise that the United States government could be forced to negotiate with Negro leaders when those leaders had the power of the masses behind them.* Second, the MOWM can be extended in space as well as in time. Because the United States was fighting a war against fascism, and *ipso facto* against racism, it was vulnerable to the charge of tolerating "Hitlers in America"

* Two points may be added:

1. The premise was of course borrowed from Gandhi's *Satyagraha* campaigns in South Africa and India, and thereby testifies to the internationalization of the struggle against colonial domination that was occurring at this time. It also suggests the fragility of the MOWM, for there is no easy way to combine Gandhiism and Garveyism in a coherent *praxis*.

2. The MOWM was the contradicted unity of the two forces that would subsequently split and organize themselves against each other as the civil rights and Black Nationalist poles of the Movement before reunifying in and as the Black Revolution.

while fighting them abroad. Hence "a decent Respect to the Opinions of Mankind" necessitated granting at least some recognition to the rights of Negro citizens. And because the government needed Negro manpower for the military-industrial effort even more than it required Negro loyalty for the propagandistic one, it was forced to honor some of its democratic promises. Thus while the MOWM itself accomplished relatively little, the more general movement of which it was a part did wrest a certain amount of political-economic power from the white man's hands.

We have seen that the ghettoization of black people between the wars and during World War II intensified the development of both regressive, self-destructive forces (crystallized in the hustling society) and relatively progressive, self-productive forces (mobilized in the MOWM). Together they contributed to the stabilization of the existing capitalist system; but from a ruling-class perspective, that stabilization was purchased at a price. It had required the cooptation of a substantial percentage of the black population, i.e., the partial recognition of the rights of a black middle class which was at that time in the process of formation. The question then arises: how did the American system develop the capacity for improving the condition of one sector of the black working class without simultaneously undermining the relative advantage of the white ruling class? Evidently cooptation in this sense requires a rapid rate of economic development, for the so-called real standard of living of some part of the working class can be improved without simultaneously lowering the real or relative standard of the ownership class if and only if the nation's wealth is growing. And this obviously requires the accumulation and reproduction of the aggregate social capital on an extended scale, i.e., an increasing capacity to produce *and realize* surplus value. When we last considered the state of the nation, however, it was not clear that such growth was possible. During the Depression the capacity to produce and the capacity to realize surplus value had become antithetical moments of the economic process. The welfare state, an attempt to overcome that contradiction, only managed to reify it. Yet by 1943 there was virtually full employment, even for black people, and productive capacity was being expanded at an almost alarming rate. What had happened?

The answer is all too obvious: what the welfare state had been powerless to achieve, the warfare state accomplished with ease. Because military production provides employment and, therefore, increased demand for consumer goods, without at the same time throwing more consumer goods into the marketplace, it helps to offset the predominant tendency of capitalist production toward overproduction. Because it requires massive amounts of heavy industrial equipment, plant facilities, etc., it also creates a strong demand for capital goods. And in both aspects it provides additional outlets for capital investment. Prosperity returned on the wings of war, and black workers were among the beneficiaries. Then, when the hot war came to an end, the Cold War began. The United States became the principal defender of the free world against communism, with armed forces stationed around the globe and a policy of supplying armaments to any nation willing to help contain the Enemy. Military spending therefore continued to play its vital role in the economy. Moreover, World War II absorbed so much value that by the time the fighting ended there was a large, pent-up demand for consumer goods. As Baran and Sweezy argue:

> During the war, consumers paid off debts and accumulated
> vast amounts of liquid savings. When they were again free
> to spend and borrow, they could and did turn their "need"
> for automobiles and houses in the suburbs into effective de-
> mand. And once the wave got fairly started, it built up its
> own momentum. We have here a classic case of quantity
> turning into quality.[68]

Thus World War II, like World War I, provided a ground for subsequent economic growth and, by the same token, the possibility of coopting a substantial sector of the working class.

Now it might appear from the preceding argument that history—in the sense of change through class struggle—had come to an end. Through the calculated use of military spending, the United States had become a middle-class nation, in which class conflict is as unthinkable as in a classless society. But at best, the interest which unifies the warfare state is the common enemy: Hitlerism was the total negation of human interest, and hence there was a genuine human interest in negating that negation. But it was overwhelmingly the proletariat who paid the price of war, and this in a double sense. First, the labor alienated from the worker in the process of military-industrial production was appropriated by the capitalist; in this respect the war effort was just business as usual. Second, the worker's labor-power, when materialized into guns and bombs, returned to him in the form of death; and his death was the revitalization of his capitalist oppressor. Thus wartime production was not just the alienation of labor, but was the ultimate perversion of the labor-process. Finally, although the category of middle-income Americans relative to lower- and higher-income recipients was enlarged during the war, the class structure of the society was not transformed. Ownership of the means of production—hence political-economic power and, consequently, a grossly disproportionate share of the national income—remained in the hands of the bourgeoisie, so that the members of the proletariat were forced to compete against each other for the remainder. In this competition black people continued to be at a severe disadvantage. As a result, the median income for black people at its best (during the Korean War period) was only 55 percent of the median white income. This represented a substantial improvement over the 37 percent of 1939, but it certainly does not represent a racially unbiased distribution of income.[69]

In sum, during World War II the American welfare state was transformed into a warfare state which parades itself as the transcendence of all class conflict but which is in fact the ultimate alienation of the sensuous energies of the proletariat. Construction for purposes of destruction, love of country that results in the death of individuals—these forces constitute the substantive premise of warfare capitalism. The mediation of this premise is, objectively, middle-class cooptation combined with lower-class pauperization. Subjectively, it comes forth as the loyal or patriotic American's identification with the oppressor, and the resentful American's paranoid attitude. But just as the hustling society has latent within it the potential for progressive political movement, so the warfare state had its contradictory aspect. During and in the aftermath of World War II the process of decolonization was markedly accelerated. Decolonization, especially in Africa, in time came home to the American situation: it became increasingly possible for black people to think and act in terms of an international anti-imperialist struggle. The emancipatory potential of World War II was neither its immediate reality nor its intended result. But war and the warfare state have the unintended consequence of tending to destroy what they were meant to preserve by creating the very political possibilities they were meant to preclude.

In sum: when we begin with Malcolm's point of entry into the hustling society, we come first to the paranoid mentality engendered by the ghettoization process and then to the warfare state which conditioned that process at this particular time. If we state the relationship both more generally and in its logical (rather than phenomenological) order, we can posit that the state of war always latent in bourgeois life, when mediated through ghettoization, produces the paranoid mentality of the hustling society. At the same time, this regressive movement has progressive implications: the hustler's paranoid consciousness is a potential for spontaneous rebellion; ghettoization tends to produce its opposite (e.g., the MOWM); and open warfare weakens, at least temporarily, the international structure of the capitalist system.

The Hustling Society

Having specified the historical situation of the hustling society, our next step is to analyze its internal structure and its functional relationship to the larger society. Only thus can we test the validity of Malcolm's argument that "in the country's entire social, political and economic structure, the criminal, the law and the politicians are actually inseparable partners." There are, in fact, two obvious reasons for being skeptical of this contention. First, Malcolm was never more than a street hustler and a small-time burglar; he may have had an exaggerated conception of the magnitude of the criminal-power structure. Second, a man who called America "one of the most criminal societies that has ever existed on earth since time began" may be suspected of hyperbole. We shall therefore have to determine whether the hustling society is in fact an integral part or merely an incidental by-product of the larger system.

The most visible part of the criminal world is of course the three-penny opera of street life, the "sidewalk jungle" of beggars, pickpockets, petty thieves, drug peddlers, prostitutes (streetwalkers), panders (john-walkers), and numbers runners. The inhabitants of this realm are the *lumpen-proletariat* in the strict sense of the term. These people do work, in their own way, and they are the ones most subject to police power and judicial punishment. In these respects they are similar to the actual proletariat. But unlike the proletariat, their time is not controlled by the mechanism of production and they produce no surplus value. In this regard they are therefore outside of or free from the discipline (enslavement) of the capitalist economy. Thus they form the shadow or illusory working-class of which Malcolm was a member and which he describes in such rich detail. Here, therefore, we have a record of personal experience, one confirmed by numerous other accounts. For example, a *Fortune Magazine* article in 1939 described Harlem's visible underworld:

> There are reefer pads (marijuana dens), gambling houses, and countless houses of prostitution. Most 'hotels' are brothels, and it is a usual sight to see a dozen street-walkers on every corner in lower Harlem. . . .
> Almost every grocery, cigar store, beauty parlor, barbershop and tavern in Harlem is a numbers 'drop' . . . [and] Harlem . . . has . . . the city's highest record of . . . dope peddling.[70]

In part, these services are utilized by a local clientele. This is especially true of the numbers game. Primarily, however, they cater to white clients:

> Much of the vice seen in the Negro community is there, not for Negroes, but for whites; it is carried on in the Negro sections because they are disorganized, without adequate police protection, but with police and politicians looking for graft. . . . Elaborate and expensive brothels cater to whites (who have the money to pay for these pleasures) and are largely owned by whites. [But] the ordinary Negro street-walker is [in] an unprotected, economically disadvantaged and overcrowded occupation.[71]

There thus emerges a picture of vice in black-and-white. At the street level, the gambling customers—those hoping to hit a big number and escape from alienated labor—are black, and the "johns"—those hoping to be sexually stimulated and to escape from emotional alienation—are white. The sellers, by contrast, are uniformly black, and uniformly victims of the system.

The first level, however, implies a second: there are white owners of black brothels, as well as "black players"—the society of pimps who are not panders but who manage a variable number of prostitutes;[72] there are the dope dealers, con men, grand thieves, and fences, who are one step up from the street hustlers; and there are "controllers," who supervise the numbers runners. In short, this is the realm of the shadow petite bourgeoisie and the *lumpen* version of the white-collar working class. Like its analogue in the straight world, it is not entirely closed to upwardly mobile black workers; but whether black or white, it is visible to the *lumpen-proletariat*, for its members are the latter's immediate superiors. Thus Malcolm, after his marijuana peddling brought him uncomfortably close to arrest and a career as a stick-up man proved relatively unsuccessful, became first a runner for a numbers operation and then a "steerer" * for a Harlem madam specializing in exotic sex. Here again Malcolm's representations are firsthand reports, and they are consonant with what is generally known about such enterprises.[73]

The distinction noted above, between the petit-bourgeois and white-collar sides of the middle class, is a reflection of the two sectors of the shadow economy which emerge on this level. On the former side are competitive enterprises like prostitution, which lend themselves to small-scale operation, and require virtually no capital, and provide easy access to new competitors. Consequently, the fortunes of such "firms" remain subject to the laws of supply and demand, and therefore yield on the average a low rate of profit. At the other extreme are the monopolistic or oligopolistic enterprises, of which the numbers game in particular and gambling in general are the archetypal forms. Any gambling operation is based upon making a small amount of profit on each of a large number of transactions (bets), which requires a large and rationally organized administrative staff. It must also be able to pay its winning customers, including the occasional big winner whose good fortune quickens the interest of other players. Accordingly, a new gambling firm requires substantial initial capitalization, which serves to restrict entry to the market area. The result of these economic factors, when combined with a liberal use of raw force, is a sphere of business enterprise dominated by a few firms (or an actual cartel) and yielding a rate of profit that would be the envy of any legitimate monopoly. In 1939, for example, the Harlem numbers racket, "run by Negroes who have a working agreement with the white [numbers] bankers of Manhattan and Hoboken," grossed about $20,000,000.[74] And at that time the Chicago game grossed $10,000,000 annually, gave employment to more than 4,000 people, and paid weekly wages and commissions of $40,000.[75] These figures do not, of course, tell us the rate of return; but if the estimates of President Johnson's Task Force on Organized Crime are both accurate and applicable, about one-third of overall revenue was profit. * Finally, the lion's share of net income is taken by the "policy kings" and "bankers," the bourgeoisie of the shadow economy; and this class is almost exclusively white.

In sum, Malcolm was quite correct in portraying crime as a major

---

* Someone who guides clients from a designated rendezvous spot to the location of the desired sexual activity.

* "There is no accurate way of ascertaining organized crime's gross revenue from gambling in the United States. Estimates of the annual intake have varied from $7 to

form of economic activity, even without taking into consideration the invasion of the legitimate economy by capital accumulated in criminal enterprise. He was similarly correct in representing its political influence. Drake and Cayton note, for instance, that the main function of the Chicago policy syndicate was "to make the necessary political alignments so that neither the police, a crusading state's attorney, nor pressure from reform groups can jeopardize the smooth running of the business."[76] And the New York investigation into the activity of "Dutch" Schultz—one of whose former secretaries was Malcolm's boss when he was a runner—"revealed a close tie between his activities and those of the Tammany political machine."[77]* Thus it is fair to conclude with Malcolm that the legitimate political economy and its illegitimate shadow are "actually inseparable partners."

Restating our conclusion, we can say that the bourgeois ruling class of the shadow economy and its legitimate equivalent are often "partners in crime." But the legitimate bourgeoisie has criminal credentials in its own right. Indeed, Edwin Sutherland argued that what he termed "white collar criminals" are "by far the most dangerous to society of any type of criminals from the point of view of effects on private property and social institutions."[78] Their crimes include "most big fraud; restraint of trade, misrepresentation in advertising and in the sale of securities; infringements of patents, trademarks and copyrights; industrial espionage; illegal labor practices; violations of war regulations; violation of trust; secret rebates and kickbacks; commercial and political bribery . . . etc., etc."[79] The "plain unvarnished facts" thus seem to show that the United States "is a very criminal society, led in its criminality by its upper socioeconomic classes."[80]

It can be argued that the typical modern business enterprise is criminal in an even more fundamental sense. We observed earlier that the shadow economy was divided into monopolistic and competitive sectors and that enterprises in the former category were not

---

$50 billion. . . . Analysis of organized criminal betting operations indicates that the profit is as high as one-third of gross revenue—or $6 to $7 billion each year" [Task Force Report: Organized Crime (Annotations and Consultants' Papers, 1967), p. 3].

* Again, the Task Force on Organized Crime indicates that such corruption is localized in neither time nor space: "All available data indicate that organized crime flourishes only where it has corrupted local officials. . . . In recent years some local governments have been dominated by criminal groups. Today, no large city is completely controlled by organized crime, but in many there is a considerable degree of corruption" [Task Force Report, p. 6].

strictly bound by the laws of the marketplace. The same structure, with the same functional consequence, exists in the legitimate economy; indeed, the practices of the shadow economy are determined by and reflective of the practices of its substantial equivalent. We are confronted, in other words, not with competitive capitalism but with monopoly capitalism, not with a system structured by the interaction of an indefinite number of small firms but by a system dominated by a small number of powerful enterprises. The laws of political economy hold, however, only in the competitive case; insofar as a firm lacks competition, it is not forced to lower prices when supply exceeds demand (although ultimately, to be sure, it must sell some given quantity of its product in order to realize an acceptable profit). It can routinely sell the commodities it produces above their costs of production. But the first law of bourgeois political economy is that every commodity must be sold at its cost of production, i.e., at its value; the selling of commodities above their values is the essence of hustling. Thus, monopoly capitalism is the systematic practice of hustling! Moreover, insofar as the economic system as a whole maintains even a semblance of equilibrium, the super-profits of monopolies must be balanced by the marginal and sub-marginal profitability of competitive firms. In this regard, therefore, the large enterprises have a parasitic relationship to their disadvantaged rivals. Finally, because even monopolistic firms are under constant pressure to enter and/or create new markets, they tend to invade the competitive sector of the economy, where capital can still be profitably invested in the rationalization of production. As Marx said in *Capital*, one capitalist always kills many.* Thus we may fairly term monopoly capitalism the criminal form of bourgeois political economy.

We now recognize how accurately Freddie's dictum on hustling reflected Malcolm's general situation. One question, however, still remains: what is the interest of the legitimate bourgeoisie in the preservation of the shadow economy? The interest of the shadow

---

* It may be noted that the concentration of capital in the United States has advanced through three successive phases. The first occurred between 1890 and the outbreak of World War I, during which horizontal mergers (mergers in which a firm absorbs a direct competitor) resulted in the monopolization of such fundamental areas as oil and steel production, the railroads, and banking. Then in the 1920s a wave of vertical mergers developed, in which many large corporations absorbed the suppliers of their means of production and the distributors of their products. Finally, during the 1950s and 1960s conglomerative mergers among unrelated firms resulted in the formation of the vast economic empires that constitute the objective basis of what Malcolm and others term the international power-structure.

bourgeoisie is clear: criminal activity is economically parasitical and politically vulnerable; it therefore requires a host economy, and its organizers must be willing to pay for legal toleration when they cannot command it. But why do politicians and business leaders collude in the corruption of their system?

Stated generally, the answer is that criminal activity serves the interests and gratifies the sexual desires of the bourgeoisie. Illegal enterprises funnel a certain amount of capital into legitimate businesses, and a large amount of money into politicians' pockets. Hence for the individuals who are directly involved, self-interest dictates the acceptance of criminal parasitism. Furthermore, the shadow economy, especially through the numbers racket, returns to the bourgeoisie an additional part of the surplus value produced by the proletariat—the so-called "nigger pennies" that, like shale oil or low-grade coal, are difficult to retrieve by conventional means. In addition, the sexual side of the shadow economy satisfies the bourgeois demand for perverse and taboo forms of erotic pleasure: "Rich men. . . . Society leaders. Big politicians. Tycoons. . . . Harlem was their sin-den, their fleshpot. They stole off among taboo black people, and took off whatever antiseptic, important, dignified masks they wore in their white world."[81] White masks, black skins—in this case the skins of prostitutes and "studs" who provided the desired excitement, and whose emotional energies were directly appropriated by their customers.

In sum, the hustling society is a vehicle for the bourgeois appropriation of sensuous energy, from which it follows that the apparent parasitism of the shadow economy is in fact a symbiotic relationship between the substantive economy and its shadow. That symbiosis is limited, however, to the legitimate bourgeoisie and its interpenetrated illegal equivalent: there is no common interest uniting the ruling classes with their economically and sexually exploited masses. But the two proletariats, the substantive one and its *lumpen* equivalent, do have a common interest *against* their bourgeois exploiters, against the parasites who suck out their life's blood, who alienate them from their sensuous energies. The street hustlers and the squares have a common enemy.

Yet if the masses experience the same oppression, they experience it in opposing ways. They are products of the same objective situation, but they are antithetical developments of that situational potential: while both classes are proletarian insofar as they own no means of production and must therefore sell their labor-power (and sometimes their emotional energy) to the bourgeoisie, only the substantive proletariat produces surplus value. Consequently, the *lumpen-proletariat*, like its bourgeois and shadow-bourgeois masters, is parasitical: directly or indirectly, it feeds upon the vital substance of the genuine working-class. Thus it is and is not proletarian, it is simultaneously exploited and exploiter. This existential contradiction is essentially reflected in the hustler's way of life, his cheap elegance, his *machismo*, and his street-corner prestige; and it collapses back into itself in the form of a falsified self-consciousness, i.e., as an internally contradicted code of conduct and an illusory sense of freedom. Because the hustler believes he is free, or is soon to be freed, through the magical intervention of Lady Luck, he does not struggle to become free. His false consciousness of freedom helps to perpetuate his slavery. Against his will, he serves the interests of his bourgeois master.

Thus the *lumpen-proletariat*, the body and soul if not the mind of the hustling society, is an instrument of bourgeois domination—an unreliable instrument, as we shall later see, for at least some of its members have grasped the principle that "everything is a hustle," and hence are "internally restrained by nothing." But because the hustler is not yet able to see beyond the limits of his situation, because he has been carefully taught to see his situation as universal in time and space instead of as particular to certain historical circumstances, he draws an incorrect inference from his correct premise and becomes involved in a nihilistic, self-destructive war of all against all. Moreover, by so doing the black hustler in particular gives additional comfort to his enemy: through the invalid generalization of the hustler image, black people are seen as a race of criminals, pimps, prostitutes, gamblers, dope fiends, murderers, and thieves. By logical inversion, the whole is subsumed into a part, and the part thus magnified becomes the stereotypical "bad nigger." In the process the criminalizing impact of white bourgeois economic interests and emotional needs disappears, so that the illusion is created that black people are just naturally "that way." Thus the hustling society creates the possibility for the group-emotional transformation of the white population's repressed emotional energy into one form of its racist false consciousness.

Finally, the members of the black proletariat, in their attempt to escape from this stereotypical house of mirrors, are forced to blind themselves to their racial identity. To be black is to be bad, to be a criminal; hence to be good, the black person must be white. If he cannot be white in physical fact, then he must be doubly white in attitude and action. He must, in Malcolm's words, "love the master more than the master loves himself"; and he must deny his kinship with his criminalized brothers and sisters. He will then find it easy to believe that the victim is the criminal, and the criminal is the victim. So believing, he will be the "good Negro" the master is glad to have working in the house. But good or bad, house or field, when push comes to shove "they can use any kind of brutal methods to suppress blacks because they're criminals anyway."[82]

The Dream World

We now understand why Malcolm considered the United States to be a criminal society. Not only is the hustling society a logically determined and essential side of American capitalism, not only is the continued existence of this shadowy realm contingent upon the criminalization of black people who have been kept "oppressed, and deprived and ignorant, and unable to get decent jobs,"[83] but those people who have been driven to criminal activity are used to criminalize the image of all black people. And that, to use Malcolm's terms, is "tricky logic," a "con game," a "hustle."

Needless to say, Malcolm did not see either himself or his situation in this light during his own hustling period. He was mesmerized by the Harlem underworld, and he viewed himself as an heroic outlaw—an image that was reinforced not only by the Code but also by the movies:

> It was about this time (mid-1943) that I discovered the movies. Sometimes I made as many as five in one day, both downtown and in Harlem. I loved the tough guys, the action, Humphrey Bogart in "Casablanca," and I loved all of that dancing and carrying on in such films as "Stormy Weather" and "Cabin in the Sky."[84]

Watching Bogart in action, Malcolm would project himself into the hero's role; when the action came to an end, he would introject the composite character thus formed. In this way Bogart became a white image of the black hero, and Malcolm in turn became a black incarnation of the white one. The movie experience was a form of hypnosis: the theater was a looking-glass world populated by fictionalized and highly erotized images of his past; the screen was a magic mirror in which he saw himself reflected larger than life. By suspending

all disbelief in these shades and shadows, Malcolm emerged from
the theater into the Harlem twilight as a cool, tough, and sensual
young hustler who had risen above the antinomies of class, race, and
morality.

Malcolm's transcendence of his situation was of course more
fiction than fact. In reality he was falling below it, sinking into a
nightmarish state of unconscious subjectivity. His successful and
self-conscious practice of hustling, which we glanced at during our
passage through the hustling society, lasted only about two years. At
the end of that time he was already beginning to lose control:

> [During the winter of 1944/45,] I began to be sick. I had
> colds all the time. It got to be a steady irritation, always
> sniffling and wiping my nose, all day, all night. I stayed so
> high I was in a dream world. Now, sometimes, I smoked
> opium with some white friends, actors who lived down-
> town. I didn't smoke the usual wooden-match-sized sticks
> of marijuana. I was so far gone by now that I smoked it al-
> most by the ounce.[85]

Malcolm was narcotizing himself into a "dream world" in order to
escape from the insecurity and uncertainty of the real one. He was
not unique in so doing: alcoholism and narcotics addiction are familiar ghetto diseases. Like gambling or the sexual "Game," they
help one to forget the misery and shame of ghetto existence. But unlike these other escape mechanisms, they invade the mind physically. Numbing both conciousness and conscience, blurring the
sharp edges of the objective world, they transport the user into a
hazy realm of movies-come-to-life. It is for this reason that alcohol
and narcotics are the most valuable commodities in the shadow
economy and that the haute bourgeoisie of the hustling society
maintains an oligopolistic control over their production and/or im-
portation.* The risks of distribution it leaves to the petite bourgeoisie and the proletarians of the realm.

Thus Malcolm was the victim of narcotization, just as he was of
criminalization. There was a bourgeois interest realized in his loss
of consciousness. Yet those interests, to be thus realized, had to be
mediated by his individual motives, by the contradictory forces in
his de-formed character. Malcolm was trying to escape from an in-

---

* During prohibition, alcohol and narcotics shared this honor equally. Alcohol is now
a legal hustle, so that the profits for the falsification of consciousness go directly to
the legitimate bourgeoisie.

ternal as well as an external danger: the realistic anxiety of living in an objective state of war was magnified by the moral anxiety aroused by his unconscious sense of guilt. He was a haunted as well as a hunted man:

> Got to keep movin', got to keep movin'
> Blues fallin' down like hail . . .
> Blues fallin' down like hail.
> Got to keep movin', blues fallin' down like hail.
> And the day keeps 'mindin' me, hellhound on my trail . . .
> hellhound on my trail.[86]

Like Robert Johnson (the writer of this song), Malcolm was bedeviled. He was being followed by the ghostly images of his past life, his half-forgotten "crimes." He drank, smoked reefers, and sniffed cocaine in a desperate effort to lay those ghosts to rest.

We may say, if a bit too simply, that Malcolm was trying to destroy his consciousness of the present and the conscience of his past. As he notes, the increasing amounts of narcotics required to accomplish this literal self-negation took an increasing toll on his physical and mental health; but he managed to struggle on until the day the ghosts materialized—in the form of West Indian Archie. Archie was the numbers runner with whom Malcolm placed his bets. He was a tough character, a survivor of the halcyon days when Dutch Schultz ran the rackets in Harlem. He "had the kind of photographic memory that put him among the elite of numbers runners. He never wrote down your number; even in the case of combination players, he would just nod. . . . This made him the ideal runner because cops could never catch him with any betting slips."[87] On this occasion Malcolm had "combinated" a number for three hundred dollars.* At least, so he thought. But Archie, after first paying Malcolm and then checking the number, concluded (or said he concluded) that Malcolm was "hyping" him. He came after him with a gun, and gave him one day to pay back the money.

It was a "classic hustler code impasse." Malcolm responded to it by first trying to figure out who was right and who was wrong; but with the "muddled thinking characteristic of the addict," he was unable to form a clear picture of the facts. In any case, the facts no longer mattered: once the situation had been created, neither party could withdraw without loss of face. Malcolm's manhood was at

---

* A three-digit number was combinated by placing an equal amount of money on each of its six possible combinations.

stake, in a double sense. In the hustling society, status and manhood were essentially identical: if he let Archie face him down, he would be effectively emasculated. In addition, by his authoritative action Archie had placed himself in the lineage of Malcolm's paternal enemies, the castrative fathers against whom the seventh son had no choice but to rebel. Malcolm therefore had to stick to his position and not repay the money. But this placed him in imminent danger, because if Archie didn't back down—and he wasn't likely to—then one of them would take the "Dead On Arrival ride to the morgue," and the other would be sent "to prison for manslaughter or the electric chair for murder."[88]

There was no practical way out of the impasse, so Malcolm fled headlong into his drug-induced dream world. He was already high on cocaine and the feel of a .32 caliber revolver in his pocket. Then he started drinking, and sniffed some more cocaine. At a bar he ran into Archie, who was also up on something. Archie cursed him out; but Malcolm saved face by sitting impassively through the tirade, waiting until Archie's friends pulled him away, and then walking slowly and calmly out the door.

The deadline was approaching, however, and Malcolm was increasingly frightened. "I knew I had to stay high," he reports. The cocaine and alcohol were followed by opium. The opium made him drowsy so he took some benzedrine: "The two drugs working in me had my head going in opposite directions at the same time." The benzedrine was followed by marijuana, and the marijuana by more cocaine. "I felt sensations I cannot describe, in all those different grooves at the same time. The only word to describe it was a *time-lessness*. A day might have seemed to me five minutes. Or a half-hour might have seemed a week."[89] He passed out in a hotel room.

When he woke up, the deadline had passed and, as he found out, the police were looking for him. It was "all over the wire" that he was armed and dangerous. Then he got into a fight with a "scared kid hustler," and there were some Italians looking for him, who thought he had "stuck up their crap game." "Everything was building up, closing in on me. I was trapped in so many cross turns."[90] The drugs no longer helped, the paranoia that is the essential spirit of the hustling society was enveloping him in a phantasmagoric play of malign forces, half palpable, half insensible, and totally terrifying. But Malcolm did have one real friend in New York, Sammy the Pimp, who knew about his trouble. Sammy called Shorty in Boston to come collect Malcolm before he got killed:

When I heard the car's horn, I was walking on St. Nicholas Avenue. But my ears were hearing a gun. I didn't dream the horn could possibly be for me.

"*Homeboy!*"

I jerked around; I came close to shooting.

Shorty—from Boston!

I'd scared him nearly to death.

"*Daddy-o!*"

I couldn't have been happier.[91]

Malcolm "didn't put up any objections to leaving." But "through just about the whole ride [to Boston], I talked out of my head."

Malcolm had been bloodied in the war of all against all, but he had not been bowed. He had been forced to beat a retreat, but he had not simply turned tail and run. He was, however, physically and mentally exhausted; his energy stores were completely depleted. For two weeks he slept, smoked marijuana, and slept some more. At the end of that time he connected for some cocaine; and with the "snow" producing its familiar feeling—"an illusion of supreme well-being and a soaring over-confidence in both physical and mental ability"—he gradually woke up. Then, "after about a month of 'laying dead,' as inactivity was called, I knew I had to get some kind of hustle going."[92]

Malcolm had been resurrected, but his life depended upon cocaine and marijuana. He was a walking corpse, a zombie, artificially kept alive and half hoping to die:

I think I really was at least slightly out of my mind. I viewed narcotics as most people regard food. I wore my guns as today I wear my neckties. . . . I expected then, as I expect now, to die at any time. But then, I think, I deliberately invited death in many, sometimes insane ways.[93]

Once, for example, a sailor tried to sell him a stolen gun. Malcolm took it from him, pointed it at him, and the sailor ran: "He knew I was crazy enough to kill him. I was insane enough not to consider that he might just wait his chance to kill me."[94]

Stating it briefly, Malcolm wanted to kill *and* be killed. He wanted to annihilate himself and the world. The presupposition of this nihilistic desire was, on the one hand, the kill *or* be killed nature of the hustling society, where every man was at least potentially an enemy to every other man. On the other, it was Malcolm's unconscious sense of guilt, the moralized form of his own aggressive energy, which threatened to erupt into a murderous rage and therefore recoiled upon the self as a suicidal impulse. The combined force of circumstance and character thus threw him into a paranoid nightmare, from which he tried to escape through the use of narcotics. This apparent escape was in fact the confirmation of his captivity: the drugs weakened his conscious control over his emotions, augmenting the unconscious tendency to magnify dangers and multiply enemies through the projection of aggressive energy. This in turn produced an increased propensity toward hostile actions on Malcolm's part, which then heightened his need to be punished for his offenses. At the same time, there was of course cocaine's "illusion of supreme well-being," i.e., the narcissistic magnification of the self. But in the context of the hustling society's state of war, this self-idealization is potential self-negation. The cocaine *Übermensch*, feeling that he can get away with anything, takes unnecessary chances. Even if this does not lead directly to his downfall, it makes his situation more dangerous, and thus increasingly subject to paranoid magnification. In the end, therefore, only one comforting thought is left—"I'm going to take Them with me when I go." The hustler's world, the war of all against all, is to end with a bang, not a whimper.

Thus for Malcolm, the circle of self-destructive aggressivity was almost closed: criminality from a sense of guilt, through the narcotic magnification of the hustling society's paranoid subjectivity, was resulting in what we may call *paranoid nihilism*, i.e., an impulse toward killing and *therefore* being killed. Within this tightening circle, on this narrowing ground, Malcolm built an illusory life during his last months in Boston. But an illusory life is not yet death; and the emotional energies of the paranoid nihilist, although increasingly under the control of the It, are not totally alienated from the I until or unless the individual becomes psychotic. The progressive tendency in Malcolm's character had not been entirely destroyed; he was still struggling, although with diminishing strength as time passed, to be a success in life, to work and love as a free man.

Malcolm sought to realize this ambition through the formation of a burglary ring. As we have seen, he knew he had to find a hustle; and he wanted to find one that would also liberate Shorty from the slavery of an underpaid musical career. Burglary had that potential. Moreover, "burglary, properly executed, though it had its dangers,

offered the maximum chances of success at the minimum risk."[95]
Proper execution involved finding and "casing" good locations; the
commission of the crime; and the disposal of the take. It was also
necessary to specialize in the most suitable "category" of the "science." Finally, the ring itself had to be unbreakable—absolutely
trustworthy and unquestioningly loyal to its "boss."

Keeping these lessons of his schooling in mind, Malcolm designed
what he hoped would be the "perfect operation." The ring would
consist of himself, Shorty, a friend of Shorty's who had wearied of
the straight life, Sophia (with whom he was again deeply involved),
and Sophia's younger sister, who shared Sophia's taste for black men
and taboo pleasures. The particular area was to be nighttime house-
burglary, with Shorty's friend and the two women as "finders," all
three men as the actual thieves, and a smart, reliable fence to buy
the merchandise. (Of course, Malcolm knew that "fences robbed
burglars worse than the burglars robbed the victims";[96] but that
was, it might be said, an unavoidable cost of running a small, competitive enterprise.) And he established himself as boss by faking a
solitary game of Russian roulette: with his cohorts watching, he
held a gun to his head and pulled the trigger, twice—after carefully
palming the one bullet he had apparently left in the chamber. He
then said:

> " 'I'm doing this, showing you I'm not afraid to
> die. . . . Never cross a man not afraid to die. . . . Now, let's
> get to work.' "[97]

The hype had the desired effect, and Malcolm "never had one moment's trouble with any of them after that."[98]

For some time thereafter, the burglary ring was an economic success. But the ring was not only the materialization of Malcolm's labor-power; it was also the embodiment of his emotional energies. As
he put it, his robber gang was "like a family unit." Shorty had paired
off with Sophia's sister, Malcolm and Sophia acted "as though we
had been together for fifty years," and the other fellow was cool and
congenial.[99] There was thus a certain amount of group love and solidarity. But if the unit was like a family, it more nearly resembled a
horde-family than a human one. We have seen that Malcolm ruled
over his subjects with a tyrannical hand, with a mixture of narcissistic authority and raw power. Moreover, he often terrorized Sophia:

> Always, every now and then, I had given her a hard time,
> just to keep her in line. Every once in a while a woman

seems to need, in fact *wants*, this. . . . But now, I would feel
evil and slap her around worse than ever.[100]

Malcolm's consciousness of his actions reflects the Code, the
pimp's version thereof, which posited that "a woman was nothing
but another commodity"; that like all human commodities, she
should be exploited as fully as possible; and, like all human beings,
she should be trusted not at all. It is evident, however, that his actions were also unconsciously determined both by his identification
with his father's behavior within the Little home and by his undying
bitterness toward his mother for her betrayal of his Oedipal passions
and her subsequent inattention to his needs and desires. In other
words, he had placed *himself* in the analogic series of malevolent paternal authorities, had become his own enemy—the seventh son
had become an imitation primal father.

Malcolm had become an evil caricature of Earl Little on the one
hand and the Man on the other. Yet even this falsified realization of
his characteristic tendencies demanded self-control. In his own
words, "in any organization someone must be the boss. If it's even
just one person, you've got to be the boss of yourself."[101] But narcotics were making it more and more difficult for him to be his own
boss: "Always before, I had been able to smoke the reefers and to
sniff the snow and rarely show it very much [but] by now it was not
that easy."[102] The drugs were telling him what to do; his *internal*
defenses against paranoid nihilism were being battered down. And
as they fell, it became proportionately more difficult to defend himself and his "family" from their *external* enemies. He was no longer
able to live by the Code, to obey the laws of illegal activity. These
laws, specified to his particular situation, were essentially two: the
burglar must not retain possession of stolen goods, i.e., of anything
that, in the hands of the police, would constitute incriminating evidence; and the black lover of a "respectable" white woman must
never allow himself to be seen in her company by any "respectable"
white man of her acquaintance.

Sometime shortly after Christmas, 1945, he broke both commandments. One night he came into a nightclub and saw Sophia,
her sister, and a white man sitting at a table. Prudence dictated leaving the club, or at least ignoring the trio. But that is not what Malcolm did: "I don't know how I ever made such a mistake as I next
did. I could have talked to her later. I didn't know, or care, who the

white fellow was. My cocaine told me to get up." [103] The man was a friend of Sophia's husband. He was entertaining the "girls" while the husband was out of town on business, and he had insisted on coming to "'niggertown' to be amused by the 'coons.'" The women were "sitting there with drinks before them, praying that no Negro who knew them would barge up to their table." Then up came Malcolm, making it plain he knew them well. The women turned "chalky-white," the man went "beet-red," and Malcolm moved on. [104]

The cocaine, Malcolm says, told him to do it. But neither he nor we are satisfied with that explanation, for the drug in itself provides no motive for his action. There is, however, a motive implicit in the action itself: by going up to the table, Malcolm was lifting the veil of secrecy in which his relationship to Sophia was enshrouded. He was demanding recognition of his status: he wanted Sophia to acknowledge that she knew him, so that in turn her companion would know who he was; and he was asserting his right to know her, and to know who her companion was. He was tired of being the invisible man! More than that: he was tired of being the other man. As we deduced earlier, Malcolm loved Sophia; and despite his proclaimed indifference to her life outside the hustling society, it is therefore a good guess that he was jealous of her husband's relationship to her—a jealousy that would have been intensified by the racial and Oedipal aspects of the Man's seignioral privilege. Hence we may infer that when Malcolm saw Sophia in *his* territory with a man who might have been her husband, he was suddenly overcome by a long-suppressed and repressed jealous rage. With cocaine weakening the repressive forces in his character, he half-consciously decided to bring things to their proper conclusion. His action thus takes on the meaning of a challenge: "Here I am," he is almost saying, "not ashamed, not afraid, not just another 'amusing coon.' Here I am, your wife's lover—now come and do something about it, if you're *man* enough."

The man did not take up the challenge . . . then. But later that night, he showed up at Malcolm's apartment. Malcolm was lying in bed, feeling sick and groggy. He heard a knock on the door: "I knew something was wrong. We all had keys. No one ever knocked at the door. I rolled off and under the bed; I was so groggy it didn't cross my mind to grab for my gun on the dresser." [105] Of course, it was the man, Sophia's husband's friend. He quickly found Malcolm, who came out from under the bed "fake laughing," trying to pretend the whole thing was a joke. The man wasn't fooled, and he was too cool

to start a fight. Having found out what he wanted to know, he simply left. Malcolm was left alone, wondering how he could have
trapped himself without his gun.

Malcolm's question becomes ours: why didn't he go for his gun?
Even considering his illness and the emotional regression indicated
by the childish action of hiding under a bed, one would have thought
that Malcolm would have reached for the gun almost instinctively.
The complete hustler who is "internally restrained by nothing," the
paranoid nihilist at the world's end, would have been dominated by
that one thought. But Malcolm was not essentially a hustler. He
could *think like* a hustler, but in the limiting situation he did not
entirely *feel* like one. Thus according to the Code women were to be
exploited and enjoyed, but they were not to be trusted or loved. To
trust a woman with one's love was to give her a powerful weapon in
the war of all against all—to leave oneself open to looking foolish or
being hurt. Yet Malcolm loved Sophia, loved her for her human soul
instead of simply lusting after her white body. Correspondingly, although he was no more than mortally afraid to die, he was morally
afraid to kill. He was certainly not lacking in human courage, but he
lacked a killer's instinct. He was not, in short, internally restrained
by nothing, and he was not completely alienated from his own emotions. He was therefore neither a true nihilist nor a successful hustler. This failure in fact saved his life when, two days after the preceding incident, he broke the commandment against holding or
displaying stolen goods.

Malcolm and his robber band had been holding "hot" merchandise
from the outset; the women had even worn some of the furs and
jewelry in public. In time, one policeman or another would have
noticed this conspicuous display and busted the ring. But Malcolm
cut the process short by making the burglar's worst possible mistake: he took a stolen watch into a jewelry shop to be repaired! Not
surprisingly, when he arrived to pick it up, the police were waiting.
He paid for the watch, and "a fellow suddenly appeared from the
back. . . . One hand was in his pocket. I knew he was a cop. He said,
quietly, 'Step into the back.'" It was all over, the game had been
played . . . but then:

> Just as I started back there, an innocent Negro walked
> into the shop. . . . The detective, thinking he was with me,
> turned to him.
> There I was, wearing my gun, and the detective talking to
> that Negro with his back to me. Today I believe Allah was

with me even then. I didn't try to shoot him. And that saved my life. . . . I raised my arm, and motioned to him, "Here, take my gun."[106]

Malcolm was disarmed—and then two other detectives appeared from the back: "They'd had me covered. One false move, I'd have been dead."[107] *

Allah, or at least his own moral character, did in truth save Malcolm: because he was unable to kill, he was not killed. The regressive unfolding of Malcolm's character thus did not reach its logical conclusion. This may be an adequate explanation of why he asked the detective to take the gun, but it does not explain why he made the mistake that set up the confrontation. The solution to that problem, however, lies close at hand. As any well-schooled hustler would say, by "thinking he could get away with it," Malcolm was "asking to be caught." He was, in the first place, breaking the law and defying his own conscience; his criminality was therefore immoral as well as illegal, but his actions were not irrational in and of themselves. When he violated the Code as well as the law, however, he was offending against consciousness as well as conscience. He was regressing into a phantasy world of infantile omnipotence, a dream world in which he could "get away with" anything. In reality, he was getting away with less and less; and as his criminality from a sense of guilt increasingly took on the character of paranoid nihilism, it was becoming quite likely that he would not even escape with his life. In his words, "I had gotten to the point where I was walking on my own coffin."[108] And when the drugs were not beclouding his mind, he was painfully aware of this contradiction between phantasy and reality. He knew he was destroying himself, but there was nothing he could *choose* to do about it.

The magical power of the seventh son was becoming simply the power of self-negation; the regression to infantile omnipotence was in fact a lapsing back into infantile impotence. But if Malcolm could not consciously choose to save himself, he could unconsciously ask to be saved from himself. As we have seen, his characteristic mechanism for escaping from situations that were constraining, frustrating, or even traumatizing was to break the rules, time and again if necessary, until the relevant authorities were left with no choice but to remove him. In the present instance, he was asking the police to

---

* Malcolm goes on to observe: "If I hadn't been arrested right when I was, I could have been dead another way." Sophia's husband was out looking for him, with a gun.

catch him and thereby bring to an end his participation in the war of all against all. Furthermore, if we view the regression of Malcolm's character from an extended temporal perspective, we recognize that its premise was his moral identification with his oppressor, i.e., his whitened-out conscience. It follows from this premise that his criminal actions were produced by and reproductive of an unconscious sense of guilt, and that paranoid nihilism followed in turn as the attempted narcotic negation of the unconscious negation of his conscious activity. This negation of the negation is clearly not an affirmation, but, rather, a retreat into madness, if not a plunge into the void of nonexistence. Short of this fatal conclusion, however, the premise remains determinative, so that the process of psychological regression entails an ever-increasing need for punishment. Thus we may conclude: in order to escape the maximum penalty of death, Malcolm was forced to accept the lesser one of imprisonment.

Charlestown Prison

"Then we were looking up at the judge in Middlesex County Court. . . . I got ten years. . . . They took Shorty and me, handcuffed together, to Charlestown State Prison."[109]
"Any person who claims to have deep feelings for other human beings should think a long, long time before he votes to have other men kept behind bars—caged. . . . Any former convict will tell you he can't forget those bars. . . . Your prison number became a part of you. You never heard your name. . . . I don't care how strong you are, you can't stand having to smell a whole cell row of defecation."[110] Confined to a cage, choked by the smell of urine and feces, and "suddenly without drugs," Malcolm was "physically miserable and as evil-tempered as a snake."[111] The prison psychologist who interviewed him "got called every filthy name" he could think of, and the prison chaplain "got called worse." Even members of his family, when they attempted to place moral claims upon him, became objects of his wrath: "My first letter, I remember, was from my religious brother Philbert in Detroit, telling me his 'holiness' church was going to pray for me. I scrawled him a reply I'm ashamed to think of today."[112] He was obviously not interested in either secular or sacred reformation.
His physical misery was soon eased by a ready supply of nutmeg (which, when properly used, produces a marijuana-like high) from

the prison kitchen, and then by marijuana itself, nembutal, and benzedrine, all purchased from other prisoners or the guards. But the drugs, while numbing his mind, did not cool his temper:

> [The] first year-plus I spent at Charlestown . . . runs all together in a memory of nutmeg and other semi-drugs, of cursing guards, balking in the lines, dropping my tray in the dining hall, refusing to answer to my number—claiming I forgot it—and things like that.[113]

Thus Malcolm fought against the identity of *prisoner* that was being forced upon him, against the penal negation of his humanity. He attempted to preserve a semblance of freedom and individuality within the narrow limits set by prison walls. The immediate consequence of this effort was to narrow the limits even further: defiance resulted in solitary confinement. Yet this additional punishment was at the same time a reward, for at least in solitary he was alone, with no other prisoners to mirror his own imprisonment. He was, in other words, relying upon his most familiar and characteristic escape mechanism, through the use of which he won freedom from the usual prison routine of line-ups and work in the license-plate shop, freedom to use his infinitely small space and his endless time in his own way: "I would pace for hours like a caged leopard, viciously cursing aloud to myself. And my favorite targets were the Bible and God."[114] There was, however, a legal limit to the number of consecutive days one could spend in solitary. At periodic intervals empty time and meaningless space were again particularized into the prison routine, from which Malcolm would again liberate himself by his defiance of divine and earthly authority. It was not long before his behavior led his cellmates to give him a new name, one that he was quick to accept. The hustler-in-chains became "Satan."

Thus in its first phase Malcolm's imprisonment reduced him to a condition of bestial and blasphemous rage. He became a satanic caricature of the aggressively inclined bad boy he once had been— which is to say, the prison experience was *infantilizing*. It stripped Malcolm of his adult character and left him exposed to uncontrollable eruptions of his own anger. That anger was, of course, not in itself irrational: the prison authorities were his enemies, and they were the deserving objects of his hatred; it was also rational, if less self-evidently so, to attack God, i.e., the moral authority that was presumably concretized in the prison system. As the chaplain's presence indicates, the prison was in a certain sense a Christian institution, a kind of earthly purgatory men passed through on their way to civic redemption, or, at least, so it was claimed. In fact, it was more nearly an inferno, with *"Lasciate ogni speranza, voi ch' entrate!"* written above its iron gates.

Although Malcolm's outrage at the blatant hypocrisy was not unwarranted, his anger was controlling him, he was not controlling himself. He was still trapped in the vicious circle of self-destructive aggressivity, a circle circumscribed by his identification with his oppressor; that is, Malcolm-as-Satan was still defined in Christian terms. His ceaseless cursing indicates that he was no true atheist, no true nihilist, but, rather, like Milton's fallen archangel, an enemy of "hee whom Thunder hath made greater." The Man's power, a power that in Malcolm's present circumstances was more nearly absolute than it had ever been before, testified to the reality of his God and the rectitude of his laws. Moreover, these were the laws in which Malcolm still believed, the standards of right and wrong that had first been incarnated in the Christian Earl Little and then in the paternalistic authorities of his later childhood, and which had consequently become his own punitive conscience. As a result, Malcolm could stand in opposition to the Christian God but not outside the boundaries of the Christian universe. He was imprisoned in his own character as well as his situation.

This extreme phase of Malcolm's self-destructive aggressivity came to an end during his second year at Charlestown, when he managed to regain a degree of self-control. The impetus for this disciplining of the spirit came from an older Negro prisoner named Bimbi, who "could command total respect . . . with his words," even from the guards and white prisoners.[115] Malcolm, who loved to talk and had always prided himself on his verbal prowess, admired Bimbi's skill and knowledge. So when the older man told him he "had some brains" if he would only use them, and that he therefore ought to take advantage of the prison correspondence courses and library facilities instead of blindly lashing out at his surroundings, Malcolm moderated his swearing and enrolled in an English course. As he studied, the mechanics of grammar gradually came back to him, but because his vocabulary was terribly limited, reading was more of a problem.

In any case, neither reading nor writing was fundamental to Malcolm's re-education at this time, or to his regained self-control. The determining force was Bimbi himself, the successor to the older hustlers who had taken a benevolent paternal interest in Malcolm when he worked in Small's Paradise. Bimbi became Malcolm's teacher, and the lesson he taught was rationalized nihilism:

> What made me seek his friendship [Malcolm reports] was when I heard him discuss religion. I considered myself beyond atheism—I was Satan. But Bimbi put the atheist philosophy in a framework, so to speak. That ended my vicious cursing attacks. My approach sounded so weak alongside his, and he never used a foul word.[116]

The argument that there was no God struck Malcolm as more powerful than his own emotional attack against God. And once divine authority was thus dispatched, it was easy to accept Bimbi's second argument, that "the only difference between us [the prisoners] and outside people was that we had been caught."[117] In other words, if everything in the world is a hustle, then the only law is: don't get caught hustling. From this follows the rest of the hustling code and its applicability to present circumstances: "Under Bimbi's tutelage, too, I had gotten myself some little cellblock swindles going."[118]

After two years in prison, Malcolm had certainly not been reformed. He had recovered a measure of emotional control and he was learning new skills and redeveloping old ones, but the skills were being used as a means to a hustler's ends and the increased self-control implied no disenchantment with his criminal vocation. He was not now, as he once had been, a naive boy who was ready to believe that reform meant "to change and become better," to "start a new life and become somebody everyone would be proud of." He had learned in the meantime that reform was a hype, a game run by the Man to his own advantage. Imprisonment (as such) only served to confirm his hustler identity and to rationalize his criminal nihilism. In this respect Malcolm's experience was hardly unique: as he observes with essential accuracy, "Behind bars, a man never reforms."[119]

Although we cannot undertake an extensive exploration of penal servitude, we may briefly mention certain of its relevant features.

The prison experience begins when the criminal is caught, held for trial, tried, sentenced, and sent to prison. In current penal practice, the sentence will usually be more or less indeterminate. (In Malcolm's case, the sentence was for ten years with possibility of parole after six; hence de facto he was sent to prison for from six to

ten years.) It ends in the process of being released, which typically
includes appearances before a parole board, the members of which
will arbitrarily grant liberty to one man and deny it to another; being
released on parole without money, decent clothing, or the likelihood
of employment; and then bearing the stigma of being an ex-convict
for the rest of one's life. In between there is the process of "doing
time." During this period the prisoner is subject to the absolute authority of guards, wardens, and, ultimately, the state. These authorities exercise their power over the prisoner primarily through
penalties for being bad and unruly, and secondarily through rewards
for being, or appearing to be, good and docile. Hence for Malcolm,
solitary confinement in the hell-holes of Charlestown and (as we
shall see) the privacy of his own room in the heaven of Norfolk were
the extremes of prison life.*

The penal system reflects the instrumental tendencies of the
larger social system: it is on the one hand an institutionalized state
of war, and on the other the most malevolent possible form of welfare paternalism. It is a system in which the incarcerated individual
is cared for by those who care nothing about him—or who care for
him only insofar as there is profit to be made from the prison business, and who care about him only as an object for their literally sadistic impulses. It is the subjugation of the individual to totalitarian
control. Not surprisingly, therefore, prison normally has a pro-
foundly regressive impact upon the prisoner. Initially, it deprives
him of his freedom, his individual identity, and all contact with the
outside world. He is thereby reduced to a state of bestial rage or infantile anxiety. Subsequently, either his character-structure is totally undermined by his guardians so that he becomes a willing tool
of his own debasement, or he is hardened in his now more rationalized nihilism. In either case, his motives and actions continue to
serve the interests of his enemy.

This, then, was Malcolm's situation before his conversion to Islam. He was a confirmed nihilist, well on his way to becoming a
criminal for life. But imprisonment, like the experience of living
through a depression or living in the hustling society, pierces the
screen of self-righteousness behind which the oppressor hides him-

---

* The penalties extend, of course, to gross physical abuse and, ultimately, death; but
the rewards never extend to the point where the individual is free from the threat of
inhuman punishment. On all of these points, see Jessica Mitford, *Kind and Usual
Punishment: The Prison Business* (New York: Alfred A. Knopf, 1973); and Erik Olin
Wright, ed., *The Politics of Punishment* (New York: Harper and Row, 1973), especially Part I.

self and against which the oppressed person sees himself reflected as either evil or unworthy of respect; hence imprisonment makes it possible for the individual to see his situation in the light of the truth. Then if someone appears who is able to demonstrate to him who is his enemy, how that enemy has victimized him, and what he can do about his victimization, the regressive tendency of incarceration may be realized by inversion. In Malcolm's words:

> Here is a black man caged behind bars, put there by the white man. Usually the convict comes from among those bottom-of-the-pile Negroes, the Negroes who through their entire lives have been kicked about, treated like children. . . .
>
> You let this caged-up black man start thinking . . . how, with better breaks, he might have been a lawyer, a doctor, a scientist, anything. You let this caged-up black man start realizing, as I did, how from the first landing of the first slave ship, the millions of black men in America have been like sheep in a den of wolves. That's why black prisoners become Muslims so fast when Elijah Muhammad's teachings filter into their cages by way of other Muslim convicts. "The white man is the devil" is a perfect echo of that black convict's lifelong experience.[120]

Sometimes the end of the road can become the beginning.

CHAPTER VI

Only Guilt Admitted

IN CONCLUDING HIS representation of his life in the hustling society, Malcolm observes that his purpose in telling about his "sordid past" is neither to "titillate some readers" nor to boast about "how bad, how evil" he was. The first disclaimer is undoubtedly true. The second is only half true: although in Islamic retrospect his past looked sordid to him, at the time he was proud of how "evil" he was; and that of which one once was proud can never become entirely a matter of shame. Moreover, and more importantly, Malcolm continued to adhere to certain aspects of the hustling code, especially to some of its ideals of manhood, both during and after his period of membership in the Nation of Islam. Finally, his prestige with the black masses and his special status within the Nation rested in part upon his having been not only a hustler but evil incarnate—a man who had sunk so low that his conversion to the true faith was in itself almost a miracle.

But if in this latter sense the *Autobiography* is a parable of the lost sheep or the prodigal son, it is also a representation of a more general sort; as Malcolm observes at this juncture, to understand why any person is as he is, "his whole life, from birth, must be reviewed. All of our experiences fuse into our personality. Everything that ever happened to us is an ingredient."[1] We adopted this methodological and theoretical principle early in our inquiry. It led us back to the nightmare night and to the question of how the seventh son, who carries within himself the potential of bivalent aggressivity, becomes a person with an individual character and a racial identity such that the appeals of charismatic group-emotion will not be lost on him. With this question in mind we have followed Malcolm as he circled away from that originating emotional ground. We saw him become a bad boy in response to welfare or malevolent paternalism and a good boy in response to reformist or benevolent paternalism; a hustler in his attempt to escape from paternalism altogether; and a prisoner when that attempt failed. At the same time we witnessed his originally self-contradictory racial identity evolve into the dumb show of racial stereotypes; devolve into a paranoid dream; and come to rest in the rationalized nihilism of the hustler in chains. In the process we discovered that Malcolm's regressive or illusory development of his subjective potential, his movement within the vicious circle of self-destructive aggressivity, was determined by the ghettoization or internal colonization of black people, which in its turn was determined by the development of American monopoly capitalism into a welfare-warfare state.

We come now to the moment when, in Malcolm's words, "I found Allah and the religion of Islam and it completely transformed my life."[2] We must therefore analyze the process of conversion through which he was able to reverse the regressive movement of his character and begin to develop the progressive side of his heritage, namely, the potential for *racial self-identification* and *self-productive aggressivity*.

Enlightenment

In 1948 Malcolm received another letter from Philbert, this one saying that Philbert had discovered the "natural religion for the black man" and that Malcolm should "pray to Allah for deliverance." Given Malcolm's emergent atheism and his habitual hatred of all gods, it is not surprising that he wrote back "a letter which, although in improved English, was worse than my earlier reply to his news that I was being prayed for by his holiness church."[3] Then, a little later, a letter from Reginald arrived: "Don't eat any more pork, and don't smoke any cigarettes; I'll show you how to get out of prison."[4] Malcolm did not connect Reginald's letter with Philbert's, despite the fact that he knew Reginald had been spending time with Philbert, Wilfred, and Hilda in Detroit. For Reginald had always been his favorite brother, just as Philbert had been his principal rival. The latter, we remember, had consistently been Malcolm's opposite: he had loved church services, had been a successful boxer, and had become a religious man and a law-abiding citizen. Reginald, by contrast, had always looked up to Malcolm, and he had even spent a period of time with his older brother in Harlem, working a legal hustle the latter had devised for him. Consequently, Malcolm's "automatic response" was to think Reginald had figured out a way to "work a hype on the penal authorities." He could not "figure out what kind of a hype it could be"; but he wanted to "get out of prison . . . so badly" that he was willing to give it a try.

After finishing the pack of cigarettes he had opened, Malcolm gave up smoking. Then, as he describes it:

> It was about three or four days later when pork was served for the noon meal. . . . When the meat platter was passed to me, I didn't even know what the meat was; usually you couldn't tell anyway—but it was suddenly as though *don't eat any more pork* flashed on a screen before me.
>
> I hesitated, with the platter in mid-air; then I passed it along to the inmate waiting next to me. He began serving himself; abruptly, he stopped. I remember him turning, looking surprised at me.
>
> I said to him, "I don't eat pork."[5]

Malcolm's refusal of the meat immediately attracted the attention of the other inmates: "It was being mentioned all over the cell block by night that Satan didn't eat pork."[6] And this made him "proud in some odd way. One of the universal images of the Negro, in prison and out, was that he couldn't do without pork. It made me feel good to see that my not eating it had especially startled the white convicts."[7] Malcolm was proud of having *not* conformed to one of the "universal images of the Negro"; that is, he was proud of being different from and superior to the stereotypical Negro. This does not in itself imply freedom from the dominating-dominated group relationship; at this juncture Malcolm was in fact still primarily concerned about winning the respect of white prisoners, to prove that he was the exception to a universal rule he still basically accepted. His pride was not yet clearly differentiated from that of the "good Negro" who had been elected class president of Mason Junior High School. Moreover, he was being a "good boy" in another sense: by not eating pork he was obeying one of his mother's most cherished precepts; indeed, the last words he remembered her saying when he was taken to live with the Gohannas were, "Don't let them feed him any pig."[8] His feeling of pride had here a deep and firm ground. Finally, Malcolm was being good in a third sense which unified the other two at a higher level: he had consciously chosen to forego an immediate pleasure for a later and more important one, to use self-restraint rather than self-indulgence as a means to the end of freedom. And this moral *choice* was a genuine transformation of conscience into consciousness.

At the time, the nature of this transformation was obscure to Malcolm. Later he "would learn . . . that, unconsciously, [his] first pre-Islamic submission had been manifested."[9] Thus by either Malcolm's religious criterion or our psychological one, or, more generally, by the standard of racial self-consciousness, his achievement was potential rather than actual. He was just beginning to "wake up" and "clean up." But he took a large step forward when, some time later, Reginald came to visit him. After some preliminary conversation, his brother asked, "Malcolm, if a man knew every imaginable thing there is to know, who would he be?" Malcolm was a bit annoyed with both the content and the indirect form of the question—he was waiting, after all, for an explanation of the hype—so he responded somewhat sarcastically, "Well, he would be some kind of a god—."[10] His opening now established, Reginald explained that there was such a man, that the man was a god, and that his name was Allah. ("Allah. That word came back to me from Philbert's letter.") Allah was omniscient. He possessed 360 degrees of knowledge, while the Masons, a white sect claiming great powers and truth, possessed only 33 degrees. And he had come to America where he had "made himself known to a man named Elijah—'a black man, just like us.'"[11]

Malcolm was "confused"; he "didn't know what to think." Then Reginald told him the second great truth of the doctrine: "The devil," he said, "is also a man. . . . The white man is the devil." Malcolm's mind began "involuntarily flashing across the entire spectrum of white people" he had known. "Without any exception?" he asked. "Without any exception," came the reply.

After Reginald left, Malcolm reports, "I thought. I thought. Thought. I couldn't make of it head, tail, or middle." His head "swam with the parading faces of white people" he had known, from "the state white people always in our house after the other whites I didn't know had killed my father . . . the white people who kept calling my mother 'crazy' to her face . . . the white judge and others who had split up the children . . ."; through the Swerlins and Ostrowski to the white people he had known in Boston and New York; and then to the prison guards and white prisoners.[12] Finally he focused on a fellow convict who was a Mason. He asked the man, "Was three hundred and sixty degrees . . . the maximum degrees of anything?" The man said yes, and then Malcolm asked, "Well, why is it that Masons go only to thirty-three degrees?" The man had no explanation.[13]

It is not difficult to understand Malcolm's reaction. He was expecting to learn about the hype, and instead he was given religious instruction. Yet he couldn't treat Reginald's words as a hype, and he couldn't just laugh them off. Hence his initial disorientation as the idea of a Black God and a White Devil gained an uncanny hold on his mind, possessed him without his willing the possession. At the same time, this new truth was reorienting. The notion of the White Devil in particular unlocked his memory, brought the past to life, forced him to reproduce his experience in a continuous and unifying flow of images. It enabled him to do this because it permitted him, for the first time, to think about his life without either shame or guilt. More: it precisely inverted his characteristic moral valuations. The white man was not God but the Devil, the black man was not the Devil but God! Such an idea would have been literally unthinkable until that moment, although he had sensed its presence in his father's Garvey meetings.

Malcolm was beginning to reconstruct his life and his life history in Islamic terms. But he was not doing so uncritically: he was at the same time testing the truth of the doctrine against his life experience; he was demonstrating to himself that the white man was in fact the devil. And in a parallel fashion he was testing the validity of the Islamic god-idea by challenging the Mason to refute the pseudo-geometric proof of Christian inferiority. In this way he was negating the possible negations of the new truth. He was consciously taking possession of it, after it had taken possession of his consciousness.

When Reginald came to visit him again a few days later, Malcolm was ready and willing to hear his brother's words:

> "You don't even know who you are," Reginald had said.
> "You don't even know, the white devil has hidden it from
> you, that you are of a race of people of ancient civilizations,
> and riches in gold and kings. You don't even know your
> true family name, you couldn't recognize your true language
> if you heard it. You have been cut off by the devil white
> man from all knowledge of your own kind. You have been a
> victim of the evil of the devil white man ever since he
> murdered and raped and stole you from your native land in
> the seeds of your forefathers."[14]

Reginald talked for two hours, at the end of which Malcolm was left "rocking with some of the first serious thoughts" he had ever had. In the days ahead, Reginald's lessons were complemented by letters from Wilfred, Philbert, and Hilda, and finally by a visit from the latter. Thus was Malcolm instructed in the gospel according to Elijah Muhammad.

Human history, the Prophet taught, was the work of an immanent deity. The collective black man is God, world history is His life's work. In the beginning He existed in a state of paradisiacal innocence, internal unity, and contentment. Then a snake crept into the garden: an evil scientist named Yacub created a race of white devils. The devil white man transformed heaven into hell. Through brutality and tricknology he gained lordship over the black man, forced Him into bondage, and reduced Him to being precisely that which He inherently is not—i.e., ignorant, lazy, sinful, servile, and impotent. But now, in the present era, the pendulum is swinging back the other way: the dark world is rising; the white world is in decline. Through the prophetic agency of Elijah Muhammad, the black man wakes up, cleans up, and stands up, becomes actually what He has always been potentially. In the end, the forces of evil will be vanquished, and God will reign supreme in His kingdom.

In later years, Malcolm looked back upon these first lessons in Muhammad's truth and tried to assess his reactions: "Every instinct of the ghetto jungle streets, every hustling fox and criminal wolf instinct in me, which would have scoffed at and rejected anything else, was struck numb." [15] His experience, he believed, was analogous to Paul's revelation on the road to Damascus when "upon hearing the voice of Christ, [he] was so smitten that he was knocked off his horse, in a daze." [16] * Like a Platonic captive suddenly liberated from imprisonment in his darkened cave and brought up into the sunlight, Malcolm was blinded by the light of reality. But despite or, rather, because of his blindness, he recognized that Muhammad's truth was more powerful than anything he had yet encountered. First, and as noted above, it was a comprehensive explanation of his situation and a transvaluation of values—an ethically rational interpretation of the world that was clearly superior to the simply rationalized nihilism of the hustling code. Furthermore, this world view entailed a new self-conception infinitely more impressive than the hustler's self-image. Taking these two points in their unity, Mal-

* Malcolm is quick to add: "I do not now, and I did not then, liken myself to Paul. But I do understand his experience."

colm had been shown a previously unimaginable racial-religious identity, one that negated the negative identity in which he had been imprisoned. Because in Muhammad's vision the identity of the Man who had imprisoned him was also revealed, because the white man's demonic nature was fully exposed, Malcolm was being given the possibility of looking the Man in the eye without being either hypnotized or ashamed. It is therefore not surprising that he found Muhammad's truth irresistible.

Salvation

In sum, Malcolm was becoming a new and more rational self through his experience with Islam. But at this juncture his self-transformation was not yet complete:

> Not for weeks [after Reginald's visits] would I deal with the direct, personal application to myself, as a black man, of the truth. It still was like a blinding light. . . .
> I was going through the hardest thing, also the greatest thing, for any human being to do; to accept that which is already within you, and around you.[17]

His family's letters and Hilda's visit were vital mediations of that truth; they gave the doctrine progressively more intellectual substance, and they brought to life in Malcolm feelings of familial solidarity which could easily be translated into a sense of religious unity. Nonetheless, it was Malcolm himself who would have to kneel before his God and say, "Lord, I believe, help Thou mine unbelief."

We come, therefore, to the moment of Malcolm's actual conversion. We will view it first as a rational choice of action, next as an hypnotic or charismatic group-emotional experience, and finally as a particular relationship of these opposing tendencies.

Malcolm initiated this phase of the conversion process by writing to Elijah Muhammad. The Prophet wrote back, explaining that the black prisoner "symbolized white society's crime of keeping black men oppressed and deprived and ignorant, and unable to get decent jobs, turning them into criminals."[18] Like the support of his family, this response was critical to Malcolm's progress: he reports that "it had an all but electrical effect upon me to see the signature of the

"Messenger of Allah."[19] In other words, Malcolm felt for the first time the hypnotic power of Allah, mediated through the words of His chosen messenger. Moreover, Muhammad had specified the truth to Malcolm's individual situation in such a way as to devalue criminal activity (the criminal was not a hero but an ignorant victim of white oppression, a fool in spite of himself) and place the blame for his criminality on the white man's shoulders. The Prophet was therefore simultaneously drawing Malcolm toward the truth and away from his life of sin.

The next step was the big one:

> The hardest test I ever faced in my life was praying. My comprehending, my believing the teachings of Mr. Muhammad had only required my mind's saying to me, "That's right!" or "I never thought of that."
>
> But bending my knees to pray—that *act*—well, that took me a week.[20]

Malcolm was above all else a proud man. For years he had bowed down before no man: "Picking a lock to rob someone's house was the only way my knees had even been bent before."[21] But now he had to kneel, admit his guilt, and beg the forgiveness of God:

> I had to force myself to bend my knees. And waves of shame and embarrassment would force me back up. . . . Again, again, I would force myself back down into the praying-to-Allah posture. When I was finally able to stay down—I didn't know what to say to Allah.[22]

But he soon found the right words, and then:

> I still marvel at how swiftly my previous life's thinking pattern slid away from me, like snow off a roof. It was as though someone else I knew had lived by hustling and crime. I would be startled to catch myself thinking in a remote way of my earlier self as another person.[23]

He had been reborn.

It is clear from Malcolm's representation that the process of conversion was a war between two psychic forces, virtually two selves. On the one side was the Bad Self (as he calls himself, the "personification of evil"), the divided unity of satanic pride and Christian guilt, the criminal from a sense of guilt who had become a paranoid nihilist—his *actual* self, which had already become potentially his *former* self. On the other side was the Good Self, characterized by the morally unifying force of Muslim pride-through-purity—the future self who already existed in him potentially. The former resisted the efforts of the latter by sending forth wave upon wave of shame and embarrassment, painful feelings designed to overwhelm all good intentions. But in Malcolm's words, "the very enormity of my previous life's guilt prepared me to accept the truth." He had been so unmistakably a wrong-doer that he was forced to become conscious of his sins. In turn he was able to admit or accept responsibility for that which he recognized in himself. This self-acceptance was then the basis for accepting Islam. Again in his words, "only guilt admitted accepts truth."[24]

Malcolm's victory over his satanic identity could be viewed as proof of the Socratic dictum that no one knowingly chooses to be evil. But more closely considered, this phase of the conversion process raises two further questions: what roots did the Good Self have in Malcolm's character, so that Muslim doctrine could be genuinely internalized and not merely superimposed; and in what sense was he guilty, i.e., responsible for the actions of the Bad Self?

Concerning the first, we remember that Malcolm had as his individual human heritage the power of moral self-unification. He was the seventh and favorite son of his Garveyite father, the good boy who was proud of the fact that he had never struck his mother. He had inherited from his parents the two-edged sword of conscience, which divides but also unifies, which cuts but also cures. Through his father's death, his mother's insanity, and the family's disintegration—through the force of Black Legion violence and welfare paternalism—he had become a divided and morally alienated self. That internal division had seemingly been overcome during the period of his reformation with the Swerlins, but his reform then had been premised upon identification with the oppressor, with the consequence that Malcolm could only escape from psychic castration by becoming a criminal from a sense of guilt, a man who was irremediably at war with himself. The original ground of his character had not been destroyed, however, although its immanent potential had surely been perverted.

Muhammad's teachings made manifest in Malcolm a latent potential of his character. They were able to awaken this slumbering power because they restored at a higher level the lost world of his childhood. In doctrinal substance the Muslim faith reflected both his father's Garveyism and his mother's religious dietary practices. Consequently, Muhammad, who incarnated the doctrine, became the legitimate successor to *both* parents. Finally, through the doctrine and Muhammad, the older children in the family had in fact been reunited. Malcolm was therefore quite correct when he said that his conversion entailed the acceptance of that which was already in and around him: in our terms, through Islam Malcolm's self-negating identification with his oppressor was itself negated. His character-structure was henceforward to be grounded in racial self-identification.

What, then, of Malcolm's moral responsibility for his previous actions? How could he hold himself accountable for what were really the white man's crimes? The answer from his own perspective might seem to be that he did perform evil actions and that he did, if in ignorance, will them. Now recognizing that those actions were wrong, not because they were violations of the white man's law but because they were at variance with the laws of God, of Allah, he felt obliged to atone for his sins. This explanation, however, shatters on the rock of intention. By definition a person is morally responsible only for that which he *wills*, that which he intends to do. Intention in turn presupposes knowledge, for a person could obviously not intend to break a law if he could not possibly have known of its existence; nor could he be held morally accountable for violating a law he did know, if he could not know that his action constituted a violation. Hence Muhammad taught that "as long as one didn't know the truth, he lived in darkness. But once the truth was accepted, and recognized, he lived in light, and whoever would then go against it would be punished by Allah."[25] In parallel fashion, the aged Oedipus could rightfully claim against Creon:

> If I came into the world—as I did come—
> In wretchedness, and met my father in fight,
> And knocked him down, not knowing that I killed him
> Nor whom I killed—how could you find
> Guilt in that unmeditated action?[26]

Nonetheless, when Oedipus discovered his double crime of patricide and incest, he *felt* guilty, and he had to endure long years of suffering before he once again felt free from sin. The psychoanalytic point is, of course, that his sense of guilt reflected his unconscious willing of those actions. Correspondingly, Malcolm's feeling of guilt reflects not only his criminal activity as such but also the sexual-aggressive "crimes" of his childhood. He was purging himself through confession of the subsequently compounded sins of his earliest years. He was praying to his parents in the double form of Elijah Muhammad and Allah for love and forgiveness; and because he was willing to submit himself to "divine" authority in this painfully humble way, the burden of his guilt was lifted from his shoulders. His past self fell away "like snow from a roof"; the negative force of criminality from a sense of guilt or, more generally, of self-destructive aggressivity had been negated; and in its place there arose the emotional potential of self-productive aggressivity.

Malcolm was no longer either a good Negro or a bad nigger; he had become a righteous black man: a Muslim.

Through the conversion process, Malcolm had at last overcome the mutual alienation of conscience and consciousness. His emotional energies were once again—or, more accurately, for the first time—under his own control. Like the collective Black Man in Yacub's history, he had returned to himself after a long period of self-degradation in the devil's service. His first experiences with Islam were in this sense a genuine process of enlightenment, a freeing of the self from the fetters of a falsified character-structure. It follows that Muhammad's teachings were in that same sense rational, a progressively transcendent reflection of Malcolm's individual-collective situation.

There is, however, another side to the story: Malcolm's conversion can be interpreted as a regression into the looking-glass world of charismatic group-emotion rather than as a progressive movement toward self-consciousness. First, it is clear that Muhammad's doctrine is not entirely rational: like Platonic myth or Hegelian theodicy, it transforms human beings into supernatural powers, history into allegory, and life history into parables. It is manifestly idealist and metaphysical—irrational in the specific sense that its ontological ground lies outside the domain of possible human knowledge. A leap of faith, transcendence in the abstract or religious sense, is therefore required of the would-be believer. Correspondingly, it is evident that Malcolm made that leap. Islamic truth struck him with charismatic force, i.e., it overwhelmed him emotionally and thereby deprived him of his characteristic powers of critical judgment. Thus he cautiously compares himself to Paul, and comments that his "hustling instincts" were struck numb. Which is not to say that he was totally unable to think: as he listened to Reginald or read the letters from his family, ideas and images formed in his mind; but, at least initially, these ideas, instead of becoming his possession, came to possess him. His mind fell under the spell of an internalized charismatic idea. He was lost in the abstraction of an hypnotic dream.

Once the Islamic idea was thus internalized, it had to draw its animating power from internal sources, from Malcolm's own emotional reserves. But insofar as the idea was hypnotic, this source could not be the conscious self, which is in control of its own energies and which was engaged in fighting against the invading force. Nor could it be his whitened-out conscience, which in this situation was allied with consciousness against the common enemy. Hence the power animating the charismatic idea had to be repressed sexual-aggressive energy, which constantly presses for release from its captivity and which does possess an hypnotic potential. Moreover, Malcolm's existing character-structure, hence his capacity to defend himself against the combined force of the charismatic idea and his own hypnotic energies, had been severely undermined by imprisonment. His repressed emotions were able to escape from their imprisonment through the openings provided by Muslim theory and practice. Carried on the wings of prayer, these energies flowed from Malcolm's unconscious in an undifferentiated and unbroken stream toward the empty universal of the god-idea. Upon reaching their projected destination, they were split into two components: sexual energy was reflected back into the self (introjected) through the mediating notion that the collective black man is god, and aggressive energy was deflected away from the self (displaced) through the mediating notion that the collective white man is the devil. Thus Malcolm was hypnotized by idealized and demonized forms of his own repressed emotional energy.

Next, if Malcolm's conversion has both the manifest attributes and the characteristic psychodynamics of a group-emotional experience, then it follows that the experience genetically considered was a rationalized regression into childhood—that the divine and demonic content of the dynamic forms was derived from the objects of ungratified infantile wishes through a process of rationalization. This process has two principal moments: first, the original objects of desire, namely, the parents, retain the appearance of omnipotence and omniscience they present to a very young child, so that they are re-presented to consciousness in supernatural form; and, second, each parental image is split, so that the good (loving) side of the person is cleanly separated from the bad (unloving or punitive) side. Thus Allah was not simply the heir to the authority of Malcolm's parents. He was specifically an idealized (positively magnified) form of the Garveyite father and the loving mother. The White Devil was correspondingly the demonized (negatively magnified) form of the Christian father and the chastising mother.

Finally, the magnified division of parental images made it possible to split filial ambivalence. Malcolm was free to love each parent totally, in the form of Allah, while simultaneously hating each, in the form of the devil. More: he was obligated to love the one and hate the other. Hence his innermost desires fused with his moral obligations into the unity of an ethical self. The internal contradiction in his character was resolved; the double, double bind of Oedipal-racial ambivalence was dissolved. But this solution to the genetic problem was an illusion. Malcolm had not in fact analyzed the problem and thereby solved it; he had only analogized and thereby mystified it. He had converted his life history into a theological abstraction through the mediating force of group-emotion.

Now, on this reading Malcolm's conversion was not the overcoming of an intrapsychic antinomy but a return of the repressed, not the transcendence of the stereotypical dumb-show but merely its inversion—in brief, not a conscious act of self-definition but the initiating act of charismatic group membership. It is therefore conformable to our general notion of charismatic group experience, and indeed allows us to particularize the notion in two interrelated respects: first, the conversion of an individual into a group member is premised upon an initial internalization of the charismatic idea so that, second, the group relationship subsequently involves not only the interpenetration of the Self with an external Other but also its interpenetration with an internal Other. Thus the possibility arises of an auto-hypnotic group-emotional experience, in which the member produces from within himself the characteristic attributes of a leader-follower interaction. This process is routinely at work in solitary prayer and was therefore an aspect of Malcolm's everyday life once he became a Muslim. It also played a critical role in the testing of his faith which occurred when Reginald broke with Elijah Muhammad.

After his conversion Malcolm had become totally devoted to Elijah Muhammad. He wrote to him daily, and would "sit for long periods and study his photographs."[27] "Islam," he remarks, "meant more to me than anything I ever had known in my life. Islam and Mr. Elijah Muhammad had changed my whole world." Reginald, who frequently came to visit him, seemingly shared his devotion and enthusiasm. But one day "Reginald began to speak ill of Elijah Muhammad." It turned out that he had been suspended from the Nation because he was "carrying on improper relations with the then secretary of the New York Temple." Malcolm was shocked: "It caught me totally unprepared. It threw me into a state of confusion. My blood brother, Reginald, in whom I had so much confidence, for whom I had so much respect, the one who had introduced me to the Nation of Islam. I couldn't believe it! . . . I was in torment."[28]

There are good reasons for Malcolm's confusion and unhappiness. Islam provided the believer with a total ordering of the cosmos. A "great chain of being" extended from Allah through Muhammad and his ministers to each individual Muslim; and the members of the Nation were linked together by their common submission to the Truth. Because Reginald was the principal mediator between Malcolm and Muhammad and was doubly his brother, his suspension broke the chain in two directions. Moreover, his backsliding was in itself a failure of the Prophet's charisma, while his suspension threatened to destroy the apparent unity of Malcolm's natal family and his religious one. Hence in the former regard Reginald's suspension gave Malcolm reason to doubt the Truth he had hitherto accepted unquestioningly, and in the latter it forced Malcolm into the position of having to choose between the obligations of blood brotherhood and those of religious adherency. In short, Reginald's backsliding and consequent punishment shook the foundations and threatened to shatter the unity of Malcolm's group-emotional world.

With his mind sorely troubled, Malcolm first wrote to Elijah Muhammad, trying to defend his brother and appealing to the Prophet to restore Reginald's status in the Nation. "Then," he states, "all the rest of that night, I prayed to Allah. I don't think anyone ever prayed more sincerely to Allah. I prayed for some kind of relief from my confusion."[29] The next night his prayers were answered:

> As I lay on my bed, I suddenly, with a start, became aware of a man sitting beside me in my chair. He had on a dark suit. I remember. I could see him as plainly as I see anyone I look at. He wasn't black, and he wasn't white. He was light-brown-skinned, an Asiatic cast of countenance, and he had oily hair.
>
> I looked right into his face.
>
> I didn't get frightened. I knew I wasn't dreaming, I couldn't move, I didn't speak, and he didn't. . . . He just sat there. Then, suddenly as he had come, he was gone.[30]

Malcolm had experienced a hypnogogic materialization of the charismatic idea. Although he says, and says honestly, that he had never seen his "visitor" before and "had no idea whatsoever who he was," we would surmise that he had formed a pre-conscious image of W. D. Fard, the Messiah, by filling in the verbal picture he had been given of Fard with the condensed features of Elijah Muhammad, various light-skinned Negroes or "Asiatics" he had known—and his mother. He then projected this image out into the darkness of his cell, where it appeared before him as a supernatural presence. It was in fact, however, an hallucination, a moment of visually mediated auto-hypnotic experience.*

Since the apparition neither identified itself to Malcolm nor told him how to resolve his doubts, it may well be asked what purpose was served by this self-mystification. How did it help him to solve his problem? The obvious answer is that the mere existence of his visitor proved to Malcolm that there was a miraculous power in the universe, and one that surely was not Christian. Muhammad's truth was immanent in the mystery of the visitation. Moreover, because the experience brought Malcolm into direct contact with this super-natural force, it eliminated the need for Reginald's mediation. Hence by the time the reply from Muhammad arrived, Malcolm had already implicitly found the required solution. The Prophet had only to explicate the solution, to speak the words the mysterious visitor had left unspoken: "He wrote, 'If you once believed in the truth, and now you are beginning to doubt the truth, then you didn't believe in the truth in the first place. What could make you doubt the truth other than your own weak self?'"[31] The truth did not have to prove itself worthy of men, men had to prove themselves worthy of the truth. The weakness of belief did not call into question the strength of the doctrine. Reginald's backsliding was his personal failure; Malcolm's doubts were his own responsibility. The Prophet was acting properly in suspending the one and gently chastising the other. In Malcolm's words, "I knew that Elijah Muhammad was right and my blood brother was wrong. . . . All doubt and confusion in my mind was removed." And any lingering doubts were removed when, over the next several months, Reginald sank into a state of

---

* Later, presumably after he had seen a picture of Fard, Malcolm came to believe he had had a "pre-vision" of the Messiah. A "pre-vision" he defines in this way: "It's impossible to dream, or to see, or to have a vision of someone whom you have never seen before—and to see him exactly as he is. To see someone, and to see him exactly as he looks, is to have a pre-vision" (Autobiography, p. 189). The present argument is that a pre-vision, like the experience of déjà vu, results from the eruption of the past into the present with such suddenness and force that the latter is transformed into an uncanny semblance of the former.

insanity. Clearly it was the "chastisement of Allah," who "executes justice by working upon the five senses of those who rebel against His Messenger."[32]

Through auto-hypnotic delusion and Muhammad's eristic reasoning, Malcolm was transformed from a doubting Thomas into a confirmed disciple. What at first seemed to be a progression toward self-consciousness thus takes on the appearance of a regression into the abstraction of group-emotion. The contradiction between these two interpretations cannot be resolved, however, by choosing one instead of the other, for the interpretive contradiction reflects the antipodal movement of the conversion process itself. The problem is, therefore, to determine the relationship between the two extremes.

The problem has only to be formulated to be solved: it is evident that, judged against the baseline of Malcolm's life history, his conversion to Islam was a progressive development, i.e., that the progressive tendency was the principal aspect of the contradiction and hence the controlling principle in the process as a whole. This is true in the first instance because Muhammad's doctrine was grounded in a conception of racial identity that was substantially more rational than the stereotypical notions it superseded. Through Islam Malcolm was able to negate his identification with the oppressor and thereby affirm himself as a black man. Second, because Muhammad did—in Malcolm's words—"identify who is our enemy," he made it possible for Malcolm to convert his criminality from a sense of guilt, his nihilism in its paranoid and rationalized forms, into righteous anger. Finally, because Yacub's history contained a rational historical kernel within its mystical shell, and because Muslim theory has its corresponding practice, after his conversion Malcolm was able to work self-productively for the first time in his life.

Thus unless we subject Malcolm's experience to a critique of pure reason—unless we abstract him from his situation and re-create him as an artifact of our own imagination—our judgment must be that his conversion was predominantly a progressive development of his character and consciousness.* Nonetheless, a regressive force was opposing the controlling tendency. Malcolm's racial identity was religiously mystified and therefore historically irrational; his

---

* In the next chapter we will be able to assess the historical rationality of the Nation of Islam; but here we are limited to the consideration of its life-historical rationality.

sense of righteousness was still dependent upon the will of an Other; and in the end, the work that he was now about to undertake would prove not to have been truly his own. At a later time, the idealist limit of his Islamic beliefs would be revealed as a limitation. For the moment, however, Malcolm was able to use his characteristic energies and extraordinary intelligence productively, first to provide himself with a working knowledge of the English language and then to "document [Muhammad's] teachings in books."[33]

Spiritual Liberation

In late 1948, after he had manifested his first pre-Islamic submission but before Reginald's first visit, Malcolm had been transferred to the Norfolk Prison Colony. Compared to Charlestown and to Concord (where Malcolm also had spent a short time) the Colony was a "heaven": "It had flushing toilets; there were no bars, only walls—and within the walls you had far more freedom. . . . There were twenty-four house units, fifty men living in each unit . . . and, greatest blessing of all, each inmate had his own room."[34] The Colony also offered a variety of rehabilitation programs; and it had a large library, which was open to interested inmates. It was, in short, more like the Swerlins' detention home than a normal prison.

Malcolm's transfer to Norfolk resulted from the efforts of his half-sister, Ella. Ella, despite her disapproval of Malcolm's way of life, had remained loyal to him throughout the years of his hustling in Harlem and Roxbury. She even, Malcolm felt, somehow admired his rebellion during that period; and now she used all her perseverance and whatever influence she possessed to arrange the transfer. Just as Malcolm's religious salvation came through the mediation of one branch of his family, so the possibility for re-education came through the other. Family solidarity was, therefore, a critical factor in Malcolm's progress toward enlightenment. Without that support, and hence without Islam, he would inevitably have been, in his own words,

> a dead criminal in a grave, or, if still alive, a flint-hard, bitter . . . convict in some penitentiary, or insane asylum. Or, at best, I would have been an old, fading Detroit Red, hustling, stealing enough for food and narcotics, and myself

being stalked as prey by some cruelly ambitious young hustlers such as Detroit Red had been.[35]

The Norfolk library, which was to play such an important part in Malcolm's education, was at first of little use to him:

> Every book I picked up had few sentences that didn't contain anywhere from one to nearly all of the words that might just as well have been in Chinese. When I just skipped those words, of course, I really ended up with little idea of what the book said.[36]

Furthermore, his writing ability was similarly primitive: "In the street, I had been the most articulate hustler out there—I had commanded attention when I said something. But now, trying to write simple English, I not only wasn't articulate, I wasn't even functional."[37] Malcolm had always been proud of his verbal skill, and he had respected those like Bimbi who used words well. Indeed, it is not too much to say that he was in love with words. Using words cleverly and effectively gave him a genuine pleasure, and their skillful use by others fascinated him. But now he could neither understand what he was reading nor communicate to those outside of prison what he was thinking. What was to be done?

Malcolm got a dictionary, some pads of paper, and some pencils. Then, after spending two days "just riffling uncertainly through the dictionary's pages," he began copying the first page, "just to start some kind of action."[38] It took him a full day to complete the page in his "slow, painstaking, ragged handwriting"; but when he had finished, he got his reward:

> Then, aloud, I read back, to myself, everything I'd written on the tablet. Over and over, aloud, to myself, I read my own handwriting.
>
> I woke up the next morning, thinking about those words —immensely proud to realize that not only had I written so much at one time, but I'd written words that I never knew were in the world.[39]

Moreover, he could remember what most of the words meant; and those he couldn't remember, he looked up again. The experience fascinated him so much that he went on to the next page, and the next, until he had copied the whole dictionary.

In certain respects, this first step of Malcolm's self-education resembles his earlier schooling in Mason, Boston, and New York, on the one hand, and his auto-hypnotic experience, on the other. But in contrast to the former, the content of this work was neither alien nor alienating; and in contrast to the latter, the process was consciously determined. Through the autonomously planned use of his work-energy, Malcolm was transforming his means of self-production—the dictionary and his writing tools—into knowledge. He was creating an object, a set of his own words, through the fusion of his emotionally interpenetrated work-energy with those means of production; and he was then mentally appropriating or internalizing his self-objectification. To state the same point genetically: he was engaged in a real labor of love, in unalienated or self-realizing work, for the first time since he grew peas to put on his mother's table; and he was rewarded with that same sense of pride in work well done. Then, of course, his pride resulted from his mother's loving recognition of his efforts; now it was a reflection of the anticipated favorable recognition from Muhammad. Nonetheless, the relationship between the two moments is not merely analogical: Malcolm's work at the later time was not *like* his earlier activity; it was the further development of that potential. Correspondingly, his love for Muhammad was a higher form of his love for his mother, and for his father.

As indicated above, Malcolm's work with words was only the first step in his re-education. It served to broaden his "word-base," so that soon he was able to build upon that foundation by giving himself a course in black history. Muhammad's teachings stressed that history had been "whitened," that the crimes of white people and the achievements of black people had simply been left out of the official record. Malcolm therefore set out to uncover this buried knowledge; and over the next three years he did manage to document Muhammad's doctrine. In the writings of DuBois, Woodson, and others, he discovered the American Negro's African heritage, which had been destroyed when the "'Christian trader' white man began to ply the seas in his lust for Asian and African empires, and plunder, and power."[40] He learned about the British rape of India and the Opium War in China; and, most importantly, he learned about "slavery's total horror." He also dabbled in philosophy and, seeking to verify the genetic argument implicit in Yacub's history, read Gregor Mendel's *Findings in Genetics*.

Thus, through his attempt to document Muhammad's teachings in books, Malcolm progressively transformed the empty universals of the Word of God and words themselves into a particularized racial-historical understanding. But while his work constitutes a proof of Muhammad's truth and of his own devotion to that truth, it also testifies to his residual skepticism and foreshadows his eventual apostasy. Malcolm was seeking to uncover the historical ground of Muhammad's theology; by so doing, he was continuing to test the validity of the doctrine, just as he had after first hearing it from Reginald. He was not content, as the true believer is, to place his faith entirely in revelation; he needed in addition the assurance of historical verification. This need was in itself an heretical tendency, for it indicates a respect for empirical reality that is ultimately incompatible with theological ideality. Moreover, in pursuing the quest for earthly knowledge with such avidity, Malcolm was transforming himself into a unique individual, a person with a wealth of information and his own point of view. He was therefore destined to be an idiosyncratic member of the Islamic community and, in the end, a threat to Muhammad's charismatic authority.

These last comments, however, take us beyond our current context; at this juncture Malcolm was working productively within the limits set by his Muslim beliefs, and he soon began to transform his developing theoretical knowledge into practice:

> Two other areas of experience which have been extremely formative in my life since prison were first opened to me in the Norfolk Prison Colony. For one thing, I had my first experiences in opening the eyes of my brainwashed black brothers to some of the truths of the black race. And, the other: when I had read enough to know something, I began to enter the Prison Colony's weekly debating program—my baptism into public speaking.[41]

Malcolm observes that before he had accepted the truth, he "so loved being around the white man" that he "disliked how Negro convicts stuck together so much." Once Muhammad's teachings had "reversed" his attitude, in his "guilt and shame" he began to recruit new members for the Nation.[42] In this way he was publicly acknowledging his new-found racial identity, and he was demonstrating his love for his black brothers. Proselytizing was a precise reversal of his previous behavior pattern and therefore served to expiate his guilt. In addition, if he were zealous in the performance of this duty, he could expect to win the praise of Elijah Muhammad who, as Allah's appointed messenger to the Lost-Found Nation, was charged with saving the souls of black folk. Finally, through the recognition and acceptance of the truth by others, the proselytizer confirms that truth and therefore the validity of his own individual-collective identity.* Hence Malcolm's recruitment activity was a rational, practical mediation of his theoretical premises.

His participation in the debating program is not, however, so clearly rational. He states that he decided to participate because "my reading had my mind like steam under pressure. Some way, I had to start telling the white man about himself to his face."[43] But why should Malcolm have desired to confront the white man? Defense of the Nation was not involved, and he was obviously not seeking white converts. But by defeating the white man in debate he was proving, to himself and to other black prisoners, the superiority of his position. He was demonstrating that, armed with Islamic doctrine, he could overpower the presumably omnipotent white man. Such a demonstration was sure to help his recruiting activities, and it would give him the status that hustlers grant to anyone who is really "tough." In this sense, therefore, it was organizationally rational activity. It is evident from Malcolm's own statements, however, that his decision to join the debating society was not determined solely or even primarily by this rational consideration. He had learned about the glorious history of the black man and of the evil history of the white man, and he *needed* to communicate this knowledge to the white man himself. The question therefore still remains, why the desire for confrontation?

Given our prior work, two interrelated interpretations suggest themselves. First, Malcolm had been unjustly judged a criminal and condemned to imprisonment by the white man; it was therefore only just that he judge and condemn the white man in turn. Moreover, the delivery of that judgment permitted the release of aim-inhibited aggressive energy, just as proselytizing permits the release of aim-inhibited sexual energy; that is to say, taking revenge is the first active form of self-productive aggressivity, just as proselytizing is the active form of racial self-identification. Together they constitute an appropriate practical mediation of the theoretical principles of a progressive racial movement. Vengeful action is not, however, a necessary consequence of the premise that the white man is the devil, for in a theological syllogism the Lord can be His own mediator. Consequently, Muhammad could argue that vengeance could and

---

* We touch here, for the first time, upon the psychology of leadership. We shall return to the subject more substantially in the following chapters.

should be left to Allah. And, given a separatist conception of racial identity, aggressive activity is organizationally rational only insofar as it aids in recruitment. But Malcolm needed to do battle with the enemy in the same way that he needed to bring the truth to his brothers and sisters. Once he discovered that "debating, speaking to a crowd, was as exhilarating . . . as the discovery of knowledge had been," he was "gone on debating" and, in his words, "it was right there in prison that I made up my mind to devote the rest of my life to telling the white man about himself—or die."[44] By so doing, he was consecrating himself to a duty he believed was inherent in Muhammad's theology; but in fact he was accepting an obligation that only follows from a de-mystified version of that doctrine.

Leaving aside this additional intimation of things to come, the second point follows directly from the first. Malcolm's theoretical work had his mind "like steam under pressure." All of his extraordinary energies had been poured forth into his work, and they now returned to him as a powerful interpretation of reality, one in which the world was viewed as changing and changeable. Conscious activity designed to change the world was therefore the rational realization of this theoretical position. Such activity, i.e., both his proselytizing and his polemical confrontations, in turn generated a demand for new knowledge, which then became a greater pressure for practical activity. Thus Malcolm became fully engaged in a Muslim practice grounded in racial self-identification and mediated through self-productive aggressivity. No wonder he states of his years in Norfolk that "up to then, I never had been so truly free in my life."[45]

In one sense Reginald's original promise to show his brother "how to get out of prison" had been kept. Malcolm had been liberated from his identification with the oppressor and hence from the vicious circle of self-destructive aggressivity, from his falsified racial character and consciousness. But in another, it obviously had not been kept. Malcolm was still imprisoned and, in fact, his last year in prison was spent back at Charlestown because the authorities at Norfolk were disturbed by his polemical and proselytizing activities. He was even worried for a time that his actions would cause the parole board to deny him parole—although he also reasoned that they might be glad to get rid of him. Be that as it may, despite his spiritual freedom, his body was still in chains. He looked forward eagerly and anxiously to the day of his physical liberation.

The great day came in August, 1952. The prison authorities gave him a "lecture, a cheap L'il Abner suit, and a small amount of money," and he walked out the gate. His first stop was at a Turkish bath where he "got some of the physical feeling of prison-taint steamed off." Then, with some money he received from Hilda, he purchased a good pair of eyeglasses (he had developed astigmatism while in prison), a watch, and a suitcase. He remarks: "I have thought, since, that [with these purchases and] without fully knowing it, I was preparing for what my life was about to become."[46] Each of these items signifies a vital aspect of his later life as a Muslim minister: his reading, his time-consciousness, and his traveling. At a minimum, they were expressions of his intention to be an ex-slave and an ex-Negro, but not a typical ex-convict.

Having thus purified his soul in prison and his body in the Turkish bath, and having equipped himself with what were to be the tools of his trade, Malcolm was ready to begin life anew in what he now understood to be the white man's America.

CHAPTER VII

We Have a Common Enemy

AFTER HIS RELEASE from prison, Malcolm went to live with Wilfred in Detroit. "The warmth of a home and a family was a healing change from the prison cage for me. It would deeply move any newly freed convict, I think. But especially this Muslim home's atmosphere sent me often to my knees to praise Allah." Malcolm had been without a home and family for years, and he had never known family life of this kind. The daily routine was regulated by Muslim law and interpersonal relations were grounded in mutual respect. Wilfred was the "family protector and provider"; but while he was the leading member of the family, he did not rule over it in the manner of his father. There were no arbitrary paternal rules, no beating of the children and no overt friction between the parents.[1] Wilfred's Muslim family, as the negation of Malcolm's original family experience, was its restoration at a genuinely higher level.* Similarly, meetings and services at Detroit's Temple Number One were a higher and combined form of the UNIA meetings and church services of Malcolm's childhood. They fused the quiet, serious tone and the racial self-consciousness of the one with the divine sanctification of the other to create a feeling of warmth, self-respect, and dignity.

For the first time, Malcolm was living in a world unified by racial self-identification—hence in an "atmosphere" reflecting the character-structure of "black people who had learned to be proud they were black, who had learned to love other black people instead of being

---

* It was not yet, however, a familial form that had gone beyond patriarchal limits; it was a type of benevolent paternalism, in which the power of the earthly father depended upon and was governed by that of the heavenly one.

jealous and suspicious."[2] But that world ended abruptly at the edge of the marketplace: every morning Malcolm and Wilfred went off to work at a local furniture store that specialized in "cheap, gaudy looking junk" and "highway robbery interest rates."[3] There they slaved for the Man just as obediently as any other black workers. After about six months, Malcolm got a job in the automotive industry and thus became a member of the industrial proletariat. His physical freedom was therefore limited to the hours after work, just as it had been when he was a young cat slaving in Roxbury. This is to say that his subjective liberation, his spiritual freedom, had no objective ground. His mind was free, but his body was enslaved. In this sense he was still in prison, still trapped in the iron cage of capitalist exploitation and racist domination. He, like virtually all black people in this country, was condemned to existence in a ghettoized, internally colonialized world.

But as Malcolm's membership in the Nation suggests, the world was changing, was in fact decolonizing. Our task in this chapter is to analyze the process of decolonization in the United States during the postwar period. We will begin with the potential for a decolonization movement as it existed for Afro-Americans at that time. Then we will consider the opposing tendencies constituting the movement—the integrationist civil rights movement and the separatist Nation of Islam. We will also follow Malcolm's evolution within the Nation from member to neophyte minister to leading minister. Finally, we will come to Malcolm's critical contribution to the liberation movement, i.e., the practice of polemical confrontation with white America.

"A Nation within a Nation"

Malcolm's job in the auto industry brings immediately into focus the critical role of the automobile in postwar economic life and the wave of suburbanization which accompanied its expanded production. Although we cannot in the present context fully analyze these phenomena, it is generally acknowledged that they were premised upon the pent-up consumer demand of the war years and were facilitated by the rapid expansion of available credit, especially for the purchase of durable goods. When combined with the judicious use of military spending, which functioned domestically as a hedge against crises of overproduction, the consequence was the longest period of prosperity in the nation's history. Moreover, the United States had emerged from the war as the leading power in what euphemistically came to be called the Free World. This hegemonic position brought with it the largest share of the responsibility for keeping not only Western Europe but also the still colonized, decolonizing, and neocolonial areas of the world free from communist economic and political penetration. There were, however, direct economic gains for the United States in accepting these responsibilities, for they created both the opportunity for imperialist expansion and the necessity for maintaining a high level of military spending. As one writer sums up the situation, "The main outcome of the war was . . . the overriding development of the federal government's eventually enduring responsibility to provide a supply of capital and a level of economic demand hitherto unimaginable—but on the behalf of arms procurement and appeals to 'national security.'"[4]

Having thus survived the crises of its immaturity, American monopoly capitalism seemed capable of lasting until, in Max Weber's prescient words, "the last ton of fossilized coal is burnt."[5] In the virtually endless meantime, the "technical and economic conditions" of the "modern economic order" would continue to "determine the lives of all individuals who are born into this mechanism . . . with irresistible force," while the objective situation would continue to be reflected in the "iron cage" of an obsessive concern for "external goods."[6] With the empty souls of the prosperous few thus mirroring the empty bellies of the impoverished many, the age of the hollow men would truly have arrived.

Those whose interests were realized in the existing situation were of course quick to proclaim and celebrate its immortality; and many of those who recognized that their interests were negated in it resigned themselves to its infinite duration. Yet the hosannas and the lamentations were equally premature. First, the stability of the American economy was not really as great as it appeared. Soon after the war, the familiar problems of capacity underutilization and unemployment reappeared, along with a marked tendency toward generalized inflation of prices which was not checked even by the recessions of 1948/49, 1953/54, and 1957/58. Unemployment during the 1950s averaged over 4 percent, capacity utilization declined from an index number of 100 in 1950 to the low 80s by the end of the decade, and the consumer price index rose 59 percent between January, 1946, and December, 1958.[7] Thus even with the aid of enlarged overseas economic activity, a permanently high level of defense spending, and a more or less Keynesian governmental fiscal and monetary policy, the system continued to produce more surplus value than it could readily realize, while the resistance of monopolistic enterprises to downward shifts in price contributed importantly to the inflationary tendency just noted. By the end of the 1960s the combined force of these contradictions would create major economic problems.

During this period very little was done to alleviate the misery of a large portion of the working population, namely, the members of the nonunionized and disproportionately black proletariat who comprised the better part of the industrial reserve army and fought with each other for the low-paid jobs available in the competitive sector of the economy. This in itself is obviously of no concern to the monopolist, who (if he is honest) recognizes in the suffering of the masses his own satisfaction. Under certain circumstances, however, a ghettoized industrial reserve army can become an important basis for an army of national liberation, and that possibility is of concern not only to the monopolist but also to the bourgeois ruling class as a whole.

This was also a time when the specter of national liberation was haunting the imperialist powers: just as World War I had fanned the flames of nationalism around the world, so the renewed defense of the rights of man during World War II encouraged colonial peoples to seek their freedom. More concretely, the weakened condition of the European nations made resistance to imperial power possible. Between 1947, when India gained her independence, and 1963, when Kenya and Zanzibar won their freedom, virtually the whole of the dark world threw off the yoke of colonial domination. Many of the countries formerly dominated by the Western powers turned toward socialism; in North Korea (1948), China (1949), North Vietnam (1954), and Cuba (1959), communist regimes were established; and at certain junctures, most notably at the time of the Bandung Conference in 1955, there were intimations of a united front against both the colonial and neocolonial powers. Although such a united effort did not materialize during the 1950s, it was evident that (as Elijáh Muhammad, and Marcus Garvey before him, had proclaimed) the dark world was rising.

The implications of decolonization were not lost upon black Americans. In 1947, for example, W. E. B. DuBois petitioned the newly formed United Nations Commission on Human Rights to take up the case of the American Negro. He argued that "prolonged policies of segregation and discrimination had involuntarily welded the mass [of Negroes] almost into a nation within a nation with its own schools, churches, hospitals, newspapers, and many business enterprises." The United States, in seeking to preserve this situation, was forced "to deny its political ideas, to falsify its philanthropic assertions and to make its religion to a great extent hypocritical." With the United Nations centered in New York, and with most of the world's population having "more or less colored skin," this contradiction between American ideals and American reality would be internationalized; it was incumbent upon the United Nations to concern itself with the problem.[8]

DuBois's appeal was unsuccessful, but the tactical point had been made. The United States would in the future increasingly have to negotiate with dark-skinned peoples. Because it would be disadvantaged in such negotiations by its racist image, enlightened self-interest dictated at least token changes in racial policy; which is to say, black people had been given a new counter in the game of American politics.

World War II had other implications for Afro-American life. As we noted when discussing the hustling society, the economic position of black people had advanced during the war. This advance was parallel to but far more dramatic than the progress made during World War I. The number of black people employed in manufacturing and mechanical work increased from 693,000 to 960,000 between 1910 and 1920, and from 738,000 to 1,336,000 between 1940 and 1950.[9]* Moreover, the number employed in trade and transportation increased from 375,000 in 1910 to 452,000 in 1920, and from 589,000 in 1940 to 1,029,000 in 1950. Between 1940 and 1950 the number of blacks in public service went from 56,000 to 180,000, and those engaged in professional or semi-professional activities (mainly the latter) increased from 177,000 to 356,000. Thus the two wars created a black industrial proletariat, a substantial class of black white-collar workers, and a sizable petite bourgeoisie.†

These occupational gains were of course accompanied by generally higher incomes, and even by a narrowing of the income gap between white and black members of the labor force: the median income of black families jumped from 37 percent of white-family income in 1939 to 53 percent in 1951.[10] It follows that the way of life

---

* The gains in manufacturing attained during World War I and the 1920s were substantially eliminated during the Depression, so that in 1940 black people had fallen back almost to their 1910 position.

† It may be noted that included in the professional/semi-professional category in 1950 were 1,450 lawyers and judges, 4,026 doctors, 4,039 college professors, 86,620 schoolteachers, and 18,150 clergymen (Ross and Hill, *Employment, Race, and Poverty*, p. 7).

of the black population was in general more tolerable than it had been. It might therefore seem that there were no valid economic grounds for racial protest: after all, great progress was being made within the existing situation.

There is, however, another side to this story. A substantial part of the black advance in economic status resulted from the continuing migration of black people from the small towns and farming regions of the South to the cities of the North, i.e., from lower-income areas to higher ones, rather than from advancement within the urban labor-market; insofar as new positions did become available to black workers, they were typically the ones left behind by white workers in their own climb toward middle-class status. Moreover, black people with the same qualifications and doing the same work as white people were usually paid at a lower wage-rate; and very few high-paying, high-status jobs were accessible to blacks. Finally, the income gap between black and white families did not narrow any further after the end of the Korean War. The ratio of black to white median family income remained at about 50 percent. Given that incomes were generally rising, it follows that the dollar amount of the difference was actually increasing. As late as 1960 only 17 percent of black families had incomes in excess of $7,000, and only 6 percent had incomes of $10,000 or above; the corresponding figures for white families were 41 and 18 percent, respectively.*

Thus by 1960 the wartime and Cold War prosperity of the American system had not done much to change the relative economic positions of the black and white populations as a whole, nor even of the respective middle classes; and it had certainly not resulted in the emergence of a genuine black bourgeoisie. Furthermore, the economic situation of the great mass of black people actually deteriorated after the end of the Korean War. Although the number of families with incomes below $3,000 declined from 65 percent to 44 percent of the black population between 1947 and 1960, the unemployment rate of black workers rose from its low point of 4.5 percent in 1953 to 9.9 percent in 1954, and it averaged about 9.5 percent for the rest of the decade. In addition, in 1960 68 percent of black families had incomes under $5000, but only 36 percent of white families were forced to exist on that little.[11] The great majority of black people were losing ground to both the white population and the black middle class in the competitive struggle for economic survival, with the consequence that the social situation of the masses was sim-

* Adjusted to the purchasing power of 1965 dollars.

ilarly depressed. In 1960, 44 percent of black people were living in substandard housing and 77 percent of blacks living in large cities were confined to "poverty areas," i.e., to the "town" sections of the ghettoes in Roxbury, Harlem, Hough, Watts, etc.[12]

In a moment we shall have to attend more closely to the class differential within the black community, but those differences are less significant than the uniformity imposed by white oppression. As Malcolm commented, "Any Negro in the community can be stopped in the street. 'Put your hands up,' and they pat you down. Might be a doctor, a lawyer, a preacher or some other kind of Uncle Tom, but despite your professional standing, you'll find that you're the same victim as the man who's in the alley."[13] The ghetto cage was gilded, or at least painted gold, for a few; but it was nonetheless a cage. The segregation of black people insured that they would become a nation within a nation, bound to each other by their common enemy. The group-emotional distortion of class lines not only divided the proletariat into opposing racial factions, it also created an inter-class racial group with a unifying interest in overcoming racist oppression.

The civil rights movement and the Nation of Islam can now be understood as the products of the continuing segregation (ghettoization) of black Americans in an era of decolonization. Such an interpretation fails to explain, though, how these objective conditions were subjectively transformed into conscious activity and why the transformation resulted in integrationist and separatist movements. With respect to the first issue, the most direct argument linking objective conditions to conscious activity was formulated by Marx in *"Wage-Labour and Capital"*:

> A house may be large or small; as long as the surrounding houses are equally small it satisfies all social demands for a dwelling. But let a palace arise beside the small house, and it shrinks from a little house to a hut. The little house shows now that its owner has only very slight or no demands to make; and however high it may shoot up in the course of civilisation, if the neighboring palace grows to an equal or greater extent, the occupant of the relatively small house will feel more and more cramped within its four walls.[14]

Marx is surely correct in arguing that the individual's objective situation generally determines his subjective tendencies; that an objective situation of relative disadvantage—in the present instance, the negated racial interest constituted by economic inequality, social injustice, and political oppression—results in a subjective feeling of relative deprivation; and that the critical factor in producing feelings of restlessness and dissatisfaction is an unfavorable change in the relative position of the individual and some specified Other. Marx's position is in fact sufficient to explain the persistent tendency toward protest activity that we have seen developing in the course of our inquiry, i.e., the historical movement from the UNIA through the MOWM to the organized efforts now coming into view. But Marx's general argument requires further specification.

For present purposes, let us assume three bases for judgments of relative deprivation, each of which has three components. The individual who lives in the small house may evaluate himself in economic, social-psychological, or political terms. He may judge his present position against his own past or projected future position; against the position of others in his own class or group; or against the position of other classes, groups, or even nations. He has three possible relationships with respect to these positions and each form of activity: getting better, getting worse, or staying the same.

When we apply these criteria to the situation of black Americans, we find that during the period 1940 to 1953 their economic, social, and political position was improving, measured against the record of their own past or the relative status of white people, and even against that of black Africans. The black house was still separate and unequal; but it was growing faster than the white house. Consequently, any residual sense that white supremacy was natural, eternal, rational, and right was rapidly disappearing. Black people were becoming increasingly aware that the structure of racial relations was historical, therefore mutable and, ultimately, subject to human control. Then, after 1953 (or 1954, if one wishes to use *Brown* vs. *Board of Education* as the point of division), economic progress slowed markedly in self-referential terms and ceased altogether or became regression when measured against the advancing prosperity of the white population. The relative social position of the two races was frozen as well; and the political situation deteriorated dramatically when the white South constituted itself as a kind of de facto Ku Klux Klan in its attempts to forestall school integration. At the same time, expectations of continued or even accelerated progress had been engendered by the experience of the World War II and Korean War years; and some black people were beginning to see themselves in the light of black Africa's rapid advance toward freedom. Thus we find a pattern similar to but more pervasive than the one resulting in the rise of the UNIA after World War I, a pattern resembling to a great extent what James C. Davies calls "the J-Curve of rising and declining satisfactions." In his words: "Revolution [or rebellion] is most likely to take place when a prolonged period of rising expectations and rising gratification is followed by a short period of sharp reversal during which the gap between expectations and gratifications quickly widens and becomes intolerable."[15]

Looked at from another angle, the J-curve of first decreasing and then increasing relative deprivation brings to the surface the deep-seated anger and resentment of the oppressed individual or group. We have encountered this anger many times before; we will meet it next in the form of a more openly acknowledged black rage. Taken together with the political-economic position of Afro-Americans during the 1950s and 1960s, it constitutes the potential for a movement toward decolonization.

The Civil Rights Movement: Decolonization as Integration

The movement as it first developed was not self-consciously anticolonialist: it was integrationist and separatist. The former tendency, embodied in the civil rights movement, represented the interests of the rising black middle class. The latter tendency, embodied in the Nation of Islam, represented the interests of the increasingly beleaguered black masses. Neither of them adequately represented the interests of all black people, yet the interests of all black people were advanced through their activities. This common interest, along with the motives appropriate to it, became increasingly apparent as the struggle progressed.

We turn first to the civil rights movement. Prior to 1955, its unquestioned leader was the NAACP (the National Association for the Advancement of Colored People). Founded by W. E. B. DuBois and his co-workers in 1909, it had been working patiently against segregation by applying pressure whenever possible to legislative bodies and, most importantly, by pressing the courts to enforce the Fourteenth and Fifteenth Amendments to the Constitution. The Supreme Court's decision in *Brown* vs. *Board of Education* that racially separate schools were inherently unequal was the organization's greatest victory; thereafter, the initiative in the struggle passed on to other organizations. This shift was the product of both the success and failure of the NAACP approach: on the one hand, by its legal victories it had demonstrated that *de jure* racism could be overcome; on the other, white resistance to integration and continued de facto segregation indicated that legal victories were insufficient. A different program was needed to solve these more difficult problems.

The NAACP was not capable of developing such an alternative. Although it had a substantial membership and a larger following, and despite the fact that even its legal victories were based upon the emerging political power of black voters in urban areas, the organization was a vehicle of and for the Negro middle class—of and for what Malcolm called "the modern counterpart of the slavery time Uncle Tom," the "twentieth century house Negro." It embodied the interest of the narrow stratum of the black population that had been partially integrated into the American economy without at the same time being integrated into the nation's social and political life. As we have seen, this economic integration was at best petit-bourgeois, and more commonly working-class. The black bourgeoisie was therefore economically disadvantaged in comparison to the white bourgeoisie. It was also socially and politically inferior to the white working-class, and it was this disadvantage that the NAACP was attempting to overcome; it was, implicitly, working to end the racial division of the American proletariat. But because the consciousness of its leaders was at least partially falsified through identification with the white-bourgeois oppressor, its members did not see its activities in this light. Consequently, the NAACP did not challenge the legitimacy of the existing system but, rather, asked that Negroes be treated as if they were white and bourgeois. Except for the happy few who were relatively wealthy (and preferably light-skinned), however, even such a semblance of integration was impossible. It follows that in class-racial terms the NAACP embodied an ultimately unrealizable interest. Nonetheless, by overturning certain of the legal barriers to racial progress and, in the process, by pushing legalism to its limit, the organization prepared the ground for the next phase of the struggle.

The second phase of the civil rights movement began on December 1, 1955, when Mrs. Rosa Parks refused to yield her seat on a Montgomery, Alabama, bus to a white passenger. Subsequently she was arrested, tried, convicted of breaking the law (a local segregation ordinance), and fined $14.

Ten years earlier, that would have been the end of the incident, if indeed such an incident would even have occurred. Or, perhaps, since Mrs. Parks was a leading member of the local NAACP chapter, her action would have become the basis for a judicial challenge to the law's constitutionality. But the time of automatic compliance with unjust laws or strictly legalistic opposition thereto was passing. The local Negro leadership decided to test the constitutionality of the law in the courts and to boycott the Montgomery buses until the bus company agreed to accord equal treatment to all passengers.

Approximately one year later, the boycott ended in success when the United States Supreme Court ruled that bus segregation was unconstitutional. In itself this victory was not unimportant; but of far greater significance was the emergence of a new Negro leader and a new (or renewed) racial movement. During the early days of the boycott a twenty-seven-year-old Baptist minister named Martin Luther King, Jr., was elected president of the boycott organization. In his first speech after being elevated to this position he defined the principles of the protest in this way:

> One of the great glories of democracy is the right to protest.
> The White Citizens Councils and the Ku Klux Klan are protesting for the perpetuation of injustice in the community.
> We are protesting for the *birth* of justice in the community.
> Their methods lead to violence and lawlessness. But in our protest there will be no cross burnings. No white person will be taken from his home by a hooded Negro mob and brutally murdered. There will be no threats and intimidation. . . . We will only say to the people, "let your conscience be your guide." [16]

The bus boycott itself was a practical expedient: by depriving the company of a substantial percentage of its income, the protesters could hope to force a change of policy. King proposed transforming the protest into a moral crusade, an appeal to the conscience of the enemy. But in such a crusade, the protester had to be worthy of his protest. He had to eschew the use of violent means, which would destroy the moral purity of his ends, and he had to purge himself of all evil intentions toward his enemies:

> Once again we must hear the words of Jesus echoing across the centuries: Love your enemies, bless them that curse you, and pray for them that despitefully use you. . . . In spite of mistreatment that we have confronted, we must not become bitter and end up by hating our white brothers. As

Booker T. Washington said, "Let no man pull you down so low as to make you hate him."[17]

Over the next several months these principles of politicized Christian love evolved into a full-blown theory and practice of nonviolent direct action—Satyagraha (Truth-force), to use Gandhi's name for the practice he originated. In 1957 King founded the Southern Christian Leadership Conference (SCLC) as an organizational vehicle for promoting the use of Satyagraha.

As we shall see in a moment, in the end the practical interest and the moralized motives involved in nonviolent protest are self-contradictory; but in the first instance, the contradiction was only latent. The economic losses and negative publicity that result from a well-managed protest tend to quicken the moral sensibilities of responsible political-economic leaders. Such a protest forces re-definition of their enlightened self-interest. To be sure, the dedicated Klansman or member of a White Citizens Council is unlikely to have his conscience touched by such demonstrations of Christian love, but nonviolent protest can bring about considerable changes in official policies—so long as the protester is willing to absorb without retaliation the violence that all protest involves, and so long as he does not substantially challenge the interest of the ruling class.

We cannot here detail the activities of SCLC and the other protest organizations that comprised the Movement, the violent white-racist response to these activities, or the role of the federal government in the protest process. But we may observe that the Movement properly so-called consisted, on one side, of the NAACP, which continued to carry the legal and political lobbying burdens of collective action, and the SCLC and CORE (Congress of Racial Equality), on the other. CORE, founded in 1942, was from its inception dedicated to the use of nonviolent protest. It had been the first organization to adapt the sit-in technique of industrial unionism to the context of racial struggle. (This technique, it may be added, was passed on to a new generation of black people when four black college students in Greensboro, North Carolina, sat in at a Woolworth's lunch counter and thereby initiated the modern use of sit-ins as a weapon to be used against segregation of public accommodations.) CORE also organized the Freedom Rides through the South, beginning in 1961, that led first to violence against the riders and mass arrests but eventually to an ICC ruling banning all segregation in interstate public transport.

The attempt to integrate the South generated massive and violent white resistance. This was of two far from mutually exclusive types. On the one hand, there were attempts by public officials to circumvent or defy the Supreme Court and the federal government, e.g., Orville Faubus's attempt to stop school integration in Little Rock, Arkansas, in 1957; Virginia's Massive Resistance in 1958; and the arrest of Freedom Riders on charges of disorderly conduct or disturbing the peace. On the other, there were direct, violent assaults upon the protesters by a variety of vigilante groups or vigilant individuals. This heavy use of the stick by Southern officials and the poor whites who were the pawns in their game made it easy for the federal government to appear in a benevolent light, especially after the election of John F. Kennedy in 1960. By playing a mediating role between the protesters and the reactionaries, and by proffering a sufficient number of legislative carrots to give the impression that substantial progress was being made, the federal government and the Democratic Party were able to retain the loyalty of most Negroes and Negro leaders.

The single most dramatic demonstration of the Movement's strength was the March on Washington in 1963. By that time, however, its organizational weaknesses were also becoming apparent. The black members of the Student Nonviolent Coordinating Committee (SNCC), which had been formed under King's leadership in 1960 to do just what its name implies, were becoming increasingly impatient with the relatively modest goals of the Movement. At the March, which was intended to persuade Congress that it could not in good conscience fail to pass President Kennedy's Civil Rights Bill, John Lewis (then chairman of SNCC) proposed to say:

> In good conscience we cannot support the Administration's civil rights bill, for it is too little, and too late. There's not one thing in the bill that will protect our people from police brutality. . . . What is in the bill that will protect the homeless and starving people of this nation? What is there in this bill to insure the equality of a maid who earns $5.00 a week in the home of a family whose income is $100,000 a year? [18]

But Lewis's remarks were censored by the March's leaders, who thereby demonstrated the validity of Malcolm's charge that Negro leaders were "being used against the Negro Revolution," i.e., against a movement that would be in the interest of *all* black people, not just the members of the black middle class. Moreover, even those whose interests were concretized in the Movement, insofar as they had actually been involved in confrontation with the racist enemy, were beginning to feel the strain of nonviolent restraint. Alfred Poussaint, a black psychiatrist who worked extensively with SNCC workers in the South, observed:

> After a period of time it became apparent that they [the black SNCC workers] were directing [their hostility] mostly at each other and the white civil-rights workers. Violent verbal and sometimes physical fights often occurred among the workers on the civil rights projects throughout the South. While they were talking about being nonviolent and "loving" the sheriff that just hit them over the head, they rampaged around the project houses beating each other up. I frequently had to calm Negro civil-rights workers with large doses of tranquilizers for what I can describe clinically only as *acute attacks of rage*.[19]

These young people, who were becoming concerned about the plight of the black masses and who were suffering not only the physical but also the emotional consequences of nonviolent protest, emerged in the mid-1960s as the originators of the Black Power Movement— or, as one writer called them, "the angry children of Malcolm X."[20]

The Nation of Islam: Decolonization as Separation

The weapons of class-racial struggle were thus being forged in the lunch counters, bus stations, polling places, and streets of the South. They were also being molded and sharpened in the Northern ghettoes; and there the principal agency of racial education was the Nation of Islam.

The ghetto situation, as we noted earlier, was deteriorating throughout the 1950s. Most fundamentally, the deterioration reflected the unemployment or underemployment of the black masses, whose consignment to the industrial reserve army was determined on the one hand by their substantial exclusion from the monopoly-union sector of the economy, and on the other by the pervasive job discrimination that limited them to unskilled and semi-skilled positions which were (and are) particularly vulnerable to technological elimination. Thus they were becoming more and

more a surplus population, subject to the greatest possible alienation of their labor when they were able to find work, and alienated
from productive use of their labor-power altogether when jobs were
not to be found. Welfare slavery and *lumpen-proletarian* hustling
were increasingly the only available means to the end of simply
staying alive. Moreover, the fight for survival was made all the more
difficult by other advantages the white ruling class derived from the
ghettoization of black people. Under this system the direct appropriation of black labor could be supplemented through such indirect
means as high rents for substandard housing, high interest rates for
the purchase of durable or semi-durable commodities, high prices
for low-grade food and clothing, and gross underinvestment in the
essential social services (education, health, recreation, transportation, etc.)—to say nothing of the value appropriated through gambling and the sale of the various illegal commodities. This pervasive
pattern of exploitation produced a process of generalized social dis-
organization, familial disintegration, and individual disorientation
which resulted in the various forms of emotional alienation we have
previously uncovered, i.e., falsified racial identity, the dumb show of
good and bad Negro stereotypes, the internally divided family or the
fragmented one, and an individual-collective character-structure
grounded in identification with the oppressor and activated through
self-destructive aggressivity. As Kenneth Clark argues, "The dark
ghetto is institutionalized pathology; it is chronic, self-perpetuating
pathology."[21] It need only be added that during this period it was
self-perpetuating on an expanding scale.

Muhammad's program was intended to be the remedy for these
ghetto ills, the "absolute cure" for the Negro's ailments; and, in fact,
for those who were able to accept the truth, Islamic adherency did
perform this function. As we have already seen in Malcolm's case,
and earlier in that of Benjamin Goodman, the convert to Islam was
able to stabilize his economic situation, re-form his personal and
family life, and re-unify his character structure on a ground of racial
self-identification. Through membership in the Nation, moreover,
the individual became part of a community of proud black people,
whose trust in and loyalty to each other contrasted markedly with
the hostility and paranoia of the hustling society and of the ghetto
way of life in general. And through Muhammad's teachings, he was
enabled to develop a groundwork of racial self-consciousness, a
black self-conception as well as a black identity. This self-conception, finally, contained the vital political notions that all black

people were entitled to equality, justice, and freedom, that the white man was the enemy who precluded the realization of these ideals, and that the dark world was rising up against the white man's devilish dominion.

In all of these respects the Nation was a progressive movement, an historically and life-historically rational response to the increasingly pathological ghetto situation. Its program was grounded in the interests of the black masses and mediated through their emotional needs; hence it was a vehicle for their political education and liberation. It was, in short, the rightful successor to the UNIA. There were limitations upon its rationality, however. Stating the point most generally, the Nation was not a nation, and therefore could not realize its universal notions. Economically, most of its members held unskilled or semi-skilled positions in white-owned businesses. They were not economically self-determining; their ability to earn a decent living depended upon the demand for their labor. But that demand was limited and, as we have seen, was becoming ever more limited. Consequently, the number of individuals who could take Muhammad's economic cure of a modified Protestant work ethic was limited as well. This limitation could not be overcome by some form of economic nationalism, for in an age of monopoly capitalism the Nation could do no more than build a chain of retail outlets and develop a marginal agricultural operation. It lacked the economic ground for an autonomous or separate national life; hence it also lacked the power to transform the ghetto situation. Membership in the Nation could help an individual free himself from the worst aspects of ghetto living, and it could insulate him from some of the frustration of living in the white man's America; but it could not bring him equality, justice, or freedom within the American system, and its program of territorial separation was politically unrealizable. Finally, its theologically falsified racial doctrine was a decided step back from Garvey's secular conception of the racial situation.

In sum, the Nation was a movement of opposing progressive and regressive tendencies: on the one side, it was racially self-conscious, nationalist, and militant; on the other, it was chiliastic, separatist, and politically inactive. It thus reflected in inverted form the contradictions of the civil rights movement, which was secular, socially involved, and activist, but also racially false-conscious, integrationist, and nonviolent.

Although Muhammad's program was an appropriate remedy at least for certain ghetto ills, in 1952—when Malcolm received his

"X" and became a full member of the Nation—not many people had taken the cure. Malcolm reports that meetings at Temple Number One in Detroit were not well attended:

> I thought it was outrageous that our small temple still had some empty seats. I complained to my brother Wilfred that there should be no empty seats, with the surrounding streets full of our brainwashed black brothers and sisters, drinking, cursing, fighting, dancing, carousing, and using dope—the very things that Mr. Muhammad taught were helping the black man to stay under the heel of the white man here in America.[22]

Yet despite the small size of the membership, "the recruitment attitude at the temple seemed . . . to amount to a self-defeating waiting view, . . . an assumption that Allah would bring . . . more Muslims" into the fold. To be sure, members of the storefront congregation did recruit among family and friends; but they were not going out into the streets, where the devil's victims were mainly to be found. They were not *hustling* for souls, the way Malcolm had once hustled marijuana, or the way the communists in Harlem had pushed the *Daily Worker*. For the moment, however, there was nothing Malcolm could do about the situation.

Then in the fall of 1952 a caravan of ten automobiles, containing the entire Detroit congregation, made its way to Chicago's Temple Number Two to hear the Prophet himself. Malcolm was more excited than he had been "since childhood"; he states that as he entered the Chicago temple, "I experienced tinglings up my spine as I've never had since."[23] He was about to see the Messenger of Allah, the man whose "small, sensitive, gentle, brown face" he had studied in photographs "until I dreamed about it." The beloved image was about to materialize. Even so, "I was totally unprepared for the Messenger's . . . physical impact upon my emotions."[24] He sat "riveted" until Muhammad, pausing for breath, called his name and asked him to stand. "It was like an electrical shock," to be recognized by the man he idolized, to feel the flow of energy as a direct circuit uniting him with that man. Then "standing there, feeling the eyes of the two hundred Muslims upon me, I heard him make a parable about me."[25] The Prophet compared him to Job, whom the devil wagered would not remain faithful to God once the "hedges" of his good fortune were removed. Malcolm had been faithful while in prison, but prison itself had been a hedge against sin. Now that he was again a free man, the devil (the white man) would say that his faith would disappear. "'Well, now, our good brother Malcolm's hedge is removed and we will see how he does,' Mr. Muhammad said. 'I believe that he [like Job] is going to remain faithful.'"[26] The electrical circuit uniting him with his leader (and the less intense but still gripping emotional relationship he had with his fellow believers) was converted into a specifically moral charge: he was made to feel the obligation or responsibility to confirm through his faithfulness Mr. Muhammad's faith in him.

The obligation was of course all the more binding because Muhammad had singled Malcolm out, given him a special status within the small Nation—a status that echoed, albeit vaguely and tentatively, Malcolm's relationship to his Garveyite father. The relationship thus implied was as yet a bare potential, but Malcolm took the first step toward its actualization that evening. His family and Minister Lemuel Hassan of the Detroit temple had been invited to dine with Muhammad. At dinner Malcolm seized an opportunity presented by a lull in the conversation to ask how large the Nation was supposed to be. Muhammad responded, predictably enough, that it should be very large indeed. Malcolm then asked Muhammad how that "ought" could be transformed into an "is"; and Muhammad answered, by recruiting new, young members. In this way Malcolm obtained official sanction for initiating a more active recruiting program for the Detroit temple. Once he was back in Detroit and with Hassan's full support, he began hustling the bars, pool halls, and back alleys of the ghetto for converts. He used the same techniques he had learned in Harlem, but now these means had an entirely different meaning. Instead of serving the white bourgeois interest in the narcotization of the masses, they had become instruments of racial-religious liberation—more effective ones than simply praying to Allah and waiting for his divine intervention. In a few months the membership in the Detroit temple had tripled; and Malcolm gained his reward in the form of "warm praise" from Muhammad, as well as the latter's "interest" in his "potential."[27]

A perfect complementarity of interests and motives was now beginning to develop between the Prophet and his young follower. The former needed "more young men willing to work as hard as they would have to in order to bear the responsibilities of his ministers";[28] and he was nourished by the love of his adherents. The latter needed an outlet for his abundant energies, which were grounded in his worship for his leader. Malcolm's elevation to ministerial status was practically a foregone conclusion. Nonetheless, he did not become a minister immediately. First his proselytizing activity in the streets of the ghetto was augmented by giving personal testimony to Muhammad's truth at temple meetings, and then by giving short, extemporaneous lectures on the interrelationship of Christianity and the horrors of slavery. These experiences were enormously stimulating to him:

> Today when thousands of Muslims and others have been out before me, when audiences of millions have been beyond radio and television microphones, I'm sure I rarely feel as much electricity as was then generated in me by the upturned faces of those seventy-five or a hundred Muslims, plus other curious visitors, sitting there in our storefront temple with the squealing of pigs filtering in from the slaughterhouse just outside.[29]

The sensations Malcolm had first felt when debating in prison were now being amplified by the atmosphere of Muslim meetings; he was beginning to experience a group's emotion as his own. He was learning to lead, and he was simultaneously learning to need the emotional satisfaction of oratorical leadership. After hours of hustling the streets for converts, he notes, "My head would reel sometimes, with mingled anger and pity for my poor blind black brothers. I couldn't wait for the next time our Minister Lemuel Hassan would let me speak."[30] As it had been when he was in prison, his knowledge, now concretized through the activity of proselytism, had his mind like "steam under pressure."

Muhammad created a more regular outlet for that pent-up energy when he appointed Malcolm assistant minister of the Detroit temple in the summer of 1953. A new phase in Malcolm's education began. He would go frequently to Chicago to visit Muhammad, where he was treated as if he were "one of the sons of Mr. Muhammad and his dark, good wife Sister Clara Muhammad."[31] In this familial atmosphere, which superseded the family situation of his childhood and even the comforting warmth of his brother Wilfred's home, Malcolm was nurtured by Muhammad's wisdom. He was given systematic instruction in Muslim theology; and he was told all of the Nation's synoptic tales. From Muhammad's mother he learned of the Prophet's childhood deeds; from Muhammad himself he learned of the later ones. In particular the Prophet told him about the sacred moment when W. D. Fard admitted that He was the Savior, the Mahdi:

"I said to Him again," said Mr. Muhammad, "What is your true name?" And then He said, "My name is Mahdi. I came to guide you into the right Path."

Mr. Elijah Muhammad says that he sat listening with an open heart and an open mind—the way I sat listening to Mr. Muhammad. And Mr. Muhammad said he never doubted any word that the "Savior" taught him.[32]

The manifest implication of the lesson is that Malcolm was to learn undoubting faith from Muhammad, whose faith came directly from God. But we may observe a suggestive analogical aspect of the incident: Fard was to Muhammad as Muhammad is to Malcolm—an analogy that implies, however quietly, that Malcolm was destined to be Muhammad's successor . . . that he would one day come into the estate of the seventh son.*

For the moment this latent implication need not concern us, nor need we detail the substance of Malcolm's instruction in Islamic ritual practices or the particulars of his training in organizational activity. Suffice it to say that he was learning both the theoretical content and the practical forms of Islam from Muhammad, and that he was repaying his teacher's time and attention with interest. He was a rapid learner, and he was absolutely devoted to his mentor:

> My adoration of Mr. Muhammad grew, in the sense of the Latin root word *adorare*. It means much more than our "adoration" or "adore." It means that my worship of him was so awesome that he was the first man whom I had ever feared—not fear such as of a man with a gun, but the fear such as one has of the power of the sun.[33]

Muhammad was the *arche*, the determining principle, of Malcolm's existence. The Prophet's truth had transformed Malcolm, re-created him: the unity of his conscience and consciousness, hence the stability of his character-structure and the totalizing tendency in his practical activity, depended upon the vivifying potency of that truth; and his sense of self-respect, as well as his happiness, was the product of Muhammad's paternal benevolence. Thus it is not surprising that Malcolm spontaneously used a Platonic analogy of the sun in order to explain his relationship to his leader or, better, that he should have had recourse to the revelation of Saint John the Divine:

---

* But blood is blood: when Elijah Muhammad died on February 25, 1975 (almost ten years to the day after Malcolm), it was *his* seventh son, Wallace Muhammad, who ascended to the throne.

I was in the Spirit on the Lord's day, and heard behind me a
great voice, as of a trumpet, saying, I am Alpha and Omega,
the first and the last. . . .

And I turned to see the voice that spake with me. And
being turned, I saw seven golden candlesticks; and in the
midst of the seven candlesticks *one* like unto the Son of
man. . . . And he had in his right hand seven stars: and out
of his mouth went a sharp two-edged sword: and his counte-
nance *was* as the sun shineth in his strength.[34]

Muhammad was for Malcolm Alpha and Omega; in his own words,
the "lamb of a man" whose two-edged sword (his teachings) "cut[s]
back and forth to free the black man's mind from the white man."[35]
In our terms, Malcolm's conscience was an internalized reflection of
Muhammad's two-edged sword, which possessed the power to unify
or divide the self. In a moral sense it was the power of life and death,
i.e., the power to determine conscious activity as either self-productive or self-destructive. Consequently, Malcolm adored his leader
and was in awe of his charismatic (divinely revealed) truth.

Yet it is not sufficient to say that Malcolm worshipped Muhammad as the Messenger of Allah, any more than it is to say that John
received revelation or that Plato was divinely inspired. There is a
fundamental falsification involved in the attribution of human energies to an abstract or spiritual image. In the present instance, this
consequence followed from the projection of Malcolm's repressed
emotional energies onto Muhammad, who was thereby idealized.
Stating the point genetically instead of dynamically, Muhammad was
the successor to Malcolm's parents, the inheritor of their powers.
Furthermore, because Muslim doctrine made possible the splitting
of Malcolm's original filial ambivalence, these powers returned to
him in the double form of *filial adoration* for Elijah Muhammad and
heroic hatred of the white man. Hence he could honestly say to the
little congregation of Detroit's Temple Number One: " 'I have sat at
our Messenger's feet, hearing the truth from his own mouth! I have
pledged on my knees to Allah to tell the white man about his crimes
and the Black man the true teachings of our Honorable Elijah Muhammad. I don't care if it costs my life.' "[36] Truly Malcolm was his
father's seventh son.

In sum, through his purified filial relationship to Elijah Muhammad, Malcolm's objective situation—in general, the situation of the
black masses under postwar American monopoly capitalism, and

more particularly, the existing state of the Nation of Islam—was transformed into a ground for proselytizing and polemical conscious activity. By 1954 that ground was secure, and Malcolm was sent forth "to establish more temples among the twenty-two million black brothers who were brainwashed and sleeping in the cities of North America."[37] His first assignment was in Boston, where after three months he had awakened and cured enough of his brothers and sisters to open a small temple.* Next he went to Philadelphia, where again in three months' time a small temple was established; then back to New York, there to be the minister in charge of Temple Number Seven in Harlem.

Malcolm had not been in New York since his near-fatal confrontation with West Indian Archie, and it is therefore not surprising that he felt an indescribable "welter of emotions" upon returning. He had left the city in a state of drug-induced insanity; he had been buried in a prison graveyard and left for (mentally) dead. But he had been resurrected from that premature grave and been reborn into a new life; now he was once again to face the challenge of being a success in the Mecca of Black America: "For Mr. Muhammad's teachings really to resurrect American black people, Islam obviously had to grow, to grow very big. And nowhere in America was such a single temple potential available as in New York's five boroughs."[38] He had been given the responsibility for realizing that singular potential, hence also the potential for singular service to his people and his leader. His future was here and now, present in that project. The prospect must have been both exciting and somewhat frightening, but the omens were good: the seventh son was to be the minister of the seventh temple and, more concretely, he had been an effective proselytizer in Detroit, Boston, and Philadelphia.

Malcolm's welter of emotions did not, however, simply reflect the immanence of his future in his present. He was also feeling the force of his past, which lived here in the external form of the people he had formerly known—the people whose lives had actually been what his life would have been if . . . : "And so many of the survivors whom I had known as tough hyenas and wolves of the streets in the old days . . . in the space of nine years had been reduced to the ghetto's minor, scavenger hustles to scratch up room rent and food

---

* It may be noted that Malcolm had a friendly reunion with Shorty while he was in Boston, but that the latter was not interested in Islam. Malcolm's half-sister Ella, on the other hand, came to temple meetings. She did not, however, join the Nation at this time.

money. Some now worked downtown, messengers, janitors, things like that." Cadillac Drake, who had been a pimp in the old days, had gotten hooked on heroin and had become "the dirtiest, sloppiest bum you ever laid eyes on."[39] Sammy the Pimp was dead, perhaps murdered, and West Indian Archie was a sick old man, living in a cheap rented room in the Bronx. Malcolm went to see him, went to make peace with the man he had once felt it necessary to kill. It was a sad reunion. Peace was made; Malcolm told Archie how often he had thought about his incredible memory, and about how the Man had negated the possibility of using it productively; and Archie understood. But they both also understood that it was too late for the old man: "Neither of us would say that it was not too late. [But] I have the feeling that he knew, as I could see, that the end was closing in. . . . I became too moved about what he had been and what he had now become to stay much longer. I didn't have much money, and he didn't want to accept what little I was able to press on him. But I made him take it."[40] The tough, proud, and independent hustler had become a charity case, while the boy he once had terrified, and who through divine good fortune had escaped the same fate, materialized his pity and sorrow in the form of a charitable donation. No victorious messenger, but only a compassionate friend, at the end of this three-penny opera.

Hustlers thought of themselves as the happy few who could defy with impunity the laws and logic of American democracy; in the end they were the system's unhappiest victims. "They had known all the angles, but beneath that surface they were poor, ignorant, untrained black men; life had eased up on them and hyped them."[41] Malcolm, too, had been hyped, trapped in first one version and then another of the American dream. But he had been awakened, he had uncovered the latent nightmare content of the manifest dream, and he was prepared to awaken his brothers and sisters. Taking his past and future together as they determined and were determined by his present activity, we may say that his project was to transform the hustling society or, more generally, the Harlem ghetto into a community of Muslim believers.

More easily said than done: Malcolm preached to the members of his congregation and to such friends as they were able to rope into attending, but very few of these prospective members were willing to accept Islam. So Malcolm, this time assisted by five or six Muslim brothers, again took to the streets and began "fishing" for converts on the edges of the street meetings of other groups, at the doorsteps of the storefront Holy Roller Christian churches, and even by handing out leaflets to people as they passed. Attendance at meetings increased; the fundamentalist Christians were especially attracted to the temple, hoping to hear "good preaching." And good preaching they did hear, although not of a kind they would have anticipated. Malcolm, adapting his message to the character of his audience, sought to free his listeners' minds from the fetters of their mistaken religious beliefs by arguing that Christianity was the white man's religion; that it was used to make them worship the Man and to wait until the "dreamy heaven-in-the-hereafter" for the "milk and honey" white people had here on earth; and that their own collective poverty was proof of what he was saying. He would stress that Muhammad taught the mutual respect of men and women, and that the strict Islamic moral code was necessary to overcome the corruption of the ghetto way of life. But at the end of the meeting, when he called for his listeners to stand up and follow Elijah Muhammad, only an "agonizing few" would respond.[42]

Still, membership in Temple Number Seven was expanding. At the same time Malcolm succeeded in organizing temples in Springfield, Massachusetts; Hartford, Connecticut; and Atlanta, Georgia. By 1956 the Nation had in fact become "sizable"; and Malcolm, although somewhat discontented with the slow rate of growth, could take pride in his work on Muhammad's behalf. In turn, Muhammad was proud of Malcolm and gave him the reward of praise for his accomplishments, gentle chastisement for his impatience, and ever-increasing responsibilities. Far more than either Malcolm's parents or the Swerlins, Muhammad played for his young adherent the role of a benevolent parent. Moreover, an increasing percentage of the Nation's membership was being converted to Islam through Malcolm's personal ministry, and under his tutelage a new generation of ministers and administrators was being formed from among these recruits. Consequently, Malcolm was beginning to feel in himself the power of mediation, i.e., a double movement of energy between himself and his leader, on the one hand, and his followers and himself, on the other—which is also to say that the growth of the Nation was simultaneously the expansion of Malcolm's racial-religious identity: his proselytizing activity was being realized in the formation of an expanded collective self so that, seeing himself in the mirror thus formed, his own sense of potency and rectitude were proportionately magnified.

The experience of self-magnification was at its greatest during the mass rallies the Nation was able to conduct by the early 1960s.* On such occasions a large hall in a major city would be secured, the event would be well publicized, and bus caravans would bring Muslims from other areas to hear Muhammad's message. The meeting would be open to any black person interested in attending, but white people would be excluded. As the hour of the rally approached, the great hall would fill to overflowing:

> Many hundreds arrived too late for us to seat them. We always had to wire up outside loudspeakers. An electric atmosphere excited the great, shifting masses of black people. The long lines, three or four abreast, funneling to the meeting hall, were kept in strict order by Fruit of Islam men. . . . In anterooms just inside the halls, more Fruit of Islam men and white-gowned, veiled mature Muslim sisters thoroughly searched every man, woman and child seeking to enter. Any alcohol and tobacco had to be checked, and any objects which could possibly be used to harm Mr. Muhammad.[43]

At the doorway of the hall, one world ended and another began. The white man's heaven/black man's hell was left behind, and the believer or the visitor entered a Muslim paradise guarded by the Fruit of Islam and populated with "white-garbed beautiful black sisters" and "dark-suited, white-shirted brothers."[44]

This, then, is the first act in the drama of the black man's redemption. The exploitation, frustration, humiliation, temptation, and sin—in a word, the alienation—of ghetto existence is about to be temporarily transcended in racial communion. The well-guarded walls of the great hall and the self-defined uniformity of the Muslim brothers and sisters are the objective significations of the impending transformation, while the feeling of electrical excitement is its subjective intimation. This feeling we have no difficulty in understanding. Repressed emotions are being called forth from the unconscious by the internalized image of a truth about to be revealed; and the identical experience in each member of the mass generates a sensation of free-flowing energy that is magnified in the mirror of that mass identity and reflected back into each individual psyche as a

---

* Malcolm's own interpretation of these events stresses the "electrical" feeling which would unify those in attendance. We will follow his lead in emphasizing the energic aspect of this emotional bonding.

compelling sense of anticipation. At the same time, each member of the mass is experiencing, perhaps as an intense curiosity, the arousal of hitherto slumbering intellectual powers. Taking these points in their unity, the physical act of leaving a situation of racial alienation and entering the realm of racial freedom is simultaneously the psychological act of liberating a mass of hitherto repressed sensuous energy.

Now, in certain respects the act of entering a Muslim rally is analogous to entering a Christian church on a holy day, or even a theater when a particularly gripping performance can be anticipated. But the purely emotional similarity of these experiences must not be mistaken for the experiences themselves, for the meaning of the emotion is given in the situation and content of the event. Both Christ and, say, Humphrey Bogart are images of the white man; hence the emotion evoked by coming into their presence only reinforces the black person's falsified racial identity. But Muhammad's message reflected the interests of the black masses, so that the apparently analogous emotional evocation has precisely the opposite implications. That is to say, in one case the domination of repressed emotional forces over the conscious self is strengthened, while in the other these forces are in the process of being subjected to conscious control. This is true at least insofar as Muhammad was reflecting the class-racial interest of the masses in an undistorted form. Conversely, insofar as that interest was religiously mystified, the entering individual was being prepared for an experience of charismatic group-emotion that would falsify his conscious activity.

With this comment we come to the second act: the meeting itself. The "great audience's restless whisperings . . . cease" as the voice of one of the Nation's leading ministers begins to convert the labile mass-energies into particularized Islamic forms. Then Malcolm comes to the microphone, "specifically to condition the audience to hear Mr. Muhammad": "I would raise my hand, 'As-Salaikum-Salaam—' 'Wa-Alaikum-Salaam!' It was a roared response from the great audience's Muslim seating section."[45] Later we shall analyze the impact of the audience's response upon Malcolm himself; for the moment, the point is that the mass-emotional potential initially manifested as an electrical excitation is here becoming a verbally unified action expressing mutual love and a common identity. As such, the greeting is the ground of the truth Malcolm is now to deliver, just as his words will be the premise of Muhammad's teaching.

Malcolm's message is briefly and simply articulated, and forcefully delivered. First he verbalizes and thereby strengthens the feeling of racial unity that is already filling the great hall: "My black brothers and sisters . . . we all have in common the greatest binding tie we could have . . . we all are *black* people."[46] An undeniable (but not for that reason necessarily undenied) truth in the form of a proud affirmation, a statement of fact which is also an ethical first principle. . . . For the audience, the feeling of racial identity starts to become a consciousness of racial unity. Then Malcolm develops a twofold implication of the common racial ground: first, that Elijah Muhammad's "greatest greatness" was identifying to black people their enemy, defining them against their white oppressor; and second, that the Prophet had revealed the enemy's devilish techniques of domination. This double claim for Muhammad and allegation against the white man is then defended by asking the members of the audience to compare their own experience with the white man's claim that his Christian god "stands for the same thing for all men." In this way a preliminary awareness that Christianity is a racial particularity masking as a human universal arises. Malcolm now derives the appropriate conclusion from his mediated premise:

> "My black brothers and sisters—*no* one will know *who*
> we are until *we* know who we are! We never will be able to
> *go* anywhere until we know *where* we are! The Honorable
> Elijah Muhammad is giving us a true identity, and a true
> position—the first time they have ever been *known* to the
> American black man!"[47]

By this time Muhammad has entered the hall surrounded by Fruit of Islam guards, moving rapidly down the center aisle from the back of the auditorium. The Prophet mounts the stage alone, where he is greeted by his ministers, including Malcolm. Finally Malcolm turns back to the microphone and delivers the introduction proper:

> "You can be around this man and never *dream* from his
> actions the power and authority he has—" (Behind me, be-
> lieve me when I tell you, I could *feel* Mr. Muhammad's
> *power*.) "He does not *display*, and *parade*, his *power*! But no
> other black leader in America has followers who will lay
> down their lives if he says so! . . . My black brothers and sis-
> ters, you have come from your homes to hear—now you are
> *going* to hear—America's *wisest* black man! America's
> *boldest* black man! America's most *fearless* black man!

This wilderness of North America's most *powerful* black
man!"[48]

And the Prophet begins to speak, specifying the general position
Malcolm had formulated with telling effectiveness, until the walls
are echoing with the responses of the audience: "YAH, Man!" . . .
"Un-huh!" . . . "*Teach*, Messenger!" . . . "Yah!" . . . "Tell 'em!" . . .
"Oh, yes!"[49] Finally, as his strength gives out, the Prophet stops
abruptly, and those on stage face "a solid wall of sound" as Muhammad is given a standing ovation.[50]

It is clear from Malcolm's representation that his "conditioning"
of the audience was designed to magnify the Prophet's charisma and
that Muhammad was able to convert the emotional potential thus
created into an intense group-emotional experience. First, Malcolm
attributed to the Prophet possession of a hitherto unrevealed truth,
hence an unparalleled wisdom; an equally unequalled fearlessness
derived from that truth; and, in consequence, unrivaled power, of
which the great assembly and its feeling of electrical excitation, on
the one hand, and the alarmed attention of the Man, on the other,
were the preliminary significations. Thus even before Muhammad
started to speak, his charismatic authority had been established
through Malcolm's *derived* charismatic power. And the members of
the audience had been warned that the Prophet's charisma would be
manifested subtly ("You can be around this man and never dream
from his actions the power and authority he has"), so that when
he proved to be physically unimposing, with a weak voice and a
marked lack of rhetorical skill, they were not disappointed. Moreover, because they had already felt his power through Malcolm, who
was directly inspired by his leader's presence ("Behind me . . . I could
feel Mr. Muhammad's power"), the listeners transformed Muhammad's words into divine utterances and responded to them with ec-
static cries of religious communion. Stating the argument more for-
mally, the mass anticipation of a charismatic experience is, in
substance, labile sexual energy, with which Malcolm's image of
Muhammad as the Truth incarnate could be grasped and thereby internalized. This erotized image was then projected onto Muhammad
as he began to speak, so that the man and his words were reflected
back into the self in an hypnotically magnified form. But having
passed through the double movement of projection and introjection,
the flow of sexual energy had been crystallized as the Prophet, with
the result that the return of this emotional power was experienced
as the penetration of the Self by a beloved Other, as an aim-inhibited

orgasmic moment. Finally, the consequence of this experience was that the Prophet's truth became a part of the Self—which is to say, the Self itself was re-formed, to a greater or lesser extent, in Muhammad's image.

Now it follows from our prior investigations that the Other generated in the group-emotional process is a composite figure, a condensation of the parental deities of childhood and the person(s) actually speaking. In a strictly psychological sense, it is the immanent presence of these archaic gods that gives the speaker his charismatic aura, and thus his ability to mesmerize his audience through the return of its own repressed emotions. But the phenomenon as a whole cannot be understood in this sense, which after all fails either to distinguish it from or to relate it to any other mass-emotional experience. This can be done only through the analysis of the conscious content and objective context of the event. In the present instance, Malcolm reports that Muhammad emphasized the political side of the doctrine, with its devastating critique of Negro identity and white Christianity on the one hand and its plaintive cry for territorial separation on the other. Hence the event is immediately differentiated from evangelical church meetings and identified with Garveyite mass meetings.

Further, we may ask this question: what if Muhammad's political position had been only a call for separation? What if his ideas were not premised upon a critique that makes both intuitive and intellectually reflective sense? Then we would have before us an irrational doctrine, for the existence or acceptance of which a group-psychological explanation would be sufficient. We would be entitled to treat consciousness as we did when first evolving the group notion, i.e., as merely the outer surface of the unconscious. But such a doctrine would make no sense; and as such, it would be essentially unthinkable. Here, however, the irrational notion appears as a conclusion derived through subjective falsification from an objectively sound premise. Consequently, the audience reaction is not entirely explicable in group-psychological terms. The cries of "teach" and "oh, yes" were also spontaneous expressions of intellectual comprehension, of work-energy being used to take possession of a particular cognitive content, i.e., of racially conscious activity. At the same time they expressed the listener's moral affirmation of Muhammad's truth, while the wall of sound that arose when he had finished was the collective or ethical form of that judgment. Thus taking the emotional and work-energetic sides of the event in their interpenetrative unity, we may say that the Muslim rally was a religiously falsified racial-ethical experience—a political drama in the form of a passion play.

Before touching upon the final act of the play we must consider one further point, namely, the role of aggression in the experience. Since white people were excluded from the rally, the role is necessarily abstract, or purely spiritual; but in a spiritual sense the Man is present, as a mental image of the enemy whom it is legitimate to hate. Thus the mass meeting does permit the release of aggressive energy. Furthermore, through the hypnotic projection and displacement of repressed aggression that enemy is demonized, with the consequence that the antithetical political interests of the white elite and the black mass are magnified into a Manichean dichotomy. Interracial relations are pictured as a holy war between the Black God and the White Devil. But that war, too, is entirely abstract, a spiritual confrontation; for the Prophet's practical policies amounted to avoiding a power he was powerless to overcome: the Muslim believer was left to wait more or less passively for the War of Armageddon. Yet in the electrified atmosphere of the mass meeting this fateful contradiction between practical passivity and spiritual aggressivity temporarily disappeared. The intersubjective flow of reflectively magnified emotional forces generated a sense of collective omnipotence, while at the same time Muhammad's message had as its latent or genetic content the image of a benevolent parental deity who would provide lovingly and absolutely for the well-being of his children. Thus the group came to share the chiliastic illusion that the devil would be destroyed and heaven-on-earth created through an act of Allah.

The last act of the drama has these moments: Muhammad abruptly finishes his speech, and Malcolm returns to the microphone, exhorting the audience to contribute generously to the collection which is now being taken—thereby to insure that Muhammad's efforts on the behalf of all black people will be grounded economically in the resources of black people. At this juncture "the audience atmosphere [is] as if people [have] gone limp."[51] Their mass energy has been expended; the experience is already becoming a memory. Finally the hall empties as people return to the harsh reality of the dark ghetto streets and tenements, there to test the validity of Muhammad's teaching in their daily lives.*

---

* Two notes may be added: (1) Eventually Muhammad permitted a few selected white visitors to attend these rallies. This change in policy was a move in the direction of

For those who were not members of the Nation and who were not persuaded to become members, the end of a Muslim rally might well be the end of their Islamic experience, although the critical aspects of Muhammad's teachings were almost sure to have some lingering effect on their consciousness. And of course the Muslim's everyday life was not filled with the ecstasy of such occasions, or even with the more contained excitement of temple meetings. Yet whether he was slaving for the Man or looking for a job, the believer could take comfort in the memory and anticipation of these experiences, and in the thought that the enemy's period of dominion was coming to a close. He could draw strength from his racial self-knowledge, from knowing who he was, how he was to act, and why he was to act that way. In part this strength was illusory, an imaginary or magical sense of being able to go beyond one's objective situation; in part it was substantive, at least if the judgmental standard was the person's past life or the present lives of his brainwashed brothers and sisters. In any case, the Muslim had the assured knowledge that he was no longer a brainwashed so-called Negro, no longer under the mental domination of his enemy.

The nominal symbol of this negation of a negative identity was of course the "X"—which, as Benjamin Goodman observed, had "something magic about it." That magical quality was not comprehensible when we began our work. Then we could only say that it signified racial negation (the loss of tribal identity, slavery, and the pseudo-selfhood of being an American Negro); the negation of that negation (becoming an ex-slave, then an ex-Negro); and therefore the affirmation of being a Muslim: a member of the Islamic family, community, and nation; a loyal follower of Elijah Muhammad; and one who had submitted himself to Allah. Now we are in a position to analyze that magical potency.

In the first place, it is clear that the "X" would possess no such power if all black people were content with their Negro identity and with the objective ground of that identity. But that ground is negated racial interest and its subjective reflection is self-negation; hence a symbol of an identity that negates that negation is rationally attrac-

---

confrontation, hence was more reflective of Malcolm's activism than the Prophet's separatism. (2) For the non-Muslim Negroes who attended, Muhammad included in his remarks well-chosen words of pity and contempt. Thus a double pressure was put on such individuals to join the Nation, for only by so doing could they participate in the loving communion of black souls and escape the ridicule Muhammad skillfully heaped upon them.

tive. The "X," however, is also magically attractive, i.e., an object having the power to bring forth from the unconscious self energies that become its (the object's) possession, and through which the conscious self is in turn possessed. We must look for the basis of its power in the character-structure of the individual who is mesmerized by it; and this, given our analysis of Malcolm's conversion, is easily done. The "X" is the outward or nominal form of a re-formed self, a self freed from internal division, from the shame and guilt that result from identification with the oppressor. It is a new self-image. Because the old self is not in conscious possession of its emotional energies, initially it cannot preclude the projection of unconscious forces into that new image, so that the image is magically magnified. Its bearer therefore appears to be a hero, invulnerable in the war against an enemy previously thought to be invulnerable; a member of a brother band united in love for and identified with the divine father; and, withal, more of a man than any street-corner *macho* or even than the Man himself. Further, when the individual joins the Nation and is rewarded with his "X," i.e., when the "X" becomes *his* name, the powers he has projected into it become once again his own possession—or, rather, they become for the first time his conscious possession. They then constitute a potential for racially self-conscious activity, albeit one that can be realized without contradiction only within theological limits.

By 1960 these limits had been considerably expanded. The Nation provided its members with a communal life which shielded them from much of the surrounding ghetto pathology. Malcolm had been instrumental in actualizing the potential for this communal experience, and so was more than fulfilling his promise to "tell the black man the true teachings of our Honorable Elijah Muhammad." He was only beginning to find a way, however, to "tell the white man about his crimes." Before seeing how that way was opened up to him, we must first consider briefly the other side of his life during the present phase, namely, his reluctant courtship of and marriage to Sister Betty X.

In 1956, when Betty joined Temple Number Seven, she was a nursing student; previously she had attended Tuskegee Institute. Thus she was unusually well-educated by either white or black working-class standards; and she was using her education for the benefit of the Nation by teaching hygiene classes at the Temple. She was quite tall, darker than Malcolm, and decidedly attractive. Initially, however, Malcolm paid her, or pretended to pay her, no special attention. He believed that his "total commitment to Islam demanded having no other interests, especially . . . no women."[52] Mr. Muhammad shared this view, at least in part, and had encouraged Malcolm to remain single. Taking these two aspects in combination, we may infer that Malcolm's work, which was infused with his love for Muhammad, was an adequate outlet not only for his work-energy but also for his emotional energy. But that is not the end of the matter:

> But in those days, I had my personal reasons [for talking "hard against women when I taught our special classes about the different natures of the two sexes" and for avoiding marriage]. I wouldn't have considered it possible for me to love any woman. I'd had too much experience that women were only tricky, deceitful, untrustworthy flesh. . . . Women talked too much [and to the wrong people]. And for anyone in any kind of leadership position, such as I was, the worst thing in the world that he could have was the wrong woman.[53]

To some extent, Malcolm's misogynous attitude reflects what he had learned from prostitutes in New York, i.e., that the wives of their clients had (in one way or another) deprived their husbands of manhood, thus leading the latter to seek sexual satisfaction away from home. But that analysis, quite apart from its inherent irrationality, was not germane to Malcolm's current circumstances: the Muslim marriage code was grounded in a form of benevolent paternalism that entailed feminine submission to male domination. Hence if Malcolm believed in the inherent powers of Muslim law, his suspicions and doubts should have been laid to rest. But clearly he believed that women were virtually the devil incarnate, surely castrative and perhaps even deadly—thus more akin to the white devil than to the black man. The question is, why?

At first glance it might appear that he was simply generalizing from his experience with Sophia. She had betrayed him, first by getting married and then, so we may surmise, by telling her husband's friend Malcolm's name and address after the scene in the bar. The woman whose white skin he had worshipped and whose soul he had loved had proved untrustworthy, and he was not going to expose himself to the possibility of again being betrayed. But this explanation, like the previous one, founders on the rock of his racial-religious identity. The relationship with Sophia was objectively grounded in the hustling society and mediated through epidermal fetishism. An inherently alienative relationship, it degenerated readily into a horde-familial life before dissolving altogether into mutual betrayal and imprisonment. Now, however, Malcolm was a member of a Muslim community within which relationships were not epidermally determined (in the eyes of Allah, all believers were equally black); hence he had no reason to expect that a Muslim sister would betray him as the white woman had.

It would thus seem that Malcolm's misogyny was irrational, and in fact it was; but this does not and could not mean that his attitude lacked an experiential ground. If we move regressively through both time and consciousness, we arrive at his relationship to his mother, who can be viewed, from the perspective of Malcolm's early childhood, as the archetypal verbally castrative woman. Moreover, because Earl Little left home on the day that he was killed as the result of a quarrel with Louise, Malcolm may have felt that she was partially responsible for his death. In this sense she would conform to the prostitute's conception of the destructive wife. Finally, she had betrayed Malcolm himself, both through her sexual involvement with his father (the Oedipal betrayal) and through open hostility and/or maternal neglect. We may infer that Malcolm projected the negative side of his maternal image onto womankind in general, just as he projected the positive side onto Elijah Muhammad. This in turn permitted the displacement of his own repressed hostility onto women and simultaneously freed his relationship with his leader from any trace of ambivalence.

By 1956 or 1957, however, Malcolm's irrational misogyny was beginning to break down. On the one hand, there was the progressive impact of Islamic belief, which for all its defects was a considerable advance over the hustling code or rationalized forms of horde-familial emotion; on the other, there was Betty, whose good character, intelligence, and beauty Malcolm found it increasingly difficult to resist. He began engaging her in casual conversation, and he was startled to find that he was beginning to think, albeit abstractly, about marrying her. This realization sent him into a full-scale retreat for some months, at the end of which his attraction to Betty overcame his repulsion toward women in general; and on January 14, 1958, they were married. Their first child, a girl, was born in November of that year, and three more girls were born in the years ahead.*

* It should be noted that Malcolm describes his "courtship" in a self-mocking, ironical tone that reflects both his eventual acceptance of Betty's role in his life and the residual perseverance of his old attitudes.

Decolonization as Polemical Confrontation

By 1958 Malcolm had substantially overcome the alienation of his sensuous energies. He loved his work, and he was working at loving and trusting his wife; he had his own family within the larger Islamic one; and he was serving his chosen leader with complete devotion. He had become, in a way Ostrowski could never have predicted, a success in life. But at that time he had not found a way to fulfill his promise to confront the white man. In the spring of 1957, however, just such an opportunity presented itself, when a Muslim brother named Hinton Johnson became a victim of police brutality.

The event itself, which foreshadows in most respects the initiating actions of the rebellions of the 1960s, originated in the deteriorating social and economic condition of ghettoized America. This condition was reflected in the complementary and opposing forms of increased ghetto pathology (including criminal activity) and increasing police paranoia: the police were more inclined to use direct coercion than persuasion with black people, and black people were forced to resist as best they could these assaults upon their persons. Usually such resistance was individual and hence ineffective; but when in the present instance Johnson and two other Muslims were present as the police started to work over a man accused of beating an unidentified woman, Johnson protested that the police were "not in Alabama"—an act which reflects in its content the struggle for integration in the South and in its form Johnson's Muslim adherency. The police responded by first telling the three men to move on and (when the witnesses to their brutality refused to accept this directive) then beating Johnson senseless and arresting him.

There the incident, like Rosa Parks' act of defiance, would have ended, had it not been for Malcolm and the Muslims. Just as the Negro community of Birmingham rallied around Parks, so now the Muslims rallied around their fallen brother. In serried ranks they surrounded the police outpost while Malcolm went in to negotiate with the authorities; and the police, seeing in the situation the possibility of an explosion, acceded to Malcolm's demands. Malcolm, like Martin Luther King, had won an unprecedented victory; but where King's victory had been secured through the use of nonviolent protest, Malcolm's had been won through national self-defense.

This incident awakened the ghetto to the presence of the Muslims. The influential *Amsterdam News* covered the story in detail, and the word went out over the "wire" that the Muslims were a tough, powerful organization. More people were attracted to Muslim meetings, and temple membership started to expand at a somewhat faster rate. Then in 1959 television newsman Louis Lomax, who was preparing a documentary on black nationalism in Harlem, "discovered" the Muslims: since his informants kept referring to "Brother Malcolm X," he decided he should investigate the man and his organization. The result of this investigation was the television report, "The Hate That Hate Produced," in which both Malcolm and Elijah Muhammad articulated the major principles of Muslim activity against a background of film footage showing Islamic family life, schooling, etc. The consequence was that "within a fortnight every major magazine and news media was carrying long stories about the Black Muslims and particularly about Malcolm. Within a month Malcolm had received invitations to speak from every major university on the East Coast."[54] The Muslims, as Malcolm later remarked, were "hot copy."

In the *Autobiography* Malcolm acknowledges that it was the mass media which "thrust the Muslims into international prominence." The media provided Malcolm with his long-awaited opportunity to tell the white man about himself, which in turn enabled him to earn the Muslims an international reputation for racial militancy. This process began in the immediate aftermath of "The Hate That Hate Produced," when white reporters en masse approached Malcolm with the same basic question: "Mr. Malcolm X, why do you teach black supremacy, and hate?" It was, of course, an accusation in interrogatory form, the same accusation that had earlier been delivered against Garvey. Malcolm, grasping the Garveyite sword, responded by turning the accusation back against the accuser:

> I tried to pour on pure fire in return. "The white man
> [who is] so guilty of white supremacy can't hide *his* guilt
> by trying to accuse the Honorable Elijah Muhammad of
> teaching black supremacy and hate! All Mr. Muhammad is
> doing is trying to uplift the black man's mentality and the
> black man's social and economic condition in this
> country.[55]

The white man was accusing the black man of his own crimes; as Malcolm said on other occasions to black audiences: "Do you know *why* the white man really hates you? It's because every time he sees your face, he sees a mirror of his crime—and his guilty conscience can't bear to face it!"[56] Consequently "the white man is in no moral *position* to accuse anyone else of hate!"[57]

The argument was conclusive. The white man—the colonial and neocolonial bourgeoisie—had brutally alienated the dark-skinned peoples from their labor and their emotional energies. He had appropriated their human substance as his own while simultaneously projecting his own bestial essence into them. The black man had thereby become a "Negro"—a product of the white man's inhumanity, the living refutation of his universal human laws, and the veritable negation of his self-righteous moral judgments. Now Malcolm and the Muslims were threatening to bring that contradiction to the level of mass consciousness; by so doing, they were forcing the white man to recognize himself in his victims. Consequently, Malcolm was often able to leave his accusers sputtering with defensive rage or making resentful admissions of guilt, or both.

The effect upon Malcolm himself of these polemical confrontations was entirely different. Their accusations were like a "red flag" to him; "something chemical" happened to him when he heard them. But the "pure fire" that he "poured on in return" was not an uncontrollable eruption of satanic rage, and it certainly was not cooled in the waters of self-punishing humility.[58] It was, rather, aggressive energy that had been grounded in racial self-identification and developed through the work of conscious activity into a moral passion: the fire set long ago in Malcolm's soul by the Black Legion attack was at last bursting forth in flames of righteous anger and racial militancy. The white devil was being burned on his own fiery cross.

The white man was beginning to reap as he had sown. But the devil was not the only object of Malcolm's holy wrath: "My bitterness was less against the white press than it was against those Negro 'leaders' who kept attacking us."[59] Muhammad viewed these attacks as "the white man's tricks," an attempt to keep "the black race divided and fighting against each other." At first, therefore, he instructed Malcolm to contain his anger. But as time passed and the attacks did not abate, he allowed Malcolm to begin "returning their fire."

Drawing freely from black history—in particular, E. Franklin Frazier's *Black Bourgeoisie*—Malcolm developed the critique of Negro leadership and nonviolent protest we represented at the beginning of our work, and which we redeveloped into our own critique of the civil rights movement. If it had not been for the Movement, however, Malcolm's polemical attack upon white America would not have been possible: his audience would have been limited to the membership of the Nation of Islam. Conversely, if it had not been for the organizational strength of the Nation, there would have been no interest in his arguments, no matter how skillfully articulated. The possibility of polemical confrontation with white America resulted from the conjuncture of the two anticolonial forces, while the limitations of each of these forces created at the same time the necessity for a critical reappraisal of the liberation struggle. It was only in such a context that Malcolm could play his polemical role; and it was only through the effective development of polemical, politically critical argument that the contradictions within and between the two sides of the liberation movement could be brought into consciousness and (at least partially) resolved.

The same point can be reached from a somewhat different direction. The internal colony of ghettoized black America resembles the classical colonized society in being territorially distinguishable from its "mother country" (the rest of American society), and in being a source of cheap and abundant labor for the latter. But the black ghettoes do not constitute an autonomous economic unit; they are not, from the standpoint of economic production, a nation. Black people are only a minority population within a national economic unit; they do not have the power to separate themselves from white America in the manner of classical decolonization or national liberation. But neither can they, given the structure of capitalist production in the United States, be integrated into the larger society. This is the fateful contradiction of internal colonialism. Of course, the contradiction can be resolved through the revolutionary transformation of the existing situation; but black people by themselves cannot effect such a change. They are therefore forced into opposing separatist and integrationist positions. Each of these positions expresses, in a distorted form, one side of the contradiction. Neither articulates a realizable racial interest. The polemical confrontation between them does effect a kind of rough unity, however, in the form of a militant struggle against the common enemy. It also makes manifest the class basis of the intraracial opposition. Polemical confrontation in this double sense is therefore comprehensible as a rational response to the contradictions of the internal colonial situation.

Thus we gain an initial appreciation of Malcolm's contribution to the struggle for racial liberation. But so long as his opportunities for polemical activity were limited to interviews with reporters, the power of his arguments disappeared in prejudiced misquotation by the time they were printed in newspapers or magazines. The general public was not able to feel the heat of his charismatic fire. But when he appeared on television or radio, no such distortion was possible; there his verbal pyrotechnics became a vehicle for producing racial self-consciousness in the form of righteous anger among his black listeners or viewers. On television and radio, his polemical activity immediately became proselytism. His appearances on college campuses did not have this same double character; but because they kept Malcolm and the Muslims in the news, they did produce the same effect indirectly. Moreover, Malcolm found college audiences particularly stimulating:

> Challenges, queries, and criticisms were fired at me by the usually objective and always alive and searching minds of . . . [the] students and their faculties. [Therefore these] sessions never failed to be exhilarating. They never failed in helping me to further my own education. I never experienced one college session that didn't show me ways to improve upon my presentation and defense of Mr. Muhammad's teachings. . . . It was like being on a battlefield—with intellectual and philosophical bullets.[60]

It was heady stuff, as addicting in its own way as any narcotic—especially for a black man whose formal education had ended in the eighth grade and whose subsequent schooling had come from hustling the streets of the Harlem ghetto and from the library of the Norfolk Penal Colony. But Malcolm never lost sight of the overriding racial-religious purpose of his college appearances, and he never forgot that his intellectual and emotional powers were derived from Allah and his chosen Prophet. The Alpha and the Omega of Malcolm's life remained his filial relationship to Muhammad, and his highest "peaks of emotion" would come at mass rallies when the older man would mount the stage: "Tears would be in more eyes than mine. He had rescued me when I was a convict; Mr. Muhammad had trained me in his home, as if I was his son."[61] As he commented in an interview with Louis Lomax at a time when rumors were spreading of growing differences between him and his leader: "How could there be any differences between the Messenger and me? I am his slave, his servant, his son."[62]

CHAPTER VIII

Think for Yourself

ON MARCH 24, 1961, Malcolm spoke to the Harvard Law School Forum. As he was about to begin, he happened to look out the window: "Abruptly, I realized that I was looking in the direction of the apartment house that was my old burglary gang's hide-out." The realization "rocked" him "like a tidal wave." He recognized that without Islam he would inevitably have been dead by this time, or stuck firmly in "the muck and the mire of this rotting world," i.e., the white man's world. But Islam had saved him. Then the story of Icarus flickered into his mind. He remembered that Icarus had believed his wings were his own, that he could fly as high as he personally wished. So Malcolm vowed that he would never commit Icarus's act of hubris: "Standing there by that Harvard window, I silently vowed that I would never forget that any wings I wore had been put on by the religion of Islam."[1]

By this comparison Malcolm is acknowledging his personal pride in his achievement. He also tells the story without any mention of Icarus's father Daedalus, who made the boy's wings—by analogy, without reference to Elijah Muhammad, who gave Malcolm his. The omission does not necessarily imply that Malcolm was straining against the limits and limitations of his disciple's position; but his thoughts at Harvard seem to indicate a growing consciousness of his individual value to the Nation of Islam and the struggle for racial liberation. He no doubt continued to think of himself as Muhammad's slave; but he was beginning to recognize that the slave empowered the master:

> I had helped to bring about the progress and national impact such that none could call us liars when we called Mr.

Muhammad the most powerful black man in America. I had helped Mr. Muhammad and his other ministers to revolutionize the American black man's thinking, opening his eyes until he would never again look in the same fearful, worshipful way at the white man. I had participated in spreading the truths that had done so much to help the American black man rid himself of the mirage that the white race was made up of "superior" beings. I had been a part of the tapping of something in the secret black soul.[2]

Viewing the matter in these terms, it is no wonder that he felt he had "every personal gratification" he could want.

Yet Malcolm did "harbor" one personal disappointment: "Privately I was convinced that our Nation of Islam could be an even greater force in the American black man's overall struggle—if we engaged in more action."[3] To be sure, with his history of activism, he might be suspected of undue impatience with Muhammad's "non-engagement" policy; but in fact, his unique position in the Nation transformed his general tendency toward activity into the desire for political participation:

> It could be heard increasingly in the Negro communities: "Those Muslims *talk* tough, but they never *do* anything, unless somebody bothers Muslims." I moved around among outsiders more than most other Muslim officials. I felt the very real potentiality that, considering the mercurial moods of the black masses, this labeling of Muslims as "talk only" could see us, powerful as we were, one day suddenly separated from the Negroes' front-line struggle.[4]

His analysis of the situation was quite correct. The masses were eager for action, and the Nation was beginning to lose contact with its mass base. The premise of Malcolm's argument was that freedom would come through political participation of one kind or another, and that consequently the Nation had a *part* to play in the overall movement. Muhammad, however, believed that politics was merely a vehicle through which Allah would destroy both the White Devil and unbelieving Negroes (that political conflicts were a prelude to an international war of Armageddon), and therefore that the Nation must be a *separate* as well as separatist organization.

Furthermore, by 1962/63 the Nation was developing a substantial middle-class membership and an even more substantial treasury. Malcolm had been instrumental in bringing about both of these conditions: his voice had reached the middle-class Negro who was not in the Nation and his organizational concepts had helped to rationalize the Nation's financial structure. His hope had been that middle-class Negroes would thereby be converted into militant black men and that the treasury would be used at least partly as a war chest. But in fact the class structure of ghettoized America was reflected into rather than dissolved in the Nation, while the economic strength of the organization constituted an ever-growing stake in the existing system.

Such a result was basically predictable. Muhammad's "economic blueprint" was little more than a carbon copy of the white man's actual business practices. As such, it was a plan that could not be followed by the mass of Muslims, who were forced by their objective situation to slave for the Man; but Muhammad and most of his leading ministers followed it with admirable consistency. Thus even if the Nation had not been able to recruit middle-class members, it would still have developed an internal class-structure through this process of theocratic self-enrichment. Malcolm therefore had not only political but also economic grounds for his feeling of disappointment.

At this juncture, Malcolm felt confident that any differences between his position and his leader's could be worked out privately; in any case, he was completely devoted to Muhammad and would continue to do his bidding. But two years later, he was suspended from the Nation; and shortly thereafter he was out of the organization altogether. We must now represent and interpret the process through which this separation took place.

Chickens Come Home to Roost

Malcolm's principal fear during the period from 1960 to 1963 was that the Muslims were losing their position as the militant side of the Movement. Through the Hinton Johnson incident and "The Hate That Hate Produced," they had won a reputation for being tough. They, and Malcolm in particular, were "scaring these white folks to death." One might say that by combining Garveyite pride with the hustler's *machismo* they had arrived at a new form of black manhood. But now people were beginning to wonder if this form had any content: maybe Muslim black manhood was a front, a hype, all sound and fury, signifying nothing. It was necessary to demonstrate in action that this skepticism was ill-founded.

By 1963 the time was ripe for such a demonstration. In the spring of that year Martin Luther King and the SCLC were leading a massive nonviolent protest movement to bring desegregation to Birmingham, Alabama. They were met by even more massive resistance from the local political and police authorities who, under the leadership of chief of police "Bull" Connor, brutalized and arrested demonstrators by the thousands. A compromise between the two sides was arranged, and it appeared that the confrontation had come to an end. On May 12, however, only two days after peace had been declared, white racists bombed both the home of King's brother and the Movement's headquarters at a local motel. This in itself was hardly a novelty, but what followed thereafter was new, at least within the situation generated by the Movement's activity. To cite Bennett, the bombing "detonated a mass explosion by Birmingham adults, many of whom had held themselves aloof from the nonviolent demonstrations. The Birmingham riot [sic] of May 11–12 sent shock waves across the country and announced the entry of a hitherto uncommitted group: the so-called underclass, the permanently depressed strata of the Negro working class."[5] About a month later, a protest campaign in Cambridge, Maryland, led by Gloria Richardson and SNCC and including in its ranks members of the "underclass," erupted violently in response to white racist attack. Thereafter a new, militant mood spread like wildfire through the grassroots of the black ghettos. By mid-summer "scores of communities teetered on the edge of miniature civil wars";[6] and people were once again talking about a March on Washington, a real one this time, a mass invasion that would completely immobilize the government.

Thus the black industrial reserve army and the irregular units of the *lumpen-proletariat*, those whose alienation from their labor was most complete and those who had been completely alienated from laboring, were taking to the streets in armed insurrection. These were the strata of the proletariat who had not been "corrupted" by middle-class status and whose conscious activity was consequently not so deeply rooted in a good Negro character structure. Moreover, during the preceding decade their position in relation to the white bourgeoisie, the Negro middle class, and their own status at the time of World War II and the Korean War was weakening. Their relative deprivation was increasing, while at the same time they were being told that conditions were improving for the American Negro. They were becoming painfully aware that their regression was the other man's progression. So when reactionary violence began to edge over into mass terror, they began to fight back against their enemies. In a spontaneous—conscious but not yet self-conscious—burst of righteous anger, in a collective action grounded in a sense of racial identity, they were breaking the vicious circle of self-destructive aggressivity. As Malcolm said, they were starting to wake up from a bad dream, the American dream. In the harsh light of day they were coming to recognize themselves as suckers in a political con game, as victims of democracy, and they were willing to *act* on the basis of that recognition.

As July turned into August, government leaders became increasingly alarmed at the prospect of a mass March on Washington. Such an event would be "the grass roots out there in the street"; and the prospect "scared the white man to death, scared the white power structure to death."[7] Yet when the March actually took place nearly a quarter of a million people assembled to petition their government for redress of grievances—nonviolently. As one commentator observed, "Instead of the emotional horde of angry militants that many had feared, what Washington saw was a vast army of quiet, middle-class Americans who came in the spirit of a church outing."[8] President Kennedy, the *New York Times* reported, "declared that the cause of twenty million Negroes had been advanced by the March."[9] To be sure, the ostensible aim of the March—passage of then-pending civil rights legislation—was not realized. But there were many who shared Martin Luther King's judgment that it had been "the greatest demonstration for freedom in our Nation's history."[10]

Malcolm agreed that the event had been transformed from a militant action into a church outing but, in his judgment, it was not a freedom demonstration; it was another demonstration of how Negro leaders are "used against the Negro Revolution."[11] Initially, he believed, "the white man had plenty of good reasons for nervous worry. The right spark—some unpredictable emotional chemistry—could set off a black uprising. The government knew that thousands of milling, angry blacks could not only completely disrupt Washington—but they could erupt in Washington."[12] But then government leaders, anxious to defuse the situation, called in the "national Negro leaders" and told them to call off the March. But "Old Tom said, 'Boss, I can't stop it, because I didn't start it. . . . I'm not even in it, much less the head of it.'"[13] The matter now appeared doubly dangerous: not only were Negroes taking to the streets, but they were acting without the restraining influence of their leaders. Their leaders, moreover, were too busy seeking financial support for their organizations and fighting among themselves for such support as was available to respond effectively to the danger. Therefore, Malcolm argued, the white man's usual policy of keeping the leadership internally divided had to be temporarily suspended. President Kennedy arranged a meeting of the major civil rights leaders, at which they were given $800,000 to be used cooperatively by a "United Civil Rights Leadership Council," with a comparable sum to be made available "later on, after the March . . . obviously if all went well." [14] Then the white man "began to project these Big Six [Negro Leaders] as the leaders of the march," while these men in turn invited the participation of white liberals who integrated the March. The March thereafter "ceased to be angry, it ceased to be hot, it ceased to be uncompromising. Why, it even ceased to be a march. It became a picnic, a circus." [15]

Malcolm's analysis of the March, stated in our terms, is that in this instance the Negro middle-class leadership functioned as an instrument of internal colonial power, in the interest of its own integration into white American society. It was, from this perspective, another act in the stereotypical dumb-show. On the other hand, the March helped to break down the stereotype of black people as a "rabble of paupers" or an undisciplined criminal mob. In parallel fashion, the Birmingham uprising began the process of breaking down the Good Negro stereotype. But so long as the discipline demonstrated in the March remained detached from the militancy displayed in the uprising, it would continue to be possible to cast black people as either the Bad Nigger or the Good Negro. It was necessary to transform these self-defeating images into the reality of the Black Militant, and hence to transform the stereotypical dumb-show into a revolutionary drama.

From his own perspective, Malcolm could see that a new situation was coming into existence. The Black Revolution was being born, but it might be stillborn. Militant leadership was literally a vital necessity. There was clearly a tendency toward increased militancy in the Movement, which was organizationally and generationally embodied in SNCC, but only the Muslims at this juncture were strong enough to provide leadership to a spontaneously evolving revolutionary army. Just as Malcolm was the cutting edge of the Nation, so now the Nation would be the cutting edge of the Movement. Muhammad's two-edged sword would cut back and forth through the ranks of the enemy, and national liberation would be won.

Malcolm's hope was the establishment's fear. A *New York Times* columnist wrote after Birmingham:

> One urgent question raised by the Birmingham episode is what form the inevitably growing Negro protest is going to take. Will it be the peaceful route of the Reverend Dr. Martin Luther King, Jr.? Or will it be the road of black nationalism preached by the Black Muslims? [16]

In a general sense, the writer was raising the right questions; the Movement was at a crossroads. But his fears of the Muslims were as ill-founded as Malcolm's hopes. Muhammad had no intention of endangering his Nation by permitting its members to become soldiers in a revolutionary army; consequently, no demonstration of Muslim manhood was forthcoming, and Malcolm was left understanding a world he was once again powerless to change. His hour had come, the time was ripe for action, and ripeness was all; but it seemed that he was destined to remain a spectator as the revolutionary drama began to unfold.

Although by the summer of 1963 Malcolm had become fully conscious of the contradiction between his leader's spiritual militancy and his political passivity, he did not yet recognize that the contradiction was inherent in the notion of territorial separation, that no project of national liberation could be brought forth from that ground. His potential conflict with Muhammad was attenuated by his inability to formulate a clear theoretical alternative to the latter's position. Moreover, the Prophet could always shift the issue to a more general level and argue with Malcolm that proselytism was more important than polemic, that the only valid concern for a Muslim was the growth and preservation of the Nation, and that Allah would destroy the enemy in His own good time. But the strength of that argument, which might have been sufficient to quiet Malcolm's discontent, had been undercut the previous year. In April of 1962 one Muslim had been killed and a number of others injured in an altercation with officers of the Los Angeles police department. Islamic doctrine entailed self-defense; and effective self-defense in turn entailed retaliatory action. So immediately after the incident, Malcolm flew into Los Angeles to direct the counterattack. But Muhammad knew that any open act of vengeance constituted a gilt-edged invitation to the government to crack down on the Nation. He also knew that if he did not permit such an action, he would be vulnerable to the charge of being "all breath and no britches" . . . a coward. Faced with this dilemma, he came down on the side of prudence rather than glory; at the last minute he "stayed the Black Muslim's hand."[17]

Malcolm was disappointed, but he accepted his leader's tactical judgment of the situation. As an alternative form of self-defense, he attempted to initiate a national campaign to defend those brothers who had been unjustly arrested during the police attack. In Breitman's words, "A campaign in defense of the Los Angeles victims and around the issue of police brutality could, if skillfully and boldly conducted, forge bonds of solidarity and unity between Muslim and non-Muslim Negroes strong enough to discourage or deter government persecution of the Nation of Islam."[18] Such an action would have been a rational response to the existing situation; but after giving the campaign his preliminary approval, during the summer of 1962 Muhammad decided to de-emphasize it. Meanwhile, a little over a month after the Los Angeles incident, a plane crash at Orly Airport killed 121 members of the Atlanta, Georgia, Art Association—needless to say, 121 white members. Hearing of the event, Malcolm announced at an open meeting that he had good news for the Nation: Allah had struck down a planeload of "crackers" in an act of divine retribution for the death of the Muslim brother in Los Angeles. Muhammad's restraint had been justified after all! But when his statement resulted in a great hue and cry against the Muslim's hate-mongering, Muhammad chastised Malcolm for his comments, and told him to moderate his public comments.

This second act of restraint constituted a genuine betrayal of Muhammad's proclaimed beliefs and of Malcolm's trusting articulation of those claims. For years he had been saying that the Prophet was America's "boldest," most "fearless" black man. Now it was evident that he did not even have the courage to acknowledge the intervention of his god against the common enemy, much less to take arms himself. Muhammad had proven to be the prophet unarmed, not the prophet armed; consequently Malcolm was disarmed as well.

Thus the ground of self-productive aggressivity was slipping away from beneath Malcolm's feet. At the same time, the ground of racial identity, insofar as it was mediated by Muhammad's theory and practice of ethical interpersonal relationships, was being eroded. There was, first, the problem that orthodox Islam was not a racially defined doctrine (something which Malcolm had learned since the time that the Nation achieved national prominence); and, corresponding to this contradiction on the practical level, the problem resulting from Malcolm's growing recognition that at least a few white people were genuinely interested in equality, freedom, and justice for all human beings. But he was not to confront this twofold question until after the break; it was not yet a point of contention.

Second, he had long heard rumors that Muhammad was given to forming sexual liaisons with his secretaries. The thought of the man he worshipped so blatantly disregarding his own commandment against fornication was so repugnant to Malcolm that he had simply closed his mind on the subject: "The very keel of my teaching, and my most bone-deep personal belief, was that Elijah Muhammad in every aspect of his existence was a symbol of moral, mental and spiritual reform among the American black people."[19] As the winds of gossip continued to blow, he "totally and absolutely rejected [his] own intelligence": "I simply refused to believe. I didn't want Allah to 'burn my brain' as I felt the brain of my brother Reginald had been burned for harboring evil thoughts about Mr. Elijah Muhammad."[20] Reginald had been driven out of the Nation for fornication and verbal insurrection against Muhammad, but if Muhammad were guilty of the same crime, then his punishment of Reginald was hypocritical and hence unjustified. Malcolm would also have wronged his blood brother in rejecting him. Finally, his religious-racial practice would have been falsified by the Messenger's unwillingness to live up to his own beliefs. Malcolm believed totally in the Prophet: this was the man he loved and feared, the man to whom he attributed the life-and-death powers of an archaic deity. He attempted to remain true to his own beliefs: just as he had worked hard to ward off the thought of arrest or death when he was a cocaine-addicted burglar, now he tried to push this problem out of his mind. But it kept coming back. It invaded his dreams, turning them into "nightmares" of headlines exposing Muhammad. In time his days became filled with that same "leaden fear"—and with an increasing sense of his own shameful foolishness:

> I felt like a total fool, out there every day preaching, and
> apparently not knowing what was going on under my nose,
> in my own organization, involving the very man I was praising so. To look a fool unearthed emotions I hadn't felt since
> my Harlem hustler days. The worst thing in the hustler's
> world was to be a dupe.[21]

His Muslim manhood presumably involved a higher level of consciousness than his hustler's *machismo*. Now it almost seemed as
if the Code was a more accurate reflection of reality than Muhammad's Truth. At least the Code did not expose its believers to
ridicule.

Finally, one day early in 1963 he was talking to black humorist
and political activist Dick Gregory when the latter made the allegation openly and bluntly. Malcolm reluctantly decided he had to investigate the matter for himself.

The rumors centered on several young women who had borne
children out of wedlock, had been tried by a Muslim court for adultery, and had been condemned to a state of "isolation" in which no
Muslim was allowed to have contact with them. The well-guarded
secret was that Muhammad had fathered their babies. In his desperation Malcolm went to visit the women: "I broke the rule that no
Muslim is supposed to have contact with another Muslim in the
'isolated' state. I looked up, and I talked with three of the former secretaries of Mr. Muhammad. From their own mouths, I heard their
stories of who had fathered their children." [22] For the first time since
he had become a Muslim, Malcolm had broken a law; given our
prior analysis of his criminal activity, we may infer that the action
was not unmotivated by aggressive inclinations toward the lawgiver.
It was also, however, clearly justified by the lawgiver's law-breaking.
To state the point in our terms, Elijah Muhammad was proving himself to be more a primal father than a benevolent parental leader, a
chief who sought sexual possession over the women in his horde
rather than a holy man whose aim-inhibited sexual energies infused
his followers with love for him and with mutual respect. If, therefore, Malcolm was half-consciously rebelling against Muhammad,
his action was sanctioned by the birthright of the seventh son.

The practical question Malcolm now faced was what to do with
his certain knowledge of Muhammad's immorality. He decided to
consult with the Prophet himself; the latter acknowledged his sins
unhesitatingly. Malcolm then suggested that these sins had been
prophesied, and that a man's public strengths outweighed his private weaknesses. Like the adultery of David or the drunkenness of
Noah, the Prophet's misdeeds were both predestined and of secondary significance. This was, to be sure, a somewhat risky argument
for one who had freely accused others of moral hypocrisy, and it
therefore should not be used unless needed. But if the issue threatened to become public, then this line of defense would have to be
taken. Meanwhile attention should be shifted away from the moral

aspects of the doctrine, and the Nation's ministers should be prepared for the possibility of having to defend the Prophet with this
argument.

Muhammad seemed to agree with his approach; Malcolm returned to Temple Number Seven much relieved. But when he tried
to prepare the East Coast ministers for the possibility of having to
confront the issue, he was accused of being a rumormonger: "Chicago Muslim officials were [making] it appear that I was throwing
gasoline on the fire instead of water. . . . They were [trying] to make
it appear that instead of inoculating against the epidemic, I had
started it."[23]

This last comment brings to our attention the final and fatal contradiction in Malcolm's situation, namely, the fight for organizational power and authority that was more and more disrupting the
harmonious life of the Nation. This conflict had a double basis: on
the one hand, the Prophet was sixty-five in 1962, and in ill health;
consequently the question was being asked, albeit *sotto voce*, who
would ascend to Muhammad's throne after his death? On the other
hand, by this time the complexity of the Nation's affairs necessitated a routinization of the Prophet's charisma and the rationalization of the organization's structures and functions; consequently,
positions of power and authority were being created which the more
able and ambitious ministers hoped to occupy. Thus there developed
an intense struggle for organizational power that was at the same
time a conflict within the Muslim brotherhood over who would succeed the primal father.

Malcolm's position in this struggle for power was at once overwhelmingly strong and terribly weak. He was surely the best known,
most influential, and most highly respected man in the Nation, with
the possible exception of Muhammad; and he had always been the
latter's favorite disciple. In 1963 he had been appointed the Nation's
first National Minister; and at a "late 1963" rally, Muhammad had
introduced him by saying, "This is my most faithful, hardworking
minister. He will follow me until he dies."[24] But as Malcolm learned
when he talked to the isolated secretaries, in private Muhammad
was convinced that one day Malcolm would "turn against him": "So
I was 'dangerous.' I learned from these former secretaries that while
he was praising me to my face, he was tearing me apart behind my
back."[25] The ultimate basis of Malcolm's organizational strength
and the rock upon which his character had been built—i.e., his filial
adoration of Muhammad, which was presumably mirrored in the
Prophet's parental loving-kindness and trust—was essentially non-

existent. Moreover, his proselytizing and polemical activities had left him little time for administrative work, with the consequence that the Nation's bureaucratic apparatus was coming totally under the control of John 3X and his assistants at the Chicago headquarters. And while Muhammad may have loved Malcolm like a son, it seemed evident that one of his actual sons would inherit the throne. Thus Malcolm, the most talented member of the Nation, was effectively barred from entering its highest office. Muhammad, who fully understood the soaring extent of Malcolm's individual and collective ambitions, therefore had reason to fear that his leading disciple would attempt to usurp his position or subvert the normal functioning of the organization; this reasonable anxiety was transformed, as a result of Muhammad's own betrayal of his beliefs, into a paranoid certainty that Malcolm would betray him. That is, his follower's unsullied devotion to the Truth he taught served as a mirror in which he was forced to see the contradiction between his theory and his practice. He therefore wished, perhaps half-audibly, that someone would shatter the glass.

Malcolm's world was crumbling. The Nation, which had been the embodiment of black racial identity, pride, and mutual self-respect, was becoming a hustling society filled with paranoid suspicion, ugly jealousy, and ruthless competition. Its benevolent spiritual leader was turning into an aging leader of a primal horde, still coveting his wives and daughters but increasingly fearful that his children would band together behind the heroic seventh son to kill him and take possession of his power and position. In this new nightmare realm, Malcolm "felt almost out of [his] mind" and every action he undertook to restore his own peace of mind or the lost Islamic paradise became self-negating.[26] If he tried to fill ministerial posts with qualified men, thereby serving the interests of the organization, he was accused of favoring his own followers, of appointing "Malcolm's ministers," so he stopped selecting his New York brothers for these positions. If he accepted speaking engagements, he was being self-aggrandizing; therefore, to avoid conflict he turned down offers of magazine cover-stories and curtailed his public appearances at a time when he felt it was of "arch importance for a militant black voice to reach mass audiences."[27] If when he was speaking he stressed political issues—both because they were of critical importance to the black masses and because moral ones had become almost embarrassing—he was accused of transforming the doctrine in his own image, making it a vehicle of his "truth" rather than Muhammad's. There seemed to be nothing left for Malcolm to do or say. He was being circled round with tightening coils of contradiction.

The penultimate moment in this process of intensifying self-negation came in the wake of President Kennedy's assassination. Muhammad had been scheduled to speak in New York in early December and, as was still usual, Malcolm was expected to substitute for him. His text, selected well in advance of the President's death, was "God's Judgment of White America." Under the circumstances, this was a touchy subject, but in the speech itself Malcolm confined himself to appropriately abstract fulminations. Then, as he described it:

> The question-and-answer period opened, I suppose inevitably, with someone asking me, "What do you think about President Kennedy's assassination?" . . . Without a second thought, I said what I honestly felt—that it was as I saw it a case of "the chickens coming home to roost."[28]

The comment was natural enough, much like his reaction to the Orly air disaster. Each was merely a specification of Muhammad's general doctrinal position. Yet specification was exactly what the Prophet was working hard to avoid. The condemnation of the white man was intended to create an insurmountable barrier of hatred between black and white, to isolate the two communities from each other; it was not designed to generate a confrontation between the Nation and the white world. Because in the Orly matter Malcolm had embroiled the Muslims in unwanted controversy, Muhammad had chastised him. And because he wanted to avoid such controversy in the future, immediately after Kennedy's death he handed down strict orders that no minister was to comment upon the assassination. From Muhammad's perspective, Malcolm's remark was both imprudent and disobedient: using a forum the Prophet had provided, he was endangering the Nation and directly challenging his leader's authority. Yet to Malcolm the remark was only a slip, an inadvertent statement of how he "honestly felt." This indicates, of course, that what Malcolm honestly felt was no longer compatible with what Muhammad just as honestly felt. The latter was acting in his own and in what he conceived to be the Nation's interest when he ordered Malcolm to be "silent" for ninety days. In this way Malcolm would be punished for his willfulness and the Nation would be dissociated from Malcolm's comment.

For Malcolm, too, the chickens had now come home to roost: the contradiction inherent in his relationship to Muhammad was at last fully manifest. He could no longer be Muhammad's son and his own man. He could no longer convince himself that, as he once put it, "It is my mouth working, but the voice is [Mr. Muhammad's]."[29] He had a mind and a voice of his own, almost in spite of himself. Malcolm had fallen back into the mode of semi-volitional action that had been characteristic of his life before he had been awakened to Islam. Once again he had been possessed by a compulsion to disobey lawful authority and thereby bring to an end both an untenable situation and a subjective mental state of unbearable ambivalence. He wanted to be loyal to his leader and to possess his powers; he loved Muhammad and, increasingly, he hated him, hated the man who was castrating him, imprisoning him in a cage of political impotence. But Malcolm's very being had been grounded in that loyalty and that love; he could not conceive of himself except as Muhammad's adoring follower and son. He therefore could not consciously resolve upon an independent course of action but, rather, expressed his desire for freedom unwillingly. That on the one hand. On the other, by his action he was asking Muhammad to chastise him, to punish him for his disloyalty and his renewed Oedipal hostility—to relieve the pressure of unconscious guilt by transforming it into manifest suffering for and expiation of his sins.

The chastisement turned out to be far more severe than he could possibly have foreseen, and his freedom was thrust upon him far more sharply than he could have wished. He learned of the Prophet's decision the day after his speech, when he flew to Arizona for his regular monthly meeting with his leader. While he was on the airplane he had a "strong intuition" that something was about to happen. The intuition became a palpable feeling when he and Muhammad greeted each other: "I was suddenly tense. . . . For years I had prided myself that Mr. Muhammad and I were so close that I knew how he felt by how I felt. If he was nervous, I was nervous. If I was relaxed, then I knew he was relaxed. Now, I felt the *tension*."[30] Malcolm loved Muhammad unreservedly (although not unambivalently) and he identified with him totally. He had felt their separate existences as a unity. Now a feeling of *difference* had arisen between them—the feeling of the Prophet's alienation from him being reflected into him and thereby constituting the contradictory duality of their relationship. Muhammad commented that the "chickens come home to roost" remark was politically unfortunate. "And then, as if Mr. Muhammad's voice came from afar, I heard his words: 'I'll have to silence you for the next ninety days—so that Muslims everywhere can be disassociated from the blunder.'"[31] Malcolm was "numb," stunned by the sudden reversal in the reciprocal flow of their mutual energies, by the feeling of his adored leader's love being withdrawn. But he managed to respond: "Sir, I agree with you, and I submit, one hundred percent."[32]

Silenced for ninety days for a slip of the tongue: it was making the punishment fit the crime, but with a disproportionate vengefulness. Still, when Muhammad handed down this verdict Malcolm submitted himself to his leader's authority. Then, Malcolm reports, "an announcement was made throughout the Nation of Islam that I would be reinstated within ninety days, 'if he submits.' This made me suspicious—for the first time. I had completely submitted. But, deliberately, Muslims were being given the impression that I rebelled."[33] We who are analyzing this sad twist of fate know that in an intrasubjective sense Malcolm *was* rebelling, and that Muhammad, who was similarly motivated by half-conscious compulsions, was punishing that rebellion. But in the only terms that make juridical sense, in the terms of conscious activity, Malcolm had submitted. Accordingly, he became justifiably suspicious: he recognized that he was "being set up," that he was being hustled. Almost immediately, his hustler's intuition was confirmed:

> Three days later, the first word came to me that a Mosque Seven official who had been one of my most immediate assistants was telling certain Mosque Seven brothers: "If you knew what the Minister did, you'd go out and kill him yourself."
>
> And I knew. As any official in the Nation of Islam would have instantly known, any death-talk for me could have been approved of—if not actually initiated—by only one man.[34]

Malcolm had once cautiously likened himself to Saint Paul; now, if he had been searching for an historical analogy, he could have seen himself as Thomas à Beckett.

The Autobiography of Malcolm X

Each of the principal aspects of Malcolm's Muslim ministry had now been inverted by the combined force of the Nation's self-contradictory role in the struggle for black national libera-

tion and its intranational war of all against . . . Malcolm. * The negation of organizational militancy (self-productive aggressivity) and
organizational unity (racial-religious identity) had culminated in the
falsification of Malcolm's filial relationship to Muhammad. In other
words, a conflict of interests between the leader and his adherent,
through the mediation of a revivified struggle between the primal
father and the seventh son, produced the latter's unwilling rebellion
against the former and the former's suspension of the latter's conscious activity. As Malcolm himself expressed his feeling at this
time:

> I was in a state of emotional shock. I was like someone
> who for twenty years had had an inseparable, beautiful mar-
> riage—and then suddenly one morning at breakfast the mar-
> riage partner had thrust across the table some divorce
> papers.[35]

Malcolm's interest and the Prophet's had become mutually exclusive. The one was working for the freedom of the Black Nation, the
other for the preservation-in-isolation of the Nation of Islam. Their
separation was unavoidable. But Malcolm could not yet face the objective fatality of his situation, the situationally determined necessity of separation; he was fully exposed to the pain of being per-
secuted by the man who had been father and mother, husband and
wife, to him. He was bewildered: "I felt as though something in *nature* had failed, like the sun, or the stars."[36] The hidden meaning of
the Book of Revelation had not been revealed, after all.

As we know, Malcolm was able to weather this spiritual, emotional, and political storm. His wife Betty's strength and her faith in
him and in Islam of course helped to make this possible, but his relationship to Alex Haley and, through Haley, to his own past history
equally determined this favorable outcome. That relationship, as
Cedric Robinson was the first to argue, has much in common with a
psychoanalytic one.[37] We shall interpret the writing of the autobiography along these lines, that is, as an interpersonal process
of self-understanding through which Malcolm came to know himself as himself—through which he reclaimed and recreated his
individual-collective past as a moment of his present activity and

---

* As he comments, the Chicago faction had found their own solution to the problem
of Muhammad's moral failing: "Hating me was going to become the cause for people
of shattered faith to rally around" (*Autobiography*, p. 299). We shall return to this
point later.

thereby constituted it as a self-conscious ground for a projected *praxis* of national liberation.

Malcolm's relationship with Haley began in late 1959, when Haley wrote a story on the Nation of Islam for *Reader's Digest*. The story pleased Muhammad, Malcolm, and the Muslims generally. In 1962 Malcolm agreed to do a *Playboy* interview with Haley. Then a publisher suggested to Haley that an "as told to" autobiography would be an attractive project. Malcolm was "startled" by the idea when Haley presented it to him, but two days later he agreed: "I think my life story may help people to appreciate better how Mr. Muhammad salvages black people."[38] There were certain conditions: the project would have to receive Muhammad's blessing, all profits would go to the Nation, and Malcolm would have complete control over the content. These conditions were accepted, and early in 1963 the two men got down to work.

Two or three times a week Malcolm would come down to Haley's Greenwich Village apartment late in the evening. Haley would sit at his typewriter, and type in a personal shorthand whatever his visitor said. At first Malcolm would not talk about himself. As Haley admits, "We got off to a very poor start. To use a word he liked, I think both of us were a bit 'spooky.'"[39] Leaving aside the reasons why Haley was uneasy, Malcolm's spookiness reflected his mistrust of the writer: after all, Haley was clearly a "bourgeois" Negro and, for all Malcolm knew, he might be covertly working for the Man.

As his initial suspicions began to fade, a new difficulty arose. He had decided to do the book for three interrelated reasons. First, he believed that, as he put it, "my . . . life *mirrors* [the] hypocrisy" of the Northern white man's "attitude toward the Negro."[40] Telling his life's story would give him yet another opportunity for holding up to the white man a reflection of his crimes, a glass in which he would see himself as the guilty party in the American racial confrontation. Second, Malcolm recognized that other black people might be awakened to the truth through reading about his experience. In this sense the autobiography would have proselytic value. Finally, the unifying force in his life and hence in the book would be Muhammad; the narrative would form a paean of praise to the man he worshipped. But a necessary condition for the success of this threefold project was that Malcolm be willing to *individualize* himself; and any such individuation was both ethically unacceptable and emotionally painful. On the one hand, it would inevitably suggest that *he* was worth knowing about, that he was not just another follower of Elijah Muhammad: presenting himself to others as the content of his communication constituted an act of *hubris*. On the other, it would necessitate freeing the ghosts of his pre-Islamic past from their imprisonment in his unconscious and hence losing himself once again in the nightmare days and nights of his former life. He therefore resisted entering fully into the project to which he had consciously committed himself, and he manifested this resistance by refusing to discuss anything other than "Black Muslim philosophy," the "evils of the white devil," and the amazing powers of Mr. Muhammad. And "he would bristle when I [Haley] tried to urge him that the proposed book was *his* life."[41]

Malcolm was thus very much like a psychoanalytic patient who, after agreeing to being analyzed and accepting in principle the idea of free association, cannot or will not relinquish conscious control over his thoughts, one who defends himself against revealing his unspoken wishes to the analyst and his unconscious ones to himself by excluding from his communications any idea which he does not consider to be morally acceptable. The analyst must then find a way to help the patient circumvent, penetrate, and, ultimately, break down the defensive barriers so that the suppressed and repressed wishes that have been negating his conscious activity can be brought into consciousness, where their energy can then be transformed through mental work into a potential for self-conscious activity. In the present instance, since Haley's concern was not of course therapeutic, he was willing to obtain additional information by any means possible. Hence when he noticed that Malcolm was an inveterate doodler, he started leaving paper napkins near him. As he had anticipated, by the time Malcolm left, they had been filled with unintentional communications. From these scraps of information he was able to develop somewhat more productive lines of questioning.

In spite of this, after about two months of work Haley was almost ready to give up. But then:

> One night, Malcolm X arrived nearly out on his feet from fatigue. For two hours, he paced the floor delivering a tirade against Negro leaders who were attacking Elijah Muhammad and himself. I don't know what gave me the inspiration to say when he paused for breath, "I wonder if you'd tell me something about your mother?"
>
> Abruptly he quit pacing, and the look he shot at me made me sense that somehow the chance question had hit him. When I look back on it now, I believe I must have caught him so physically weak that his defenses were vulnerable.[42]

Malcolm began talking, and kept talking almost until morning. For the next several months he talked freely and without prodding about his life, until at the end of that time Haley had most of the material he needed for the book.

Why did Haley's question penetrate Malcolm's defenses? Haley suggests that the weakness of Malcolm's defenses at that moment provides the explanation; but such an interpretation provides necessary but not sufficient grounds for the break-through. As Freud argues repeatedly, such external or circumstantial factors do not explain the particular or determinate attributes of the phenomenon. If, however, we consider the *content* of the evening's interaction, Malcolm's response becomes more intelligible. He had been talking about Negro leaders who were serving the white man by attempting to destroy the Nation of Islam—who were attacking both Malcolm and the man who was mother and father to him. This suggests an analogy: the present attackers were to the Nation of Islam as the Black Legion was to the Little family or as the Christian Earl Little was to his wife. In other words, the nightmare night and the nightmare of everyday life constituted the latent content of the manifest situation. When Haley mentioned Malcolm's mother he created a conscious *form* for that unconscious content, an opening through which it could penetrate defenses weakened by fatigue.

Summing up thus far, we may say that the unconscious content of Malcolm's self-in-situation, through the mediation of his growing trust in Haley and his fatigue, became a conscious communication. This interpretation is not yet satisfactory, for it fails to specify the dynamus, the motive force, in that content, and therefore remains at the level of analogy. But if we remember that at this time Malcolm's filial adoration for Muhammad was being undermined by the latter's unwillingness to live up to his proclaimed beliefs, then we may infer that Malcolm's emotional energy was no longer flowing quite so freely through its customary interpersonal circuit; that, instead, it was circulating intrapersonally; and that in so doing, it revivified his love for his mother. Taking the genetic content and the dynamic process in their unity, the Prophet's failure to actualize his apparent charismatic potential was subjectively reflected in Malcolm's de-idealization of his leader; de-idealization in turn entailed the decomposition of the hypnotic identity, Muhammad equals mother equals father; and decomposition in its turn entailed an intrasubjective flow of emotional energy such that Malcolm's memory of his mother was emotionally reanimated—reanimated, it may be added, in proportion to his rejection of Muhammad.

Thus the bonds of Malcolm's absolute submission to Muhammad began to loosen. His self-abnegation was being negated, which of course implies a movement toward self-affirmation. In this sense the weakening of Malcolm's defenses was a progressive development. At the same time, however, the experience was a regression, a re-entry into the world of childhood and the decomposition not only of Muhammad's charismatic identity but also of Malcolm's character. Yet it was a "regression in the service of the ego," i.e., the making conscious of an unconscious content rather than the making unconscious of a conscious one. It had the consequence of transforming hitherto suppressed if not quite repressed thoughts, emotions, problems, and wishes into a ground which could be worked up into and through conscious activity. It constituted, in short, the necessary premise for an (almost) psychoanalytic reconstruction of the self.

Thinking back upon that night, Malcolm recognized that it was the first step toward the opening up of his mind. He told Haley that he had formerly "blocked" his mother out of his mind: "It was just unpleasant to think about her having been twenty-one years in that mental hospital."[43] But Haley's question, he continued,

> made me face something about myself. . . . My mind had
> been closed to our mother, I simply didn't feel the problem
> could be solved, so I had shut it out. I had built up
> subconscious defenses. . . . I've opened it up again. That's
> one of the characteristics I don't like about myself. If I meet
> a problem I feel I can't solve, I shut it out. I make believe
> that it doesn't exist. But it does.[44]

On the basis of our own work, we can testify to the accuracy of Malcolm's self-criticism. Indeed, the unintentional actions which resolved contradictions in his life were a return of the repressed conditioned by his "subconscious defenses." But this defensive process —the denial of a problem through the suppression of the subject matter in which it inheres—was not a freely chosen "characteristic"; it was, rather, the product of repeated traumatization, a manifestation of the racially magnified division of his psyche; in short, the price he paid for growing up black in white America. But further, Malcolm is here taking a position of moral responsibility. We might hear him saying, in paraphrase of Sartre: "This is what I have been made; now we shall see what I can make of myself." In the present instance he accepted Yvonne's initiative and, together with his brothers and sisters, liberated his mother from her captivity. Louise was released from the mental institution and taken home to Philbert's, there to live out the rest of her life in the midst of her family.

Thus one apparently insoluble problem was solved. His problematical relationship with Muhammad was not so easily resolved. Yet Malcolm progressed toward such a resolution over the next several months (from late spring through early autumn of 1963). Using Haley as a mirror against which to reflect the various facets of his personality, he developed a new perspective on or conception of himself. First, he came to see his life as developing through three phases, each of which was nominally differentiated from the others: there was the childhood of Malcolm Little, which ended in Ostrowski's revelation of American racism; the hustling career of Detroit Red, which ended in Muhammad's revelation of Islamic Truth; and the ministerial career of Malcolm X, which was coming to an end in part through the process of Malcolm's self-revelation. Second, he saw each of these phases as his history, as the history of black people at that time, and as an American or even world history. Finally, he constituted the unity of this temporal and spatial manifold through an interpretive process having as its moments empirical representation, psychological understanding, and racial-religious knowledge.

It should be apparent to the reader who has also read the *Autobiography* that Malcolm self-consciously reconstructed the moments of his life in this way. It should be equally evident that our interpretation has been a reflection of his interpretation, with this critical difference: where for Malcolm the ultimately determining principle in his life was Allah, who guided his steps at every point without his knowledge, for us this principle is human activity, which in its alienated form—as the class/group structure of American monopoly capitalism—acts upon men against their will. We therefore have been obliged throughout to explain changes and relationships which for Malcolm were self-evidently the work of an immanent deity.

Nonetheless, Malcolm has recourse to theological interpretation only in the last instance. In the substantial meantime, he attempts to solve his problems—which in most cases are also our problems—with concepts that are markedly similar to our own. Thus the *Autobiography* was his attempt to understand his relationship to his parents and their relationship to each other; the death of his father, the disintegration of the family, and hence his delinquency; his unwillingness to remain a house Negro in Mason or, to say it differently, the reasons why he became a hustler; and the reasons why he joined the Nation of Islam. At the same time he was trying to explain why black people have allowed themselves to be dominated by white people, and why they are no longer willing to accept domination. And he was attempting to expose the structure of the white mind, so that both white people and black people would be freed from the spell of the "racial mirages, clichés [stereotypes], and lies that this country's very atmosphere has been filled with for four hundred years."[45] Finally, he was attempting to represent the interests and motives of the black masses, the most victimized of the victims of democracy; and to persuade and/or force the Negro middle class and the Man to recognize the legitimacy of that interest, the inevitability of those motives. In his words:

> I think that the objective reader may see how in the society to which I was exposed as a black youth in America, for me to wind up in a prison was really just about inevitable. It happens to so many thousands of black youths.
>
> I think that the objective reader may see how when I heard "The white man is the devil," when I played back what had been my experiences, it was inevitable that I would respond positively; then the next twelve years of my life were devoted and dedicated to propagating that phrase among black people.
>
> I think, I hope, that the objective reader, in following my life—the life of only one ghetto-created Negro—may gain a better picture and understanding than he had previously had of the black ghettoes which are shaping the lives and thinking of almost 22 million Negroes who live in America.[46]

As indicated above, Malcolm's individual-collective self-understanding was the product of a partial psychoanalysis, the moments of which may be briefly specified as follows. Once the resistance to self-revelation is initially overcome, a free flow of associations from the self becomes possible. This flow continues until new resistance points are reached, at which time these resistances must be overcome. But in any case, free association is the objectification of the unconscious self; it is the implicit subjectivity of the self becoming explicit, the transformation of that which the person is *in* himself into an object that exists *for* himself. Thus Malcolm projected a self he had not formerly been able to see against the screen that Haley thereby became, so that he was then able to see himself as that reflection. Further, he was able to recognize the reflection as *his* image, as the representation, through memory, of his life. Finally, this act of recognition was implicitly a repossession or reappropriation of that object, i.e., a process of internalization. It was not, however, a return of the repressed; rather, it was the creation of himself in and for himself through the work of systematically unifying his life experience.

This psychoanalytic dialectic was not, however, carried through to the end. Although in the relationship with Haley (through the project of the *Autobiography*) Malcolm was able to uncover the suppressed or preconscious determinants of his behavior, he did not in fact penetrate to the region of the unconscious repressed; and while during this time his political understanding was developing with great rapidity, he had not yet worked his way down to the economic foundation of American society. Consequently, the actual determinants of his class-racial character remained hidden behind a veil of religious abstraction and were present to him only in the illusory form of a play of divine forces. In a more immediate sense, his work with Haley and in American politics was insufficient to destroy Muhammad's charismatic domination of his character and conscious activity. Hence it was once again an accident and not a willed action that expressed Malcolm's rebellion against authority; and it took the unjust punishment of that unwilling defiance to force him finally to confront the insoluble problems that had arisen in his relationship to Muhammad and the Nation of Islam.

My Sincerity Is My Credentials

As we have already noted, Malcolm understood why the Chicago faction of the Nation wanted him suspended, and also how that suspension was likely to end. National solidarity was being undermined by the Prophet's immorality, and would be undermined even further if his sins were to be widely publicized; but with Malcolm cast in the role of Judas, the Nation could be reunited against him and, just as importantly, the fire of the press would be drawn away from Muhammad's private life and onto the renegade disciple. Malcolm deduced that step one—giving out the impression that he had not submitted to Muhammad's commandment—having been taken, step two would be the indefinite extension of that suspension. Then "step three would be either to provoke some Muslim ignorant of the truth to take it upon himself to kill me as a 'religious duty'—or to 'isolate' me so that I would gradually disappear from the public scene."[47] National unity would thus be restored under the leadership of the Chicago clique. Despite this understanding, which as far as it goes is consonant with our own organizational and group-emotional analysis of the situation, Malcolm was not able to divorce himself psychologically from Muhammad and the Nation. As he put it, "I could not yet let myself psychologically face what I knew: that already the Nation of Islam and I were physically divorced."[48] He simply could not "conceive betrayal," the repayment of his total loyalty to Muhammad and the Nation with suspension, public humiliation, and the threat of death. Consequently, he was in a state of "emotional shock. . . . My head felt like it was bleeding inside. I felt like my brain was damaged."[49] The pain was so great that he asked the family physician to give him a "brain examination." No pathology was found, but it was evident to the doctor that he was under great strain and needed a rest.

It requires no great insight to recognize that Malcolm feared and, at some level, even believed that Muhammad was "burning his brain" as he had Reginald's; given our prior work, the psychodynamics of this illusion are easily inferred. Malcolm's conversion to Islam had entailed the projection onto Muhammad of his repressed emotional energies, with the immediate consequence that Muhammad became in his mind a figure of awesome power and charismatic authority. Because, however, his sexual energy had been returned to him in the form of both an affirmative racial identity and his leader's benevolence, while his aggressive energy had been displaced onto the White Devil, he had experienced a profound peace of mind. He had seemed to be at one with himself. Now, his aggressive tendencies, instead of being displaced through Muhammad onto the White Devil, were being reintrojected, just as the impending doom with which he had been threatening the Man was returning to him in the form of his imminent death. Furthermore, the aggressive energy now flooding his mind was a reflection of his earlier rejection of Reginald; it was an hysterical identification with his brother's insanity determined by the return of the aggression that this prior action involved.* By the same reasoning, his mental anguish was an identification with his mother's insanity. In each of these respects, therefore, the chickens were coming home to roost. Yet in the terms thus

---

* After Malcolm had finally broken with Muhammad, he was able to see and accept his responsibility for Reginald's illness: "After Elijah Muhammad himself was later

far specified, it was not really a case of Hammurabian justice, of an eye for an eye. Malcolm initially believed that his brain was bleeding, not that he was going insane: he understood his mental state as a physical symptom. At a deeper genetic level, this punishment precisely fit the crime: "My father's skull, on one side, was crushed in"; Oedipal assault, paternal revenge.

Thus Malcolm was once again trapped in a vicious circle of self-destructive aggressivity, this time in the form of an hysterical identification with the personal objects of his unconscious aggressive desires, mediated through his moral identification with Muhammad. We may say, Muhammad had put a curse upon him, voodooed him. He therefore had to find a way to break the hypnotic spell.

Although he did not realize it, Malcolm had already taken the first steps toward self-liberation. In his work with Haley, he had overcome his resistance to talking about himself, and this action then served as a ground for the reintegration of his life history. The alienated, lost reaches of his pre-conscious mind, the memories of his childhood and young manhood, had once again become his own. Simultaneously he had begun to detach himself from Muhammad, or at least to de-idealize him. These two complementary processes, which mainly moved through free-associative channels, were beginning to crystallize into an interpretation of his experience that was at once individual and universal. He was becoming self-conscious in spite of himself—which implies that he was potentially but not yet actually capable of free self-conscious activity. When Muhammad suspended him from the Nation, this newly born free self was able to struggle with the old submissive one for the possession of Malcolm's mind.

This battle was initially conducted on the field of memory:

> Whatever I was saying at any time was being handled by a small corner of my mind. The rest of my mind was filled with a parade of a thousand and one different scenes from the past twelve years . . . scenes in the Muslim mosques . . . scenes with Mr. Muhammad . . . scenes with Mr. Muhammad's family . . . scenes with Muslims, individually, as my audiences, and at our social gatherings . . . and scenes with the white man in audiences, and the press.[50]

---

accused of being a very immoral man, I came to believe that it wasn't a divine chastisement upon Reginald, but the pain he felt when his own family totally rejected him for Elijah Muhammad, and this hurt made Reginald turn insanely upon Elijah Muhammad" (*Autobiography*, p. 189).

At two other points in his life Malcolm had found it necessary or unavoidable to test a new truth against the reality of his own experience. The first time was when Ostrowski told him niggers could not be lawyers. Malcolm had accepted this judgment as authoritative, but after comparing himself to his classmates, he had also judged it to be unjust. Consequently he had taken it to its logical extreme: if not a lawyer, then a criminal. The second time was when Reginald told him that the black man was God and the white man was the devil. In this instance he had wanted to believe the proposition put forward, just because it was the negation of Ostrowski's dictum. But he had to negate its possible negations in his own experience in order to affirm it. This necessity produced first a free-associative reliving of his life and then the argumentative testing of the proposition. Islamic doctrine passed the test and Malcolm became a Muslim. Now Muhammad's truth had once again become an hypothesis requiring empirical testing: Malcolm brought forth from his memory all of the experience that testified to Muhammad's divine inspiration and benevolence, the holiness of the National community, and the devilish hostility of the white man. He "still struggled" to persuade himself that Muhammad in his adultery "had been fulfilling prophecy."[51]

His argument with himself was unpersuasive:

> What began to break my faith was that, try as I might, I couldn't hide, I couldn't evade [the fact], that Mr. Muhammad, instead of facing what he had done before his followers, as a human weakness or as fulfillment of prophecy . . . had instead been willing to hide, to cover up what he had done.[52]

Malcolm was, perhaps above all else, an honest man—as an old family friend in Lansing had once told him, during his hustling days: "Malcolm, there's one thing I like about you. You're no good, but you don't try to hide it. You are not a hypocrite."[53] His conversion to Islam had been realized through that honesty: he had been willing to admit his guilt, accept responsibility for his actions, and pray for forgiveness; as a result, he had been saved and the Truth had become a living force in his character. Subsequently, his whole life had been dedicated to telling that Truth to others, black and white alike. Now he had discovered that Muhammad was not living the Truth. This in itself was a terrible shock, but not a fatal one. After all, sins openly confessed would be forgiven. But Muhammad would not accept responsibility for his actions, and therefore his sins could not be remitted. He was a hypocrite, doubly a hypocrite, unworthy of Malcolm's filial adoration.

Thus Malcolm freed himself from the bonds of Muhammad's charisma. He had tested the Prophet's belief in his God and found it to be wanting. "And that was how," he states, "after twelve years of never thinking for as much as five minutes about myself, I became able finally to muster the nerve, and the strength, to start facing the facts, to *think for myself*."[54] Thinking for himself, however, meant facing an apparently insoluble problem. If Muhammad did not believe in his Truth, then that Truth was not true: the assurance of its validity rested entirely upon the Prophet's charismatic (divinely given) legitimacy, not upon rational argument. In other words, Muslim doctrine was a hype. But if it were only a hype, then how could it possess the power to change men's lives? How was Malcolm to explain his own reformation and the success of his proselytism and polemical activity? And how could he claim to have been or to be a Muslim, a true servant of Allah? The solution to the problem, Malcolm finally reasoned, was that he "had believed in Mr. Muhammad more than he believed in himself."[55] That is, Muhammad did in fact possess the Truth, or at least a certain form of the Truth. His own belief in it was not strong, and he had therefore falsified it in practice. But because it was the Truth for all that, his followers were able to receive its blessings despite his imperfections. And from this (as it were) Lutheran position, it follows that Malcolm could remain a Muslim without being a follower of Elijah Muhammad.

As we shall see, Malcolm's argument was not really conclusive either in his own terms or in ours; but it was sufficient to restore his racial-religious identity, this time on a consciously self-determined basis. Once this had been accomplished, he was able to see that his conversion to Islam and his success as a Muslim minister had been as much a product of his work as of Muhammad's inspiration. In his words: "I was going downhill until he [Muhammad] picked me up, but the more I think of it, we picked each other up."[56] Malcolm was not only rebuilding his racial-religious identity, he was also repossessing what he now recognized as the alienated process and product of his proselytizing and polemical labors—which is to say, he was beginning to understand that as Muhammad's leading disciple he was implicitly or potentially an independent Black Muslim leader.

Not a leader of the Black Muslims, however: the Nation of Islam, firmly under Muhammad's charismatic sway, held no future for Malcolm. But as his free-associative search for himself in the memories of the preceding twelve years reveals, Malcolm was as wedded to and in love with the Nation as he was with Muhammad. He therefore had to achieve a psychological divorce from the organization.

Again, the first step in this direction had already been taken in his prior work with Haley and his current immersion in his past; each time he relived the moments of his Muslim years it was with the implicit admission: "This can never happen again." He was, at least half-consciously, *mourning* for the Black Muslim brothers and sisters he was no longer free to love, thus relinquishing them as objects of his affection. But this process of mourning was not completed until it was objectively reflected in the "first direct order" for his death.* That was when, Malcolm states, "I began to arrive at my psychological divorce from the Nation of Islam."[57] He could not identify with or love a group that was trying to kill him, any more than he had been able to accept the psychic castration that would have been entailed if he had remained a "good Negro" in Lansing. He decided to leave the organization rather than wait for Muhammad to have him killed, expelled, or indefinitely isolated.

Malcolm was once again on his own. The bonds of charismatic-group membership had been cut in both directions, just as formerly the illusions of benevolent paternalism and the stereotypical dumb-show had been destroyed. This time there was no possibility of sinking into the *lumpen-proletariat*: through the mediation of his quasi-psychoanalytic relationship to Alex Haley, he had survived what he calls his "psychological and spiritual crisis."[58] His character structure had been re-formed through his conscious activity, and he had reappropriated (at least subjectively) his past work. His life was "inseparably committed to the American black man's struggle"; he could admit to himself that he was "generally regarded as a 'leader'"; and he accepted responsibility for using his leadership potential in the interests of the black masses. The question was, what was he to do? "I had to honestly ask myself what I could offer, how I was genuinely qualified to help the black people win their struggle for human rights."[59]

Answering this question entailed carefully analyzing his power resources: "I had enough experience to know that in order to be a good organizer of anything in which you expect to succeed—including yourself—you must almost mathematically analyze cold facts."[60]

---

* A Muslim brother had been given a "contract"—as it is revealingly called—to wire the ignition of Malcolm's car so that a bomb would explode when the ignition was turned; instead of carrying out his assignment, he told Malcolm, who then told him the real reason why they wanted him dead and won the brother to his cause.

He had always wanted to be a success in life, and now his success had become identified with the project of black national liberation. He had always been analytical, a thoughtful observer of whatever situation he happened to be in; now the time had come to think for himself about himself—but about himself as a participant in the struggle. As he viewed it, in this regard he had two principal strengths: "I had, as one asset, I knew, an international image. . . . [And] more immediately, in New York City, where I would naturally base any operation, I had a large, direct personal following of non-Muslims."[61]* In addition, we may observe for Malcolm that his objective power base was subjectively reflected in the organizational and theoretical skills he had developed within the Nation of Islam. That on the one hand. On the other, any project of his own would have to overcome the limitations of Muhammad's practice. It would have to "embrace all faiths of black men" in order to achieve a genuine racial unity; it should "carry into practice what the Nation of Islam had only preached"—it would have to be militant in practice as well as in theory.[62] To state the same point in its opposite form, it would have to overcome the limitations of the Movement, which was interdenominational but not nationalist, activist but not militant. In sum, it would have to be an organization that "would help to challenge the American black man to gain his human rights, and to cure his mental, spiritual, economic, and political sicknesses."[63]

On March 8, 1964, at a press conference in the Hotel Theresa in Harlem, Malcolm announced the formation of Muslim Mosque, Inc., the organization he hoped would serve this purpose. He began by stating his intention of being "very active in every phase of the American Negro struggle for *human rights*"; and he emphasized the critical importance of political action in a year of national elections. Then he paused to clarify his relationship to both the Nation and the Movement. He affirmed his Islamic faith and belief in Muhammad's analysis of and solution to the American racial problem. He acknowledged that he had not left the Nation of his "own free will," and he indicated his willingness to use the freedom thus thrust upon him to develop "a more flexible approach toward working with others to get a solution to this problem." With respect to the Movement leadership, he admitted that there had been "bad things" said on every side, but he stated his intention of letting the dead bury their

---

* The full implications of this double potential were not to become clear to him until somewhat later; for the moment, he saw his international image primarily as a counter in the domestic political game.

dead and his desire to work in unity with other leaders and organizations. As for himself:

> I do not pretend to be a divine man, but I do believe in divine guidance, divine power, and divine prophecy. I am not educated, nor am I an expert in any particular field—but I am sincere and my sincerity is my credentials.[64]

We who have been witnessing Malcolm's struggle to free himself from his bondage to Muhammad and the Nation both feel and understand the anger, sadness, and pride in his self-representation. He was not the man-god Muhammad hypocritically pretended to be. He was not the respectable middle-class citizen Movement leaders believed themselves to be. But he did have faith in his God, and in the power of the collective black man; and he would sincerely serve the interests of both.

Having articulated the personal grounds for his new position, Malcolm next proceeded to outline his first attempted solution to the problem of unified racial practice. His own base of political and spiritual power was to be Muslim Mosque, Inc.; this organization would develop political, economic, and social programs in which all black people could participate. These programs would be black nationalist in character, i.e., they would be oriented toward bringing the black community under genuinely black control. Moreover, Muslim Mosque would work collaboratively with any other black organization sharing its general purpose. It would even work with white people, at least to a certain degree:

> The Muslim Mosque, Inc., will remain wide open to ideas and financial aid from all quarters. Whites can help us, but they can't join us. There can be no black-white unity until there is first some black unity. There can be no workers' solidarity until there is first some racial solidarity.[65]

Finally, he affirmed unconditionally the right of any black person to "fight back in self-defense whenever and wherever he is being unjustly and unlawfully attacked."[66]

Genuinely militant black nationalism, the guiding principle of the Black Revolution, had finally appeared on the American political stage. A new act in the racial drama was about to begin.

CHAPTER IX

Freedom by Any Means Necessary

SHORTLY AFTER HE ANNOUNCED his separation from the Nation of Islam, Malcolm spoke at the Militant Labor Forum of the Socialist Workers' Party on the topic of the Black Revolution. He defined his subject in this way:

> Now the black revolution has been taking place in Africa and Asia and Latin America; when I say black, I mean non-white—black, brown, red or yellow. Our brothers and sisters in Asia, who were colonized by the Europeans, our brothers and sisters in Africa, who were colonized by the Europeans, and in Latin America, the peasants who were colonized by the Europeans, have been involved in a struggle since 1945 to get the colonialists, or the colonizing powers, the Europeans, off their land, out of their country.[1]

The Black Revolution as he conceived it was thus an anti-imperialist struggle for national liberation. And, as the Essian-Udoms argue, "He regarded the Afro-American liberation movement as part and parcel of this Black Revolution or Third World rebellion against colonialism and imperialism."[2] The Afro-American role was first to "overturn" the American system which in "1964 still colonizes 22 million Afro-Americans, still enslaves 22 million Afro-Americans."[3] Further, "the racial sparks that are ignited here in America today could easily turn into a flaming fire abroad, which means it could engulf all the people of this earth into a giant race war."[4] The white man who correctly perceived this situation was frightened, and the one who really understood it would attempt to right the wrongs before it was too late. Meanwhile, however, the American black man who thought for himself—the black nationalist—was not waiting for the day when the white man would get religion. He was ready to "fight for independence," confident that he was the spark "necessary to fuse or ignite the entire black community," which in turn would ignite the "world-wide powder keg."[5]

Muslim Mosque, Inc., was intended to be the vanguard of the Black Revolution. Yet a little more than three months after its formation Malcolm relegated it to an exclusively religious role, and replaced it politically with the OAAU. By then he had decided that the Mosque was an inadequate organizational vehicle for radical political action. To determine how and why he arrived at this decision we must first represent at least schematically the theory and intended practice of Muslim Mosque.

Muslim Mosque, Inc.

We can best approach this subject by representing a speech Malcolm gave in April of 1964 in which he systematically articulated his analysis of the existing situation, the appropriate course of action to be taken, and the black nationalist idea which was immanent in both his analysis and his choice of action. This speech, entitled "The Ballot or the Bullet," was delivered at a meeting sponsored by a CORE chapter in Cleveland, Ohio, which in itself is indicative of the tendency toward racial unification that Malcolm was attempting to strengthen. He began by stating that he was a Muslim, but that his religion was a personal matter. What was not personal was the collective interest of black people who have suffered "political oppression at the hands of the white man, economic exploitation at the hands of the white man, and social degradation at the hands of the white man."[6] This common interest necessitated unified action; all personal differences would have to be set aside.

Having defined black people's common interest, Malcolm next discussed the existing political situation. Nineteen hundred sixty-four was a presidential election year. This meant that "all of the political crooks will be right back in your or my community with their false promises, building up our hopes for a letdown, with their trickery and their treachery, with their false promises that they don't intend to keep." But because "the type of black man on the scene today . . . just doesn't intend to turn the other cheek any longer," the false promises of the politicians, which result in rising expectations, will lead to an "explosion."[7] That explosion will be justified because the "22 million black people" in America are "the victims of democracy, nothing but disguised hypocrisy." Hence Malcolm could say: "I see America through the eyes of a victim. I don't see any American dream; I see an American nightmare."[8]

Given "the type of black man on the scene," it follows that insurrectionary bullets are one potential of the situation. The other is the intelligent use of the ballot. Because black people will be the swing vote in the coming election, they can use their ballots to put in people of their own choice—but not if they continue to be fooled by the old Democratic Party "con game" of blaming inaction on the Dixiecrats. A Dixiecrat, Malcolm stressed, was "nothing but a Democrat"; and the game the Demo-Dixiecrat plays is simply this: "One of them [the liberal] makes believe he's for you, and he's got it fixed where the other one [the conservative] is so tight against you, he never has to keep his promise."[9] A policy of nonalignment is the only rational alternative, and the exercise of that policy calls for coordinated collective action. This electoral strategy must be framed with the certain knowledge that its failure entails more aggressive measures: "It's got to be the ballot or the bullet. The ballot or the bullet. If you're afraid to use an expression like that, you should get on out of the country, you should go back in the cotton patch, you should get back in the alley."[10]

Malcolm had now moved almost imperceptibly from representation of the existing situation to a general conception of situationally rational action. In the process he had interpreted the situation in such a way that conventional civil rights activity was revealed as irrational: "It is the government itself, the government of America, that is responsible for the oppression and exploitation and degradation of black people in this country."[11] It follows that "when you take your case to Washington, D.C., you're taking it to the criminal who's responsible; it's like running from the wolf to the fox."[12] It follows, then, that "the entire civil rights struggle needs a new interpretation, a broader interpretation,"[13] and this means that "we need to expand the civil rights struggle to a higher level—to the level of human rights."[14] Such an expansion is both morally justified and strategically necessary. It permits black people to take their case to the U.N., to a level of international balloting or judgment where the influence of the Third World can be mobilized. Internationalizing the struggle will also serve to link it to the guerrilla efforts of the dark world, efforts the white man is powerless to defeat (witness the Korean War, the French Indo-Chinese war, and the Algerian freedom movement): "Just as guerrilla warfare is prevailing in Asia and in parts of Africa and parts of Latin America, you've got to be mighty naive, or you've got to play the [American] black man cheap, if you don't think some day he's going to wake up and find that it's got to be the ballot or the bullet."[15]

Having established his conception of situationally rational action, Malcolm proceeded to define the role of Muslim Mosque in relation thereto. He first articulated its basic principle, namely, the concept of black nationalism: "The political philosophy of black nationalism means that the black man should control the politics and politicians in his own community. . . . The economic philosophy of black nationalism . . . only means that we should control the economy of our community. . . . The social philosophy of black nationalism only means that we have to get together and remove the evils that are destroying the moral fiber of our community."[16] In other words, black nationalism was simply racial self-determination in the ghettoized situation. It was not a separatist notion à la Muhammad, for it entailed taking power away from the white man through the organized use of the ballot or the bullet; but neither was it a fully developed revolutionary concept, for it presupposed the continued existence of the larger, alien society against which the black community would have to determine itself.

Just because black nationalism was not *yet* a truly revolutionary idea, Malcolm had reason to believe that the more militant members of the Movement would find it acceptable—if a way could be found to create a racially unified black-nationalist practice without threatening the status of any existing organization, i.e., without turning the Movement into a self-destructive war of organizational all against all. Consequently Malcolm defined for Muslim Mosque a limited proselytizing role:

Our gospel is black nationalism. We are not trying to threaten the existence of any organization, but we are spreading the gospel of black nationalism. Anywhere there's a church that is also preaching and practicing the gospel of black nationalism, join that church.[17]

Rather than replace the Movement with Muslim Mosque, Malcolm was encouraging its militant members to transform it from within.

If its leaders refused to allow this tendency to develop, it would become necessary to overturn the leadership or split from the organization; but until or unless that happened, members of the Movement should attempt to radicalize it, so that by summer it would be possible to hold a "black nationalist convention" as an alternative to participating on a second-class basis within the established political parties and for the purpose of choosing a political path to follow:

> At that time, if we see fit . . . to form a black nationalist party, we'll form a black nationalist party. If it's necessary to form a black nationalist army, we'll form a black nationalist army. It'll be the ballot or the bullet. It'll be liberty or it'll be death.[18]

Muslim Mosque was thus intended to be a black nationalist organization with an international revolutionary orientation. We shall see presently why Malcolm decided to redefine his position as Afro-American rather than black nationalist, and why he gave his redefined position a new organizational embodiment. But Muslim Mosque cannot be adequately comprehended in exclusively political terms, for it was also a religious institution. As such, it represents Malcolm's continuing faith in Islam and the practical necessity of providing his Muslim followers with an alternative to membership in the Nation of Islam.

In order for Muslim Mosque to serve these purposes, Malcolm's own Islamic position had to be reestablished. His religious identity and ministry had come to him through Elijah Muhammad. Now that he was no longer a follower of Muhammad, his religious standing was uncertain. Besides, he had often been told, and he inwardly admitted, that Islam was not a racially defined theology. Over the past few years, the public denial of that reality had become increasingly problematical, but the public admission of the fact presented problems from the standpoint of his racial legitimacy. Both of these difficulties could be resolved, however, if he were successfully to complete a pilgrimage to Mecca, for only orthodox Muslims were permitted to enter the Holy City, and those who entered the city were not exclusively black. If Malcolm were allowed to visit Mecca, he could return to America with his religious status confirmed and a change in his racial-religious views experientially justified. Finally, we may deduce from our prior knowledge of Malcolm's character that the pilgrimage was not only a public but also a private necessity: he needed to prove to himself that he was a Muslim, and he needed to establish an unmediated relationship between himself and his God.

In April, 1964, Malcolm flew from New York to Cairo. In the Cairo airport, surrounded by pilgrims of "all complexions," he was immediately struck by the atmosphere of "warmth and friendliness": "The feeling hit me that there really wasn't any color problem here. The effect was as though I had just stepped out of prison."[19] Later he was to conclude that in leaving the United States he left behind the racist atmosphere in which all Americans were suffocating; in Cairo he was free for the first time from the constant tension of struggling to determine himself against an imposed racial identity. Stating the point positively, in the Middle East he believed he was free to be a member of a religious community in which race had no exchange value, no currency. The fact that he was black gave him a distinctive character but no position of either superiority or inferiority in relation to any other Muslim. Islam was for Malcolm already beginning to lose its racial quality and to take on a human one instead, while at the same time his self-conception was being deracialized.

The prelude to the pilgrimage was pleasant and stimulating; the first act of the pilgrimage itself, i.e., getting to Mecca, was painful and disorienting. Malcolm was "nervous" as he changed from his ordinary clothing into the "two white towels" all pilgrims wear to symbolize the *Ihram* or consecration state of one who is going to Mecca. He was more than nervous when he reached the passport officials who could grant him permission to proceed or require that he appear before a tribunal that would judge his Islamic authenticity. The permission was not granted, and Malcolm had to stay behind as the other pilgrims in his party went on ahead. He watched them go, and then he was alone: "It was then about three in the morning, a Friday morning. I never had been in such a jammed mass of people, but I never had felt more alone, and helpless, since I was a baby."[20] He was far from home, wearing strange clothing, unable to "speak anybody's language" or properly perform the Islamic rituals. He had been partially detached from his racial identity, and his religious authenticity was in doubt. To be sure, the masses who surrounded him were friendly; but for the reasons mentioned, he could not partake fully of their friendship. Thus he was separated from both himself and the others who were all too unlike himself, and this separation resulted in alternating waves of anxious activity and weary depression. Finally, after about sixteen hours of "feeling blue and alone," "out of the darkness came a sudden light": he remembered seeing a telephone at a table in the airport, and he had in his possession the number of a local notable named Omar Azzam. He easily persuaded an English-speaking official to put through a call for him, and in almost no time he was at the Azzam family home, being greeted as if he were a "long-lost child."[21]

After the hours he had just spent feeling like a helpless, abandoned infant, it is hardly surprising that Malcolm was touched by the Azzams' warm welcome and their subsequent hospitality. He needed, at least temporarily, to feel loved and cared for, to experience the healing warmth and spiritual purification of Muslim family life. The Azzams gratified that need. There the matter might have ended—except that the Azzams were white. Malcolm observes:

> Nothing in either of my two careers as a black man in
> America had served to give me any idealistic tendencies. My
> instincts automatically examined the reasons, the motives,
> of anyone who did anything they didn't have to do for me.
> Always in my life, if it was any white person, I could see a
> selfish motive.[22]

Not this time: Malcolm could find no self-interested motive in the Azzams' action, and he was therefore forced to conclude that they were simply motivated by the Muslim spirit of brotherly love. Consequently:

> That morning was when I first began to reappraise the
> "white man." It was when I first began to perceive that
> "white man," as commonly used, means complexion only
> secondarily; it described attitudes and actions. In America,
> "white man" meant specific attitudes and actions toward
> the black man. . . . But in the Muslim world, I had seen that
> men with white complexions were more genuinely broth-
> erly than anyone else had ever been.[23]

The white devil was dying. Malcolm was being reborn into a world inhabited only by human beings.

Potentially Malcolm now had a religious identity and a ministerial vocation freed from racial particularity. That potential could not be actualized, however, unless he were permitted to enter the Holy City and complete his Hajj. He had therefore to appear for judgment before the Hajj court. An immediate appearance was arranged by the Azzams, and the next morning he was in a courtroom:

> [The judge] was a kind, impressive man. He asked me some
> questions, having to do with my sincerity. I answered him

how to seek for and take possession of the political kingdom.
sequently, when he returned to the United States, he defined
position in this way:

> Because of the spiritual rebirth which I was blessed to
> undergo as a result of my pilgrimage to Mecca, I no longer
> subscribe to sweeping indictments of one race. . . . I am not
> a racist and do not subscribe to any of the tenets of racism.
> In all honesty and sincerity it can be stated that I wish
> nothing but freedom, justice and equality—life, liberty and
> the pursuit of happiness—for all people. My first concern is
> with the group of people to which I belong, the Afro-
> Americans, for we, more than any other people, are de-
> prived of these inalienable rights.[35]

Islam was a universal truth which transcended without transforming the existing situation. It was therefore no longer vital to the
struggle for racial liberation. It was not opposed to the struggle: it
was, after all, an important part of the *cultural* heritage of Afro-
Americans, and it could still serve as a source of spiritual identification. But it no longer provided a definition of the enemy. Moreover, as Malcolm had often emphasized when black Christians
attacked the Nation of Islam, the public airing or accentuation of religious differences among black people only served the interests of
the white ruling class. Muslim Mosque, which defined Malcolm's
role in religious terms, was not an adequate vehicle for his political
interests. Thus, when he was asked upon his return to this country
if he would now call himself "El-Hajj Malik El-Shabazz," * he responded: "I'll continue to use Malcolm X as long as the situation
that produced it exists. Going to Mecca was the solution to my personal problem; but it doesn's solve the problem for my people."[36]

Malcolm's decision to separate his religion from his politics does
not in itself tell us why he reformulated his political position. To
understand the change, we must consider the impact his two visits
to sub-Saharan Africa had upon him.

After he left Mecca, Malcolm visited several other Middle Eastern
and African nations, with most of his time south of the Sahara spent

---

* Malik El-Shabazz had been Malcolm's official name within the Nation. It signified
his descent from the tribe of Shabazz, but it did not define him *against* his white
oppressor. "El-Hajj" signifies that he had completed the pilgrimage to Mecca. Hence
if he had intended to be primarily a religious leader, this is the name he would have
used.

as truly as I could. He not only recognized me as a true
Muslim, but he gave me two books, one in English, the
other in Arabic. He recorded my name in the Holy Register
of true Muslims, and we were ready to part. He told me, "I
hope you will become a great preacher of Islam in America."
I said that I shared that hope, and I would try to fulfill it.[24]

Twice before, Malcolm had stood before the judicial bench awaiting
judgment; both times, he had been condemned. Seeing himself in
his judges' eyes, he had recognized himself as a criminal. Now he
had been recognized not only as a Muslim but as a Muslim minister.
His sincerity had proved to be adequate "credentials."

Later that day Malcolm entered Mecca and performed the ritual
actions of Islamic submission in the Great Mosque that housed the
Ka'ba. There in the presence of the huge black stone he prayed, sending forth his love to Allah. There he experienced a profound "numb-
ness" as his sensuous energies, reflected against the adamantine
surface, returned to him as the overpowering spiritual presence of
his god. Then came the other rituals performed at Mecca: the journey to Mina and Mount Ararat; the night at Muzdalifah; and the final
sacrificial ceremony, during which Malcolm cast the traditional
seven stones at the devil. The *Ihram* phase of his pilgrimage had
been completed.

Looking back upon his experience, Malcolm said: "In my thirty-
nine years on this earth, the Holy City of Mecca had been the first
time I had ever stood before the Creator of All and felt like a complete human being."[25] This confession is as moving as it is honest;
but it is clear that the ritual submission to Allah was an hypnotic
experience and, as such, an act of emotional alienation. The *Ihram*
is, however, the ultimate form of Islamic group-emotion, in which
the particularity of the group experience is finally overcome. The
group's leader here is not a man but Allah himself, the group's membership is not a class, a race, or a nation but (at least potentially) all
of humankind. Consequently, the individual is immediately identified with the abstract universal of the God-idea and the potentially
concrete universal of a unified humanity. Stating the former point
psychodynamically, the emotional energy the pilgrim projects into
the Ka'ba returns to him as the intrasubjective presence of the Infinite and the Good, hence as a feeling of perfect moral unification.
In genetic terms, the emotionally charged and authoritative parental
images that typically have haunted, falsified, and negated his conscious activity are here transformed into a unifying moral presence.

Consciousness becomes conscience, conscience becomes conscious-ness. All traces of moral alienation disappear: "True Islam teaches
. . . that it takes *all* of the religious, political, economic, psychologi-cal, and racial ingredients or characteristics, to make the Human Family and the Human Society complete."[26] It then becomes the pilgrim's obligation to bring Islam to his brothers and sisters and thereby help them to transform the family of a class-divided society into the human family of a human society.

Furthermore, the universal experience of the *Ihram* had for Mal-colm a particular implication. Again in his words:

> In Mecca, too, I had played back for myself the twelve
> years I had spent with Elijah Muhammad as if it were a
> motion picture. I guess it would be impossible for anyone
> ever to realize how complete was my belief in Elijah
> Muhammad. . . . [But] there on a Holy World hilltop, I real-
> ized how very dangerous it is for people to hold any human
> being in such esteem, especially to consider anyone some
> sort of "divinely guided" and "protected" person.[27]

We remember that Malcolm had replayed his years in the Nation at the time of the split, detaching himself from the experience and con-signing it to the storage chambers of memory. Now we realize that he did not completely separate himself from Muhammad until, through ritual authentication and humanly unmediated charismatic experience, his religious identity was freed from its dependence upon his relationship to the Prophet. His filial adoration of his for-mer leader now became his unqualified devotion to the One God. He could finally see that Muhammad was merely a man among men; his own past was a bad dream from which he had at last awakened. As he said in an interview some time later, "I feel like a man who has been asleep somewhat and under someone else's control. I feel what I'm thinking and saying now is for myself. Before, it was for and by the guidance of Elijah Muhammad. Now I think with my own mind, sir."[28] The Black God had died in mortal combat with the White Devil, Muhammad's spell had been broken, and Malcolm was at last a spiritually free individual.

Finally, with the distortive group-emotional structure of his rela-tionship to the Prophet at last annihilated, the moments of Mal-colm's individual past returned to his consciousness with unex-pected clarity. During the night at Muzdalifa, he lay awake on a hillside beneath the open sky, "surrounded by snoring brother pil-grims." Then:

> my mind took me back to personal memories I would have
> thought were gone forever . . . as far back, even, as when I
> was just a little boy, eight or nine years old. . . . I remem-
> bered there in the Holy World how I used to lie on the top of
> ["an old, grassy" knoll] we called Hector's Hill, and look up
> at the sky, at the clouds moving over me, and daydream.[29]

We remember the daydreaming in his mother's garden, and con-sequently we find in his recollection the wishfully fulfilled ambi-tions of the seventh son. He continues:

> And then, in a funny contrast of recollections, I remem-
> bered how years later, when I was in prison, I used to lie on
> my cell bunk—this would be especially when I was in
> solitary . . . and I would picture myself talking to large
> crowds.[30]

The unlimited phantasies of a restless child, the pre-visions of the imprisoned hustler . . . different and yet the same, each of them the realization of apparently unrealizable ambitions. But these mo-ments of the past recaptured have a deeper meaning: in their unity they are Malcolm in his religious solitude, alone among his brothers and sisters on a Holy World hilltop, at peace with himself, his fellow men, and his god—a complete human being.

While he was still in Mecca, Malcolm wrote to his family and fol-lowers, sharing with them his "new insight into the true religion of Islam, and [his] better understanding of America's entire racial di-lemma."[31] He argued that "America needs to understand Islam, be-cause this is the one religion that erases from its society the race problem":[32] "True Islam removes racism, because people of all col-ors and races who accept its religious principles and bow down to the one God, Allah, also automatically accept each other as brothers and sisters, regardless of differences in complexion."[33] Islam re-moves the "white" from the minds of white-skinned people: "If white Americans would accept the Oneness of God, then perhaps, too, they could accept *in reality* the Oneness of Man—and cease to measure, and hinder, and harm others in terms of their 'differences' in color."[34]

Malcolm had been awakened to the true faith, but he would still have been dreaming if he really thought that he could awaken many Americans, black or white, from their white Christian slumbers. His practical task was not, therefore, to preach Islam to the (es-pecially white) non-believer but, rather, to teach oppressed people in Nigeria and Ghana. In Nigeria his principal contacts were with university students.† Speaking to the student body of Ibadan University, he argued for the necessity of bringing the United States before the international bar of justice at the U.N., and he emphasized the need for American black people to become pan-Africanists. In other words, his argument reflected the same objective conditions that had led both Garvey and DuBois to seek international solutions to an apparently intranational problem. But the stay in Nigeria also had an important subjective meaning. The Nigerian Muslim Students' Society made him a member and gave him a Yoruba name, Omowale, meaning " 'the son who has come home.' "[37] The seventh son had finally realized the ambition of the homeless Garveyite father. No wonder that Malcolm says: "I meant it when I told them [the students] I had never received a more treasured honor."[38] Still, his personal homecoming was not a solution to his political problem—although the solution was implied in the statement of a Nigerian official who argued that "the world's course will change the day the African-heritage peoples come together as brothers."

Malcolm's emergent pan-Africanism was further developed during his visit to Ghana. He viewed Ghana, which was then under Nkrumah's leadership, as both a living expression of pan-Africanism and as a realization of the Garveyite vision:

> Indeed, it was Marcus Garvey's philosophy that inspired
> the Nkrumah fight for the independence of Ghana from the
> colonialism that was imposed on it by England. It is also
> the same Black Nationalism that has been spreading
> throughout Africa and that had brought the emergence of
> the present independent African states. Garvey never failed.
> Garvey planted the seed which has popped up in Africa—
> everywhere you look![39]

Nowhere did that seed seem more firmly planted than in Ghana. Not surprisingly, therefore, Malcolm was struck by the militant attitude of the people he met. Because he was widely and correctly regarded as the most militant leader of Black America, he was given the opportunity to meet Nkrumah himself and a variety of Ghanaian dignitaries, as well as students, Afro-American exiles, and the ambassadors to Ghana from China, Mali, British Guiana, and Algeria. From these meetings he came away with a strong impression

†His host in Nigeria was Essien-Udom, whom he had come to know when the Nigerian scholar was in the United States preparing his definitive study of the Nation of Islam.

of "Africa seething with awareness of itself, and of Africa's wealth, and of her power, and of her destined role in the world."[40] That on the one hand. On the other, he saw all too many signs of America's neocolonial penetration of the continent. He therefore decided "that as long as I was in Africa, every time I opened my mouth, I was going to make things hot for that white man, grinning through his teeth wanting to exploit Africa again—it had been her human wealth the last time, now he wanted Africa's mineral wealth."[41]

In the African context, however, Malcolm's polemical role was partially redefined. He was very much impressed by the Algerian ambassador to Ghana, who seemed to be "dedicated totally to militancy, and to world revolution, as the way to solve the problems of the world's oppressed masses."[42] But the Algerian did not view the revolutionary process in racial terms:

> When I told him that my political, social and economic philosophy was black nationalism, he asked me very frankly, well, where did that leave him? Because he was white. He was an African, but he was an Algerian, and to all appearances, he was a white man. And he said if I define my objective as the victory of black nationalism, where does that leave him? . . . So he showed me where I was alienating people who were true revolutionaries dedicated to overthrowing the system of exploitation that exists on this earth by any means necessary.
>
> So, I had to do a lot of thinking and reappraising of my definition of black nationalism.[43]

Malcolm was coming to accept the idea that the struggle for the liberation of black people could not be racially defined, could not be defined so as to exclude true revolutionaries. A more inclusive definition emerged when, in talking to the Ghanaian press, he referred to the plight of the American "Negro." He was immediately corrected by one of those in attendance: " 'The word is not favored here, Mr. Malcolm X. The term Afro-American has greater meaning, and dignity.' "[44] Malcolm had been familiar with the idea of Afro-American identity before he came to Africa, but the name only became self-definitional for him at this time. Once he became conscious of himself as an Afro-American, he took action with characteristic energy: in conjunction with the Afro-Americans in Ghana, he formed the first chapter of the OAAU.

Malcolm returned to the United States on May 21. One month

as truly as I could. He not only recognized me as a true
Muslim, but he gave me two books, one in English, the
other in Arabic. He recorded my name in the Holy Register
of true Muslims, and we were ready to part. He told me, "I
hope you will become a great preacher of Islam in America."
I said that I shared that hope, and I would try to fulfill it.[24]

Twice before, Malcolm had stood before the judicial bench awaiting
judgment; both times, he had been condemned. Seeing himself in
his judges' eyes, he had recognized himself as a criminal. Now he
had been recognized not only as a Muslim but as a Muslim minister.
His sincerity had proved to be adequate "credentials."

Later that day Malcolm entered Mecca and performed the ritual
actions of Islamic submission in the Great Mosque that housed the
Ka'ba. There in the presence of the huge black stone he prayed, sending forth his love to Allah. There he experienced a profound "numb-
ness" as his sensuous energies, reflected against the adamantine
surface, returned to him as the overpowering spiritual presence of
his god. Then came the other rituals performed at Mecca: the journey to Mina and Mount Ararat; the night at Muzdalifah; and the final
sacrificial ceremony, during which Malcolm cast the traditional
seven stones at the devil. The *Ihram* phase of his pilgrimage had
been completed.

Looking back upon his experience, Malcolm said: "In my thirty-
nine years on this earth, the Holy City of Mecca had been the first
time I had ever stood before the Creator of All and felt like a complete human being."[25] This confession is as moving as it is honest;
but it is clear that the ritual submission to Allah was an hypnotic
experience and, as such, an act of emotional alienation. The *Ihram*
is, however, the ultimate form of Islamic group-emotion, in which
the particularity of the group experience is finally overcome. The
group's leader here is not a man but Allah himself, the group's membership is not a class, a race, or a nation but (at least potentially) all
of humankind. Consequently, the individual is immediately identified with the abstract universal of the God-idea and the potentially
concrete universal of a unified humanity. Stating the former point
psychodynamically, the emotional energy the pilgrim projects into
the Ka'ba returns to him as the intrasubjective presence of the Infinite and the Good, hence as a feeling of perfect moral unification.
In genetic terms, the emotionally charged and authoritative parental
images that typically have haunted, falsified, and negated his conscious activity are here transformed into a unifying moral presence.

Consciousness becomes conscience, conscience becomes consciousness. All traces of moral alienation disappear: "True Islam teaches
. . . that it takes *all* of the religious, political, economic, psychological, and racial ingredients or characteristics, to make the Human
Family and the Human Society complete."[26] It then becomes the
pilgrim's obligation to bring Islam to his brothers and sisters and
thereby help them to transform the family of a class-divided society
into the human family of a human society.

Furthermore, the universal experience of the *Ihram* had for Malcolm a particular implication. Again in his words:

> In Mecca, too, I had played back for myself the twelve
> years I had spent with Elijah Muhammad as if it were a
> motion picture. I guess it would be impossible for anyone
> ever to realize how complete was my belief in Elijah
> Muhammad. . . . [But] there on a Holy World hilltop, I real-
> ized how very dangerous it is for people to hold any human
> being in such esteem, especially to consider anyone some
> sort of "divinely guided" and "protected" person.[27]

We remember that Malcolm had replayed his years in the Nation at
the time of the split, detaching himself from the experience and con-
signing it to the storage chambers of memory. Now we realize that
he did not completely separate himself from Muhammad until,
through ritual authentication and humanly unmediated charismatic
experience, his religious identity was freed from its dependence
upon his relationship to the Prophet. His filial adoration of his former leader now became his unqualified devotion to the One God. He
could finally see that Muhammad was merely a man among men;
his own past was a bad dream from which he had at last awakened.
As he said in an interview some time later, "I feel like a man who
has been asleep somewhat and under someone else's control. I feel
what I'm thinking and saying now is for myself. Before, it was for
and by the guidance of Elijah Muhammad. Now I think with my
own mind, sir."[28] The Black God had died in mortal combat with
the White Devil, Muhammad's spell had been broken, and Malcolm
was at last a spiritually free individual.

Finally, with the distortive group-emotional structure of his relationship to the Prophet at last annihilated, the moments of Malcolm's individual past returned to his consciousness with unex-
pected clarity. During the night at Muzdalifa, he lay awake on a
hillside beneath the open sky, "surrounded by snoring brother pilgrims." Then:

> my mind took me back to personal memories I would have
> thought were gone forever . . . as far back, even, as when I
> was just a little boy, eight or nine years old. . . . I remem-
> bered there in the Holy World how I used to lie on the top of
> ["an old, grassy" knoll] we called Hector's Hill, and look up
> at the sky, at the clouds moving over me, and daydream.[29]

We remember the daydreaming in his mother's garden, and consequently we find in his recollection the wishfully fulfilled ambitions of the seventh son. He continues:

> And then, in a funny contrast of recollections, I remem-
> bered how years later, when I was in prison, I used to lie on
> my cell bunk—this would be especially when I was in
> solitary . . . and I would picture myself talking to large
> crowds.[30]

The unlimited phantasies of a restless child, the pre-visions of the
imprisoned hustler . . . different and yet the same, each of them the
realization of apparently unrealizable ambitions. But these moments of the past recaptured have a deeper meaning: in their unity
they are Malcolm in his religious solitude, alone among his brothers
and sisters on a Holy World hilltop, at peace with himself, his fellow
men, and his god—a complete human being.

While he was still in Mecca, Malcolm wrote to his family and followers, sharing with them his "new insight into the true religion of
Islam, and [his] better understanding of America's entire racial dilemma."[31] He argued that "America needs to understand Islam, because this is the one religion that erases from its society the race
problem":[32] "True Islam removes racism, because people of all col-
ors and races who accept its religious principles and bow down to
the one God, Allah, also automatically accept each other as brothers
and sisters, regardless of differences in complexion."[33] Islam re-
moves the "white" from the minds of white-skinned people: "If
white Americans would accept the Oneness of God, then perhaps,
too, they could accept in reality the Oneness of Man—and cease to
measure, and hinder, and harm others in terms of their 'differences'
in color."[34]

Malcolm had been awakened to the true faith, but he would still
have been dreaming if he really thought that he could awaken many
Americans, black or white, from their white Christian slumbers.
His practical task was not, therefore, to preach Islam to the (especially white) non-believer but, rather, to teach oppressed people

how to seek for and take possession of the political kingdom. Consequently, when he returned to the United States, he defined his position in this way:

> Because of the spiritual rebirth which I was blessed to
> undergo as a result of my pilgrimage to Mecca, I no longer
> subscribe to sweeping indictments of one race. . . . I am not
> a racist and do not subscribe to any of the tenets of racism.
> In all honesty and sincerity it can be stated that I wish
> nothing but freedom, justice and equality—life, liberty and
> the pursuit of happiness—for all people. My first concern is
> with the group of people to which I belong, the Afro-
> Americans, for we, more than any other people, are de-
> prived of these inalienable rights.[35]

Islam was a universal truth which transcended without transforming the existing situation. It was therefore no longer vital to the struggle for racial liberation. It was not opposed to the struggle: it was, after all, an important part of the *cultural* heritage of Afro-Americans, and it could still serve as a source of spiritual identification. But it no longer provided a definition of the enemy. Moreover, as Malcolm had often emphasized when black Christians attacked the Nation of Islam, the public airing or accentuation of religious differences among black people only served the interests of the white ruling class. Muslim Mosque, which defined Malcolm's role in religious terms, was not an adequate vehicle for his political interests. Thus, when he was asked upon his return to this country if he would now call himself "El-Hajj Malik El-Shabazz,"* he responded: "I'll continue to use Malcolm X as long as the situation that produced it exists. Going to Mecca was the solution to my personal problem; but it doesn't solve the problem for my people."[36]

Malcolm's decision to separate his religion from his politics does not in itself tell us why he reformulated his political position. To understand the change, we must consider the impact his two visits to sub-Saharan Africa had upon him.

After he left Mecca, Malcolm visited several other Middle Eastern and African nations, with most of his time south of the Sahara spent

---

* Malik El-Shabazz had been Malcolm's official name within the Nation. It signified his descent from the tribe of Shabazz, but it did not define him *against* his white oppressor. "El-Hajj" signifies that he had completed the pilgrimage to Mecca. Hence if he had intended to be primarily a religious leader, this is the name he would have used.

in Nigeria and Ghana. In Nigeria his principal contacts were with university students.† Speaking to the student body of Ibadan University, he argued for the necessity of bringing the United States before the international bar of justice at the U.N., and he emphasized the need for American black people to become pan-Africanists. In other words, his argument reflected the same objective conditions that had led both Garvey and DuBois to seek international solutions to an apparently intranational problem. But the stay in Nigeria also had an important subjective meaning. The Nigerian Muslim Students' Society made him a member and gave him a Yoruba name, Omowale, meaning "'the son who has come home.'"[37] The seventh son had finally realized the ambition of the homeless Garveyite father. No wonder that Malcolm says: "I meant it when I told them [the students] I had never received a more treasured honor."[38] Still, his personal homecoming was not a solution to his political problem—although the solution was implied in the statement of a Nigerian official who argued that "the world's course will change the day the African-heritage peoples come together as brothers."

Malcolm's emergent pan-Africanism was further developed during his visit to Ghana. He viewed Ghana, which was then under Nkrumah's leadership, as both a living expression of pan-Africanism and as a realization of the Garveyite vision:

> Indeed, it was Marcus Garvey's philosophy that inspired
> the Nkrumah fight for the independence of Ghana from the
> colonialism that was imposed on it by England. It is also
> the same Black Nationalism that has been spreading
> throughout Africa and that had brought the emergence of
> the present independent African states. Garvey never failed.
> Garvey planted the seed which has popped up in Africa—
> everywhere you look![39]

Nowhere did that seed seem more firmly planted than in Ghana. Not surprisingly, therefore, Malcolm was struck by the militant attitude of the people he met. Because he was widely and correctly regarded as the most militant leader of Black America, he was given the opportunity to meet Nkrumah himself and a variety of Ghanaian dignitaries, as well as students, Afro-American exiles, and the ambassadors to Ghana from China, Mali, British Guiana, and Algeria. From these meetings he came away with a strong impression

†His host in Nigeria was Essien-Udom, whom he had come to know when the Nigerian scholar was in the United States preparing his definitive study of the Nation of Islam.

of "Africa seething with awareness of itself, and of Africa's wealth, and of her power, and of her destined role in the world."[40] That on the one hand. On the other, he saw all too many signs of America's neocolonial penetration of the continent. He therefore decided "that as long as I was in Africa, every time I opened my mouth, I was going to make things hot for that white man, grinning through his teeth wanting to exploit Africa again—it had been her human wealth the last time, now he wanted Africa's mineral wealth."[41]

In the African context, however, Malcolm's polemical role was partially redefined. He was very much impressed by the Algerian ambassador to Ghana, who seemed to be "dedicated totally to militancy, and to world revolution, as the way to solve the problems of the world's oppressed masses."[42] But the Algerian did not view the revolutionary process in racial terms:

> When I told him that my political, social and economic philosophy was black nationalism, he asked me very frankly, well, where did that leave him? Because he was white. He was an African, but he was an Algerian, and to all appearances, he was a white man. And he said if I define my objective as the victory of black nationalism, where does that leave him? . . . So he showed me where I was alienating people who were true revolutionaries dedicated to overthrowing the system of exploitation that exists on this earth by any means necessary.
>
> So, I had to do a lot of thinking and reappraising of my definition of black nationalism.[43]

Malcolm was coming to accept the idea that the struggle for the liberation of black people could not be racially defined, could not be defined so as to exclude true revolutionaries. A more inclusive definition emerged when, in talking to the Ghanaian press, he referred to the plight of the American "Negro." He was immediately corrected by one of those in attendance: " 'The word is not favored here, Mr. Malcolm X. The term Afro-American has greater meaning, and dignity.' "[44] Malcolm had been familiar with the idea of Afro-American identity before he came to Africa, but the name only became self-definitional for him at this time. Once he became conscious of himself as an Afro-American, he took action with characteristic energy: in conjunction with the Afro-Americans in Ghana, he formed the first chapter of the OAAU.

Malcolm returned to the United States on May 21. One month

later, on June 28, he led the first OAAU rally in Harlem. He began by observing that earlier in the year he had spoken of creating a "black nationalist party or a black nationalist army." Meanwhile he had gone to Africa, hoping to discover how Africans had been able to free themselves from "colonization, oppression, exploitation, degradation, humiliation, discrimination, and every other kind of -ation."[45] He had learned that in addition to their separate national struggles, Africans had formed a "coalition," the OAU, through which they were able to work "in conjunction with each other to fight a common enemy." In like fashion, he announced,

> We have formed an organization known as the Organiza-
> tion of Afro-American Unity which has the same aim and
> objective—to fight whoever gets in our way, to bring about
> the complete independence of people of African descent
> here in the Western Hemisphere, and first here in the
> United States, and bring about the freedom of these people
> by any means necessary.[46]

Thus we return to the historical moment with which our inquiry began.

The OAAU

In less than a year Malcolm had shifted from black nationalism to Afro-American internationalism. The first of these positions was racial-religious in nature; the second was political-cultural. It could be argued that Malcolm was changing from racial militant to political radical and that by so doing he was abandoning the perspective which gave him his historical significance; but such a judgment would be valid only if Malcolm ceased being a racial militant as he became a political radical. We shall now see, however, that Malcolm's radicalism was really a politically self-conscious racial militancy. More specifically, we will find that the idea of Afro-American unity was a rational theoretical reflection of the existing situation; that the intended practice of the OAAU was the appropriate practical mediation of that theoretical position; and that the unity of theory and practice both derived from and resulted in an ethic of revolutionary responsibility signified by the expression "freedom by any means necessary."

Like the Nation of Islam or Muslim Mosque, Inc., the OAAU was based upon the idea that all black people had a common enemy; that the critical task in the existing situation was to develop a program which would serve the interests and meet the emotional needs of the black masses; and that such a program must be aimed at transforming ghettoized black America into a virtual nation—into a black national party *and* army. The Afro-American concept added to these premises expanded grounds for black cultural identity and an enlarged field of political activity.

Ever since his conversion to Islam, Malcolm had stressed the importance for black Americans of recognizing their African origins and the role the white man had played in physically and spiritually removing them from Africa. The nominal sign of the white man's criminality was the American Negro identity. What, Malcolm asked, does it mean to be a "Negro"?

> Negro doesn't tell you anything. I mean nothing, absolutely nothing. What do you identify it with?—tell me—nothing. What do you attach it to, what do you attach to it? Nothing. It's completely in the middle of nowhere. And when you call yourself that, that's where you are—right in the middle of nowhere. It doesn't give you a language, because there is no such thing as a Negro language. It doesn't give you a culture,—there is no such thing as a Negro culture, it doesn't exist. The land doesn't exist, the culture doesn't exist, the language doesn't exist and the man doesn't exist. They take you out of existence by calling you a Negro. And you can walk around in front of them all day long and they act like they don't even see you. Because you made yourself non-existent.[47]

When Afro-Americans allowed themselves to be called, and called themselves, Negroes, they were acknowledging themselves to be imitation white men, creatures whose very existence depended upon the white man's recognition. Or at least their civilized existence: hidden beneath the Negro self-image was the specter of the jungle savage. "Europeans created and popularized the image of Africa as a jungle, a wild place where people were cannibals." This image was so "hateful to Afro-Americans that they refused to identify with Africa."[48] But in hating Africa, they were in fact hating themselves. For years past Afro-Americans had been condemned to self-hatred by this falsified image of Africa:

> We hated the color of our skin, hated the blood of Africa
> that was in our veins. And in hating our features and our
> skin and our blood, why, we had to end up hating our-
> selves. . . . Our color became to us a chain.[49]

Conversely, "to the same degree that your understanding of and
attitude toward Africa becomes positive, you'll find that your understanding of and attitude toward yourself will also become positive."[50] Reconnection to African culture would provide the foundation for an affirmative self-conception, and this self-conception
would in turn provide the inner strength necessary for the struggle
against the white oppressor. Pride would replace shame, and a sense
of power would replace the feelings of impotence with which black
people had been afflicted. Their knowledge of their African past
would provide the inner strength and determination they needed in
order to work for their Afro-American future.

Our own analysis supports Malcolm's argument. We have seen
how a "whitened-out" conscience can split the black self, falsify
black consciousness, compel black people to play their ordained
roles in the stereotypical dumb-show, or trap them in the dream-
world of paranoid nihilism. But once self-identification replaces
identification with the oppressor, aggressive energies can be used
self-productively rather than self-destructively, sexual energies can
be utilized for the expansion of racial identity rather than alienated
in epidermally fetishized relationships, and work energies can be
used in one's own individual and collective interests. The Black Militant replaces the stereotyped Good Negro and Bad Nigger; and the
Black Militant, through the process of testing the realities of the existing situation, becomes self-consciously Afro-American. An Afro-
American identity is, therefore, a psychologically rational response
to the existing situation—a rational response, but not an automatic
one: in the years ahead black people would struggle in varying ways
and with varying degrees of success against the hypnotic power of
the American dream. Only a few would achieve Malcolm's degree of
psychological liberation, but many more would experience a birth,
rebirth, or qualitative intensification of black pride, "a reintegration
of self-concept . . . which entails the assumption of a positive sense
of self-esteem and a rejection of adaptive inferiority."[51]

Although the combination of emergent Black Pride, Black Militancy, and Afro-American identity constituted a powerful motive-
force for political action, any judgment concerning the situational
rationality of these psychological factors ultimately depends upon

the possibilities for Afro-American and African unity. In Malcolm's view, political unity followed from the existence of the common enemy. But do all Africans and Afro-Americans have a common enemy?

When the enemy is defined as white racism—the vicious circle of racist oppression—then virtually all dark-skinned peoples do have a common enemy. Decolonization is simultaneously a struggle for racial liberation, from which only those individuals benefitting directly from the continued existence of the black ghettoes or colonial regimes are excluded. This was the reality of the immediate situation. Moreover, Malcolm was not being unrealistic when he asserted that the international "bases of power" were changing, and that the "rise of the dark world [was] producing the fall of the white world."[52] Many of the nations of Africa, the Middle East, and Asia were winning their freedom from colonial domination and were attempting to avoid neocolonial domination. Thus after the Bandung Conference there emerged a policy of nonalignment which formed nations from Indonesia to Ghana into a third force in world politics, into the Third World. Although economically underdeveloped and politically divided, the Third World was nonetheless a new and potentially powerful force in international affairs. Of greater short-run concern to the former colonial or neocolonializing powers, however, was the possibility that Third World countries would become communist or would align themselves with the Soviet Union or China. On one count or the other, many policymakers believed they were threatened with the loss of the vital raw materials, exploitable labor power, outlets for capital investment, and strategic military positions of the dark world. It was also widely believed that the loss of any one unaligned nation to direct communist control would create a "domino" effect with respect to other such nations, so that in time the existing structure of international power would be undermined.

The most dramatic attempt upon the part of the United States government to preserve its international position was of course the war in Vietnam, a war which Malcolm early predicted would end in American defeat. At the same time, local police authorities, White Citizens Councils, and a revivified Ku Klux Klan maintained a steady resistance to integration—and a bloody one, as in the murder of three civil rights workers during the Freedom Summer voter registration campaign in Mississippi, or in the unchecked police brutality in every ghetto in the country. Consequently there arose a picture of white America attempting to halt the rise of the dark world both internationally and intranationally. Intranationally, these sup-

pressive policies had a further unintended consequence: the violence being used against the black activists radically decreased their
own willingness to remain nonviolent. Thus in the spring of 1964,
John Lewis of SNCC was advocating the use of "aggressive nonviolent action," meaning nonviolent protest not premised upon loving one's enemy, oriented, rather, toward a "social revolution" that
would "overthrow" the country's "racist political and economic
structure."[53] He was also willing to contemplate the use of force if
nonviolent means proved inadequate to bring about that revolution.
And that same spring Robert F. Williams, an NAACP branch president in Monroe, North Carolina, was arguing for "effective self-
defense" of black communities against "racist terrorists" and "forces
of the state."[54] *

In sum, Malcolm had good reason to believe that there was a common enemy, that the enemy was in retreat, and that Africans and
Afro-Americans had a common interest in its defeat. It is for this
reason that we can speak meaningfully of a black revolution, a
worldwide process of decolonization, or of Afro-American unity.
Afro-American identity is in fact a psychological reflection of this
political-economic reality; hence it is rational in the same sense and
to the same degree. But once the struggle is defined in political-economic terms, a more complicated picture comes into view. Already
in 1961 Fanon was seeking to warn the emerging African nations
about the "pitfalls of national consciousness." He argued that the
mere fact of national independence did not insure the advent of national liberation. It was possible that the bourgeois classes of the
new nations would put their interests ahead of national ones:

> Seen through its eyes, [the national bourgeoisie's] mis-
> sion has nothing to do with transforming the nation; it
> consists, quite prosaically, of being the transmission line
> between the nation and a capitalism, rampant though
> camouflaged, which today puts on the masque of neo-
> colonialism.[55] *

* As is well known, Williams was driven into exile when he began advocating the use
of guerrilla tactics. Malcolm, who was arguing a similar line, was therefore careful to
state his position in objective or hypothetical (rather than advocatory) terms. He
thereby hoped to encourage the growth of revolutionary consciousness without being
forced into political isolation.
* With the advantage of hindsight we may see that the African situation contained
the possibilities for a less dependent line of capitalist development than the analysts
of neocolonialism anticipated—a line of development more nearly like the one originally postulated by Marx in his analysis of colonial relations. But for our purposes

Which is to say, Malcolm's possibilities for support were inversely proportional to the neocolonial involvement of the African nations. Considering the relatively fluid situation and the intensity of racial consciousness characteristic of the early 1960s, it was not unrealistic for Malcolm to expect some support for his position from some African nations; but he discovered during his second African sojourn that there were to be no African solutions to Afro-American problems.

Malcolm assigned a high priority to gaining both OAU recognition of the OAAU and OAU support for his plan of bringing the Afro-American struggle into the U.N. If he were successful, he could then hope to establish the OAAU as the vanguard of the black revolution. Accordingly, about two weeks after the OAAU founding rally Malcolm traveled to Cairo, where an OAU summit meeting was taking place. He succeeded in gaining admission to the meetings as an observer; he was housed with the leaders of the African liberation movements, which gave de facto recognition to his leadership of oppressed Afro-Americans; and he was permitted to submit a memorandum to the assembled delegates. As Essien-Udom emphasizes, "This was quite a feat! It must be remembered that this was a heads of state summit meeting. It was an extraordinary concession to Malcolm and the Afro-American community he represented since he was neither a head of an existing state nor a leader of a state in exile."[56] Moreover, the OAU did pass a resolution on racism. In Essien-Udom's words:

> The wording of the resolution, as might be expected from
> an international body with diverse and often conflicting
> interests, was mild, but its intent was clear. The Heads of
> State Summit noted "with satisfaction the recent enactment
> of the Civil Rights Act designed to secure for American
> Negroes their basic human rights." The OAU was "deeply
> disturbed, however, by continuing manifestations of racial
> bigotry and racial oppression against Negro citizens of the
> United States of America." The resolution reaffirmed the
> OAU's "belief that the existence of discriminatory practice
> is a matter of deep concern to the member states of the
> OAU," and urged "the government authorities in the United
> States of America to intensify their efforts to insure the

---

there is no need to enter into the contemporary debates on the issues of underdevelopment, dependency relations, etc.

total elimination of all forms of discrimination based on race, color or ethnic origin."[57]

Although the resolution did not in itself advocate bringing the United States before the World Court, it did provide grounds for such an action at a future date. Some of the delegates at the meeting even "promised officially to assist the OAAU in its plan and to give their support during the following session of the United Nations."[58] Malcolm felt justified in writing to his followers in America that as a result of his work in Cairo "our problem has been *internationalized.*"[59]

Malcolm had helped to place the Afro-American problem on the international agenda. But he did not attain in Cairo the widespread and militant support for which he had really been hoping. Consequently, he decided to spend some time

> visiting and speaking in person to various African leaders . . . giving them a firsthand knowledge and understanding of our problems, so that all of them will see . . . the necessity of bringing our problem before the United Nations this year, and why we must have their support.[60]

Although he remained in Africa until late November, he was unable to gain that support. He gained instead an appreciation of the complicated nature of African affairs, and of the limits which these complications imposed upon his own aims.

If neocolonial relationships in Africa constituted one limit upon Malcolm's political activity, the class structure of the Afro-American community constituted the other. At least in the short run, the masses and the middle class had partially divergent interests. The middle class was, of course, largely proletarian. Its income, consumption patterns, and life style were middling, neither rich nor poor; but because its membership was overwhelmingly comprised of wage-laborers, it shared with the masses an ultimately revolutionary interest. It also, obviously, shared with the masses an interest in ending racism. But the middle class had a realizable interest in integration—in gaining the social and political rights commensurate with its economic standing, and in opening up new avenues for advancement within the existing system. The black masses, who filled the ranks of the industrial reserve army and the *lumpen-proletariat*, did not have such an interest in reform. More: a successful reform movement would increase their relative deprivation; separate them from their middle-class allies, who were bound to them only by the existence of the common racist enemy; and, consequently, leave them even more isolated, segregated, and alienated from American society than hitherto. For the black masses, the struggle for racial liberation was necessarily revolutionary.

Malcolm was the leading spokesman for the revolutionary interest of the masses; through the OAAU, he hoped to bring the Negro middle class into his projected mass struggle. But as we shall see later in this chapter, the end result of his activity was to bring the black masses into the middle-class reform movement. He helped to create the revolutionary means needed to realize racial reformist ends. By so doing, however, he also helped to weaken the lines of racial division within the working class and clarify the lines of class division within the black community. In the former regard, the Black Revolution tended both to shatter white racist stereotypes and to ease somewhat the racist restrictions upon black participation in American national life. Through their efforts black people won at least the grudging respect of many white people, and a reluctant recognition of their rights. The veil of racist false-consciousness was thereby partially lifted. In the latter regard, the class divisions within the black community became more important politically in proportion to the success of the racial reform movement, for to the extent that black people have a common enemy, they have a common interest. If the enemy's power weakens, the common interest tends to disintegrate. It then becomes both possible and necessary to carry forward the class struggle within the black community (as in fact Malcolm was doing) and, by so doing, to advance the cause of proletarian revolution.

We may therefore conclude that Malcolm's conception of Afro-American unity was situationally rational both because black people did have a common enemy and because by struggling together against that enemy they were also engaging in and preparing the way for class struggle—which is also to say that the situational rationality of Malcolm's revolutionary project can be seen most clearly in the light of his own consciousness that the "world's oppressed masses" have a common emancipatory interest.

A revolutionary project requires a revolutionary organization. Our next step must be to analyze Malcolm's conception of how the OAAU was to embody and thereby help to realize the situational possibilities for Afro-American unity.

Malcolm wanted the OAAU to be both a coalition of Afro-American organizations and a vanguard party. In the latter regard it was to be as autonomous as possible: by raising funds internally and publishing its own newspaper, it would seek to minimize its reliance on any outside group. It was to have a secretariat or executive committee under Malcolm's personal direction, the members of which would be in charge of the eight policy (cultural, economic, educational, political, publications, social, self-defense, and youth) and four staff (finance, fund-raising, legal, and membership) committees. The parent body would help to generate local chapters, so that ultimately there would be an OAAU branch in every major black community in the country. The local groups would then channel information and ideas to and from the secretariat.[61] Thus the internal operations of the organization would fuse the functional specialization and capacity for coordinated action of the OAU General Secretariat with the powerful leadership principle of the Nation of Islam. The weakness of the OAU, a body entirely dependent upon the cooperation of its sovereign members, would be offset by Malcolm's authority within the relatively self-sufficient core organization. At the same time, an active secretariat would help Malcolm to avoid the concentration of authority in one man that had hampered the Nation's day-to-day operations and contributed to its doctrinal rigidity.[62] The core OAAU was, in other words, to be governed by a kind of democratic centralism.

Within this governmental structure, the local chapters were to perform a double function: first, to defend each community against the unlawful incursions of white America, "to protect its people against mass murders, bombers, lynchers, floggers, brutalizers and exploiters,"[63] and to do so "whatever the price and by any means necessary";[64] and second, to work for the total revitalization and purification of the black communities. OAAU branches were to establish their own schools, "wage all-out war on organized crime . . . and drug addiction,"[65] "launch a cultural revolution to unbrainwash an entire people,"[66] and engage in an "unrelenting struggle" against "economic exploitation." By creating semi-autonomous enclaves within white society, by transforming each ghetto into a unified and militant alternative to either integration or territorial separation, the OAAU branches would make it possible for black people—within limits—to gain "control of their destiny: economic, political and social."[67]

The black nationalist aspect of the OAAU program, modeled upon the Nation of Islam, brought Malcolm into direct competition with his former leader for the support of the black masses. In this confrontation Muhammad had the advantage of the organization that Malcolm had done so much to construct, and of a situationally transcendent, charismatic group-emotional doctrine. Malcolm, by contrast, would have to build his organization from the ground up, by appealing to the mass interest in situational transformation. Unlike the Prophet, he would not be able to present his followers with magical solutions to practical problems. The considerable success of the Black Power movement after Malcolm's death indicates, however, that Malcolm's disadvantages were not insurmountable.

Just because Malcolm was not offering magical solutions to his people's problems, he could not be content with building relatively autonomous institutions within the nation's ghettoes. He was working for the elimination of ghetto conditions altogether, and therefore needed the cooperation of other black organizations. His possibilities for gaining such cooperation rested upon his support among the masses, and upon increasing mass impatience with politics as usual. Early in 1964 Malcolm had predicted that this would be "one of the most explosive years yet in the history of America on the racial front." [68] Because it was an election year, politicians would be "back in the so-called Negro community jiving you and me for some votes." But their "false promises, building up our hopes for a letdown," would only "nourish dissatisfaction" and result in an explosion. [69]

Malcolm's reasoning is consonant with our own. During the late 1950s and early 1960s the black masses were experiencing an intensified relative deprivation. Their consciousness of their condition had been clarified by both the civil rights movement and the Nation of Islam. Their frustration and rage had been intensified by white racist assault and the white man's assurances that things were, or were about to be, improving. A mass explosion was the predictable outcome of these circumstances and, true to Malcolm's prediction, the masses did explode. In July an instance of police murder touched off a massive uprising in Harlem and then in Bedford-Stuyvesant. As the U.S. Riot Commission described the events:

> For several days thereafter . . . despite exhortations of
> Negro community leaders against violence, protest rallies
> became uncontrollable. Police battled mobs in Harlem and
> in the Bedford-Stuyvesant section of Brooklyn. Firemen
> fought fires started by Molotov cocktails. When bricks and
> bottles were thrown, police responded with gunfire. Wide-
> spread looting followed and many persons were injured. [70]

It was a spontaneous and only half-conscious insurrection, and a police "pogrom" (as Malcolm later called it).[71] But it lent credibility to Malcolm's analysis of the existing situation and provided him with counters in the game of coalition politics.

We should observe that Malcolm was skeptical about the possibilities of working cooperatively with the Movement's leadership. They had not supported, and seemed not to comprehend the meaning of, black mass-action. Thus at the OAAU founding rally he stated:

> I don't know if I'm right in saying this, but for a period of time, let's you and me not be too hard on other Afro-American leaders . . . let's give them a little time to straighten up. If they straighten up, good. They are our brothers, and we're responsible for our brothers. But if they don't straighten up, that's another point.[72]

We have seen that the other Afro-American leaders were unlikely to straighten up. Their organizations embodied the interests of the black middle class; and the only way the middle class and the masses could work together was through an on-going process of polemical confrontation. Organizational unification under OAAU leadership was therefore unlikely. Malcolm could realistically hope, however, that at least some Movement people would be drawn toward more militant positions as the masses became less passive and as white racism became more overt; and as we have seen, such a shift was already underway among the younger Movement activists of CORE and SNCC.

The presidential election provided important opportunities for cooperative effort. Presidential election campaigns have the advantage of focusing issues at the national level, thereby permitting organizations to transcend local differences in pursuit of more general ends. In Malcolm's view, moreover, a massive and properly run registration campaign could result in minimizing the violence of the developing black revolution. We have seen that he believed there were fundamentally two forms of power, the bullet and the ballot. The angry energy of the black masses had to be channeled toward use of one or the other. If freedom could be won by means of the ballot, the bullet would not be needed. This was conceivable. The 1960 election had shown that "the Negro in this country holds the balance of power." Thus if he

> were given what the Constitution says he is supposed to have, the added power of the Negro in this country would

sweep all of the racists and the segregationists out of office. It would change the entire political structure of the country. It would wipe out the Southern segregationism that now controls America's foreign policy, as well as America's domestic policy.[73]

The OAAU was willing to cooperate with voter registration efforts, if they were properly handled. To Malcolm, this meant two things in particular. First, black people should register as independent voters "who are not committed to any man until we find out what we're going to receive from that commitment."[74] Otherwise black voters would have no bargaining power. The model for this strategy was the nonalignment policy of the Third World nations, who "take from East and West and don't take sides with either one."[75] Second, they should defend themselves from attack while they are seeking to gain their political rights. The OAAU was to "provide defense units in every area of this country where workers are registering voters or are seeking voting rights, in every area where young students go out on the battlefront."[76]

Viewed in one way, Malcolm's idea of self-defense for Movement workers was simply an extension of the Nation's official policy, but in an activist context it takes on a different meaning. Self-defense becomes retaliation, and retaliation becomes the struggle for liberation. Thus the OAAU basic unity program states that when a racist attack has occurred and

> the United States government has shown itself unable and/or unwilling to bring to justice the racist oppressors, murderers, who kill innocent children and adults, the Organization of Afro-American Unity advocates that the Afro-American people insure ourselves that justice is done— whatever the price and *by any means necessary.*[77]

It follows logically enough that Malcolm argued for the formation of an Afro-American Mau Mau: "In Mississippi we need a Mau-Mau. Right here in Harlem, in New York City, we need a Mau-Mau."[78] The OAAU defense units were to be not only the armed guard for the black community and the Movement, but, when necessary, guerrilla fighters as well.

We now have a clearer conception of what Malcolm meant by "freedom by any means necessary." He intended to open up options that did not exist before: anything from rent strikes to ghetto uprisings, from electoral campaigns to guerrilla warfare, was legitimate so long as it brought freedom closer. The OAAU would work with anyone who was genuinely committed to that basic goal—would even work with white people if they were willing to attack racism in their own communities, preferably in the manner of a John Brown.[79] The "ballot or bullet" formulation was a particular policy embodying the general principle of "freedom by any means necessary." It was designed to create the maximum amount of politically effective unity among Afro-Americans. The energies of the oppressed masses would be merged with those of the more middle-class Movement people in an electoral campaign for national power. If that power could not be obtained peacefully, then the same organizational structure would be adapted to a new and more violent level of struggle.

By the end of 1964, a substantial number of younger Movement members were gravitating toward Malcolm's position, and after his death a black liberation movement guided by the principle of freedom by any means necessary did develop. But the civil rights leaders were not interested in the revolutionary transformation of American society. They therefore responded to Malcolm's initiatives by disassociating themselves from principles they described as politically unrealistic and morally irresponsible.

We have already explored the situational and organizational rationality of Malcolm's position. We have seen that, despite the impossibility of the immediate realization of its aims, an Afro-American revolutionary movement was in the interests of the black masses. We have also argued that the black liberation movement tends toward working-class solidarity, augments the possibilities for proletarian class-struggle, and is therefore in the interests of the world's oppressed masses. Our present concern must accordingly be with the relationship between Malcolm's political principles and the moral issues raised by his opponents.

Let us begin with Malcolm's own articulation of his position. We know that he was not telling black people to "go out and initiate aggression":

> I don't mean go out and get violent; but at the same time
> you should never be nonviolent unless you run into some
> nonviolence. I'm nonviolent with those who are nonviolent
> with me. But when you drop that violence on me, then
> you've made me go insane, and I'm not responsible for what
> I do. And that's the way every Negro should get. Any time
> you know you're within the law, within your legal rights,

within your moral rights, in accord with justice, then die for what you believe in. But don't die alone. Let your dying be reciprocal. This is what is meant by equality.[80]

The moral principle behind the OAAU position is simply that when the white man deprives black people of their human rights he has broken all bonds of mutual responsibility. Black people are then entitled to use any means necessary to regain those rights. The reason for being willing to use violent means is, however, practical as well as moral: Malcolm believed, *si vis pacem, para bellum*; if you want peace, be prepared for war. Because a racist is a coward, a strong stance will often be sufficient to ward him off. So with respect to the archetypal racist, the Ku Klux Klansman: "He's a coward. He can be thoroughly organized and if you go like that [stamps his foot] he'll cut out."[81] The white man simply does not want to risk his own life or, for that matter, his property. He cannot afford a black rebellion:

When you're inside another man's house, and the furniture is his, curtains, all those fine decorations, there isn't too much action he can put down in there without messing up his furniture and his windows and his house. And you let him know that when he puts his hands on you, it's not only you he puts his hands on, it's his whole house, you'll burn it down . . . then the man will act right. . . . He will only act right when you let him know that you know he has more to lose than you have.[82]

An uncompromising stance could lead to progress without massive violence, although nothing short of a miracle would result in the total cessation of racist attack. Still, if black people let it be known that any assault would be met with armed resistance, perhaps the level of violence could be kept relatively low. If, however, "[the man] knows when he's playing with you that you're going to back up and be nonviolent and peaceful and respectable and responsible, why, you and me will never come out of his claws."[83] Being nonviolent may result in a good image, but "nobody who's looking for a good image will ever be free."[84] A good image is, after all, an appeal, the plea that "you should give me my rights because I am worthy of them." But only a moral man can respond to a moral argument, and "the internal moral consciousness of this country is bankrupt. It hasn't existed since they first brought us over here and made slaves out of us."[85] To be nonviolent is to put on a dumb-show, a moral pageant in the face of which the white man is blind and deaf. The actors are all "Negroes" and therefore cannot be seen; they speak the language of the meek and therefore cannot be heard: "The language that you and I have been speaking to this man in the past hasn't reached him. And you can never really get your point across to a person until you learn how to communicate with him."[86] The implication? "He's talking the language of violence while you and I are running around with this little chicken-picking type of language. . . . Let's learn his language. If his language is with a shotgun, get a shotgun. Yes, if he only understands the language of a rifle, get a rifle."[87] Or stated more generally:

> Power never takes a back step—only in the face of more power. Power doesn't back up in the face of a smile, or in the face of a threat, or in the face of some kind of nonviolent loving action. It's not in the nature of power to back up in the face of anything but some more power.[88]

In sum, the means used must be appropriate to the situation: nonviolent if possible, violent when necessary. The beginning along with the end justifies the means.

Thus in Malcolm's view, ethical questions could not be detached from political ones, and political questions could only be answered through practical activity. This is not to say that Malcolm derived his ethical principles from political reality. He was quite comfortable with the traditional liberal justifications for revolutionary action, which he used with great polemical effectiveness against his liberal critics. "You fought for your freedom," he would say:

> But now when the time comes for our freedom, you want to reach back in the bag and grab somebody who's nonviolent and peaceful and forgiving and long-suffering. I don't go for that—no. I say that a black man's freedom is as valuable as a white man's freedom. And I say that a black man has the right to do whatever is necessary to get his freedom [just as] other human beings have done [anything necessary] to get their freedom.[89]

Malcolm refused to accept the idea that "give me liberty or give me death" was Patrick Henry's private property.

There is, however, another line of criticism which can be taken regarding Malcolm's position. One might abandon the right of revolution in favor of the categorical imperative. Then the Afro-American would be told, "So act that the maxim of your will could always hold at the same time as a principle establishing universal law."[90]

You cannot will that the right to revolution by any means necessary be a universal law, for that would result in a war of all against all. But this argument misrepresents the revolutionary position. It suggests that the idea of "any means necessary" can be reduced to the notion of violent means only, when in fact it is the most inclusive conception of the ends-means relationship. Moreover, this view ignores the fact that oppressed individuals do not create a state of war. We have seen in our exploration of the hustling society that the state of war is the limiting condition of bourgeois reality; and as Malcolm would have argued, it was the white man who declared war upon black people when the first slave ships reached Africa. A categorical imperative cannot, in other words, be one-sidedly imposed upon the oppressed masses: they cannot be asked to abide by an ethic of human responsibility or to accept universal moral obligations in an historical situation determined by the clash of particular—class and racial—interests. Accordingly, Malcolm claimed that "what is logical for the oppressor isn't logical for the oppressed." If the oppressed individual is to act responsibly in terms of his collective interest, he must define the rules of the struggle for himself: "Don't let anybody who is oppressing us ever lay the ground rules. Don't go by their game, don't play the game by their rules. Let them know that this is a new game, and we've got some new rules, and these rules mean anything goes."[91]

In other words, Malcolm was advocating an ethic of revolutionary responsibility. At the limit this meant that he was willing to kill or die to win equality, justice, and freedom for his fellow Afro-Americans.

"Cool It, Brothers . . ."

When Malcolm was in Egypt in July, 1964, he wrote to his followers:

> You must realize that what I am trying to do is very dangerous, because it is a direct threat to the entire international system of racist exploitation. It is a threat to discrimination in all its international forms. Therefore, if I die or am killed before making it back to the States, you can rest assured that what I've set in motion will never be stopped.[92]

Unfortunately, what Malcolm had set in motion depended upon his individual mediation for its realization; in this regard he underestimated his personal importance. But he was precisely correct in believing that he was a threat to the international power-structure. Accordingly, it does not surprise us that while in Cairo he "became violently ill one night after dinner at the Nile Hilton and was briefly hospitalized. He suspected he had been poisoned and guessed that American agents had done it."[93] Needless to say, such suspicions are not easily verified; but it is a matter of record that by mid-August the American "State Department and the Justice Department [had] begun to take an interest in Malcolm's campaign to convince African states to raise the question of persecution of American Negroes at the United Nations."[94] The State Department and the CIA actively pursued that interest. They followed him through Africa, so that by the end of his journey Malcolm had reached "that point in the life of a revolutionary where paranoia and reality intersect."[95] We would say: the paranoia of the neocolonialist had become the reality of the anticolonialist. Thus in Ghana, shortly before he returned to America, his friends observed that "there was a sense of— not desperation, you know, but it was like the hand of fate was on him."[96] Whose hand? He told Julian Mayfield, leader of the Afro-American community in Accra, "that if anything happened to him in the States they shouldn't necessarily think it was solely the doing of the Black Muslims."[97]

Malcolm's friends in Africa encouraged him to remain with them, but he chose to return to Afro-America. He reached New York on November 24, 1964; he was assassinated on February 21, 1965. During the three intervening months, his actions were determined by the play of mutually antagonistic progressive and regressive forces. On the one hand, he was coming back from Africa with a groundwork laid for internationalizing the Afro-American problem; the increasing militancy of the black masses and the younger members of the Movement was generating the subjective potential necessary for the utilization of that objective ground; and Malcolm himself possessed precisely the character and consciousness which could transform that potential into organizationally unified revolutionary action. On the other hand, the international power-structure, the American ruling class, and the leadership of the Nation of Islam had every interest in destroying this revolutionary potential—by any means necessary. Malcolm recognized his situation. He knew that unless he threw off the responsibilities of revolutionary leadership the hellhounds of his enemies would be constantly on his trail. But he had accepted those responsibilities willingly and without reservation. He had chosen to live for his people rather than for himself; and he was ready to pay the price that choice entailed . . . the price of almost certain death.

Given that choice, Malcolm had to continue the work he had begun, hoping that he would be able to outwit if not overpower his enemies. His most important task was to find a way of describing his theoretical position that would extend black nationalism into some kind of revolutionary internationalism. He was looking for, in his words, "a specific definition of the over-all philosophy which I think is necessary for the liberation of black people in this country."[98] But such a definition was not easy to establish. His relationship to his followers when he had been in the Nation had of course been grounded in a racial-religious identity. When he left, those who left with him—and these men were the core of the OAAU—expected him to preserve that identity, to preserve the old dream in all its hypnotic power. Thus when Malcolm attempted to transform their racial-religious identity into a racial-political one, he was in danger of undermining the foundations of his leadership. Yet if he did not effect such a transformation, he would be continuing to mis-lead his people. That on the one hand. On the other, he had to define his new position in such a way that the younger members of the Movement would be attracted to it—or, to state the point in negative form, so they wouldn't be red-scared away from it.

Malcolm's first problem was thus the establishment and expansion of a new racial-political identity. The second was the development of an effective form of self-productive (i.e., revolutionary) aggressivity. Polemical activity with a revolutionary content was, of course, one such form; but it was not in itself direct action and, increasingly, Malcolm was being called upon to match his words with deeds. What, in fact, was to be done? If he were to organize a direct attack upon the Klan in Mississippi or the police in New York, his nascent organization would be totally destroyed. If he avoided militant action, then he, like Muhammad before him, would be vulnerable to the charge of being all breath and no britches. His angry words would be seen as a hype, a hustle, especially by those re-formed *lumpen-proletarians* who followed him because he was tough and cool, a "bad nigger." If, however, he could inspire the younger Movement members while simultaneously calming down his more volatile followers, then the problem might be solved: the OAAU might become a broad-based mass organization, a true revolutionary vanguard. And with winter keeping people off of the streets up North and a voter-registration campaign heating up down South, this was not an impossible task. In fact, in early February, 1965, Malcolm gained his long-sought-after point of entry into the Movement. At the invitation of SNCC, he spoke to demonstrators in Selma, Alabama. He argued with his usual skill the distinction between field Negroes and house Negroes; he indicated his belief in the "absolute right" of black people to use "whatever means necessary to gain the vote"; and just before concluding, he stated that "I'm not intending to try and stir you up and make you do something you wouldn't have done [a slight pause, just long enough to leave the unmistakable implication of things left unsaid] anyway."[99] After he was done, "the kids [sic] applauded furiously; the SCLC people thought better of sending them out on a march that day and hastily got King's wife, Coretta, to say a few inspirational words to quiet them down."[100]

Finally, there was the problem of internationalizing his emergent revolutionary practice. This was in certain respects the most difficult aspect of the situation, for the member states of the OAU could initiate no action in the U.N. unless they were presented with a petition from a massive Afro-American national liberation movement. Since such a movement did not yet exist, no such petition was forthcoming. Nonetheless, in the U.N. debate over the Congo, several African delegations developed with great effectiveness Malcolm's argument that American racism in the Congo was parallel in form and identical in substance to American racism in Mississippi—an argument that American Ambassador to the U.N. Adlai Stevenson was at embarrassed pains to deny.

In sum, by the beginning of February, the Movement was moving toward Malcolm and, through Malcolm, toward an Afro-American practice. Simultaneously the revolutionary forces in Africa and the Third World, again through Malcolm, were moving toward Afro-America. Malcolm was thus becoming the middle term in a logic of international revolutionary action.

On February 9, perhaps at the request of the United States government, perhaps at the request of Senegal and the Ivory Coast, Malcolm was barred from France, where he had been scheduled to address the Congress of African Students. On February 21, he was dead.

On the one side, there were the soldiers of the Black Revolution, young, untrained, not yet able to fill their positions but developing that capability with great speed. On the other, there were the soldiers both of the state and of the Nation of Islam, well-trained and in command of the strategic positions in ghettoized Afro-America. In between, but increasingly being encircled by the reactionary forces, there was Malcolm with his OAAU. This is the regressive side of the logic of revolutionary action, i.e., a state of siege.

Malcolm's defensive battle began in the spring of 1964. While he was still in the Nation, the FBI visited him with an offer to pay him generously for the organization's membership rolls. He of course refused the cooptive bribe, and thereby affirmed for them his position on the wrong side of the law. Then just after the split, the Nation's leaders demanded that he surrender possession of the house, owned by the Nation, which he and his family occupied. They also began a campaign of vilification, the low point of which was a statement by Malcolm's brother Philbert "likening Malcolm to Judas, Brutus and Benedict Arnold and suggesting that he was crazy in the bargain. . . .: 'I am aware of the great mental illness which beset unfortunately many Americans,' said Philbert, 'and which besetted my mother whom I love and one of my other brothers and which now may have taken another victim, my brother Malcolm.'" [101] Thus Muhammad was using both legal and psychic coercion in an attempt to break Malcolm, to humiliate him and/or drive him insane.

Malcolm was not about to break under the Nation's threats of punishment any more than he was going to beg for the State's monetary rewards. The house, he believed, was rightfully if not legally his. It was all he possessed after twelve years of working in and for the Nation; and it was the only *thing* of substantial value that he had provided for Betty and his children. He therefore refused to be alienated from this solitary product of his labor. And he certainly wasn't going to fall victim to Muhammad's old hypnotic hustle, not after having fought for and won control over his emotional energies. But at the same time, he was not interested in fighting a war with his former leader. Accordingly, he offered Muhammad a *quid pro quo*: he would not speak out against the Prophet or reveal any of the Nation's closely guarded secrets if the Prophet would leave him the house and leave him alone. The offer was refused. Consequently, on June 16, Malcolm appeared with representatives of the Nation in a Queens courtroom, there to have a white judge decide who owned the house. The Nation stated its case, which was legally persuasive; Malcolm entered his charge that Muhammad was an adulterer, which may have been morally persuasive but was legally irrelevant. The judge ruled in the Nation's favor; and with this action the line had been drawn, the curse had been cast.

Muhammad now began a more intense campaign of intimidation,

although it was not yet one of terror. Fruit of Islam units began to materialize wherever Malcolm was speaking, reminding him by their grim presence that his days were numbered. In early July, four men with knives were waiting for him outside his house, but Malcolm managed to escape. At about this same time Muhammad published a short article on the subject of hypocrites, in which he told his followers, "They are not to be killed, for Allah desires to make them examples for others, by chastising them like a parent does a child. He chastises one with a strap to warn the other not to disobey. [102] Malcolm was not a child; he knew that the Messenger's message would be treated by loyal Black Muslims as a not very cryptic cryptogram.

In July, Malcolm went abroad, leaving his enemies in the Nation behind. But the United States Information Service and the CIA now picked up his trail. As we have seen, they may have tried to kill him in Cairo; and during the rest of his African mission they kept him under tight surveillance while doing everything possible to discredit him. After he returned to this country, the Nation escalated its offensive into an open campaign of terror. It continued to hound him from one place to another; *Muhammad Speaks* began to print more direct threats; one of his followers was beaten and almost killed; and Malcolm himself was nearly trapped by members of the Fruit of Islam in Los Angeles and again in New York. Next came his abortive trip to France. Finally, during the night of February 13–14, his house was fire-bombed. Malcolm and his family barely escaped with their lives, but the Muslims accused him of setting the fire himself and, as Goldman puts it: "The authorities did not precisely agree with the Malcolm-did-it theory but quietly encouraged it with the matter-of-fact mention that, oh, by the way, they had found a whiskey bottle containing a clear liquid standing upright on a dresser in the girls' room and that the liquid had turned out upon analysis to be gasoline." [103]

At that point, Malcolm finally concluded that the Nation and the state were conspiring to kill him. This conclusion is not incompatible with the known facts; but it must be observed that no proof is available that the two enemy forces were conducting a unified and coordinated campaign to end his life. Without a doubt there were government agents in both the Nation of Islam and the OAAU; hence it is a safe inference that information flowed freely—although not necessarily directly—between the operatives in the two organizations, and that in each case these men did all they could to feed the fires of intraorganizational rivalry and interorganizational hostility. It is also true that there were a number of peculiarities in the actions taken and those *not* taken by the police during Malcolm's last days. Finally, the state's case in the murder trial raised far more questions about who was responsible for Malcolm's death than it answered. Be that as it may, the uncovering of conspiratorial linkages is a matter of secondary concern: the interests of the country's ruling class were being served, no matter who was actually giving the order. Whether the men who were stalking Malcolm were really Muslims or were government agents pretending to be Muslims, they were still pawns in the bourgeois game, black soldiers in what was ultimately the white man's army.

Against these alien forces Malcolm could marshall only a small band of revolutionary brothers, the inner circle of the OAAU. These men were his soldiers, his last line of organizational defense against the state and the Nation, against the malevolent paternal authorities the brothers called "the Old Ones in the power structure," against the charismatic leader turned bourgeois executive who had once been Malcolm's loving father. But as we saw earlier, the OAAU at this juncture was more a potential for conscious activity than a real political force. Furthermore, Malcolm had little time to devote to its internal development, at first because he was obliged to accept one paying speaking engagement after another in order to keep the OAAU alive financially, later because he was forced to use almost all of his energies in order simply to stay physically alive in what was once again a kill-or-be-killed world—which is to say, during these final months the always tenuous distinction between the hustling society and bourgeois society was collapsing altogether. Malcolm could trust no one outside of his own closed circle, and even its members could not be trusted absolutely. But as long as he stayed cool, the circle would not break.

Everything was building, closing in on him. He was trapped in so many cross turns. But despite the desperate nature of the situation he refused to lose control, even when his friends were openly alarmed and his organizational defenses were becoming inadequate. He had hustled the Harlem streets for years, and he understood the mentality of his enemies; he knew that if there were even one break in his apparent calm, if he gave any sign of fear, his enemies would know that he was weakening and would attack him all the more boldly: *homo homini lupus*. Furthermore, rigid self-control was his only defense against anxiety—realistic anxiety, the emotional reflection of his situation. Utter stoicism was thus a matter of both objective and subjective necessity.

Yet it is not enough to say that Malcolm's self-control was necessary; we must also determine how it was possible. Of course, a studied coolness was his characteristic attitude. It was the product both of the years he had spent in the hustling society and the Nation of Islam, and of his ability to compartmentalize or categorize his thinking. But coolness in this sense, a radically transformed hustler's *machismo*, was predicated upon the limiting assumption that in the end Allah would protect him, his luck would not desert him, his sixth sense would not fail him. It was the cool assurance of the seventh son, who had been in tight corners before but had always managed to escape.

This premise was, however, increasingly unrealistic; it had become merely a wish that a benevolent parental deity, a *deus ex machina*, would intervene to save the blessed seventh son. Malcolm's luck had run out; the blessing had become a curse. He was leading his renegade brother band in rebellion against the White Christian father and the self-ordained Prophet of Allah. He would therefore have to be punished for his intended repetition of the primal crime. His guilt would have to be objectified in his chastisement, to serve as a salutary warning to others who might also be jealous or overly ambitious. So the authorities proclaimed. Malcolm's conscience was no longer under the control of these alienating, pseudo-ethical powers, however. He was neither a nihilistic hustler nor a chiliastic Black Muslim. He was a revolutionary leader, a hero to his followers. If he had to die for the people, the people would give him his just reward: a hero's funeral, revolutionary immortality. The curse becomes a blessing.

Thus we arrive at the hero's destiny. "It has always been my belief that I, too, will die by violence. I have done all that I can to be prepared." But destiny is necessity, fatality is knowledge, only in retrospect. In prospect it is possibility, choice, projection. Hence Achilleus could say before the death of Patroklos sealed his own fate, "I carry two sorts of destiny toward the day of my death. Either, if I stay here and fight beside the city of the Trojans, my return home is gone, but my glory shall be everlasting; but if I return home to the beloved land of my fathers, the excellence of my glory is gone, but there will be long life for me, and my death will not come to me quickly."[104] Achilleus chose to fight and die; Malcolm did the same. He chose to be a bad man rather than a good boy, the angriest Muslim rather than simply a Muslim, the heroic leader of the OAAU rather than an Afro-American exile in the African homeland. Only through and as these choices did his life become a fatality.

Until his house was fire-bombed, Malcolm was generally able to maintain the appearance of a man who was a stranger to fear. But in the flames of his burning home he must have seen the fiery image of his father's house, felt again the terror of the nightmare night. Then at last he knew that the circle had been closed, that he had no more time. Then, too, he was afraid, not for himself but for his family. Perhaps also there were times when he wanted to die, wanted to end the fear and the meaningless waiting. . . . He had never wanted to wait.

At times his composure cracked, his self-assurance disintegrated. At other times he was possessed of an almost superhuman calm. He told a reporter, "I live like a man who's already dead."[105] He was torn between an agonized attachment to life and the painless detachment of death. These extremes resolved themselves into one last attempt to outwit death: he yelled as loudly as he could that Muhammad's men were trying to kill him, hoping that by so doing he could force them to stop. But the Muslims, unlike his mother, did not care if the "neighbors" were listening; and the neighbors (the police, the press, the public), if they were listening, did not care about what they heard. There was nothing more to do but to go on working and loving as if he were not already dead.

A speech in Detroit, a lecture at Columbia University, a search for a new home, a reorganizational meeting of the OAAU. Then an open meeting of the OAAU on Sunday, February 21. In his waiting room he told his brothers, "I don't feel right about this meeting. I feel I should not be here. Something is wrong, brothers." He sensed it, he almost knew it . . . he was prepared that day to make public the names of the five men who had been assigned to kill him.

Betty was there, backstage. Benjamin Goodman was finishing the introduction: "I present a man who would give his life for you." Malcolm walked to the podium. "As-Salaam Alaikum," he said; the audience responded, "Wa-Alaikum Salaam." A sudden commotion, attention drawn to the illusion of a fight in the back of the room. Three men converging on the stage, unseen. "Hold it! Don't get excited. Let's cool it, brothers! . . ."[106]

"Black Awakening in Capitalist America"

On February 22, the *New York Times* editorialized:

He was a case history, as well as an extraordinary and twisted man, turning many true gifts to evil purpose.

> . . . Malcolm X had the ingredients for leadership, but
> his ruthless and fanatical belief in violence not only set him
> apart from the responsible leaders of the civil rights move-
> ment and the overwhelming majority of Negroes, it also
> marked him for notoriety and a violent end. . . . Malcolm
> X's life was strangely and pitifully twisted. But this was
> because he did not seek to fit into the society or into the life
> of his own people.

Then on February 28 it reported: "Mourners and the curious lined
the sidewalks on both sides of Amsterdam Avenue behind police
barricades to watch as the procession of friends and relatives moved
into the church. Hundreds more pressed against the window panes
of the red brick and wooden tenements across the street, or stood
shivering on their fire escapes." Perhaps Harlem's black masses did
not accept the editorial judgment of America's newspaper of record.
Thus we come to the legacy of Malcolm's life work.

In what is sometimes referred to as his "last message" (the speech
in Detroit after the bombing), Malcolm argued that "colonialism or
imperialism, as the slave system of the West is called," forms an "international power structure" that "is used to suppress the masses of
dark-skinned people all over the world and exploit them of their
natural resources."[107] But, he continued, there is a revolution against
that suppressive structure taking place, particularly in Africa but
also in Asia and Latin America. Consequently the "Western interests" unified in the power structure are worried. They were also worried about the work Malcolm was doing in Africa, where he was "almost fanatically stressing the importance of the Afro-Americans
uniting with the Africans and working as a coalition, especially in
areas which are of mutual benefit to us all."[108] Furthermore, while
the revolution in Africa—the one "on the outside of the house, or
the outside of the structure"—is troublesome, "now the powers are
beginning to see that this struggle on the outside by the black man is
affecting, infecting the black man who is inside of that structure.
. . . Just as the external forces pose a grave threat, they can now see
that the internal forces pose an even greater threat."[109] Initially the
threat posed is ghetto rebellion on an expanding scale:

> 1965 will be the longest and hottest and bloodiest year of
> them all. It has to be, not because you want it to be, or I
> want it to be, or we want it to be, but because the condi-
> tions that created these explosions in 1963 are still here; the

conditions that created explosions in 1964 are still here.
You can't say you're not going to have an explosion when
you leave the conditions, the ingredients, still here. As long
as those explosive ingredients remain, then you're going to
have the potential for explosion on your hands.[110]

That potential will be realized in effective anticolonial action when
black people "have properly analyzed the situation and know what
the stakes are."[111] More concretely: "It is for this reason that it is so
important for you and me to start organizing among ourselves, intel-
ligently, and try to find out: 'What are we going to do if this happens
or the next thing happens?'"[112]

During the early part of the summer of 1965, it appeared that Malcolm had not properly analyzed the situation. Outside of the South,
everything was quiet. Then on August 11, an incident of police brutality provided the needed spark for the explosive ingredients that
were piled up in Los Angeles. For ten days thereafter, first police
and then the National Guard used every means at their disposal to
put down the insurrection, while the "rioters" smashed windows,
looted stores, and burned buildings. There was no method to the
madness of the government's armed forces, or at least no limit to the
amount of fire-power they were willing to use; but the "rioters"
were not so indiscriminate: the U.S. Riot Commission reported that
"few white persons were attacked"; rather, "the principal intent of
the rioters . . . seemed to be to destroy property owned by whites, in
order to drive white 'exploiters' out of the ghetto."[113] Thus the people of Watts attempted to burn out their oppressors in very much the
way one would cauterize a wound.

The Watts war cry was "Burn, baby, burn," a spontaneously generated slogan which expressed a willingness to destroy the objective
conditions of internal colonial oppression. As such, it implied a profound psychological transformation, i.e., the (at least temporary)
shattering of the vicious circle of self-destructive aggressivity. The
police and the soldiers, with their clubs, guns, and gas, destroyed the
individual's identification with his oppressor, so that the aggressive
energy which hitherto had been turned inward through the agency
of that whitened-out conscience was now turned outward. In Fanon's words: "At the level of individuals, violence is a cleansing force.
It frees the native [the colonized man] from his inferiority complex
and from his despair and inaction; it makes him fearless and restores
his self-respect."[114] It is, in short, the constitutive act of Black Pride,

identical in substance to Malcolm's self-formation as a proud and righteous black man through his conversion to Islam. Identical in *emotional* substance, but not in *conscious* form: spontaneous aggressivity is not conscious activity. Again to quote Fanon:

> Racial feeling, as opposed to racial prejudice, and that determination to fight for one's life which characterizes the native's reply to oppression are obviously good enough reasons for joining the fight. But you do not carry on a war, nor suffer brutal and widespread repression, nor look on while all other members of your family are wiped out in order to make racialism and hatred triumph. Racialism and hatred and resentment—"a legitimate desire for revenge"— cannot sustain a war of liberation.[115]

Insurrectionary violence must be organized into a rational political practice if it is to form the basis for revolutionary activity.

Spontaneous aggressivity without conscious activity is self-negating: the "intense emotion of the first few hours falls to pieces if it is left to feed on its own substance."[116] But conscious activity that is not the product of spontaneous aggressivity is, from a revolutionary perspective, also self-negating. Consequently for those who were not participants in, for example, the Watts uprising, the problem was to determine one's relationship to the event. Of course, for those who knew that if they had been there they would have joined the action, the Watts uprising was purely a moment of self-liberation. Thus Eldridge Cleaver reports that when the news reached Folsom Prison, the black prisoners assembled on a basketball court: "They were wearing jubilant, triumphant smiles, animated by a vicarious spirit by which they, too, were in the thick of the uprising."[117]

For those who were engaged in programmatic political action and who had accepted the categorical imperative of nonviolent direct action, the matter was not so simple. On the one hand, here were their black brothers and sisters, in open rebellion against their oppressor. Moreover, as their own experience in the Movement had taught them, "Nonviolence might do something to the moral conscience of a nation, but a bullet didn't have morals and it was beginning to occur to more and more organizers that white folks had plenty more bullets than they did conscience."[118] The young activists in particular were therefore suffering from the attacks of acute rage discussed earlier. Consequently many of them were pulled by their own suppressed anger toward the masses and toward aggressive, insurrectionary action. But in joining the Movement they had chosen to accept certain moral values, and spontaneous rebellion was not a possibility for them. Accordingly, they were faced with a choice of action: they could either reaffirm the values upon which their current actions were being predicated, or they could elect to follow where the masses were leading.

Not surprisingly, different individuals, moved by the determining forces of their own situations, made varying choices. Some were unable to dispel the illusion of the American dream, to bring to an end their participation in the stereotypical dumb-show. Others were able to negate the categorical imperative and thereby affirm the mass action. In this way the Movement came into possession of the aggressive energy of the masses, while the masses were given access to the consciousness that had been developing—especially through Malcolm's mediation—within the Movement. At least potentially, the contradiction between spontaneity and consciousness, masses and middle class, was overcome. Hence one might even say with Marx: "Just as philosophy finds its *material* weapons in the proletariat, so the proletariat finds its *intellectual* weapons in philosophy." [119] Or in the language of the times, "We shall overcome," when mediated by and activated through "Burn, baby, burn," emerged as the call for "Black Power."

The major statement of the Black Power position was the book *Black Power* by Stokely Carmichael and Charles V. Hamilton. In their programmatic statement, the authors argue that "the social, political and economic problems [of our urban ghettoes] are so acute that even a casual observer cannot fail to see that something is wrong." [120] It is also obvious that the existing but "outmoded structures and institutions" of the society, especially the political party system, "will not be able to serve a growing body of alienated black people." [121] Changes must be made, and these changes "will have to come from the black community." [122] What changes? "We must begin to think of the black community as a base for organization to control institutions in that community." [123] Further, because "virtually all the money earned by merchants and exploiters of the black ghetto leaves those communities, properly organized black groups should seek to establish a community rebate plan." [124] In the political sphere, "the black communities in these northern ghettoes [must] form independent party groups to elect their own choices to office when and where they can"; at the same time, black people may have to "spearhead a drive to revamp completely the present institutions of representation."[125] Finally there comes the peroration, which we cited at the outset of our work and which almost sounds like Malcolm speaking at the OAAU founding rally:

> Because one thing stands clear: whatever the consequences, there is a growing—a rapidly growing—body of black people determined to "T.C.B."—take care of business. They will not be stopped in their drive to achieve dignity, to achieve their share of power, indeed, to become their own men and women—in this time and in this land—by whatever means necessary.[126]

Almost, but not quite. For as Robert Allen observes, Carmichael "attempted to pick up the threads of Malcolm's thought and apply them to this social context. But he was uncertain how to move. He was torn between reformism and revolution."[127]

The young men who organized and were majorly responsible for leading the Black Panther Party were less divided in their political orientation. Huey Newton and Bobby Seale founded the Black Panther Party (BPP) in the fall of 1966. Their immediate aim was ghetto self-defense. Hence they began to make armed patrols of Oakland, California, following the police on their appointed rounds, intervening to advise citizens of their rights when they observed those rights being violated. As Angela Davis notes, "Their vigilance produced a marked decrease in police harassment and brutality. Black people in Oakland were impressed."[128] So were the police, who induced state assemblyman Don Mulford to introduce a bill to the California Assembly making it illegal to carry loaded weapons in incorporated areas. The Panthers then decided to exercise simultaneously their right to submit a petition against this legislation and their right to bear arms: on May 2, 1967, Seale led an armed contingent of BPP members into the legislative halls. The men were arrested, although their action was not illegal, and the Party gained immediate nationwide recognition. Moreover, they, like Malcolm and the leaders of the Black Power Movement, gained strength from the actions of the masses. The summer of 1966 had been marked by major ghetto uprisings in Chicago and Cleveland; and the summer of 1967 witnessed rebellions in Tampa, Cincinnati, Atlanta, Newark, and Detroit.* The Panthers, so their dramatic action indicated, had at least

---

* It is worth mentioning that the U.S. Riot Commission found it worth mentioning that when Stokely Carmichael was arrested in Atlanta for the crime of warning po-

the will and maybe the way to channel and organize the energies that were being released in these mass actions. Consequently, the authorities intensified their efforts to destroy the Party. Again in the short run, these attempts backfired. The arrest of Huey Newton on what proved to be trumped-up murder charges enabled the Panthers to organize a nationwide campaign to "Free Huey"; chapters of the Party were formed in other cities; and the wanton attacks upon these chapters led large numbers of people in the black community to join in the defense of an organization which they might otherwise have ignored. Finally, the rising tide of protest against the war in Vietnam made it possible for the Panthers to form a loosely structured but nonetheless potent alliance with (as they called them) "mother country radicals." In this way there arose the New Left Movement of the late 1960s, a movement which tended increasingly to identify itself as anti-imperialist and anticolonialist.

Yet by 1972 the New Left was history. After the last flurry of protest against the invasion of Cambodia, the "mother country radicals" largely disappeared back into their everyday lives; after more than 1,000 arrests and 19 killings, the Black Panther Party had been effectively dismembered; and after almost two decades of struggle, the Movement had ground to a halt. To be sure, the black middle class had won some portion of the social and political rights to which its economic standing entitled it; but the black masses still had not obtained the freedom, justice, and equality for which they had been struggling. Given our prior analysis, this outcome does not require extensive explanation, but a brief consideration of the last moments of the Black Revolution will help to bring out the salient theoretical points.

The limit of the Black Revolution was, most importantly, the international and intranational strength of American capitalism. Internationally, although the United States was not able to win the war in Vietnam, the structure of international capitalist power did not collapse. Consequently the idea of Afro-American and African unity remained situationally transcendent. Cultural nationalism, as it came to be called, continued to play a vital role within the liberation movement, but the political game was played on a domestic American field.

---

lice that if they did not pull out of the ghetto area there was going to be trouble, he was wearing a green Malcolm X sweatshirt (Report of the National Advisory Commission on Civil Disorders, p. 55).

Intranationally, the revolutionary movement was confronted, first, with wartime prosperity. Although in time the war in Vietnam was to prove economically destabilizing, in the short run it provided employment opportunities in the monopoly and state sectors of the economy, as well as jobs in the military itself; made possible increased welfare benefits for the men and women of the industrial reserve army; and resulted in easier pickings for the *lumpen-proletariat*. Next there was the War on Poverty, the velvet glove of the cooptation process, benevolent paternalism *à la* Lyndon Johnson, who fancied himself "the ultimate self in which the will of the state is concentrated,"[129] the Franklin Roosevelt of his generation. Then there was the iron fist or, as it came to be called, the "war on the poor": the systematic and brutal suppression both of spontaneous mass insurrection and of organized black-radical political activity. The net effect of these policies was to separate, once again and more definitively, the black middle class from the masses. As the 1970 census indicates, the middle class did improve its economic position, both absolutely and relative to that of the white population; and it did at long last win some of the social privileges, individual prerogatives and political rights that *ought* to accompany middle-class standing.[130] But as the "ought" became an "is," as the black middle-class interests were progressively being realized, the members of that class tended increasingly to act as the mediating agents for the ruling class. Thus, as Robert Allen observes in a slightly different context, public policy served the white bourgeois interest in "reorganizing the ghetto 'infrastructure,' in creating a ghetto buffer class clearly committed to the dominant American institutions and values on the one hand, and on the other, in rejuvenating the black working class and integrating it into the American economy."[131]

Against the background of the black masses beaten into quiescence and the black middle class well advanced in its struggle for Black Power *within* the existing system, the failure of the BPP actually to function as a revolutionary vanguard is hardly surprising. But the BPP also contributed to its own undoing. Its leaders were attempting to form a *lumpen-proletariat* revolutionary party. But the *lumpen-proletariat*, even if taken in a very loose sense to include the black industrial reserve army and the victims of the welfare system, does not have the potential for seizing state power and thereby overthrowing the existing system; and so long as that system survives, its realistic expectations must be limited to the trickle down of benefits it can receive as a result of a more or less successful racial reform movement. It was for this reason that Malcolm was working

desperately hard to unify in a vast Afro-American coalition the reformist interests of the middle class with the revolutionary interests
of the masses. He recognized that the realization of black revolutionary ends entailed the use, in the existing American situation, of
reformist means, of the ballot as well as the bullet. But the Panthers
did not fully recognize that if the middle class could not be forced to
serve mass interests, mass activity would instead serve middle-class
interests. They left the middle class to its own devices, with the
consequence that their actions functioned primarily as pressure on
the white ruling class to seek moderate solutions to the racial problem. Their revolutionary energies were harnessed to reformist ends,
and the terms in Malcolm's postulated ends-means relationship
were inverted.

It follows from the preceding analysis that the BPP conception of a
lumpen-proletariat party was not in itself situationally rational.
Moreover, the objective irrationality of the BPP was subjectively
reflected in the character and conscience of its members. As James
Boggs argues, the Party was "still caught up in the illusion that the
masses are revolutionary in themselves."[132] But the *lumpen-proletarian* is not inherently revolutionary. Although the hustler may
be "the most dangerous black man in America," he is dangerous not
only to the power structure but also to the "ghetto youth" who are
mesmerized by the man who displays "no respect for anybody or
anything"; dangerous to the black people who are his victims; dangerous, ultimately, to his friends and himself. He is either "internally restrained by nothing," a genuine sociopath—in which case
he is almost certain to become (in the revolutionary situation) "a
bribed tool of reactionary intrigue"—or he is caught in the vicious
circle of self-destructive aggressivity, in which case he will tend to
regress toward a state of paranoid nihilism if his character is not re-
formed. Hence the members of a *lumpen-proletarian* party, if they
do not pass through a secular version of the Nation of Islam's conversion process, are no more than hustlers in transition, revolutionaries in the making. They tend to mistake a good front for substantial strength, *machismo* for manhood, and restless action for
self-conscious activity. But the BPP defined itself against the preexisting cultural-nationalist tendency, and thereby surrendered the
possibilities for racial reidentification that the Afro-American concept provided. And it failed to develop either "rigorous orientation
training and tests to determine fitness for membership" or a program adequately "focused on problems that the people can learn

from."¹³³ * Consequently Black Pride became a substitute for both organized Black Power and Afro-American culture.

The BPP's proclivity for three-penny-opera politics was most clearly expressed in its somewhat fetishistic attitude toward guns. The leaders of the Party tended to attribute to the gun powers it did not possess but only symbolized. They infused it with their own energies, their desire for power and freedom, and then worshipped it as if it had a life of its own. But this identification of the gun with power is precisely a *lumpen-proletarian* illusion. In the kill-or-be-killed world of individual hustlers, the gun is an instrument through which the property of another can be possessed; it is the visible proof of one's manhood; and the firing of a gun is action itself, the ultimate action when the gunman takes a human life. Yet as Malcolm's experience in that world demonstrates, the use of guns is a last resort: the cool or rational hustler much prefers to gain his ends by other means. Moreover, if the hustler carries a weapon, he must be prepared to use it; and the more conspicuously he carries it, the more likely it is that its use will be required. Hence if he is rational, he tries to calculate what he will do if this happens or the next thing happens. Then on the basis of that calculation, he decides if and how he will arm himself. Correspondingly, the revolutionary leader, if he is rational and responsible—as Malcolm was—advocates violence only as a last resort; recognizes that the use of violent means in isolation from political power is suicidal; and does not display arms unless he has been politically empowered to do so.

In sum, the Black Revolution, as it developed after Malcolm's death, was an internally divided form of his intended OAAU practice. Basically, these divisions reflected both the strength of the existing system and the partially opposing interests of the black masses and the middle class. The black pride concomitant upon the militancy of the struggle did indeed unite its various protagonists. But Afro-American political unity did not materialize; Black Power

* It should be noted that in substance the Panther ten-point platform and program was responsive to the needs of the masses. It included demands for full employment, reparations for economic exploitation, decent housing and education, exemption for men from military service, an end to police brutality, the release of all black prisoners, trial by a jury of one's peers, and a plebiscite to allow people the opportunity of national self-determination. But these demands were not grounded in systematic theory at the one end and they did not coalesce into a program of action at the other; they remained suspended in a condition of abstraction. It should also be noted, however, that the brutal suppression of the BPP at that time left it little opportunity to develop into anything other than a self-defensive band.

became a resource of the middle class; and "freedom by any means necessary," when directly identified with the *lumpen-proletariat*, tended to regress toward the hustling code. Consequently—to repeat what Malcolm said in 1965—"the masses of [black] people still have bad housing, bad schooling and inferior jobs. . . . So the problem of the masses has gone absolutely unsolved."

CHAPTER X

The Logic of Democracy

WE HAVE NOW REACHED the historical limit of our inquiry, the point at which our interpretation of Malcolm X and the Black Revolution merges with the analysis of the class-racial struggle in our present situation. Our remaining task is to summarize in more or less logical fashion the various theoretical principles and propositions which have emerged in the course of our work.

The most general concept arising from our work is the idea that the sensuous interaction of energetic individuals constitutes a potential for self-conscious activity, a potential which is actualized through opposing and interpenetrating objectifying (work) and subjectifying (emotional) processes. From the standpoint of logical exposition, this anthropological notion or conception of human nature in general constitutes a premise from which all our other, more particular concepts can be derived. This premise was itself constituted through the phenomenological process, and hence was derived from our interest in racial and human liberation. It was this interest which initially transformed the phenomenon of American race relations into a problematical subject for phenomenological investigation—into the question of Malcolm's historical significance, the problematic of racist oppression, and the problem of false consciousness; and it is the phenomenological process which has as its product the above-mentioned premises for a possible logical exposition. If we were now to treat the phenomenological process as external to its product, as a merely propaedeutical phase of subsequently scientific activity, it would appear as if we had before us an *a priori* construction. Likewise, if we were to leave our initial purpose behind, it would appear as if this construction could stand upon the ground of a disinterested or pure scientific reason. Conversely, when we acknowledge that our premises are the product of phenomenological inquiry, we are forced to recognize that they are inherently problematical. We abandon the search for apodeictic certainty in the logical unfolding of our concepts, and content ourselves with a dialectical recapitulation of problems solved.* We also recognize that our logical premises are theoretical reflections of the political purposes with which we began our inquiry, as well as theoretical grounds for subsequent political activity.

The Potential for Self-Conscious Activity

Returning to our anthropological conception, we may say that, as *sensuous* beings, human individuals are receptive and responsive to the impact of external reality. Through touching, tasting, smelling, hearing, and seeing, the human individual experiences the reality of his intersubjective and objective world. The intercourse of human individuals with other human individuals and the non-human environment is the first phylogenetic form of sensuous experience, just as the interactions of the individual's natal family are the first ontogenetic experiences. In all actual historical circumstances, however, the nature of these interactions is determined by the situationally given play of social forces. Our inquiry therefore did not begin with the life of Malcolm's family but with the nightmare night viewed as a social and historical reality. Only after we had established the objective and subjective limits of that reality did we attempt to represent and interpret Malcolm's primary, sensuous experiences.

The next term in our premise is suggested by the fact that Malcolm was not merely the object of impinging social forces but also a subject who responded *actively* to the realities of his situation. Indeed, the critical beginning of a Marxist psychoanalysis is the recognition that human experience is not primarily the individual's contemplation of a past event or external object; it is, rather, the interaction of individuals with each other and their objective world.

---

* Hitherto our concepts have been developed when needed for the interpretation of historical representations. Now, however, historical representations are to be used when they are illustrative of conceptual relationships.

Accordingly, we speak not only of sensuous experience but also, and more importantly, of sensuous interactions or sensuous activity.

If human individuals are sensuously active, then they must also be *energetic*. They must possess a potential for activity which, *qua* potential, is experienced as both power and pressure. We think, for example, of Malcolm's statement that his reading in prison and after his conversion had his "mind like steam under pressure," a pressure he was able to relieve through proselytizing and polemical activity. Conversely, when Muhammad later denied him access to these forms of conscious activity, Malcolm again experienced his power as an internal pressure.

In sum, human life has at its foundation the sensuous interaction of energetic individuals. But sensuous activity is not *ipso facto* conscious activity. Sensuous energies must be developed through the objectification and subjectification processes if conscious or self-conscious activity is to result. The objectification process involves the constructive and destructive activation of both work instruments and the objects of work-activity (Malcolm tending the garden plot his mother assigned to him). The subjectification process involves the sexual and aggressive activation of emotional modalities, in relationship to possible objects of emotional attachment (Malcolm yelling loudly to gain cessation of maternal chastisement). The interpenetrative unity of these two processes is the relative freedom and universality of human production, which conditions and is conditioned by the mutual recognition of human individuals. And this is the immediate basis of self-conscious activity, i.e., of practical activity aimed at the realization of rationally and responsibly chosen ends.*

---

* It is evident that our conception of human nature is in essential conformity with Marx's methodological postulate that our reasoning must begin with "practical, human-sensuous activity," and that the truth of our reasoning must be proved in practice. It also includes the idea that human beings are distinctively universal (or universalizing) with respect to the natural objects of their life activity, and that they are freely creative rather than instinct-bound with respect to the instrumental forms of that activity. But the Marxist conception of "species-being" is primarily concerned with conscious life activity (material production) rather than with self-consciousness (emotionally based processes of mutual human recognition). It also emphasizes what happens *between* people rather than what goes on *within* them. The alienation of conscious life activity in bourgeois society is, however, reflected in the falsification of individual self-consciousness, a falsification which is intrasubjectively mediated by the unconscious distortion of conscious functioning. Hence the relevance of psychoanalysis to the Marxist problem of false consciousness and to the analysis of the problematic of racist oppression.

Alienated Conscious Activity

When we think of Malcolm's life, we recognize that his potential for self-conscious activity developed within a manifold of alienated and alienating social relationships: in bourgeois society, the sensuous energies of individuals constitute, not an immanent power of acting self-consciously, but an external pressure which falsifies conscious activity. This externalization of sensuous energies has two interrelated forms: the alienation of work-energy through exchange, and of emotional energy through repression. More concretely, the alienated objectification process consists of the buying and selling of labor-power; the use of labor-power in the production process, at greater length and/or with greater intensity than is required for its reproduction; and, therefore, the creation of products possessing a surplus value, a value that accrues not to its creator but to the buyer of its creator's labor-power. This accumulated value—capital—then serves to begin the cycle anew. It becomes the active subject of the objectification process: "The objective conditions essential to the realization of labour are *alienated* from the worker and become manifest as *fetishes* endowed with a will and soul of their own. *Commodities*, in short, appear as the purchasers of *persons*. . . . Hence the rule of the capitalist over the worker is the rule of things over man, of dead labour over the living, of the product over the producer."[1] Or again: "At the level of material production, of the life-process in the realm of the social . . . we find the same situation that we find in religion at the ideological level, namely the inversion of subject into object and *vice versa*."[2]

The subjectification of the object determines the objectification of the subject, creates a world in which there are "material relations between persons and social relations between things." In our own view, however, the fetishism of commodities determines and is in turn determined by the intrapersonal as well as the interpersonal materialization of the individual—by the reification of character. The fetishized commodity *par excellence* is money, "the visible god-head, the transformation of all human and natural qualities into their opposites, the general confusion and inversion of things . . . the universal whore, the universal pander between men and peoples"[3]— which is to say, the mutual recognition of human individuals is mediated by exchange relations, with the consequence that the money-god is internalized. The individual's conscience is monetized, and his monetized conscience enforces the repression by and hence separation from the self of any emotional tendencies which are not in its service. The character structure of the individual in bourgeois society becomes a foundation for self-alienation, for a divided self who judges the rationality and responsibility of his actions against the standard of his alienated reality, and who therefore acts so as to reproduce that reality.

In sum: *the alienation of sensuous energies, when mediated by the commodity-character of bourgeois social production, results in the systematic falsification of conscious activity.*

The commodity-character of bourgeois social production appeared most clearly when we were analyzing the hustling society. But on the whole, we have not attempted to work out in detail the more technical and abstract political-economic and psycho-economic concepts that connect these generalities to the problematic of racist oppression. A more complete logical exposition would involve an analysis of the production, circulation, and realization of the value of commodities; the relationship between the production of surplus value and the accumulation of capital; and the development of class structure and class conflict on the basis of capitalist production. At the same time we would have to show how variations in the quantity and quality of relative deprivation during the production process as a whole create class differentials in character structure and emotional conflict. But for our purposes it is sufficient to observe, as we did when analyzing the "great migration," that the private ownership and control of socially productive forces, when mediated by the participation of population aggregates in production and exchange, results in a class-differentiated distribution and consumption of the social product. The objective interests of the resultant classes are determined within the economic sphere by the direct relations of individuals to productive forces. Here we speak of the opposing interests of capital and wage-labor and of the purely objective distinctions within these classes (merchant, industrial, and financial capital; competitive vs. monopoly capital; unionized vs. nonunionized proletariat, etc.). When socially developed, these economic determinations emerge as the opposing interests of the American bourgeoisie, petite bourgeoisie (whether traditional individualist or modern corporatist), and proletariat, with the latter differentiated into a middle class and a lower class or mass.

Although we may take the existence of these class formations as the objective limit of the historical situation with which we have been and are concerned, we cannot adopt the view that class relations are stable and unchanging. We have seen the American economy developing into an increasingly monopolized capitalism with extensive imperialist interests, and we have analyzed the consequences of this development for the class-racial struggle. Thus in our investigation of the UNIA and the KKK we witnessed the simultaneous emergence of an urbanized black proletariat and partial dissolution of the traditional white petite bourgeoisie. We posited that the advance from rural peonage and forced labor to urban wage-labor was challenging rather than traumatizing, while the retreat from an established petit-bourgeois position into the working class was traumatizing rather than challenging. On this basis we were able to give a partial explanation of the progressive tendency of the UNIA and the regressive tendency of the KKK. When we came to the Depression, we saw that the increased relative deprivation of the black proletariat produced tendencies toward radical social change, escapist religious solutions to situational problems, and, through state intervention, the institution of welfare slavery. By contrast, World War II and the warfare state brought into existence a substantial Negro middle class and a more sharply differentiated black mass or underclass—the black industrial reserve army and *lumpen-proletariat*. The middle class was, of course, largely comprised of wage-laborers. Moreover, both classes were the victims of ghettoization (racial segregation or internal colonialization). Nonetheless, the middle class had interests in opposition to those of the masses. It could gain substantial advantages from integration into white society, while the masses could gain such advantages only through the radical transformation of the existing order. Hence the remainder of our inquiry turned upon the class struggle within the black community, a struggle bounded by the interest of all black people in liberation from white racist oppression.

So much, then, for the transformation of the generalized concept of falsified conscious activity into objective class-racial terms. We come now to the subjective terms of the problematic of racist oppression. Just as character is the subjective mediation of the commodity, so the *emotional group* or mass is the subjective mediation of class. An emotional group is the rationalized product of unconscious emotional forces developed through an hypnotically induced, double-valenced process: an intragroup dynamic involving the projection onto a leader and/or leading idea of repressed, aim-inhibited sexual energy, and its subsequent reintrojection by the group members; and an intergroup dynamic involving a similar projection of repressed aggressive energy, which is then displaced at the leader's suggestion or command onto another group. The in-group is thus narcissistically aggrandized while the out-group is contemptuously devalued. The in-group's sadistic tendencies are legitimated while the out-group is forced into a corresponding masochistic posture. Through these dynamics a collective emotional structure results which parallels the alienated individual whom psychoanalysis takes as its norm. The in-group becomes to the out-group as ego (the potentially conscious self) is to id (the repressed or alienated self), while the group membership is to its leader as receptive and largely passive ego to an active and activating super-ego.

The intergroup relationship is, then, an externalization of the divided self. But the divided self results from the internalization of primal family relations, which are themselves the product of the family's social situation. The group relationship is therefore a re-externalization of these relations, or, rather, it is their split and duplicated re-creation. In the primal family, each member is ambivalently experienced. The child feels himself, his siblings, and his parents to be both good and bad, loving and hating. The group relationship alleviates the anxiety attendant upon such ambivalence by splitting it: the group to which the individual belongs becomes a good, loving family presided over by a benevolent parental authority; the other group becomes a bad, threatening horde dominated by a malevolent parental power.* This familial dimension of the group relationship can ultimately be expanded until it replicates the objectively alienated world, but in a subjectively distorted fashion—as, for example, in any theodical transfiguration of historical reality. Group-emotion is the mechanism through which an "inverted world" produces an "inverted world consciousness."[4]

The emotional content of the group process, as just specified, takes on three social forms. First, it may occur in the form of a generalized, nonspecific social mentality. This, for example, is what Malcolm termed the American racist "atmosphere." It is generalized racial prejudice, racist false consciousness as it is experienced in everyday life. Second, there is institutionalized group-emotion, which functions as the more or less manifest content of various social structures (e.g., the white racism of American schools, courts, welfare systems, and prisons). This is situationally adapted or rou-

* When we considered the group-emotional aspect of Malcolm's conversion to Islam, we saw that Muhammad fell heir to the Garveyite Earl Little, and white people were recast in the image of the Christian Earl Little. As this example suggests, the out-group roles do not have to be as clearly defined as the in-group roles.

tinized charismatic group-emotion. Finally, there is situationally transcendent or directly charismatic group-emotion, which is the subjective aspect of regressive political and social movements such as the KKK. But in every form, the group-emotional process falsifies consciousness and, in so doing, precludes the mutual recognition of human individuals.

There are a variety of historical embodiments of group-emotion, but we have been concerned only with white racism. The white racist idea is the illusion of a natural or inherent superiority of white over black, which legitimates and rationalizes the objective domination of one race over the other. In this relationship of objective-subjective domination, the black race serves as a mirror in which white people see reflected their own unconscious repressed or alienated selves. They see themselves—or, rather, a distorted image of their childhood selves—but they think they are seeing black people: hence they do not recognize black people as adult, human individuals. Instead, they see black people as children who cannot be trusted with adult responsibilities and human rights and who therefore must live their lives under paternal domination. The attitude and actions of the white paternalist subsequently depend upon whether the black person is seen in the image of a good or bad child. The good child is rewarded and the bad child is punished. But the images of the good and bad child are themselves superimposed upon a more primitive phantasy of infantile bestiality, which is defended against by treating black people as things rather than persons. (Here we have the emotional aspect of that economic relationship in which not the labor-power but the persons of black people function as commodities, i.e., slavery or welfare-slavery.) Once the white race has emptied and purified itself of its repressed images and impulses, it appears to itself as the incarnation of both right and reason, as civilized humanity.

One side of the racist emotional relationship is the white view of self and other. The second side is the black view of the same. Because this is a relationship of domination, the black side is a reflection, in fact a negative image, of the white. The black person is what the white person is not. He is the alienated white self, the stereotypical Other of the white individual. He must grant human recognition to an individual who will not grant him human recognition; he is, therefore, individually invisible to his racial opposite. In part his invisibility results directly from white power: historically, white people in this country have had the power to demand that black people act as if they were lacking in adult, human individuality. An outward compliance with white stereotypical expectations has been a necessity for most black people most of the time. But even as black people have increasingly acted in violation of these expectations, the meaning of their actions has often been reduced to the given stereotypes. An attitude of civility and respect for white individuals has been reduced to the Good Negro stereotype, while an attitude of defiant self-assertion has been reduced to the Bad Nigger stereotype. Thus black people, as human individuals, have been neither seen nor heard by white people. White people are deaf, hence black people are dumb; white people are blind, hence black people cannot be seen. Yet black and white continue to interact within objectively determined and stereotypically defined limits. It follows that they are merely acting out their assigned roles in a stereotypical dumb-show, or racial pantomime.

If the stereotypical dumb-show were strictly an interracial relationship, if black people could simply and completely drop their masks when white people were not present, then our analysis of the racist emotional relationship would end at this point. And at this point it must be stressed that the internalization of white racist stereotypes is individually variable and never complete. Although our inquiry has not permitted us to judge the matter, we might hypothesize that internalization is inversely proportional to the solidarity and autonomy of the black individual's community and family: the more the individual, especially as he or she is growing up, is sheltered from the white world, the less that individual will tend to internalize white racist stereotypes. Malcolm, whose family was fragmented and whose community was the hustling society, was therefore particularly vulnerable to the hypnotic power of these images. Moreover, we have seen that even within the hustling society black people are able to grant human recognition to each other and, by so doing, manage to preserve their human individuality. The Bad Nigger is also a rebellious human being. Similarly, we have seen that the Good Negro (e.g., of the civil rights movement) is also a morally responsible individual. Were this not so, there would have been no potential for racial liberation within the existing American situation.

Our analysis of Malcolm's life history, however, as well as his analysis of the black experience, leads us to conclude that black people have tended to identify with their oppressors, and that the psychological work of black liberation has been to overcome this tendency.[5] The tendency results from the fact that to be black in white racist America is to be angry—if not all of the time, at least most of the time. But as long as the white man has the power to oppress black people, the direct expression of that anger is virtually suicidal. Black rage must therefore be suppressed or repressed. In Malcolm's case, the needed self-control resulted from the internalization of the Swerlins as agents of moral self-consciousness. More generally, we may surmise that the character-structure of black children will be partially formed in the oppressor's image. White power defines reality (is the reality principle); white authority fuses with black parental authority in the formation of conscience; and the desire for black self-affirmation is identified with the unconscious repressed. This reaction is reinforced when the parents have previously identified themselves with their oppressor. Even when such an identification is superficial, however, public authority is a principal heir to parental authority. It is therefore difficult for the black individual to free himself entirely from the idea that white authority is both rational and right. Consequently, rebellion and moral responsibility tend to be alienated from each other. The rebellious individual tends to define himself by his irresponsibility to (white) authority; the responsible individual tends to define himself by his obedience to (lawful, but still white) authority. And each individual is trapped in the vicious circle of self-destructive aggression. The responsible individual feels guilty for his rebellious impulses against white authority. The rebellious individual acts out his hostility in a criminal—ultimately, paranoid nihilistic—fashion. The conceptual (and in Malcolm's life, the historical) link between these two conditions is criminality from a sense of guilt, which involves a regression from a more to a less integrated level of emotional functioning. Finally, when neither obedience to white authority nor rebellion against it any longer provides a sufficient basis for self-identification, when the inherent irrationality of stereotypical identity is driven to its limit, the self is reduced to bestial rage (Malcolm in prison) or literal insanity (Louise Little). Nearly total dehumanization is the last act in the stereotypical dumb-show.

Having specified the objective and subjective aspects of the problematic of racist oppression separately, we come now to their interpenetration and mutual determination. Stated most comprehensively: *in all class-divided societies, mass motives serve ruling-class interests.* Through identification with the oppressor, mass consciousness is falsified, so that the oppressed population takes as its own the interests of its oppressor. From the standpoint of its objective interests, its actions are therefore self-defeating, a re-creation of the power of its enemy. Justice, as Thrasymachus argues in the *Republic*, is the interest of the stronger.

In bourgeois societies, the class-group relationship develops from the commodity-character of social production and serves to perpetu-ate political domination by the bourgeois ruling class. Each individ-ual in such a society is the personification of the commodity re-lationship. He must measure his human value by his success or failure, relative to other individuals, in the exchange process. At the limit, his interest and the interest of any other individual are mutu-ally exclusive. But any nation is a unity of such self-interested indi-viduals. The sum total of individual interests is, then, the national interest, just as the fetishism of commodities and reification of char-acter constitute the generalized form of bourgeois national charac-ter. It is through the mediation of the group-emotional process that national unity in this sense is transformed into the illusion that all members of the nation are equally its beneficiaries—that there is an identity of interest between wage-labor and capital or between black and white.

The group-emotional identification of the national masses with the interests of the ruling class is national identity—in our case, the American dream. But the American dream is also an American nightmare. The nation is divided into a white mass identified with its oppressor (as above) and a black mass identified by white people as an intranational, alien power. Just as national identity falsifies working-class consciousness by unifying each individual's interest with the class interest of the bourgeoisie, so the racist pantomime serves to perpetuate bourgeois rule by dividing the working class against itself. Racial divisions are superimposed upon class lines, obscuring the latter and thereby limiting the possibilities for pro-letarian class struggle. *It follows from this racist falsification of class consciousness that class struggle must take form as a move-ment toward racial liberation.*

The movement toward racial liberation has in turn a more or less national character; that is, it reflects the existing situation of inter-nal colonialism. Historically, the racist division of American society has been so thoroughgoing that black people have constituted a vir-tual nation within a nation—an economically exploited nation which serves as a source of cheap and abundant labor for the larger capitalist society. And during the twentieth century, black people have been increasingly ghettoized, territorially separated or segregated from white people: hence the appeal of black nationalism. But as we know, not all members of the black nation are equally exploited. In addition to those black people who directly benefit from internal colonialism (e.g., owners of black business enterprises, whether legal or illegal, which depend upon ghetto conditions for protection from white competition) and the small black bourgeoisie (whether ghetto-based or integrated into the white bourgeoisie), there is the black middle class (petite-bourgeoisie and upper-echelon proletariat) and the black masses (lower-level proletariat, industrial reserve army, *lumpen-proletariat*). Accordingly, where the possibilities for working-class unity are limited by racial divisions, the possibilities for racial unity are limited by class divisions. Moreover, members of the middle class, in their quest for respectability, tend to identify with the white oppressor through the internalization of the Good Negro stereotype. Conversely, members of the masses, in their rejection of a respectability they cannot hope to attain, tend to identify with the white oppressor through the internalization of the Bad Nigger stereotype. Consequently, the masses and the middle class are objectively and subjectively, economically and emotionally, alienated from each other.

Finally, while black people have been territorially separated from white people, black ghettoes are also territorially separated from each other. And even when the populations of these enclaves are combined, they constitute only a minority of the American population. It follows that national liberation in the literal sense is precluded. This, indeed, is the limiting condition and fateful ambiguity of the Afro-American situation. The middle class or, rather, its political leaders recognize that they cannot liberate themselves from American society nor, by the action of black people alone, transform it. They are, moreover, relatively advantaged within the black community and can gain further advantage through integration. They therefore take their particular class-racial interest as representing the general interest of black people, and limit the choice of political means to those which appear to be rational and responsible in the light of their integrationist ends. They play the political game by the rules, in the hope that the rules will be extended to cover interracial relations. Playing the game by the rules is, however, self-defeating even from a middle-class standpoint. (As Malcolm argued, power retreats only in the face of power.) It is doubly self-defeating from a mass standpoint, for when the masses accept the identification of their interests with those of the middle class they are surrendering the possibility of defining the struggle in revolutionary terms. But only a revolutionary struggle contains the possibility of their liberation.

Having represented both the general (commodity-character) and racially particular (class-group) forms of alienated or falsified conscious activity in American society we come now—and only now— to its concrete form, the lives of the individuals who comprise the society. In other words, if our work had been a logical exposition rather than a phenomenological investigation of Malcolm X and the Black Revolution, we would have come to his individual experience only after its general and particular presuppositions had been established. But it would not be simply *his* experience that we would be considering; rather, we would be seeing him as a typical black victim of American democracy, one of the isolated individuals who, just because they are isolated, are powerless to control their collective destiny. And when we reached the limit of his regressive development, we would see revealed the logical consequence of the commodity-character of American life, namely, the hustling society's war of all against all, the paranoid nihilism of its articulated code, and the bestial rage of its defeated warriors.

In sum: the logic of American democracy is a vicious circle of falsified conscious activity, which has as both its premise and its conclusion the alienation of the human potential for a rational and responsible collective choice of action.

Revolutionary Activity

At this point we have reproduced the anthropological conception of a potential for self-conscious activity and the psycho-economic conception of the alienated development of this potential. Phenomenologically, the anthropological notion was derived through the psycho-economic analysis of a particular manifold of historical events—a manifold rendered practically and theoretically problematical by our interest in human liberation. Logically, the anthropological notion functions as a premise from which first our understanding of the existing situation and then the project of racial and human liberation are to be derived. But even in logical exposition the potential for self-conscious activity is not to be viewed as existing apart from the historical process of its realization. It is, rather, historically immanent, in a double sense. On the one hand, every particular form of social production is the development of this potential into process, into actual human activity. On the other, the birth of each new generation of human individuals is a renewal of the potential *qua* potential. Thus each generation develops anew the human potential for self-conscious activity, but does so within its given historical circumstances.

The same point may be approached from a different direction. As far as we have considered it, the logic of American democracy is a regressive development of the potential for rationally and responsibly chosen collective activity.* It is not the destruction of that potential. If it were, then there would have been no Black Revolution. Conversely, if life activity were not alienated and conscious activity were not falsified within the existing situation, then there would have been no need to transform it. The American Creed or dream would be reality, not illusion, and a Black Revolution would not have been necessary. In other words, because an alienated reality is a negative or inverted development of a potential, it is inherently (potentially) problematical. It becomes actually problematical when the system is disrupted: when the latent contradictions of the system become manifest, it also becomes possible to recognize that the contradictions must be resolved, that the system must be transformed. A crisis in the expanded reproduction and accumulation of capital is in this sense an advance over the production of capital *per cis*, just as a regression into neurosis (or, e.g., Malcolm's regression into paranoid nihilism) is an advance over an on-going pathology of character. But this is not to say, the worse the better—that neurosis or psychosis is a higher form of sanity, that economic chaos is a higher form of social order. These are romantic illusions, simple mirror-images of an alienated reality, idealizations of the very conditions which must be overcome. It is also illusory to think that the mere manifestation of a contradiction is a sufficient condition for its progressive resolution. Rather, if a manifest social contradiction is to be progressively resolved, then such a resolution must be objectively possible; the objective possibility must be subjectively recognized; and the subjective recognition of the objective possibility must result in actual, revolutionary activity.

---

* Bourgeois society is neither the best nor the worst of all possible worlds. With respect to the relative freedom and universality of human production—of freedom from natural necessity—capitalism marks a great advance over prior economic forms. Sim-

Let us examine the matter more concretely. Generally, we may agree with Marx: "At a certain stage of development, the material productive forces of society come into conflict with the existing relations of production. . . . From forms of development of the productive forces these relations turn into their fetters. Then begins the era of social revolution."[6] But we add to this conception the recognition that social production is psycho-political as well as political-economic. Hence we are initially concerned with the conflict between the commodity-character of bourgeois production relations and the sensuous energies which are developed in this alienated form. This conflict derives from the fact that alienation is *eo ipso* a resistance to the full expression or utilization of sensuous energies. Consequently, if the production of these energies cannot be reduced or if the indirect ways of releasing them are becoming exhausted, they will constitute an increasing pressure upon the structure of the system. If the pressure is sufficient, the fetishism of commodities and the reification of character will be at least partially undermined. Exchange relations ("material relations between persons and social relations between things") will become more manifestly antagonistic, and this objective antagonism will be subjectively reflected in a return of hitherto repressed emotional forces. The implicit irrationality of the system thus becomes explicit, and this explicit irrationality provides grounds for reconsidering the nature of rational and responsible political action.

More specifically, the objective contradiction between forces and relations of production is signified by periodic crises during which the progress of capital accumulation becomes a regress—by the "industrial earthquakes, in which the trading world can only maintain itself by sacrificing a part of wealth, of products and even of productive forces to the gods of the nether world."[7] Such crises do not by themselves bring capitalism to an end, but they weaken and divide the bourgeois ruling class; they demonstrate that the existing system is not satisfying human needs which it has become possible to satisfy; and they increase the relative deprivation of the proletariat. The working class finds that its level of well-being has declined relative to its own past condition, its expectations concerning the future, the well-being of the bourgeoisie in particular, and the wealth

---

ilarly, bourgeois society universalizes in principle the mutual recognition of free human individuals. But these universalizing tendencies have the particular character of the antagonistic forces already depicted.

of society in general. Consequently, it becomes possible for the proletariat to recognize that its class interests can be realized through—
and only through—the revolutionary transformation of the existing
situation.

During the 1950s and 1960s the American economy was not in a
critical condition. The revolutionary interests of the proletariat
were therefore held in abeyance: they continued to exist as such—as
given in the relationship of the proletariat to the forces of social production—but they were not activated in and as class struggle. Even
without taking into account the problem of white racism within the
working class, the basis for a unified black-white revolutionary
movement was lacking. By contrast, the relative deprivation of the
black masses was increasing in all the above-mentioned respects
and with respect to the black middle class as well. The middle class,
for its part, was relatively prosperous, but the violent white-racist
response to its reformist activities increased its political deprivation. Accordingly, the possibility existed for the black masses and
middle class to recognize their mutual interest in ending internal
colonial domination. Even a unified racial movement, however,
would not have been powerful enough to seize control of the state
and the forces of social production. Intranationally considered, a
temporary immobilization of the system sufficient to force through
a measure of racial reform was the most that could be anticipated.
But again, when viewed from an international perspective, the situation appeared in a different light. The black nation within the
United States could then be seen as sharing a common revolutionary interest with the emerging nations of the Third World. Or at
least with the Third World masses; for national liberation does not
necessarily involve either social revolution or freedom from economic dependency upon the former colonial powers. The political
prospects for the "wretched of the earth" in these nations or in the
United States were therefore limited by the extent of native bourgeois and neocolonial domination.

It follows that the critical black-mass or Afro-American revolutionary task was to strengthen as much as possible the existing
tendencies toward racial militancy and political radicalism. This
necessitated not only striving for intranational and international racial solidarity but also carrying forward the class struggle within the
black nation and the Third World nations. These latter two aspects
of the task have, however, opposing aims. The struggle for racial solidarity obscures class lines within the racial community and thereby tends to preserve the privileged position of the "native" ruling

class, even if it is successful in combatting racist domination *per cis*. Class struggle aims at the end of bourgeois domination, whatever its color, and thereby tends to dissolve racial solidarity. The movement toward racial liberation is accordingly characterized by the interplay of these opposing tendencies.

Thus far we have considered the inherent contradictions of bourgeois social production in general and the objective side of the revolutionary process in particular without criticizing the classical Marxist position that class-conscious activity is immanent in or is a direct reflex of changing objective conditions. The idea of increased relative deprivation as a motive for revolutionary action, although apparently a subjective concept, actually expresses the direct relationship between objective forces and conscious activity. Stated negatively: it does not express the problematical nature of the subjective connection between objective forces and conscious activity. With respect to the preceding exposition, this problematical aspect of the revolutionary process commands our interest on three interrelated grounds: the resistance of the American working class to recognizing its objective interests, even when its relative deprivation has increased as a result of a crisis in capitalist production (as during the Depression of the 1930s); the white racism of the working class, which divides it against itself and thereby precludes united action against the common class enemy; and the Good Negro and Bad Nigger division of the black working class, which precludes united action against the common racial enemy. Each of these group-emotional relationships obscures the objective realities of the existing situation and falsifies—irrationalizes—the conscious activity of the working class. We must therefore turn our attention to the subjective side of the revolutionary process, i.e., to the dissolution of group-emotional relationships.

In the course of our work we have not considered the dissolution of group-emotional relationships *per cis*. It is not difficult, however, to enumerate the abstract conditions of the process. A group-emotional relationship, be it diffuse, institutionalized, or charismatic, tends to dissolve if there is a substantial change in the strength or balance of sexual-aggressive forces expressed in the relationship; if the defenses against these emotional forces are weakened or their psycho-dynamic mediation becomes inadequate; and/or if there is increased pressure (either from inside or outside the group) upon the structure of the externalized divided self and the reduplicated primal family. Which is to say, we may understand changes in group relationships in psycho-economic, dynamic, or structural terms.

These categories can then be used in analyzing each participant in the group-emotional process: a group leader in relationship to his followers, the out-group, and himself; the group members in relation to the leader, the out-group, other group-members, and themselves; members of the out-group in relation to the in-group, their own leaders, other out-group members, and themselves.

When psychological categories are stated in this abstract fashion, they apply everywhere and nowhere. Group-emotional tendencies are operative in all forms of collective life, but collective life can never be comprehended in purely group-emotional terms. Likewise, all social change involves the dissolution of certain of the existing group-emotional relationships, but no social change involves merely the dissolution of these relationships. Moreover, in the night of psychological abstraction, one cannot clearly see the difference between the beginning and the end of a group-emotional relationship—between the rationalization and the rational realization of emotional tendencies. Nonetheless, we may briefly characterize the principal transformation in group-emotional relations with which we have been concerned.

The generative emotional act of the Black Revolution was the externalization and redirection of aggression—the recognition of the common, white-racist enemy. Consequently, racial self-identification could replace identification with the oppressor, and the self-productive use of aggression could replace the vicious circle of self-destructive aggression. At the same time and through the same emotional processes, the foundation of the Good Negro/Bad Nigger antinomy was partially undermined. The Black Militant emerged as the productive fusion of these hitherto alienated emotional tendencies, i.e., as an individual-collective identity grounded in racial pride and mutual responsibility rather than in shame and guilt. As black militancy increased, white people found it proportionately more difficult to maintain the stereotypical images of their black opposites. This is not to say that the images dissolved altogether; but the emergence of the Black Militant signifies that the stereotypical dumbshow was beginning to lose its hypnotic power.

We may now take the objective and subjective dimensions of the revolutionary process as they interact with each other. Periodic crises, or their equivalents for particular collectivities, increase relative deprivation and, by so doing, free emotional energies which have hitherto been frozen into routinized group-emotional structures. New forms of collective activity therefore become possible. These new forms of activity are not necessarily premised upon the recognition of a realizable class, or class-racial, interest; rather, a significant increase in relative deprivation amounts to a traumatic experience for the individuals concerned. Traumatic experience weakens the individual's capacity for the critical analysis of his existing situation, and he becomes more vulnerable to the appeals of charismatic group-emotion, more inclined to accept magical solutions to real problems.

Thus in the first instance, crises or their equivalents tend more toward emotional regression than progression. The isolated mass-individual experiences collective failure as his personal responsibility. He finds himself unable to provide for his own or his family's needs, feels the shame of his impotence, anger at the members of his family whose neediness mirrors his impotence, guilt because he is angry at the ones he loves. (We think, for example, of Louise Little's shame and ultimate descent into madness when she was unable to provide adequately for her family.) But this regressive tendency is simultaneously a potential for progressive development; the tightening of the vicious circle of self-destructive aggression is also a condition for breaking the circle altogether. The intensification of aggression in the traumatic situation constitutes a pressure upon the character-structure of the oppressed individual, hence also a potential for directing the aggression against external objects. At the same time crises help to make manifest the objective divisions of interest which have been previously concealed within the illusion of a national identity of interest. The oppressed individual therefore begins to see himself as oppressed and, by so doing, begins to free himself from his moralized identification with his oppressor. Accordingly, the hostility he has been directing against himself, his family, and his friends can be redirected against his enemies: instead of hating his friends and loving his enemies, he loves his friends and hates his enemies. He is then able to use his aggression self-productively, i.e., as an emotional mediation of his political-economic interests.

We see, then, that objectively revolutionary conditions contain the potential for both progressive and regressive development; as we have previously argued, a realizable class or class-racial interest is a necessary but not a sufficient condition for situationally rational political action. Moreover, given this double potentiality, it is evident that all actual political movements will be fusions of progressive and regressive, organizationally rational and charismatic group-emotional tendencies. Only a political movement expressing a realizable objective interest, however, escapes the necessity of relying predominantly upon charismatic group-emotion. Finally, in movements where organizational rationality is the limiting tendency, charismatic group-emotion plays a progressive role. It mobilizes movement members against the reality principle of the existing order and enables them to challenge the accepted canons of rational and responsible action without falling into paralyzing doubt and emotional confusion. Thus, for example, the theodical dimension of the Nation of Islam, although ultimately tending toward situational transcendence rather than situational transformation, nonetheless helped isolated individual members of the black masses to "wake up, clean up, and stand up." It was therefore rational for Malcolm to accept Muhammad's truth. If we view the matter prospectively (in the light of Malcolm's eventual need to free himself from Muhammad's hypnotic domination) rather than retrospectively (in the light of his former nihilist position), then the limits of this relative rationality become apparent. But within these specified limits, we may say that *in progressive movements, mass motives (both rational and charismatic) serve mass interests.*

Regarding the Black Revolution, we have seen that the reformist interest of the black middle class, when combined with the revolutionary interest of the masses, constituted a relatively realizable interest in racial liberation or decolonization. This racial interest of course reflects the existence of the common, white-racist enemy, from which it follows that the recognition of the racial interest was directly bound up with the recognition of the common enemy. But the recognition of the common enemy both presupposes and facilitates the externalization of previously internalized aggressive tendencies. Thus the release of pent-up hostilities in the spontaneous rebellions of the early 1960s was at the same time a spontaneous act of racial self-recognition.

Spontaneous violence is not yet self-conscious, revolutionary activity, however. In it the recognition of class-racial interests is obscured by a proclivity to equate political action with paranoid nihilism—in our case, militancy with the Bad Nigger stereotype. The theory and practice of the Nation of Islam was a partial cure for this particular ghetto pathology, but the efficacy of the remedy was limited by the Prophet's separatism and religious transcendentalism. Islamic militancy was undermined by political inactivity. Conversely, the political activity of the civil rights movement was lacking in militancy. Insofar as its leaders were restricting themselves to legal and/or nonviolent political means, they were continuing to work within the limits of the Good Negro stereotype. As time passed, however, frustration at the Nation's militancy without action grew, along with an intense rage among those Movement members who were compelled to act without militancy. The result was a politically activated or radicalized black militancy, the self-consciousness of the Black Revolution.

The substantive elements of black revolutionary consciousness were Afro-American Unity, Black Power, and Black Pride. More than any other individual, Malcolm was responsible for the development of these interrelated concepts. In Robert Allen's words:

> He sought to establish an intellectual framework for revolutionary black nationalism by weaving into an integrated whole a series of disjointed ideas. He pointed up the necessity for psychological liberation and black pride. He demanded black control of black organizations and communities, and he was an advocate of self-defense for those communities. Malcolm was an unrelenting opponent of the white, capitalist power structure and its political vehicles, the Democratic and Republican parties. He identified this power structure, rather than the white population as a whole, as the primary agent of black oppression. To counter this power structure he called for independent black political action. Finally, Malcolm identified the condition of black people in the United States as domestic colonialism, explicitly calling for an aggressive internationalism among all colonial peoples if any of them are to be truly liberated.[8]

Although Malcolm laid the theoretical foundations for the Black Revolution, his work was not simply individual. Rather, his formulations must be understood as theoretical reflections of a collective racial-revolutionary practice. Correspondingly, the disintegration of this theoretical unity reflects the ultimate fragmentation of the revolutionary movement. The interests of the black masses remained unrealized, while the situational rationality of the liberation movement was found to reside in its successful use of revolutionary means to attain reformist ends. But precisely the attainment of these ends brings into focus the class structure of the black community and thereby prepares the way for black mass struggle which is self-consciously proletarian. Here again, however, we reach the historical limit of our inquiry.

In sum, the Black Revolution was a progressive movement through which the contradiction between political radicalism and racial militancy was pushed to its limit, i.e., to the point where it becomes clear that even liberation from specifically racist oppression cannot liberate the mass of black people from bourgeois domination. We can also understand on this basis a principal aspect of Malcolm's contribution to the revolutionary movement. He *represented* the interests of the black masses. In the first part of our inquiry (Chapters II–V) and in our logical exposition of the vicious circle of racist oppression he appeared simply as a *typical*, isolated, individual victim of democracy. But his isolation was overcome through participation in organized collective activity, and when he emerged as a leader of the liberation movement, his individual actions took on collective significance. Because he represented the mass interest within the movement, he was led to articulate a position of racial militancy and political radicalism. And given the class-divided character of the movement, this articulation took the form of a polemical confrontation between Malcolm and middle-class black leaders—a confrontation which, however, functioned as a two-pronged attack upon white racist domination.

Although Malcolm was the seventh son of his Garveyite father, neither his revolutionary vocation nor his heroic destiny were determined in advance, just as neither the fact of white racist oppression nor the potential of black people for self-conscious activity had as its inevitable consequence the Black Revolution. Rather, in both the individual and collective instances the potential was developed into actual revolutionary activity through a process of self-liberation from the group-emotional falsification of racial consciousness. For Malcolm this process had three critical moments. First was the confrontation with the English teacher, Ostrowski, which shattered the re-formed character structure of his Good Negro identity. This incident led in time to his half-conscious choice of the life of a hustler, a Bad Nigger. It therefore signifies the logic of American democracy, a vicious circle having as its starting point identification with the white racist oppressor, as its devolution criminality from a sense of guilt, and as its end point—failing literal self-destruction—more or less rationalized forms of paranoid nihilism. Second was Malcolm's conscious decision to accept Muhammad's truth, the conversion experience through which he escaped from the vicious circle and from his Bad Nigger identity. Here was a racial-religious solution to the problem of individual nihilism. Finally, there was Malcolm's reluctant decision to leave the Nation of Islam and found his own religious and political organization. This choice involved accepting the harsh imperative of a revolutionary struggle based upon practical human activity rather than upon divine guarantees of inevitable victory. It was mediated by his relationship to Alex Haley, which provided him with a mirror in which he could see the meaning of his life history.

We interpreted Malcolm's relationship with Haley as having certain features in common with psychoanalytic therapy. Needless to say, we did not interpret it as being a literally psychoanalytic experience. But psychoanalysis as a therapeutic process is based upon principles of more general applicability. Thus each of the three choice points in Malcolm's life involved a return of previously repressed emotional forces; a resistance to the recognition that the balance of intrapsychic forces was changing; a central "interpretation" of the situation as it was developing; the acceptance of that interpretation, or the gaining of insight; and a process of testing the meaning and implications of this new self-understanding. From this perspective, each of these choice points may be signified by the major interpretation: "a lawyer—that's no realistic goal for a nigger"; "the white man is the devil"; "I had believed in Mr. Muhammad more than he believed in himself." These are not conventional psychoanalytic interpretations; but they were productive of insight, and they did give direction to processes of internal transformation. On the other hand, they were not all equally productive of insight: the movement from first choice to last was toward increased self-understanding—toward a re-formation of character structure such that both conscience and consciousness could be joined in self-conscious activity.

Taken as a whole, we may represent the development of Malcolm's self-consciousness as the process through which he learned to think for himself, to recognize that his sincerity was his credentials, and to accept the responsibilities of revolutionary leadership. This process, which Malcolm's autobiography so clearly reveals, is a moving and dramatic affirmation of the human spirit. But its significance is neither simply individual nor abstractly universal. As Malcolm's speeches and the subsequent role played by *The Autobiography of Malcolm X* indicate, his experience became a medium for the reproduction of that experience in others. He became a mirror in which black people saw reflected their pain and rage, and he provided interpretations of that pain and rage which led to both insight and to action. His interpretation of the black American experience provided insight into the souls of black folk for black folk themselves and, by so doing, led toward organized black revolutionary action.

In sum, Malcolm both represented the interests and mobilized the emotional resources of the black masses and black people in general.

These two leadership functions can be simultaneously expressed in the ethical imperative of revolutionary action, "freedom by any means necessary." This is the position that the *New York Times* saw as a "ruthless and fanatical belief in violence." Yet three hundred years earlier John Locke had developed a similar ethic of revolutionary responsibility. In the second *Treatise of Government* he asks, with characteristic irony:

> Who would not think it an admirable peace between the Mighty and the Mean, when the Lamb, without resistance, yielded his Throat to be torn by the imperious Wolf? *Polyphemus's* Den gives us a perfect Pattern of such a Peace, and such a Government, where in Ulysses and his Companions had nothing to do, but quietly suffer themselves to be devoured. And no doubt *Ulysses*, who was a prudent Man, preach'd up *Passive Obedience*, and exhorted them to a quiet Submission, by representing to them of what concernment Peace was to Mankind; and by shewing the inconveniences might happen, if they should offer to resist *Polyphemus*, who had now the power over them? [9]

From the perspective of the oppressed individual, civil society is Polyphemus's cave. If such an individual is met with the argument that revolutionary action is unethical because it proceeds from the principle that the end justifies the means, he is entitled to respond that it is the beginning along with the end which not only justifies but also determines the means. He is also entitled to make good his escape, or to transform the cave into a human habitation.

Finally, although "freedom by any means necessary" is a morally justified conception of the relationship between political means and ends, it does not follow that the end of human freedom is historically realizable and therefore situationally rational. But speculation about whether or not class-racial struggle can lead to a society in which the "free development of each is the condition for the free development of all" is quite beside the point. We are not interested in a metaphysical or contemplative conception of historical truth but, rather, in its production: given that there can be no apodeictic certainty concerning the future except that it will not be the past; that all knowledge must be constituted in the light of a projected future if it is to be historical at all; and that history itself must be viewed as nothing more or less than the process of human self-production, then it follows that:

The question whether objective truth can be attributed to human thinking is not a question of theory but is a *practical* question. Man must prove the truth, that is, the reality and power, the this-sidedness of his thinking in practice. The dispute over the reality or non-reality of thinking which is isolated from practice is a purely scholastic question.[10]

The truth of the ethic of revolutionary responsibility can only be proven in practice.

Notes

CHAPTER I. THE PROBLEM

1. George Breitman, ed., *By Any Means Necessary: Speeches, Interviews and a Letter by Malcolm X* (New York: Pathfinder, 1970), p. 37.
2. Archie Epps, ed., *The Speeches of Malcolm X at Harvard* (New York: William Morrow, 1968), p. 133.
3. Karl Marx, *Capital* (New York: Random House, 1977), I, p. 103.
4. Malcolm X, with the assistance of Alex Haley, *The Autobiography of Malcolm X* (New York: Grove, 1964), publisher's frontispiece.
5. G. W. F. Hegel, *The Phenomenology of Mind* (New York: Harper and Row, 1967), p. 69.
6. Malcolm X, *Autobiography*, p. 150.
7. Ibid., p. 352.
8. Epps, *The Speeches of Malcolm X at Harvard*, p. 133.
9. George Breitman, ed., *Malcolm X Speaks* (New York: Grove, 1966), p. 11.
10. Malcolm X, *On Afro-American History* (New York: Merit, 1967), p. 15.
11. Ibid.
12. Ibid., p. 18.
13. Ibid., p. 30.
14. Ibid.
15. Ibid.
16. Ibid., p. 12.
17. Ibid., pp. 6–7.
18. Ibid., pp. 8–9.
19. Ibid.
20. Breitman, *Malcolm X Speaks*, p. 150.
21. Breitman, *By Any Means Necessary*, p. 86.
22. Malcolm used this phrase to describe his approach to the election-year politics of 1964. See, e.g., Breitman, *Malcolm X Speaks*, pp. 23ff.

23. Breitman, *By Any Means Necessary*, pp. 20–21.
24. Ibid., p. 159.
25. Malcolm X, *Autobiography*, p. 371.
26. Breitman, *Malcolm X Speaks*, pp. 68–69.
27. Ibid.
28. Ibid.
29. Ibid., p. 216.
30. Ibid.
31. Ibid., p. 66.
32. Ibid., p. 103.
33. Breitman, *Malcolm X Speaks*, p. 9.
34. Ibid., p. 174.
35. Ibid., p. 151.
36. Benjamin Goodman, ed., *The End of White World Supremacy: Four Speeches by Malcolm X* (New York: Merlin House, 1971), p. 137.
37. Breitman, *Malcolm X Speaks*, p. 117.
38. Ibid., p. 174.
39. Goodman, *The End of White World Supremacy*, p. 89.
40. Breitman, *Malcolm X Speaks*, p. 10.
41. Goodman, *The End of White World Supremacy*, p. 88.
42. Ibid., p. 90.
43. Ibid., p. 88.
44. Epps, *Malcolm X at Harvard*, p. 132.
45. Breitman, *By Any Means Necessary*, p. 87.
46. Goodman, *The End of White World Supremacy*, p. 137.
47. Malcolm X, *Autobiography*, p. 251.
48. Breitman, *Malcolm X Speaks*, p. 166.
49. Ibid., p. 5.
50. Malcolm X, *Autobiography*, p. 274.
51. Ibid., p. 273.
52. Ibid., p. 272.
53. Ibid.
54. Ibid.
55. Ibid.
56. Ibid., p. 273.
57. Breitman, *Malcolm X Speaks*, p. 46.
58. Epps, *Malcolm X at Harvard*, pp. 136–37.
59. Breitman, *Malcolm X Speaks*, p. 108.
60. Goodman, *The End of White World Supremacy*, p. 72.
61. Malcolm X, "God's Judgment of White America," in Goodman, *The End of White World Supremacy*, p. 13.
62. Goodman, *The End of White World Supremacy*, p. 7.
63. Ibid., p. 2.
64. Cited in ibid., p. 4.
65. Ibid., p. 6.

66. Ibid., p. 8.
67. Goodman was the second 'Benjamin' to join the Nation—hence Benjamin 2X.
68. Goodman, *The End of White World Supremacy*, p. 6.
69. Ibid., p. 9.
70. Cited in E. U. Essien-Udom, *Black Nationalism* (New York: Dell, 1962), p. 92.
71. Goodman, *The End of White World Supremacy*, p. 9.
72. Malcolm X, *Autobiography*, p. 194.
73. Cited in C. Eric Lincoln, *The Black Muslims in America* (Boston: Beacon, 1961), p. 92.
74. Ibid., p. 4.
75. Malcolm X, *Autobiography*, p. 212.
76. Ibid., p. 183.
77. Ibid., p. 36.
78. Ibid., p. 3.
79. For a general treatment of this tradition, see Theodore Draper, *The Rediscovery of Black Nationalism* (New York: Viking, 1969).
80. Cited in Lewis M. Killan, *The Impossible Revolution* (New York: Random House, 1968), p. 155.
81. Stokely Carmichael and Charles V. Hamilton, *Black Power* (New York: Vintage, 1967), p. 185.
82. Ossie Davis, "Our Shining Black Prince," in John H. Clarke, ed., *Malcolm X* (New York: Collier, 1969), p. 128.
83. Peter Goldman, *The Death and Life of Malcolm X* (New York: Harper and Row, 1973), p. 26.
84. Albert Cleage, "Myths About Malcolm X," in Clarke, *Malcolm X*, p. 21.
85. Ibid., p. 17.
86. Ibid., p. 16.
87. George Breitman, *The Last Year of Malcolm X* (New York: Schocken, 1968), p. 27.
88. Ruby M. and E. U. Essien-Udom, "Malcolm X: An International Man," in Clarke, *Malcolm X*, p. 236.
89. Ibid., p. 264.
90. John H. Clarke, "Introduction," in Clarke, *Malcolm X*, p. 12.
91. Max Weber, "Politics as a Vocation," in H. H. Gerth and C. Wright Mills, eds., *From Max Weber* (New York: Oxford University Press, 1958), p. 79. (Italics in the original.)
92. Karl Mannheim, *Ideology and Utopia* (New York: Harcourt, Brace, and World, 1936), p. 207.
93. Gunnar Myrdal, *An American Dilemma* (2 vols., New York: McGraw-Hill, 1964), I, p. lxxi.
94. Ibid., I, p. 76.
95. Ibid., I, p. 75.

96. Ibid., II, pp. 674–75.
97. Ibid.
98. Ibid., I, p. lxxiii.
99. Ibid., II, pp. 1021–22.
100. Oliver C. Cox, *Caste, Class and Race* (Garden City, New York: Doubleday, 1948), p. 512.
101. Ibid.
102. Ibid.
103. Ibid., p. 530.
104. Ibid., p. 536.
105. Ibid., p. 520.
106. Ibid., p. 528.
107. Ibid., p. 527.
108. Ibid., p. 582.
109. Myrdal, *An American Dilemma*, I, pp. 69–70.
110. Wilhelm Reich, "Dialectical Materialism and Psychoanalysis," in Lee Baxandall, ed., *Sex-Pol* (New York: Vintage, 1972), p. 37. I have discussed Reich's work in more detail, along with the work of Erich Fromm, Herbert Marcuse, and others, in "Groundwork for a Marxist Psychoanalysis," a paper presented to the American Political Science Association, 1977. Also see Bruce Brown, *Freud, Marx, and the Critique of Everyday Life* (New York: Monthly Review Press, 1973).
111. Reich, "Dialectical Materialism," p. 20.
112. Frantz Fanon, *Black Skin, White Masks* (New York: Grove, 1967).
113. Frantz Fanon, *The Wretched of the Earth* (New York: Grove, 1966), p. 29.
114. Fanon, *Black Skin, White Masks*, p. 12.
115. Ibid., p. 13.
116. Ibid.
117. Ibid., p. 114.
118. Karl Marx, *The Grundrisse* (Middlesex, England: Penguin, 1973), p. 101.
119. Ibid., p. 100.
120. Ibid.
121. Karl Marx, "Theses on Feuerbach," in Robert Tucker, ed., *The Marx-Engels Reader* (New York: W. W. Norton, 1972), p. 108.
122. Ibid., p. 109.

CHAPTER II. THE NIGHTMARE NIGHT

1. Malcolm X, *Autobiography*, p. 1.
2. Ibid., p. 2.
3. Ibid.
4. Ibid., p. 4.
5. Ibid., p. 3.

6. Ibid.
7. Kenneth T. Jackson, *The Ku Klux Klan in the City, 1915–1930* (New York: Oxford University Press, 1967), p. 143.
8. Malcolm X, *Autobiography*, p. 1.
9. Jackson, *The Ku Klux Klan*, p. 3.
10. Ibid., p. 9.
11. Ibid., p. 11.
12. Ibid., p. 12.
13. Ibid.
14. Ibid., pp. 235–36.
15. From Hiram Wesley Evans, "The Klan's Fight for Americanism," in George E. Mowry, ed., *The Twenties: Fords, Flappers and Fanatics* (Englewood Cliffs, N.J.: Prentice-Hall, 1963), p. 137.
16. Ibid., p. 140.
17. Ibid., p. 141.
18. Ibid., p. 142.
19. Ibid.
20. Jackson, *The Ku Klux Klan*, p. 19.
21. Ibid., p. 22.
22. Ibid., p. 31.
23. John Hope Franklin, *From Slavery to Freedom* (New York: Vintage, 1969), p. 480.
24. Jackson, *The Ku Klux Klan*, p. xv.
25. Malcolm X, *Autobiography*, p. 4.
26. Theodore G. Vincent, *Black Power and the Garvey Movement* (San Francisco: Ramparts, 1972), p. 101.
27. Charles S. Johnson, "After Garvey—What?" in Leslie Fischel and Benjamin Quarles, eds., *The Black American* (New York: William Morrow, 1970), p. 435.
28. Ibid., p. 434.
29. Ibid., p. 435.
30. Cited in Essien-Udom, *Black Nationalism*, p. 385.
31. Cited in Vincent, *Black Power*, pp. 205–206.
32. Cited in Essien-Udom, *Black Nationalism*, p. 385.
33. Ibid., p. 50.
34. Vincent, *Black Power*, p. 127.
35. Ibid., p. 103.
36. Cited in Essien-Udom, *Black Nationalism*, p. 385.
37. Vincent, *Black Power*, p. 102.
38. For an interesting discussion of the relationship between black religion and politics, see Gayraud S. Wilmore, *Black Religion and Black Radicalism* (Garden City, N.Y.: Doubleday, 1973).
39. Cited in Vincent, *Black Power*, p. 259.
40. Ibid., pp. 260–61.
41. Ibid., p. 114.
42. Malcolm X, *Autobiography*, pp. 6–7.

43. Franklin, *From Slavery to Freedom*, p. 473.
44. From Harold Faulkner, *The Decline of Laissez-Faire* (New York: Harper Torchbooks, 1951), p. 415.
45. Cited by Michael Reich, "The Evolution of the United States Labor Force," in R. C. Edwards, M. Reich, and T. E. Weisskopf, eds., *The Capitalist System* (Englewood Cliffs, N.J.: Prentice-Hall, 1972), p. 175.
46. George Soule, *Prosperity Decade* (New York: Harper Torchbooks, 1947), p. 7.
47. Franklin, *From Slavery to Freedom*, p. 472. A more detailed examination of the conditions of agricultural employment in the South and its relationship to the great migration can be found in Myrdal, *An American Dilemma*, chaps. 8 and 11.
48. J. A. and A. Lomax, *The Leadbelly Legend* (New York: Folkways, 1959), p. 16.
49. Myrdal, *An American Dilemma*, p. 193.
50. Johnson, "After Garvey—What?," p. 435.
51. W. T. B. Williams, "The Negro Exodus from the South," in Fischel and Quarles, *The Black American*, p. 394.
52. Franklin, *From Slavery to Freedom*, p. 472.
53. In Fischel and Quarles, *The Black American*, p. 399.
54. Bob Dylan, "Only a Pawn in Their Game," in *The Bob Dylan Songbook* (New York: M. Witmark and Sons, n.d.), p. 81.
55. Franklin, *From Slavery to Freedom*, p. 474.
56. Cited in ibid., pp. 480–81.
57. St. Clair Drake and Horace R. Cayton, *Black Metropolis* (New York: Harper and Row, 1962), I, p. 61.
58. Ibid., p. 64.
59. Jackson, *The Ku Klux Klan*, p. 244.
60. Soule, *Prosperity Decade*, p. 317.
61. Ibid.
62. Irving Bernstein, *The Lean Years* (Baltimore, Md.: Penguin, 1970), pp. 64–65.
63. Karl Marx, "Wage-Labour and Capital," in Tucker, *The Marx-Engels Reader*, p. 183. (Italics in the original.)
64. It is not possible in the present context to provide anything more than a bald statement of the relationship between the production of surplus value and the exchange of commodities in the marketplace. Similarly, the analysis of the various problems which attend these concepts is not our direct concern. In the former regard, Marx's *Capital*, Volumes I–III (Moscow: Foreign Languages Publishing House, n.d.); *Theories of Surplus Value* (Moscow: Progress Publisher, 1963); and *The Grundrisse* (Middlesex, Eng.: Penguin, 1973) remain the primary texts. A useful introduction to Marxist economics is provided by Paul Sweezy, *The Theory of Capitalist Development* (New York: Monthly Review Press, 1970), and Ernest Mandel, *Marxist Economics* (New York: Monthly Re-

view Press, 1970). Joan Robinson, in *An Essay on Marxian Economics* (New York: St. Martin's, 1967), provides a critical appreciation of Marx's work; Paul Mattick, *Marx and Keynes* (Boston: Porter Sargent, 1969) can be usefully read along with Robinson's essay. A more wide-ranging review of problems and prospects is to be found in David Horowitz, ed., *Marx and Modern Economics* (New York: Monthly Review Press, 1968).

65. The relationship between the ownership of the social forces of production and the possession of political power, like the economic relationships noted above, is complicated and controversial. Again, the best sources remain Marx's own work, especially his *The Eighteenth Brumaire of Louis Bonaparte* [in *The Selected Works of Marx and Engels* (Moscow: Foreign Languages Publishing House, 1962)]. But also see Anthony Giddens, *The Class Structure of the Advanced Societies* (New York: Harper and Row, 1975); Ralph Miliband, *Marxism and Politics* (Oxford: Oxford University Press, 1977); and for a more empirically oriented study, James O'Connor, *The Fiscal Crisis of the State* (New York: St. Martin's, 1973).

66. Jeremy Brecher, *Strike!* (San Francisco: Straight Arrow, 1972), p. 125.

67. Cited in Bernstein, *The Lean Years*, p. 52.

68. The class of self-employed entrepreneurs had in fact been substantially reduced in size by 1900, through the same historical process that created both the country's financial-industrial oligarchy and its industrial working class; but between 1900 and 1930 the size of the surviving class fraction was reduced from 30.8 to 20.3 percent of the labor force: see M. Reich, "The Evolution of the United States Labor Force." For the class composition of the KKK, see, *inter alia*, Jackson's data, especially as summarized in chap. 16.

69. Sigmund Freud, *Group Psychology and the Analysis of the Ego*, in *The Standard Edition of the Complete Psychological Works of Sigmund Freud* (London: Hogarth, 1955), XVIII, p. 88.

70. Ibid., p. 91.

71. Ibid., p. 81.

72. Max Weber, *The Theory of Social and Economic Organization* (New York: Free Press of Glencoe, 1964), p. 358.

73. Freud, *Group Psychology*, p. 112.

74. Ibid.

75. Ibid., p. 113.

76. Ibid.

77. Hypnosis is a complex and only partially understood phenomenon. Indeed, there is not even a consensus on what range of phenomena are to be considered hypnotic. I will be following Freud's example in defining hypnosis broadly and in seeking out its connection to other social phenomena. For contemporary views of hypnosis, see Merton Gill and Margaret Brenman, *Hypnosis and Related States* (New York: Interna-

tional Universities Press, 1959), Part I; and Erika Fromm and Ronald E. Shor, eds., *Hypnosis: Research Developments and Perspectives* (New York: Aldine-Atherton, 1972). Also see Paul Schilder and Otto Kauders, *Hypnosis* (New York: Nervous and Mental Disease Publishing, 1927), for a most suggestive treatment of the subject. It should be noted that hypnosis seems to penetrate into very deep layers of the self, so that it mobilizes primitive phantasies and defensive techniques. The work of Melanie Klein and her followers is therefore of considerable relevance for understanding the hypnotic state: see, for example, the essays by Klein and W. R. Bion in Part Two of Klein et al., *New Directions in Psycho-Analysis* (London: Tavistock, 1955). Finally, one of the few attempts to use the concept of hypnosis to understand politics is by Lloyd S. Etheredge, "Hypnosis and Order," a paper presented to the Yale Conference on Political Psychology, March, 1975.

78. Freud, *Group Psychology*, p. 115.
79. Ibid., p. 125. (Italics in the original.)
80. Ibid.
81. Ibid., p. 127.
82. Ibid., p. 116.
83. Freud, *Introductory Lectures on Psychoanalysis, S.E.*, XVI, p. 278.
84. Johnson, "After Garvey—What?", in Fischel and Quarles, p. 435.
85. Karl Mannheim, *Ideology and Utopia*, p. 1920.
86. Ibid.
87. Freud, *Introductory Lectures on Psychoanalysis*, p. 273.
88. Although this analysis is only hypothetical, given the empirical ground thus far established, it follows from a well-developed theoretical tradition. See, for example, T. W. Adorno et al., *The Authoritarian Personality* (New York: Harper and Brothers, 1950); Erich Fromm, *Escape from Freedom* (New York: Holt, Rinehart, and Winston, 1941); and Wilhelm Reich, *The Mass Psychology of Fascism* (New York: Farrar, Straus and Giroux, 1970).

CHAPTER III. THE SEVENTH SON

1. Karl Marx and Frederick Engels, *The German Ideology* (New York: International Publishers, 1970), p. 42.
2. Marx, *The Grundrisse*, p. 88.
3. Sigmund Freud, *Three Essays on Sexuality, S.E.*, VII, pp. 181–82.
4. Ibid.
5. Edith Jacobson, *The Self and the Object World* (New York: International Universities Press, 1964), p. 13.
6. Sigmund Freud, "Instincts and Their Vicissitudes," *S.E.*, XIV, p. 122.
7. There are certain similarities between this position and the one developed by Ives Hendrik in "Work and the Pleasure Principle," *The Psychoanalytic Quarterly* (1943): 311–29.

8. Marx, *The Grundrisse*, p. 88.
9. Malcolm X, *Autobiography*, p. 8.
10. Ibid., p. 4.
11. Ibid.
12. Ibid.
13. Freud, *Group Psychology*, p. 122.
14. Ibid., p. 123.
15. Ibid., p. 124.
16. See Freud's discussion of the primal scene in *From the History of an Infantile Neurosis*, S.E., XVII, pp. 48–60.
17. Malcolm X, *Autobiography*, p. 2.
18. Willie Dixon, "The Seventh Son," on *Memphis Slim and Willie Dixon in Paris*, Battle Records.
19. Malcolm X, *Autobiography*, p. 2.
20. Ibid.
21. Ibid.
22. Ibid., p. 4.
23. Ibid., p. 7.
24. Ibid., p. 4.
25. Ibid.
26. Ibid., p. 6.
27. Ibid.
28. Ibid.
29. Ibid.
30. Ibid., p. 7.
31. Ibid., p. 8.
32. Ibid., p. 7.
33. Ibid., p. 8.
34. Ibid.
35. Ibid., p. 7.
36. Ibid., p. 8.
37. Earl Little died on September 28, 1931 (personal communication from Bruce Perry).
38. Malcolm X, *Autobiography*, p. 9.
39. Ibid., p. 7.
40. Ibid., p. 9.
41. Ibid.
42. Ibid.
43. Ibid.
44. Ibid., p. 10.
45. Ibid.
46. Ibid.
47. Ibid.
48. In what follows I am combining Freud's descriptions of the slaying of the primal father in *Group Psychology*, pp. 135–36, and in *Totem and Taboo*, S.E., XIII, pp. 140–46.

49. See Freud's discussion of omnipotence of thought in *Totem and Taboo,* Part III.
50. Malcolm X, *Autobiography,* p. 10.
51. Ibid., p. 11.

CHAPTER IV. THE VICIOUS CIRCLE

1. Jean-Paul Sartre, *Search For a Method* (New York: Vintage, 1963), p. 91.
2. Ibid., p. 95.
3. We may observe that our analysis to this point has followed an apparently Reichian line. We have sought to show how "the economic structure of society—through many intermediary links . . .—enters into reciprocal relation with the instincts, or ego, of the newborn." But in contradistinction to Reich, we have evolved a conception of human beings as sensuously energetic and interactive individuals who develop the capacity for self-conscious activity through mutually determinative work and emotional processes. We have also conceptualized the linkages between the individual and society differently: instead of relying upon the merely descriptive and indefinite notion of "many intermediary linkages," we have connected class interests to group-emotion; and we have conceptualized the group or mass as a social formation that is neither reducible to nor derivable from the summation of individual motive-forces. In both respects, therefore, we have attempted to consider our subject matter in simultaneously subjective and objective terms. When we come to the topic of commodity fetishism in Chapter V, we will seek to extend this line of reasoning to the "economic structure of society."
4. Malcolm X, *Autobiography,* p. 11.
5. Ibid., p. 12.
6. Ibid.
7. In what follows I am not arguing that the Depression was caused by problems in realizing surplus value. It would be more accurate to say that when the process of realizing surplus value has been sufficiently disrupted, then depression or economic crisis exists. A crisis *is* a disruption in the realization process. (For more elaborated views of periodic crises, see the texts on Marxist economics previously cited.)
8. Soule, *Prosperity Decade,* p. 287.
9. Ibid., p. 288.
10. Ibid., p. 287.
11. Paul A. Baran and Paul M. Sweezy, *Monopoly Capital* (New York: Monthly Review Press, 1966), p. 237.
12. Soule, *Prosperity Decade,* p. 289.
13. Karl Marx, "Wage-Labour and Capital," in Marx and Engels, *Selected Works,* I, p. 105.

14. Ibid.
15. Cited in Arthur M. Ross and Herbert Hill, eds., *Employment, Race, and Poverty* (New York: Harcourt, Brace, and World, 1967), p. 15. These figures for white unemployment differ slightly from those in the sources previously cited.
16. Ibid.
17. Ibid.
18. Drake and Cayton, *Black Metropolis*, I, p. 89.
19. Malcolm X, *Autobiography*, p. 13.
20. Karl Marx, *A Contribution to a Critique of Political Economy* (New York: International Publishers, 1970), preface.
21. On the relationship between black workers, the union movement, and the Communist Party, see Philip S. Foner, *Organized Labor and the Black Worker, 1619–1973* (New York: International Publishers, 1974), chaps. 14–16.
22. Myrdal, *An American Dilemma*, p. 355.
23. G. W. F. Hegel, *The Philosophy of Right* (New York: Oxford University Press, 1952), p. 150.
24. Ibid.
25. Karl Marx, *The Eighteenth Brumaire of Louis Bonaparte*, I, p. 295.
26. Breitman, *Malcolm X Speaks*, p. 166.
27. Myrdal, *An American Dilemma*, p. 353.
28. Malcolm X, *Autobiography*, p. 14.
29. Ibid., p. 15.
30. Ibid., p. 12.
31. Ibid., p. 13.
32. Ibid., p. 14.
33. Ibid., p. 12.
34. Ibid.
35. Ibid., p. 13.
36. Ibid.
37. Ibid., p. 18.
38. Ibid.
39. Ibid.
40. Ibid.
41. Ibid., p. 19.
42. Ibid., p. 21.
43. Ibid., p. 11.
44. Kurt Weill and Bertolt Brecht, *The Threepenny Opera*, Act II ("Ballad about the Question, What Keeps a Man Alive"), Columbia Records, 1958. Translated from the German by Guy Stern.
45. Malcolm X, *Autobiography*, p. 14.
46. Ibid., p. 19.
47. Ibid., p. 18.
48. Ibid., p. 15.

49. Ibid.
50. Ibid., p. 23.
51. Richard Wright, "Joe Louis Uncovers Dynamite," reprinted from *The New Masses* in Daniel Aaron and Robert Bendiner, eds., *The Strenuous Decade* (Garden City, N.Y.: Doubleday, 1970), p. 396. Wright's comments were made following the Louis-Baer fight in 1935 but, as Malcolm's remarks make clear, they were equally applicable to the fight with Braddock two years later.
52. Malcolm X, *Autobiography*, p. 23.
53. Ibid., p. 24.
54. Ibid., p. 25.
55. Ibid.
56. Ibid.
57. Ibid., p. 26.
58. Ibid., p. 31.
59. Ibid., p. 25.
60. Ibid., p. 33.
61. Ibid., p. 31.
62. Ibid., p. 28.
63. Ibid., p. 32.
64. Ibid., p. 30.
65. Ibid., p. 26.
66. Ibid., p. 27.
67. Ibid.
68. Although the concept of identification with the oppressor is derived from and overlaps with Anna Freud's concept of identification with the aggressor, it differs from the latter insofar as it specifies the identification to an objectively oppressive authority. For an argument similar to the one being developed here, see Hortense Powdermaker, "The Channeling of Negro Aggression by the Cultural Process," in Clyde Kluckhohn and Henry A. Murray, eds., *Personality in Nature, Society, and Culture* (New York: Alfred A. Knopf, 1948), pp. 473–84.
69. Malcolm X, *Autobiography*, p. 33.
70. Ibid., p. 32.
71. Ibid.
72. Ibid.
73. Ibid.
74. Ibid., p. 34.
75. Ibid.
76. Ibid., p. 35.
77. Ibid.
78. Ibid., p. 35.
79. Ibid., p. 36.
80. Ibid., p. 37.
81. Ibid., p. 36.
82. Cited in Ross and Hill, *Employment, Race, and Poverty*, p. 7.

CHAPTER V. NEVER TRUST ANYBODY

1. Malcolm X, *Autobiography*, p. 34.
2. Ibid., p. 42.
3. Ibid., p. 43.
4. Ibid., p. 39.
5. This concept was originally formulated by Freud in "Some Character-Types Met with in Psychoanalytic Work," *S.E.*, XIV, pp. 309ff.
6. In what follows we will not be concerned to construct an exhaustive typology of black character structure. See in this regard William H. Grier and Price M. Cobbs, *Black Rage* (New York: Basic Books, 1968), Chapter VI; and William McCord, John Howard, Bernard Friedberg, and Edwin Harwood, *Life Styles in the Black Ghetto* (New York: W. W. Norton, 1969), Part II.
7. Malcolm X, *Autobiography*, pp. 46–49.
8. Ibid., p. 49.
9. Ibid., p. 53.
10. Ibid., p. 54.
11. Ibid., p. 51.
12. Ibid., p. 54.
13. Ibid.
14. Ibid., p. 67.
15. Ibid., p. 66.
16. Ibid., p. 45.
17. Ibid., p. 50.
18. Ibid., p. 93.
19. Ibid., p. 67.
20. Marx, *Capital*, I, p. 72.
21. Ibid., p. 73.
22. Ibid., p. 85.
23. For a similar argument see Michael Schneider, *Neurosis and Civilization* (New York: Seabury, 1975), Part III.
24. Karl Marx, *The Economic and Philosophical Manuscripts of 1844* (New York: International Publishers, 1964), pp. 167–68.
25. Fanon, *Black Skin, White Masks*, p. 63.
26. Malcolm X, *Autobiography*, p. 95.
27. Ibid.
28. Ibid., p. 75.
29. Ibid., p. 72.
30. Ibid., p. 75.
31. Ibid., p. 86.
32. Ibid., p. 83.
33. Ibid.
34. Ibid., p. 87.
35. Ibid., p. 98.
36. Ibid., p. 99.

37. Ibid.
38. In addition to the following discussion, see Julius Hudson, "The Hustling Ethic," in Thomas Kochman, ed., *Rappin' and Stylin' Out* (Urbana, Ill.: University of Illinois Press, 1972).
39. Malcolm X, *Autobiography*, p. 102.
40. Ibid., p. 139.
41. Ibid., p. 138.
42. Ibid., p. 109.
43. Thomas Hobbes, *Leviathan* (Oxford: Clarendon Press, 1909), p. 97.
44. Malcolm X, *Autobiography*, p. 311.
45. Clarence Major, *Dictionary of Afro-American Slang* (New York: International Publishers, 1970), p. 22.
46. Malcolm X, *Autobiography*, p. 127.
47. Ibid., p. 116.
48. Ibid., p. 81.
49. Ibid., p. 82.
50. Ibid., p. 83.
51. For the early history of Harlem, see Gilbert Osofsky, *Harlem: The Making of a Ghetto* (New York: Harper and Row, 1971). The linked notions of the victimization and ghettoization of black people are developed with his characteristic insight and subtlety by St. Clair Drake in "The Social and Economic Status of the Negro in the United States," an article in Talcott Parsons and Kenneth B. Clark, eds., *The Negro American* (Boston: Beacon, 1966), pp. 3–46. The classic analysis of ghetto conditions during the post-World War II period is Clark's *Dark Ghetto* (New York: Harper and Row, 1965).
52. Vivian W. Henderson, "Regions, Race and Jobs," in Ross and Hill, *Employment, Race, and Poverty*, p. 83; E. Franklin Frazier, *The Negro in the United States* (New York: Macmillan, 1967), p. 266.
53. Fanon, *The Wretched of the Earth*, p. 31.
54. Ibid., p. 42.
55. The idea that black people in the United States constitute a colonialized population gained a certain theoretical importance during the 1960s as a consequence of practical political considerations. In adopting the term here, I am signifying my agreement with the critical and emancipatory tendencies it expresses, but I am not implying that either the conditions of oppression or the possibilities for liberation are identical in the internal and external colonial situations. Most obviously, it does make a difference if the colonized population is a minority rather than a majority group. Rather than attempt a formal delimitation of the concept at this juncture, however, we shall see how its meaning evolves in the course of our work. For a thoughtful treatment of several of the relevant issues, see Robert Blauner, "Internal Colonialism and Ghetto Revolt," in Milton Mankoff, ed., *The Poverty of Progress* (New York: Holt, Rinehart, and Winston, 1972), pp. 216–30.

56. Peter Laslett, ed., *John Locke: Two Treatises of Government* (New York: New American Library, 1965), p. 311.
57. Ibid., p. 319.
58. Ibid., pp. 395–97. (This line of argument is most notably and far more extensively developed in C. B. MacPherson's *The Political Theory of Possessive Individualism* (London: Oxford University Press, 1962).
59. Cited in Richard M. Dalfiume, "The 'Forgotten Years' of the Negro Revolution," in Bernard Sternsher, ed., *The Negro in Depression and War* (Chicago: Quadrangle, 1969), p. 305.
60. Geoffrey Perrett, *Days of Sadness, Years of Triumph* (New York: Coward, McCann and Geoghegan, 1973), p. 320.
61. Cited in Dalfiume, "The 'Forgotten Years,'" p. 301.
62. Ibid., p. 302.
63. Ibid., p. 303.
64. Ibid.
65. Ibid., p. 302.
66. Ibid., p. 305.
67. Ibid.
68. Baran and Sweezy, *Monopoly Capital*, p. 245.
69. See Edwards et al., *The Capitalist System*, p. 289; and Ross and Hill, *Employment, Race, and Poverty*, p. 52.
70. Cited in Myrdal, *An American Dilemma*, I, p. clxx.
71. Ibid., p. 332.
72. See, for example, Christina and Richard Milner, *Black Players* (Boston: Little, Brown, 1972).
73. In addition to Myrdal's account in *An American Dilemma*, there is a good analysis of the "policy game" in Drake and Cayton, *Black Metropolis*, II, chap. 17.
74. Myrdal, *An American Dilemma*, I, p. clxxi.
75. Ibid., I, p. clxxiii.
76. Drake and Cayton, *Black Metropolis*, II, p. 482.
77. Myrdal, *An American Dilemma*, I, p. clxxi.
78. Cited in Ferdinand Lundberg, *The Rich and the Super-Rich* (New York: Bantam, 1968), p. 128.
79. Ibid.
80. Ibid., p. 137.
81. Malcolm X, *Autobiography*, p. 119.
82. Breitman, *Malcolm X Speaks*, p. 166.
83. Malcolm X, *Autobiography*, p. 169.
84. Ibid., p. 99.
85. Ibid., p. 123.
86. Robert Johnson, "Hellhound on My Trail," Columbia Records CL-1654.
87. Malcolm X, *Autobiography*, p. 117.
88. Ibid., p. 127.
89. Ibid., pp. 130–31.

90. Ibid., pp. 131–32.
91. Ibid., p. 132.
92. Ibid., p. 136.
93. Ibid., p. 138.
94. Ibid.
95. Ibid., p. 140.
96. Ibid., p. 144.
97. Ibid., p. 143.
98. Ibid.
99. Ibid., p. 141.
100. Ibid., p. 135.
101. Ibid., p. 142.
102. Ibid., p. 147.
103. Ibid.
104. Ibid.
105. Ibid.
106. Ibid., p. 149.
107. Ibid.
108. Ibid., p. 146.
109. Ibid., p. 151.
110. Ibid., p. 152.
111. Ibid.
112. Ibid.
113. Ibid., p. 153.
114. Ibid.
115. Ibid.
116. Ibid., p. 154.
117. Ibid.
118. Ibid., p. 155.
119. Ibid., p. 152.
120. Ibid., p. 183.

CHAPTER VI. ONLY GUILT ADMITTED

1. Malcolm X, *Autobiography*, p. 150.
2. Ibid. If we were using Lasswell's formula of the displacement and rationalization of private motives as the constitutive act of a political personality, then the conversion would be that act; or we could view it in Erikson's terms, as the resolution of Malcolm's adolescent identity crisis. See Harold D. Lasswell, *Psychopathology and Politics* (New York: Viking, 1960); and Erik H. Erikson, *Young Man Luther* (New York: W. W. Norton, 1958). For Erikson's view of racial identity, see his "The Concept of Identity in Race Relations," in Parsons and Clark, *The Negro American*, pp. 227–53.

3. Malcolm X, *Autobiography*, p. 155.
4. Ibid.
5. Ibid., p. 156.
6. Ibid.
7. Ibid.
8. Ibid., p. 19.
9. Ibid., p. 156.
10. Ibid., p. 158.
11. Ibid., p. 159.
12. Ibid.
13. Ibid., p. 160.
14. Ibid., p. 161.
15. Ibid., p. 163.
16. Ibid.
17. Ibid., p. 164.
18. Ibid., p. 169.
19. Ibid.
20. Ibid.
21. Ibid.
22. Ibid., p. 170.
23. Ibid.
24. Ibid., p. 163.
25. Ibid., p. 187.
26. Grene and Lattimore, eds., *Sophocles I: Oedipus at Colonus* (Chicago: University of Chicago Press, 1954), p. 124.
27. Malcolm X, *Autobiography*, p. 170.
28. Ibid., p. 186.
29. Ibid.
30. Ibid., p. 187.
31. Ibid.
32. Ibid.
33. Ibid., p. 178.
34. Ibid., p. 157.
35. Ibid., p. 287.
36. Ibid., p. 171.
37. Ibid.
38. Ibid., p. 172.
39. Ibid.
40. Ibid., p. 176.
41. Ibid., p. 182.
42. Ibid.
43. Ibid., p. 184.
44. Ibid., p. 185.
45. Ibid., p. 173.
46. Ibid., pp. 191–92.

CHAPTER VII. WE HAVE A COMMON ENEMY

1. Malcolm X, *Autobiography*, p. p. 193.
2. Ibid., p. 194.
3. Ibid., p. 192.
4. Gabriel Kolko, *Main Currents in Modern American History* (New York: Harper and Row, 1976), p. 311. For useful and usefully opposing views of the United States in the world economy during this period, see Michael Barratt Brown, *The Economics of Imperialism* (Middlesex, Eng.: Penguin, 1974); Gabriel Kolko, *Wealth and Power in America* (New York: Praeger, 1962); Joyce Kolko, *America and the Crisis of World Capitalism* (Boston: Beacon, 1974); Pierre Jalee, *The Pillage of the Third World* (New York: Monthly Review Press, 1968); Harry Magdoff, *The Age of Imperialism* (New York: Monthly Review Press, 1969); Ernest Mandel, *Europe vs. America* (New York: Monthly Review Press, 1970).
5. Max Weber, *The Protestant Ethic and the Spirit of Capitalism* (New York: Charles Scribner's Sons, 1958), p. 181.
6. Ibid.
7. See Baran and Sweezy, *Monopoly Capital*, p. 247; and Bert G. Hickman, *Growth and Stability in the Postwar Economy* (Washington, D.C.: The Brookings Institution, 1960), p. 362.
8. W. E. B. DuBois, "An Appeal to the World," in Walter Wilson, ed., *The Selected Writings of W. E. B. DuBois* (New York: New American Library, 1970), p. 320.
9. Arthur M. Ross, "The Negro in the American Economy," in Ross and Hill, *Employment, Race, and Poverty*, p. 4.
10. U.S. Govt., Current Population Reports, Series P-23, no. 24, "Social and Economic Conditions of Negroes in the United States"; and Charles E. Silberman, *Crisis in Black and White* (New York: Vintage, 1965), p. 42.
11. Silberman, *Crisis in Black and White*, p. 42.
12. Ibid.
13. Breitman, *Malcolm X Speaks*, p. 166.
14. Karl Marx, "Wage-Labour and Capital," in Marx and Engels, *Selected Works*, I, p. 93.
15. James C. Davies, "The J-Curve of Rising and Declining Satisfactions as a Cause of Some Great Revolutions and a Contained Rebellion," in Hugh Davis Graham and Robert Ted Gurr, eds., *Violence in America* (New York: The New York Times Co., 1969), p. 690.
16. Cited in William Robert Miller, *Martin Luther King* (New York: Avon, 1968), p. 50.
17. Ibid.
18. Cited in Robert L. Allen, *Black Awakening in Capitalist America* (Garden City, N.Y.: Doubleday, 1970), p. 24.
19. Alvin F. Poussaint, "A Negro Psychiatrist Explains the Negro Psyche," in August Meier and Elliott Rudwick, eds., *Black Protest in the Sixties*

(Chicago: Quadrangle, 1970), pp. 136–37. (Emphasis added.) For an extended discussion of this topic, see Grier and Cobbs, *Black Rage*.
20. Julius Lester, "The Angry Children of Malcolm X," in August Meier et al., eds., *Black Protest Thought in the Twentieth Century* (New York: Bobbs-Merrill, 1971), p. 469.
21. Clark, *Dark Ghetto*, p. 81.
22. Malcolm X, *Autobiography*, p. 195.
23. Ibid., p. 196.
24. Ibid.
25. Ibid., p. 197.
26. Ibid.
27. Ibid., p. 199.
28. Ibid., p. 200.
29. Ibid., p. 201.
30. Ibid.
31. Ibid., p. 204.
32. Ibid., p. 208.
33. Ibid., p. 212.
34. Revelation 1:10–16.
35. Malcolm X, *Autobiography*, p. 211.
36. Ibid., p. 210.
37. Ibid., p. 211.
38. Ibid., p. 215.
39. Ibid., p. 216.
40. Ibid., p. 217.
41. Ibid., p. 216.
42. Ibid., pp. 220–21.
43. Ibid., p. 248.
44. Ibid., p. 249.
45. Ibid., p. 251.
46. Ibid.
47. Ibid., p. 252.
48. Ibid.
49. Ibid., p. 254.
50. Ibid., p. 256.
51. Ibid., p. 257.
52. Ibid., p. 225.
53. Ibid., p. 256.
54. Louis E. Lomax, *To Kill a Black Man* (Los Angeles: Holloway House, 1968), p. 61.
55. Malcolm X, *Autobiography*, p. 241.
56. Ibid., p. 204.
57. Ibid., p. 241.
58. Ibid., pp. 240–41.
59. Ibid., p. 243.
60. Ibid., p. 282.

61. Ibid., p. 287.
62. Lomax, *When The Word Is Given* (New York: Signet, 1963), p. 179.

CHAPTER VIII. THINK FOR YOURSELF

1.   Malcolm X, *Autobiography*, p. 287.
2.   Ibid., p. 289.
3.   Ibid.
4.   Ibid.
5.   Lerone Bennett, Jr., *Confrontation: Black and White* (Baltimore, Md.: Penguin, 1972), p. 239.
6.   Ibid., p. 240.
7.   Breitman, "Message to the Grass Roots," in *Malcolm X Speaks*, p. 14.
8.   Anthony Lewis and the *New York Times*, *Portrait of a Decade* (New York: Bantam, 1964), p. 217.
9.   Ibid., p. 216.
10. Martin Luther King, from his speech at the March (August 28, 1963).
11. Breitman, *Malcolm X Speaks*, p. 13.
12. Malcolm X, *Autobiography*, p. 279.
13. Breitman, *Malcolm X Speaks*, p. 15.
14. Malcolm X, *Autobiography*, p. 279.
15. Breitman, *Malcolm X Speaks*, p. 16.
16. Cited in Lewis and the *New York Times*, *Portrait of a Decade*, p. 163.
17. Lomax, *To Kill a Black Man*, p. 97.
18. Breitman, *The Last Year of Malcolm X*, p. 16.
19. Malcolm X, *Autobiography*, p. 294.
20. Ibid., p. 295.
21. Ibid., p. 296.
22. Ibid., p. 297.
23. Ibid., p. 299.
24. Ibid., p. 293.
25. Ibid., p. 297.
26. Ibid.
27. Ibid., p. 293.
28. Ibid., p. 301.
29. Cited in Lomax, *When the Word Is Given*, p. 93.
30. Ibid., p. 301.
31. Ibid.
32. Ibid., p. 302.
33. Ibid.
34. Ibid.
35. Ibid., p. 304.
36. Ibid.
37. Cedric J. Robinson, "Malcolm X as a Charismatic Leader," a paper presented to the American Political Science Association, 1970.

38. Malcolm X, *Autobiography*, p. 386.
39. Ibid., p. 387.
40. Ibid., p. 271.
41. Ibid., p. 388.
42. Ibid., p. 390.
43. Ibid., p. 393.
44. Ibid.
45. Ibid., p. 273.
46. Ibid., p. 378.
47. Ibid., p. 305.
48. Ibid.
49. Ibid., p. 303.
50. Ibid., p. 304.
51. Ibid., p. 305.
52. Ibid., p. 306.
53. Ibid., p. 15.
54. Ibid., p. 306 (emphasis added).
55. Ibid.
56. Ibid., p. 406.
57. Ibid., p. 309.
58. Ibid., p. 210.
59. Ibid.
60. Ibid.
61. Ibid.
62. Ibid., p. 315.
63. Ibid.
64. Breitman, *Malcolm X Speaks*, p. 20.
65. Ibid., p. 21.
66. Ibid., p. 22.

CHAPTER IX. FREEDOM BY ANY MEANS NECESSARY

1. Breitman, *Malcolm X Speaks*, p. 50.
2. Ruby M. and E. U. Essien-Udom, "Malcolm X: An International Man," in Clarke, *Malcolm X*, p. 239.
3. Breitman, *Malcolm X Speaks*, p. 50.
4. Ibid., p. 48.
5. Ibid., p. 46.
6. Ibid., p. 24.
7. Ibid., p. 25.
8. Ibid., p. 26.
9. Ibid., p. 27.
10. Ibid., p. 28.
11. Ibid., p. 31.
12. Ibid., p. 35.

13. Ibid., p. 31.
14. Ibid., p. 34.
15. Ibid., p. 38.
16. Ibid., pp. 38–39.
17. Ibid., p. 41.
18. Ibid.
19. Malcolm X, *Autobiography*, p. 321.
20. Ibid., p. 325.
21. Ibid., pp. 331–32.
22. Ibid., p. 333.
23. Ibid.
24. Ibid., p. 325.
25. Ibid., p. 365.
26. Ibid., p. 375.
27. Ibid., p. 365.
28. Breitman, *Malcolm X Speaks*, p. 226.
29. Malcolm X, *Autobiography*, p. 365.
30. Ibid.
31. Ibid., p. 339.
32. Ibid., p. 340.
33. Breitman, *Malcolm X Speaks*, 60.
34. Malcolm X, *Autobiography*, p. 341.
35. Breitman, *Malcolm X Speaks*, 458.
36. From a transcript of Malcolm's press conference of May 21, 1964.
37. Malcolm X, *Autobiography*, p. 351.
38. Ibid.
39. In Epps, *The Speeches of Malcolm X at Harvard*, pp. 157–58.
40. Malcolm X, *Autobiography*, p. 360.
41. Ibid., p. 352.
42. Ibid., p. 355.
43. Breitman, *By Any Means Necessary*, p. 159.
44. Malcolm X, *Autobiography*, p. 354.
45. Breitman, *By Any Means Necessary*, p. 36.
46. Ibid., p. 37.
47. Malcolm X, *On Afro-American History*, p. 16.
48. Epps, *The Speeches of Malcolm X at Harvard*, pp. 167–68.
49. Breitman, *Malcolm X Speaks*, p. 169.
50. Ibid.
51. Roderick W. Pugh, "Psychological Aspects of the Black Revolution," in Reginald L. Jones, ed., *Black Psychology* (New York: Harper and Row, 1972), p. 355. We touch here upon the complicated question of black attitudes in relationship to both underlying emotional forces and the realities of the political situation. For representative survey data bearing on the latter issue, see Gary T. Marx, *Protest and Prejudice* (New York: Harper and Row, 1969).
52. Malcolm X, *On Afro-American History*, p. 9.

53. John Lewis, "Interview, 1964," in Meier et al., *Black Protest Thought in the Twentieth Century*, pp. 353–60.

54. Robert F. Williams, "U.S.A.: The Potential for a Minority Revolution," in Meier et al., *Black Protest Thought in the Twentieth Century*, pp. 361–72.

55. Fanon, *The Wretched of the Earth*, p. 124.

56. Essien-Udom, "Malcolm X," in Clarke, *Malcolm X*, p. 253.

57. Ibid., p. 255.

58. Ibid.

59. Breitman, *By Any Means Necessary*, p. 110.

60. Ibid.

61. The two-way flow of initiatives is provided for in the "Establishment" section of the "Basic Program": see Breitman, *The Last Year of Malcolm X*, pp. 113–14.

62. Members of the OAU could, of course, withdraw from the alliance at any time (see Article XXXIII of the Charter). On the other hand, the organization had a highly developed administrative structure (see Articles XVI–XXII). With regard to Elijah Muhammad's exercise of authority, see Essien-Udom, *Black Nationalism*, pp. 196–97.

63. "Statement of Basic Aims," in Breitman, *By Any Means Necessary*, p. 107.

64. "Basic Unity Program," ibid., p. 119.

65. "Statement of Basic Aims," ibid., p. 110.

66. Ibid., p. 111.

67. Ibid., p. 109.

68. Breitman, *Malcolm X Speaks*, p. 46.

69. Ibid., p. 25.

70. *Report of the National Advisory Commission on Civil Disorders* (New York: The New York Times, 1968), p. 36.

71. Breitman, *Malcolm X Speaks*, p. 153.

72. Breitman, *By Any Means Necessary*, p. 65.

73. Breitman, *Malcolm X Speaks*, p. 57.

74. Breitman, *By Any Means Necessary*, p. 102.

75. Breitman, *Malcolm X Speaks*, p. 132.

76. Epps, *The Speeches of Malcolm X at Harvard*, p. 174.

77. "Basic Unity Program," in Breitman, *By Any Means Necessary*, p. 119.

78. Breitman, *Malcolm X Speaks*, p. 106.

79. Breitman, *By Any Means Necessary*, pp. 81–82.

80. Breitman, *Malcolm X Speaks*, p. 33.

81. Breitman, *By Any Means Necessary*, p. 100.

82. Breitman, *Malcolm X Speaks*, p. 103.

83. Breitman, *By Any Means Necessary*, p. 154.

84. Breitman, *Malcolm X Speaks*, p. 134.

85. Ibid., p. 40.

86. Ibid., p. 106.

87. Ibid., p. 108.

88. Ibid., p. 150.
89. Ibid., p. 113.
90. Immanuel Kant, *Critique of Practical Reason* (New York: Bobbs-Merrill, 1956), p. 30.
91. Breitman, *By Any Means Necessary*, p. 155.
92. Ibid., p. 110.
93. Peter Goldman, *The Death and Life of Malcolm X*, p. 211.
94. Cited in Breitman, *Malcolm X Speaks*, p. 85.
95. Goldman, *The Death and Life of Malcolm X*, p. 212.
96. Ibid., p. 219.
97. Ibid., p. 220.
98. Breitman, *Malcolm X Speaks*, p. 212.
99. Breitman, *By Any Means Necessary*, p. 184.
100. Goldman, *The Death and Life of Malcolm X*, p. 232.
101. Ibid., p. 139.
102. Ibid., p. 203.
103. Ibid., p. 263.
104. Richmond Lattimore, trans., *The Iliad of Homer* (Chicago: University of Chicago Press, 1961), p. 209.
105. Malcolm X, *Autobiography*, p. 381.
106. As reported by Alex Haley, in the epilogue to *The Autobiography of Malcolm X*, p. 434.
107. Breitman, *Malcolm X Speaks*, p. 160.
108. Ibid.
109. Ibid., p. 161.
110. Ibid., p. 174.
111. Ibid., p. 161.
112. Ibid., p. 176.
113. *Report of the National Advisory Commission on Civil Disorders*, p. 38.
114. Fanon, *The Wretched of the Earth*, p. 73.
115. Ibid., p. 111.
116. Ibid.
117. Eldridge Cleaver, *Soul on Ice*, (New York: Dell, 1968), p. 26.
118. Julius Lester, "The Angry Children of Malcolm X," p. 473.
119. Karl Marx, "Contribution to a Critique of Hegel's *Philosophy of Right*. Introduction," in Tucker, *The Marx-Engels Reader*, p. 23.
120. Carmichael and Hamilton, *Black Power*, p. 164.
121. Ibid.
122. Ibid., p. 165.
123. Ibid., p. 166.
124. Ibid., p. 172.
125. Ibid., pp. 173, 176.
126. Ibid., p. 185.
127. Allen, *Black Awakening in Capitalist America*, p. 47.

128. Angela Y. Davis, *If They Come in the Morning* (New York: Joseph Ok-paku Publishing, 1971), p. 48.
129. Hegel, *The Philosophy of Right*, p. 184.
130. For an excellent summation of relevant data, see Dorothy K. Newman et al., *Protest, Politics, and Prosperity* (New York: Pantheon, 1978).
131. Allen, *Black Awakening in Capitalist America*, p. 194.
132. James Boggs, *Racism and the Class Struggle* (New York: Monthly Review Press, 1970), p. 184.
133. Ibid., p. 183.

CHAPTER X. THE LOGIC OF DEMOCRACY

1. Karl Marx, "Results of the Immediate Process of Production," in Ben Fowkes, trans., *Capital* (New York: Vintage, 1977), I, p. 1003. (Emphasis in the original.)
2. Ibid., p. 990.
3. Karl Marx, *The Economic and Philosophical Manuscripts of 1844*, in Tucker, *The Marx-Engels Reader*, p. 81.
4. Karl Marx, "Contribution to a Critique of Hegel's *Philosophy of Right*. Introduction," in Tucker, *The Marx-Engels Reader*, p. 11.
5. For a partially contrasting view, see E. Earl Baughman, *Black Americans* (New York: Academic Press, 1971), pp. 39–41.
6. Karl Marx, *A Contribution to a Critique of Political Economy*, preface, in Tucker, *The Marx-Engels Reader*, p. 4.
7. Karl Marx, "Wage-Labour and Capital," in Marx and Engels, *Selected Works*, I, p. 105.
8. Allen, *Black Awakening in Capitalist America*, p. 247.
9. Laslett, *John Locke: Two Treatises of Government*, pp. 465–466 (emphasis in original).
10. Karl Marx, "Theses on Feuerbach," p. 108.

Bibliography

AFRO-AMERICAN HISTORY: BOOKS

Allen, Robert L. *Black Awakening in Capitalist America*. Garden City, New York: Doubleday, 1970.

Aptheker, Herbert. *A Documentary History of the Negro People in the United States*, Volumes II and III. Secaucus, New Jersey: Citadel Press, 1973–1974.

Baughman, E. Earl. *Black Americans*. New York: Academic Press, 1971.

Bennett, Lerone. *Confrontation: Black and White*. Baltimore, Maryland: Penguin, 1972.

Boggs, James. *Racism and the Class Struggle*. New York: Monthly Review Press, 1970.

Bracey, John H., August Meier, and Elliott Rudwick, editors. *Black Nationalism in America*. New York: Bobbs-Merrill, 1970.

Breitman, George. *The Last Year of Malcolm X*. New York: Schocken, 1968.

———, editor. *By Any Means Necessary: Speeches, Interviews and a Letter by Malcolm X*. New York: Pathfinder, 1970.

———, editor. *Malcolm X Speaks*. New York: Grove, 1966.

Carmichael, Stokely, and Charles V. Hamilton. *Black Power*. New York: Vintage, 1967.

Clark, Kenneth B. *Dark Ghetto*. New York: Harper and Row, 1965.

Clarke, John H., editor. *Malcolm X*. New York: Collier, 1969.

Cleaver, Eldridge. *Post-Prison Writings*. New York: Random House, 1969.

———. *Soul on Ice*. New York: Dell, 1968.

Comer, James P. *Beyond Black and White*. New York: Quadrangle, 1972.

Cox, Oliver C. *Caste, Class and Race*. Garden City, New York: Doubleday, 1948.

Davis, Angela Y. *If They Come in the Morning*. New York: Joseph Okpaku Publishing, 1971.

Drake, St. Clair, and Horace R. Cayton. *Black Metropolis*, Volumes I–II. New York: Harper and Row, 1962.

Draper, Theodore. *The Rediscovery of Black Nationalism*. New York: Viking, 1969.

Epps, Archie, editor. *The Speeches of Malcolm X at Harvard*. New York: William Morrow, 1968.

Essien-Udom, E. U. *Black Nationalism*. New York: Dell, 1962.

Fanon, Frantz. *Black Skin, White Masks*. New York: Grove, 1967.

———. *The Wretched of the Earth*. New York: Grove, 1966.

Fischel, Leslie, and Benjamin Quarles, editors. *The Black American*. New York: William Morrow, 1970.

Foner, Philip S. *Organized Labor and the Black Worker, 1619–1973*. New York: International Publishers, 1974.

Franklin, John Hope. *From Slavery to Freedom*. New York: Vintage, 1969.

Frazier, E. Franklin. *Black Bourgeoisie*. New York: Collier, 1962.

———. *The Negro in the United States*. New York: Macmillan, 1967.

Goldman, Peter. *The Death and Life of Malcolm X*. New York: Harper and Row, 1973.

———. *Report from Black America*. New York: Simon and Schuster, 1971.

Goodman, Benjamin, editor. *The End of White World Supremacy: Four Speeches by Malcolm X*. New York: Merlin House, 1971.

Grier, William H., and Price M. Cobbs. *Black Rage*. New York: Basic Books, 1968.

Guthrie, Robert V. *Being Black*. San Francisco: Canfield, 1970.

Jackson, George. *Soledad Brother*. New York: Bantam, 1970.

Jackson, Kenneth T. *The Ku Klux Klan in the City, 1915–1930*. New York: Oxford University Press, 1967.

Jones, Reginald L., editor. *Black Psychology*. New York: Harper and Row, 1972.

Kain, John F. *Race and Poverty*. Englewood Cliffs, New Jersey: Prentice-Hall, 1969.

Killan, Lewis M. *The Impossible Revolution*. New York: Random House, 1968.

Kochman, Thomas, editor. *Rappin' and Stylin' Out*. Urbana, Illinois: University of Illinois Press, 1972.

Lewis, Anthony, and the *New York Times*. *Portrait of a Decade*. New York: Bantam, 1964.

Lincoln, C. Eric. *The Black Muslims in America*. Boston: Beacon, 1961.

Lomax, J. A., and A. Lomax. *The Leadbelly Legend*. New York: Folkways, 1959.

Lomax, Louis E. *To Kill a Black Man*. Los Angeles: Holloway House, 1968.

———. *When the Word Is Given*. New York: Signet, 1963.

McCord, William, John Howard, Bernard Friedberg, and Edwin Harwood. *Life Styles in the Black Ghetto*. New York: W. W. Norton, 1969.

McPherson, James M., Laurence B. Holland, et al. *Blacks in America*. Garden City, New York: Doubleday, 1971.

Major, Clarence. *Dictionary of Afro-American Slang*. New York: International Publishers, 1970.

Malcolm X. *On Afro-American History*. New York: Merit, 1967.

———, with the assistance of Alex Haley. *The Autobiography of Malcolm X*. New York: Grove, 1964.

Marx, Gary T. *Protest and Prejudice*. New York: Harper and Row, 1969.

Meier, August, and Elliott Rudwick. *From Plantation to Ghetto*. New York: Hill and Wang, 1976.

Meier, August, and Elliott Rudwick, editors. *Black Protest in the Sixties*. Chicago: Quadrangle, 1970.

Meier, August, Elliott Rudwick, and Francis L. Broderick, editors. *Black Protest Thought in the Twentieth Century*. New York: Bobbs-Merrill, 1971.

Miller, William Robert. *Martin Luther King*. New York: Avon, 1968.

Milner, Christina, and Richard Milner. *Black Players*. Boston: Little, Brown, 1972.

Mowry, George E., editor. *The Twenties: Fords, Flappers and Fanatics*. Englewood Cliffs, N.J.: Prentice-Hall, 1963.

Myrdal, Gunnar. *An American Dilemma*, Volumes I–II. New York: McGraw-Hill, 1964.

Newman, Dorothy K., et al. *Protest, Politics, and Prosperity*. New York: Pantheon, 1978.

Osofsky, Gilbert. *Harlem: The Making of a Ghetto*. New York: Harper and Row, 1971.

Parsons, Talcott, and Kenneth B. Clark, editors. *The Negro American*. Boston: Beacon, 1966.

Report of the National Advisory Commission on Civil Disorders. New York: The New York Times Co., 1968.

Ross, Arthur M., and Herbert Hill, editors. *Employment, Race, and Poverty*. New York: Harcourt, Brace, and World, 1967.

Silberman, Charles E. *Crisis in Black and White*. New York: Vintage, 1965.

Sternsher, Bernard, editor. *The Negro in Depression and War*. Chicago: Quadrangle, 1969.

Vincent, Theodore G. *Black Power and the Garvey Movement*. San Francisco: Ramparts, 1972.

Watson, Peter, editor. *Psychology and Race*. Chicago: Atherton, 1974.

Wilmore, Gayraud S. *Black Religion and Black Radicalism*. Garden City, New York: Doubleday, 1973.

Wilson, Walter, editor. *The Selected Writings of W. E. B. DuBois*. New York: New American Library, 1970.

AFRO-AMERICAN HISTORY: ARTICLES

Blauner, Robert. "Internal Colonialism and Ghetto Revolt," in Milton Mankoff, editor, *The Poverty of Progress*.

Dalfiume, Richard M. "The 'Forgotten Years' of the Negro Revolution," in Bernard Sternsher, editor, *The Negro in Depression and War*.

Dansby, Pearl Gore. "Black Pride in the Seventies: Fact or Fantasy?" in Reginald L. Jones, editor, *Black Psychology*.

Drake, St. Clair. "The Social and Economic Status of the Negro in the United States," in Talcott Parsons and Kenneth B. Clark, editors, *The Negro American*.

DuBois, W. E. B., "An Appeal to the World," in Walter Wilson, editor, *The Selected Writings of W. E. B. DuBois*.

Dylan, Bob. "Only a Pawn in Their Game," in *The Bob Dylan Songbook*. New York: M. Witmark and Sons, undated.

Erikson, Erik H. "The Concept of Identity in Race Relations," in Parsons and Clark, *The Negro American*.

Essien-Udom, Ruby M. and E. U. "Malcolm X: An International Man," in John H. Clarke, editor, *Malcolm X*.

Evans, Hiram Wesley. "The Klan's Fight for Americanism," in George Mowry, editor, *The Twenties*.

Haley, Alex. "Interview with Malcolm X," *Playboy Magazine*, May, 1963.

Henderson, Vivian W. "Regions, Race and Jobs," in Arthur M. Ross and Herbert Hill, editors, *Employment, Race, and Poverty*.

Hudson, Julius. "The Hustling Ethic," in Thomas Kochman, editor, *Rappin' and Stylin' Out*.

Johnson, Charles S. "After Garvey—What?" in Leslie Fischel and Benjamin Quarles, editors, *The Black American*.

Lester, Julius. "The Angry Children of Malcolm X," in August Meier et al., *Black Protest Thought in the Twentieth Century*.

Lewis, John. "Interview, 1964," in Meier et al., *Black Protest Thought in the Twentieth Century*.

Poussaint, Alvin F. "A Negro Psychiatrist Explains the Negro Psyche," in August Meier and Elliott Rudwick, editors, *Black Protest in the Sixties*.

Powdermaker, Hortense. "The Channeling of Negro Aggression by the Cultural Process," in Clyde Kluckhohn and Henry A. Murray, editors, *Personality in Nature, Society, and Culture*.

Proshansky, Harold, and Peggy Newton. "Colour: The Nature and Meaning of Negro Self-Identity," in Peter Watson, editor, *Psychology and Race*.

Pugh, Roderick W. "Psychological Aspects of the Black Revolution," in Jones, editor, *Black Psychology*.

Robinson, Cedric J. "Malcolm X as a Charismatic Leader." A paper presented to the American Political Science Association, 1970.

Ross, Arthur M. "The Negro in the American Economy," in Ross and Hill, *Employment, Race, and Poverty*.

United States Government, Current Population Reports. "Social and Economic Conditions of Negroes in the United States," Series P-23, Number 24.

Williams, Robert F. "U.S.A.: The Potential for a Minority Revolution," in Meier et al., *Black Protest Thought in the Twentieth Century*.

Williams, W. T. B. "The Negro Exodus from the South," in Fischel and Quarles, editors, *The Black American*.

Wolfenstein, Eugene Victor. "Race, Racism and Racial Liberation," in *The Western Political Quarterly*, Volume XXX, Number 2, June, 1977.

Wright, Richard. "Joe Louis Uncovers Dynamite," in Daniel Aaron and Robert Bendiner, editors, *The Strenuous Decade*.

OTHER SOURCES: BOOKS

Aaron, Daniel, and Robert Bendiner, editors. *The Strenuous Decade*. Garden City, New York: Doubleday, 1970.

Adorno, T. W., et al. *The Authoritarian Personality*. New York: Harper and Brothers, 1950.

Baran, Paul A., and Paul M. Sweezy. *Monopoly Capital*. New York: Monthly Review Press, 1966.

Baxandall, Lee, editor. *Sex-Pol*. New York: Vintage, 1972.

Bernstein, Irving. *The Lean Years*. Baltimore, Maryland: Penguin, 1970.

———. *The Turbulent Years*. Boston: Houghton-Mifflin, 1971.

Brecher, Jeremy. *Strike!* San Francisco: Straight Arrow, 1972.

Brown, Bruce. *Freud, Marx, and the Critique of Everyday Life*. New York: Monthly Review Press, 1973.

Brown, Michael Barratt. *The Economics of Imperialism*. Middlesex, England: Penguin, 1974.

Dowd, Douglas. *The Twisted Dream*. Cambridge, Massachusetts: Winthrop, 1974.

Edwards, R. C., M. Reich, and T. E. Weisskopf, editors. *The Capitalist System*. Englewood Cliffs, New Jersey: Prentice-Hall, 1972.

Erikson, Erik H. *Young Man Luther*. New York: W. W. Norton, 1958.

Faulkner, Harold. *The Decline of Laissez-Faire*. New York: Harper Torchbooks, 1951.

Freud, Sigmund. *From the History of an Infantile Neurosis*, in *The Standard Edition of the Complete Psychological Works of Sigmund Freud* (henceforth referred to as *S.E.*). London: Hogarth, dates variable. Volume XVII.

———. *Group Psychology and the Analysis of the Ego*. *S.E.*, Volume XVIII.

———. *Introductory Lectures on Psychoanalysis*. *S.E.*, Volumes XV and XVI.

———. *Three Essays on Sexuality*. *S.E.*, Volume VII.

———. *Totem and Taboo*. *S.E.*, Volume XIII.

Fromm, Erich. *Escape from Freedom*. New York: Holt, Rinehart, and Winston, 1941.

Fromm, Erika, and Ronald E. Shor, editors. *Hypnosis: Research Developments and Perspectives*. New York: Aldine-Atherton, 1972.

Gerth, H. H., and C. Wright Mills, editors. *From Max Weber*. New York: Oxford University Press, 1958.

Giddens, Anthony. *The Class Structure of the Advanced Societies*. New York: Harper and Row, 1975.

Gill, Merton, and Margaret Brenman. *Hypnosis and Related States*. New York: International Universities Press, 1959.

Graham, Hugh Davis, and Robert Ted Gurr, editors. *Violence in America*. New York: The New York Times Co., 1969.

Grene, David, and Richmond Lattimore, editors. *Sophocles I*. Chicago: University of Chicago Press, 1954.

Hegel, G. W. F. *The Phenomenology of Mind*. New York: Harper and Row, 1967.

———. *The Philosophy of Right*. New York: Oxford University Press, 1952.

Hickman, Bert G. *Growth and Stability in the Postwar Economy*. Washington, D.C.: The Brookings Institution, 1960.

Hobbes, Thomas. *Leviathan*. Oxford: Clarendon Press, 1909.

Horowitz, David, editor. *Marx and Modern Economics*. New York: Monthly Review Press, 1968.

Jacobson, Edith. *The Self and the Object World*. New York: International Universities Press, 1964.

Jalee, Pierre. *The Pillage of the Third World*. New York: Monthly Review Press, 1968.

Kant, Immanuel. *The Critique of Judgment*. New York: Hafner, 1951.

———. *The Critique of Practical Reason*. New York: Bobbs-Merrill, 1956.

———. *The Critique of Pure Reason*. New York: St. Martin's, 1965.

Klein, Melanie, Paula Heimann, and R. E. Money-Kyrle, editors. *New Directions in Psycho-Analysis*. London: Tavistock, 1955.

Kluckhohn, Clyde, and Henry A. Murray, editors. *Personality in Nature, Society, and Culture*. New York: Alfred A. Knopf, 1948.

Kolko, Gabriel. *Main Currents in Modern American History*. New York: Harper and Row, 1976.

———. *Wealth and Power in America*. New York: Praeger, 1962.

Kolko, Joyce. *America and the Crisis of World Capitalism*. Boston: Beacon, 1974.

Laslett, Peter, editor. *John Locke: Two Treatises of Government*. New York: New American Library, 1965.

Lasswell, Harold D. *Psychopathology and Politics*. New York: Viking, 1960.

Lattimore, Richmond, trans. *The Iliad of Homer*. Chicago: University of Chicago Press, 1961.

Lundberg, Ferdinand. *The Rich and the Super-Rich*. New York: Bantam, 1968.

MacPherson, C. B. *The Political Theory of Possessive Individualism*. London: Oxford University Press, 1962.

Magdoff, Harry. *The Age of Imperialism*. New York: Monthly Review
    Press, 1969.
Mandel, Ernest. *Europe vs. America*. New York: Monthly Review Press,
    1970.
———. *Marxist Economics*. New York: Monthly Review Press, 1970.
Mankoff, Milton, editor. *The Poverty of Progress*. New York: Holt,
    Rinehart, and Winston, 1972.
Mannheim, Karl. *Ideology and Utopia*. New York: Harcourt, Brace, and
    World, 1936.
Marcuse, Herbert. *Eros and Civilization*. New York: Vintage, 1962.
———. *One-Dimensional Man*. Boston: Beacon, 1964.
Marx, Karl. *Capital*, Volume I. New York: Vintage, 1977.
———. *Capital*, Volumes I–III. Moscow: Foreign Languages Publishing
    House, [n.d.].
———. *A Contribution to a Critique of Political Economy*. New York:
    International Publishers, 1970.
———. *The Economic and Philosophical Manuscripts of 1844*. New York:
    International Publishers, 1964.
———. *The Eighteenth Brumaire of Louis Bonaparte*, in *Marx and Engels,
    Selected Works*. Moscow: Foreign Languages Publishing House, 1962,
    Volume I.
———. *The Grundrisse*. Middlesex, England: Penguin, 1973.
———. *Theories of Surplus Value*. Moscow: Progress Publisher, 1963.
Marx, Karl, and Frederick Engels. *The German Ideology*. New York:
    International Publishers, 1970.
———. *Selected Works*. Volumes I–II. Moscow: Foreign Languages
    Publishing House, 1962.
Mattick, Paul. *Marx and Keynes*. Boston: Porter Sargent, 1969.
Miliband, Ralph. *Marxism and Politics*. Oxford: Oxford University Press,
    1977.
Miller, A. V., translator. *Hegel's Science of Logic*. London: George Allen
    and Unwin, 1969.
Mitchell, Broadus. *Depression Decade*. New York: Harper and Row, 1947.
Mitford, Jessica. *Kind and Usual Punishment*. New York: Alfred A. Knopf,
    1973.
Mowry, George, editor. *The Twenties: Fords, Flappers and Fanatics*.
    Englewood Cliffs, New Jersey: Prentice-Hall, 1963.
O'Connor, James. *The Fiscal Crisis of the State*. New York: St. Martin's,
    1973.
Perrett, Geoffrey. *Days of Sadness, Years of Triumph*. New York: Coward,
    McCann and Geoghegan, 1973.
Reich, Wilhelm. *Character-Analysis*. New York: Orgone Institute, 1945.
———. *The Mass Psychology of Fascism*. New York: Farrar, Straus and
    Giroux, 1970.
Robinson, Joan. *An Essay on Marxian Economics*. New York: St. Martin's,
    1967.

Sartre, Jean-Paul. *Search for a Method*. New York: Vintage, 1963.
Schilder, Paul, and Otto Kauders. *Hypnosis*. New York: Nervous and Mental Disease Publishing, 1927.
Schneider, Michael. *Neurosis and Civilization*. New York: Seabury, 1975.
Soule, George. *Prosperity Decade*. New York: Harper Torchbooks, 1947.
Srole, Leo, and Anita K. Fischer. *Mental Health in the Metropolis*. New York: Harper and Row, 1962.
Sweezy, Paul. *The Theory of Capitalist Development*. New York: Monthly Review Press, 1970.
Szymanski, Albert. *The Capitalist State and the Politics of Class*. Cambridge, Massachusetts: Winthrop, 1978.
Tucker, Robert, editor. *The Marx-Engels Reader*. New York: W. W. Norton, 1972.
Wallace, William, translator. *The Logic of Hegel*. London: Oxford University Press, 1973.
Wallace, William, and A. V. Miller, translators. *Hegel's Philosophy of Mind*. London: Oxford University Press, 1971.
Weber, Max. *The Protestant Ethic and the Spirit of Capitalism*. New York: Charles Scribner's Sons, 1958.
———. *The Theory of Social and Economic Organization*. New York: Free Press of Glencoe, 1964.
Wright, Erik O., editor. *The Politics of Punishment*. New York: Harper and Row, 1973.

OTHER SOURCES: ARTICLES

Davies, James C. "The J-Curve of Rising and Declining Satisfactions as a Cause of Some Great Revolutions and a Contained Rebellion," in Hugh Davis Graham and Robert Ted Gurr, editors, *Violence in America*.
Etheredge, Lloyd S. "Hypnosis and Order." A paper presented to the Yale Conference on Political Psychology, March, 1975.
Freud, Sigmund. "Instincts and Their Vicissitudes," in *S.E.*, Volume XIV.
———. "Some Character-Types Met with in Psychoanalytic Work," in *S.E.*, Volume XIV.
Hendrik, Ives. "Work and the Pleasure Principle," in *The Psychoanalytic Quarterly*, Volume XII, 1943.
Marx, Karl. "Contribution to a Critique of Hegel's *Philosophy of Right*. Introduction," in Robert Tucker, editor, *The Marx-Engels Reader*.
———. "Results of the Immediate Process of Production," in Karl Marx, *Capital*, Volume I, trans. Ben Fowkes. New York: Vintage Books, 1977.
———. "Theses on Feuerbach," in Tucker, *The Marx-Engels Reader*.
———. "Wage-Labour and Capital," in Tucker, *The Marx-Engels Reader*; also in Karl Marx and Frederick Engels, *Selected Works*, Volume I.
Reich, Michael. "The Evolution of the United States Labor Force," in R. C. Edwards et al., editors, *The Capitalist System*.

Reich, Wilhelm. "Dialectical Materialism and Psychoanalysis," in Lee
Baxandall, editor, *Sex-Pol*.
Weber, Max. "Politics as a Vocation," in H. H. Gerth and C. Wright Mills,
editors, *From Max Weber*.
Wolfenstein, Eugene Victor. "Groundwork for a Marxist Psychoanalysis." A
paper presented to the American Political Science Association, 1977.

Index

PAGE - 207 : What could become of a black man
In prison

Designer: Richard Hendel
Compositor: G & S Typesetters, Inc.
Printer: Vail-Ballou Press, Inc.
Binder: Vail-Ballou Press, Inc.
Text: VIP Trump
Display: VIP Trump and Trump Bold
Cloth: Holliston Roxite 50302 linen
Endsheets: Multicolor charcoal
Paper: 50 lb cream eggshell